FATHERHOOD IN AMERICA

FATHERHOOD
IN AMERICA

A HISTORY

ROBERT L. GRISWOLD

BasicBooks
A Division of HarperCollins*Publishers*

Designed by Craig Winer

93 94 95 96 ❖/HC 9 8 7 6 5 4 3 2 1

Library of Congress Cataloging-in-Publication Data
Griswold, Robert L., 1950–
    Fatherhood in America: a history/Robert L. Griswold.
      p. cm.
   Includes bibliographical references and index.
    ISBN 0–465–00140–8
    1. Fatherhood—United States—History. I. Title.
HQ756.G78   1993
306.874'2'0973—dc20

92–54516

CIP

To my father, Robert E. Griswold,
and my children, Sarah and Peter

CONTENTS

PREFACE   ix

1. Introduction: From Breadwinner to "Daddy Tracker"   1

2. Breadwinning and American Manhood, 1800–1920   10

3. Breadwinning on the Margin: Working-Class Fatherhood, 1880–1930   34

4. Fatherhood, Immigration, and American Culture, 1880–1930   68

5. The Invention of the New Fatherhood, 1920–1940   88

6. The Cultural Contradictions of the New Fatherhood, 1920–1940   119

7. Fathers in Crisis: The 1930s   143

8. Fatherhood, Foxholes, and Fascism, 1940–1950   161

9. Fatherhood and the Great American Barbecue, 1945–1965   185

10. Fatherhood and the Reorganization of Men's Lives, 1965–1993   219

11. Patriarchy and the Politics of Fatherhood, 1970–1993   243

NOTES   270

INDEX   346

PREFACE

I F I WERE NOT A FATHER, THIS BOOK WOULD HAVE BEEN FINISHED AT least a year ago. Rearing children, after all, takes commitment and time. On the other hand, if I were not a father, this book would likely have not been written at all. It was the experience of being a father that prompted my interest in the historical meaning of fatherhood. However, this book is a history and not a personal testimonial: although the research and writing have represented, in some sense, a fusion of my professional interests and personal responsibilities, my intention is to offer an interpretation of fathers' lives and fatherhood over the course of this century.

Given the complexity of the topic and the paucity of historical analyses of American fatherhood, I must emphasize that this book is *a* history, not *the* history, of fatherhood since the turn of the century. To claim the latter would be presumptuous. Rather, I have tried to present an overview and an interpretation that have required me to make difficult selections as to sources and content. For example, early on I decided against the extensive use of personal letters or diaries of individuals, not because such sources are without merit but because the national scope of the study and the long period of time under review would have made any such selection capricious at best and foolish at worst. Such a decision has meant that the history of emotional relationships between fathers and children, a worthy subject indeed, will be left to other scholars. Selecting what topics to analyze and what to omit has also presented a host of challenges. A book-length study could be written of any number of subjects that I either glide over or ignore altogether. Single

fathers, gay fathers, Hispanic fathers, and others all deserve their historians, and perhaps at some point they will find them. What I have
attempted to chart are the main lines of the story, and thus I have often
had to slight the particular experience of this or that group.

That said, I should say that I have tried to capture changes in the
history of American fathers in this century, fully aware that I have often
painted with a broad brush. I hope and expect that finer strokes will be
added by later historians. But even the broad brush strokes I have used
would have been impossible without help from a variety of quarters.
Even a cursory glance at the notes reveals my indebtedness to a host of
scholars who have helped me understand men's experiences in the
past. I also owe thanks to a number of colleagues, librarians, and editors who have helped me with this project at various stages. I would
like to thank my editor at Basic Books, Steve Fraser, for his constant
support and critical attention to the analysis. Thanks, too, to Ed Cone,
the copyeditor, who ironed out awkward sentences and highlighted
unclear passages in need of attention. Gary Murphy and Michael
Mueller were unfailingly helpful during the production phase of the
project.

Many colleagues read the manuscript at different stages, pointed me
to sources, offered critiques, and supplied the indispensible encourage-
ment that keeps scholars going when the end seems not in sight. Clyde
Griffen and Doug Mitchell read several of the chapters and provided
helpful critiques. Others who read and offered advice on various parts
of the book or who helped in other ways were Mark Carnes; Connie
Ellison; Peter Filene; Robert Hemenway; Michael Kimmel; Sarah
McMahon; Margaret Marsh; Elaine Tyler May; Martha May; Robert
Nye; Paula Petrik; Henry Tom; William Tuttle, Jr.; and Elliott West.
Margaret Cain served as an able research assistant in Washington,
D.C.; Ralph LaRossa brought my attention to the Patri Papers at the
Library of Congress; Alan Hertzke shared with me his knowledge of
the religious right; and Robert Sears allowed me to photocopy tran-
scripts of interviews of fathers he and associates recorded in the 1950s.
Librarians at the University of Minnesota's Social Welfare History
Archives, Radcliffe's Henry A. Murry Research Center, and the Library
of Congress deserve a word of thanks as well. Faculty research grants
and a sabbatical leave from the University of Oklahoma helped provide
time to research and write this book. The merits of this book derive, in
part, from the generosity of these friends and colleagues. I alone, of
course, accept responsibility for any errors or shortcomings.

Finally, a word of thanks to my father, Robert E. Griswold. It was his
stories about World War II, clearly the pivotal event for so many men

of his generation, that first ignited my interest in history. He also spent literally thousands of hours of "quality time" with me long before the term obtained its current meaning. At a time when many fathers were slaves to their jobs, my father gladly left his dental office and passed on to me his love of games and sports. As we skated, skied, swam, walked, golfed, and played endless hours of tennis, he also taught me much about life and about the art of fatherly nurture. For those hours together, I am forever grateful. My wife, Ellen, has been a constant source of sage advice and strong support; moreover, her work with troubled families has helped keep my own troubles in perspective. A fruitless day of writing hardly compares with the frustrations and difficulties of working with parents and children hurt by poverty, illness, substance abuse, and the like. My children, Sarah and Peter, deserve special thanks. I found it impossible to write a book about fatherhood without thinking constantly about my children and my life as a father. Surely few commitments are more challenging or more rewarding. In the recent movie *Parenthood,* a roller coaster serves as a metaphor for rearing children, one I find especially apt. Fatherhood has its ups and downs, but even the downs lead to new ups, and it is always exciting. The movie failed to mention that the roller coaster ultimately runs out of steam and slows to a halt, but perhaps by that time I will be ready for grandfatherhood. Until then, I have the good fortune to be rearing two children who are a constant source of joy.

1

Introduction: From Breadwinner to "Daddy Tracker"

J IMMIE CAPASSO, THE AMERICAN-BORN SON OF AN ITALIAN IMMIGRANT laborer, had high hopes of continuing his education through high school. His father, however, had different aspirations for the studious fifteen-year-old: "What's the matter you, Jimmie, you want to go to school? Sixteen years I work pick and shovel, t'ree dollar a day. Who goin' to buy clothes for the children? You big now, you fifteen. What's the matter you want more school? No more school; you get him job." Sixty years later, Gil Gordon explained why he left a high-powered corporate job to set up his own consulting firm: "[T]here has been a manifold increase in the quality of family life. I don't want to make out like I'm a superfather or the perfect husband, because that's not true. But I know I see the kids more now. I coach baseball in the spring and soccer in the fall because I've got the flexibility in my schedule. I think they appreciate that I can go on school trips with them. There are many times when I am the only man, and they think it's kind of neat. . . . I feel a little sorry for men whose only definition of success is what it says on their business cards."[1]

From hard-pressed immigrant patriarch and breadwinner to upscale "daddy tracker" and suburban soccer coach, these two men's experiences suggest some of the changes that have occurred in American fatherhood during the twentieth century. They also suggest some of the complexities: to understand twentieth-century fatherhood is to understand what men have shared and where men have differed, to comprehend not only change over time but the interplay of class, race, and ethnicity in men's lives. Both the immigrant laborer and the flextime executive were breadwinners, but while the former desperately tried to eke out an existence and exert control over his son, the latter took a pay cut to spend more "quality time" with his children. While the elder Capasso lived in a culture none too friendly to Italian immigrants, Gordon had found a secure niche in an affluent suburban community. Breadwinning gave shape to what they had in common, class and ethnicity to what pulled them apart.

Despite men's differences, breadwinning has remained the great unifying element in fathers' lives. Its obligations bind men across the boundaries of color and class, and shape their sense of self, manhood, and gender. Supported by law, affirmed by history, sanctioned by every element in society, male breadwinning has been synonymous with maturity, respectability, and masculinity. Robert S. Weiss, who has studied the work and family lives of contemporary men, concludes that breadwinning and children are inextricably bound together in men's sense of self: "Children, for men, are a commitment, an investment, an obligation, a hope. They are men's chief contribution to the world and justification for their lives." One of Weiss's respondents put it this way: "Five kids. I'm proud of that. I own my own home. I have a couple of cars, there's no sheriff knocking at my door. And the kids are all in school. I don't know what more I could ask for."[2]

Moving as they are, such testimonials conceal the impact of work on fathers' relationships with their children. In other words, if breadwinning has given meaning to men's lives, it has also structured the time fathers have available for their offspring. Time spent at the factory, store, or office is time away from children; time spent worrying about or being depressed by work likewise undermines the paternal bond with children. The daughter of a hard-pressed Southern textile worker in the early twentieth century recalled the distance she felt from her father: "He never took up any time with his children, of any description. I knew my father very well, [but] I never cared too much for him. I think we bored him. He was home to sleep. He was always there at mealtime."[3] Lillian Rubin suggests that such withdrawal remains a common response of working-class fathers beaten down by inadequate wages and poor living standards. One man recalled to Rubin his own father's unresponsiveness: "My father was a very quiet man. He almost never talked, even when you asked him a question. He'd sit there like he didn't hear you. Sometimes, an hour later (it was like he'd come out of a spell), he'd look at you and say, 'Did you want something?' Most of the time, he just didn't know you were there."[4]

If alienation has characterized the life of the working class, perhaps preoccupation is the hallmark of the middle-class father. Decades ago, a Middletown father described his own sense of failure in this regard: "I'm a rotten dad. If our children amount to anything it's their mother who'll get all the credit. I'm so busy I don't see much of them and I don't know how to chum up with them when I do."[5] Years later a middle-level manager described his own erratic efforts to separate his work from his home life: "I'm sure I have brought stress home from work. I don't think that it happens that frequently. I try to lock it in the drawer at night, to maintain some separation. But I'm sure there are times when I come home and it's because of something that has happened at work that I act differently. I may be a little shorter with the kids."[6] Survey and psychological data from throughout the twentieth century suggest that such father-child alienation remains a defining characteristic of American family life.[7]

This alienation is not, however, without political significance. The ideology of male breadwinning over the course of the twentieth century has also justified men's limited commitment to child care. Despite persistent calls in this century for more fatherly commitment to offspring, men have left most of the work of rearing children to women. They have done so because of their status as providers, and their efforts as breadwinners should not be denigrated. To support a family is no small accomplishment, and men have rightfully gained a sense of self-worth and importance from doing so. But this recognition should not obscure the fact that fathers have largely left the boring, repetitious, and vexing work of child care to their wives, a division of labor that persists despite dramatic changes in the household economy. Even in homes where both parents work full-time, mothers still do the great majority of child care, a "second shift" that leaves them exhausted and resentful. Yet, a steady rise in the number of wives and mothers in the labor force and over twenty years of feminist agitation have only now begun to dent this prerogative of patriarchy. Even today, most men resist the onerous tasks of child care because it is in their interest to do so.

Thus men's virtual monopoly of breadwinning has been part and parcel of male dominance. The seventeenth-century patriarch has long since disappeared, but twentieth-century men have profited from their status as fathers. The linkage between fatherhood and breadwinning, for example, has helped legitimate men's monopoly of the most desirable jobs. If men support families and women nurture them, then fathers need sufficient pay so their wives can remain at home "where they belong." Women's "intrusion" into the world of work outside the home only upsets this gender-based division of labor and threatens to undermine men's prerogatives. If mothers must go to work, their jobs should be temporary, supplemental, gender-segregated and, ideally, attributable to the exigencies of war or some other calamity. So, too, insurance policies, pension plans, retirement programs, tax codes, mortgage and credit policies, educational opportunities, and many more practices have bolstered men's role as providers and undermined women's ability to become breadwinners in their own right.

Such is the way male breadwinning has shaped the structure of gender and family politics in this century. And yet not all men have experienced these politics in the same way. Breadwinning did not mean the same thing to an immigrant working class plagued by un- and underemployment, periodic layoffs, and pitifully low wages as it did to financially secure Anglo middle-class fathers working in the businesses and professions. Nor were either of their experiences similar to that of black men coping with the crop-lien system and Jim Crow or to the thousands of black men who moved to Northern cities to be greeted with persistent discrimination, segregation, and menial work. Even their anxieties were different. The incredulity of an Italian immigrant father upon discovering that his son's schoolteacher had changed the spelling of the family surname—"A name is a name. What happened to the *i*?"—was a different kind of paternal worry than that of a Middletown father lamenting his alienation from his offspring: "You know, I don't know that I spend any time having a good time with my children. . . . And the worst of it is, I don't know how to."[8]

The meaning of breadwinning not only varied from group to group, it also changed over time, and nothing has changed and continues to change fatherhood more than the collapse of men's monopoly on breadwinning. This great organizing principle of men's lives began to change even before World War II but accelerated quickly in the postwar years. The image of baby boom mothers pushing strollers through suburban neighborhoods belies the fact that from 1948 to 1960, the percentage of mothers in the work force with children ages six to eighteen jumped from 21 to 36 percent, while those with children under six climbed from 11 to 23 percent. These changes accelerated in the years that followed, and by the mid-1980s the proportion of mothers in the work force with preschool children reached almost 60 percent, one-quarter of whom worked full-time.[9] Propelled by desires for self-fulfillment, economic need, expansive consumer wants, and a better life for their children, wives and mothers play an increasingly important role in family support.

Accordingly, fathers have slowly lost their hold on the privilege, power, and responsibility that came with breadwinning. But how should men change if they were no longer sole breadwinners? Were they capable of becoming companions and co-parents to their children, or were more men simply willing to condemn their wives to the "second shift"? Was it possible to reassert traditional authority, as some conservatives hoped, or was it better to get out of the rat race and on to the "daddy track," as progressives suggested? And what claims on traditional male privilege could women make in light of their contributions to the family finances? Could women insist that husbands now do their fair share of child care, and if they pressed such demands, how much would fathers resist? In short, would the wage work of women be successful in redefining the meaning of fatherhood?

Helping this redefinition was the second great force of change. Until the rebirth of feminism in the 1960s, American fatherhood existed in what amounted to a political vacuum. Without saying that fatherhood was apolitical, no political movement before modern feminism challenged the gender-based division of labor, questioned the assumption that women were innately more capable of rearing children than men, or lambasted men for their limited commitment to families. Only feminism made the connections between fatherly privileges and patriarchy. Feminists brought attention to the "second shift," analyzed the politics of housework, asked why women but not men reordered their lives to rear children, and exposed "dangerous fathers" who abused their children. Although liberal feminists have remained optimistic about men's capacity for change while more radical feminists have continued to be suspicious of men's good intentions, together they have politicized fatherhood.

Their claims, in turn, have led to a backlash. Voices on the political and religious right hope to reinvigorate the power of men within families, to bring back an age when men were breadwinners, and women, child rearers. In the pulpit and in legislative halls, these defenders of orthodoxy fight against women's rights, worry about the difficulties encountered by male breadwinners, lament the rise of mothers in the work force, and agonize over the large numbers of children being reared in families without fathers. Their ire toward feminists is well known. This debate has grown increasingly vitriolic and suggests that virtually no aspect of American family life is uncontested. Whether it is Vice President Dan Quayle worrying about Murphy Brown or evangelist Pat Robertson calling for the reinvigoration of traditional family values, the politics of fatherhood never lie too far below the surface.

The transformation of male breadwinning and the rise of feminism have also given new meaning to demands that fathers spend more time with their children. Such calls are by no means new. The "new fatherhood" originally arose in the early decades of the twentieth century when a host of writers tried to refashion men's sense of their paternal responsibilities. They did so, however, without in any sustained way challenging the gender-based division of labor that made breadwinners of men and child rearers of women. In this conception, men's involvement in the home was important, but it was a "gift" men granted to women and children and not part of a restructured conception of masculinity and parenthood. Men remained providers first, buddies and sex-role models second. This variant survives today but now shares cultural space with a vision of fatherhood informed by feminism and mothers' wage work that holds out the possibility for a genuine transformation of paternal culture.

These two versions of the "new fatherhood" still compete for cultural predominance. The earlier variant quickly became entangled with an emerging therapeutic culture heavily dependent upon expert advice. Common sense was no longer a sufficient guide to good fathering; it was far better to educate oneself with the help of the books, workshops, radio shows, advice columns, and parent education programs that began to proliferate in the 1920s and 1930s. From such sources men could learn that hobbies taught the virtues of patience and hard work, that fathers were vital sex-role models, and that family counsels were the foundation of democratic values. By the 1920s fathers were seeking information on everything from children's movies to coping with their youngsters' temper tantrums, and in the ensuing years the "new fatherhood" began to make its cultural mark as it became part of the experts' discourse on family life, personality development, and psychological well-being. After World War II, fatherhood became even more tied to the therapeutic culture, a tonic to overworked middle managers in the 1950s and 1960s and a path to good health for "Me Decade" seekers in the 1970s and 1980s. These assumptions culminated in the thousands of books, classes, and workshops on fathering that now dot contemporary America, all suggesting that fathering properly pursued is good for you.

This older variant of the "new fatherhood" could go only so far. Its message was apolitical, nonfeminist, and dependent upon the good intentions of men to become more nurturant fathers. Men and their children would profit by closer companionship, but the gender-based division of labor at the heart of male breadwinning remained more or less unquestioned. Only feminism and the transformation in male bread-winning made this challenge; hence the "new fatherhood" of the 1970s and 1980s differed from that of the earlier years of the century. In its modern incarnation, the "new fatherhood" is not a gift to women or a growth experience for men but a willingness to shoulder the burdens of child care in a society where both fathers and mothers work outside the home. It cannot occur without transformations in both private con-sciousness and public policy. Fathers must see themselves as more than "helpers," and work and other institutions must be restructured so that fathers and mothers can share child care equally. After all, breadwin-ners who build model airplanes differ fundamentally from fathers who co-parent. This basic distinction is often misunderstood.

Changes in the household economy and the reemergence of femi-nism have been the two most critical forces changing fatherhood, but other forces have been at work as well. Over the course of the century, the state absorbed increasing numbers of paternal (and maternal) func-tions. Most experts celebrated the state's increasing involvement as part of a historic shift in family life from "institution to companionship." In this view, the state progressively absorbed the traditional economic, ed-ucational, and welfare functions that had marked the patriarchal fami-lies of preindustrial America, thereby freeing men to develop more companionate attachments to their wives and children. Such a view, of course, is debatable: state intervention has had complicated and contra-dictory effects on the power of fathers. One law might save an immi-grant breadwinner from financial ruin while another might force him to send his child to a school that denigrated the youth's cultural heritage. The same state that provided unemployment insurance to a breadwin-ner with the hope of keeping the family together might use the juvenile court system to remove a recalcitrant daughter from the home. Whether the overall effect of such policies and laws undermines or shores up paternal power remains unclear, but the fact remains that the state has entered a private domain and helped to redefine the meaning of fatherhood. Paternal autonomy is thus illusory in modern society.

American fatherhood has also been shaped by shorter-term political and economic developments. Both the Great Depression and World War II prompted public concern about fatherhood. As unemployment in the Depression engulfed up to a quarter of the working population, breadwinners looked desperately for help. The poignant testimonials of men worried about the fate of their families suggest the psychic costs of breadlosing. The response of the Roosevelt administration to this calamity, in turn, reveals the importance of fatherhood and breadwin-ning to the political culture of the 1930s. So, too, the military's recommendation that fathers be drafted during World War II prompted a national debate that pitted manpower needs against the indispensability of fathers on the homefront. Not surprisingly, the former prevailed, but not before opponents rallied popular opinion to their side. The popular iconography of the war also reaffirmed the importance of private obligations: men went to war not to safeguard abstract rights but to protect their present or future families.

The twenty years after World War II saw the final flowering of men's monopoly on breadwinning. Two distinct cultural perspectives on fatherhood and breadwinning emerged. One celebrated the success of breadwinners in bringing to their wives and children a standard of living never before reached in American history. After the horrors of the Depression and the shortages of the war years, how could one help but be thrilled by the cornucopia of goods purchased by fathers' paychecks in the 1950s? This view quickly became entangled in the Cold War, and the goods that American men supplied to their families—as Richard Nixon made clear to Nikita Khrushchev in their famous Kitchen Debate—proved the superiority of the American Way.[10] The other view reflected the dark side of this male success. A group of influential postwar critics focused upon men's excessive conformity and slavish commitment to middle-management maneuvering. Entrapped within meaningless jobs and cookie-cutter tract homes, successful men of the middle class lived lives of "quiet desperation."

Against the backdrop of this debate, family experts and ordinary citizens invested fatherhood and family life with ever greater meaning. A fine home signified not only the personal success of the provider but also the political and economic success of the system that made such abundance possible. A prosperous family meant the father had done his part in promoting good personality formation—the sine qua non of successful family life in the 1950s—while simultaneously warding off juvenile delinquency, authoritarian intolerance, and even homosexuality. The private home, and fatherhood with it, would help to contain the anxieties of the age.[11]

The 1950s and early 1960s, then, represent the last hurrah of a mode of fatherhood that had prevailed, albeit with some change, since the Industrial Revolution. Men earned bread, women used it. Changes in the family economy and the rise of feminism would thereafter challenge the cultural saliency of this mode and leave fatherhood culturally unsettled. Today, a welter of voices hopes to define fatherhood. From feminist condemnation of "deadbeat dads" to paeans for "daddy trackers," from conservative hopes for the return of Old Testament patriarchs to "wildmen" searching for lost fathers, the cultural meaning of fatherhood has become unsteady under the impact of both long- and short-term forces in this century. Is today's archetypical father the man who leaves work early to attend a parent-teacher conference or the noncustodial parent who has not seen his children in three years? Is it Mr. Mom and Ted Kramer or the father who profits from the labor of his wife's "second shift"?

Such questions cannot be properly answered without recognizing that American culture changes over time and with it the relationship between fatherhood and patriarchy. War can alter the terms of the debate, but so can economic depression. "Americanization" movements can undercut the power of Old World fathers but so can the development of a youth culture with its own standards of behavior. Above all, changes in the household economy and feminism have the power to transform fatherhood, but so, too, do religious movements dedicated to more conservative visions of paternal life. These forces have all been at work on American fathers, although not all fathers have experienced them in quite the same way.

This book cannot begin to describe all these variations in detail, nor can it treat fully the histories of farm fathers, stepfathers, foster fathers, gay fathers, and divorced fathers. But the book does analyze the complex connections among fatherhood, masculine identity, patriarchy, and American culture over time. How men think about fatherhood helps us understand how they think about themselves as men, and this knowledge may, in turn, help us understand the structure of male dominance. Today, fatherhood has become politicized: its terms are contested, its significance fragmented, its meaning unstable. How we came to such a pass, how we came to expect more than ever before from fathers without knowing quite what to expect, is the story of fatherhood in the twentieth century.

2

Breadwinning and American Manhood, 1800–1920

I N THE EARLY SEVENTEENTH CENTURY, JOHN ROBINSON REMARKED that "surely there is in all children, though not alike, a stubborness, and stoutness of mind arising from natural pride, which must, in the first place, be broken and beaten down; that so the foundation of their education being laid in humility and tractableness, other virtues may, in their time, be built thereon." Three centuries later Lincoln Steffens, a first-time father at age sixty, confessed that his three-year-old son was not especially obedient: "Pete has something much better than obedience to give us; he has courtesy, and he has humor. He had these gifts from the very beginning, and a little inquiry among other parents seems to justify me in my theory that human beings are born with good will rather than subordination, and that they are governable, from infancy up, much more gently than we think."[1]

Robinson and Steffens could not have been further apart in their assumptions about children and fatherhood. The former emphasized the venality of children and the need to crush their will, the latter their essential goodness and tractability. Robinson saw fathers as stern patriarchs, Steffens as genial "dads." If their remarks were in any way representative, profound changes had reshaped American fatherhood over these years. To understand these changes, it is necessary to explore the forces that transformed fatherhood and altered the boundaries of patriarchal power in America. Thus, before we can begin to explore twentieth-century fatherhood, we must examine the key factors that shaped nineteenth-century family life.

The Roots of Change

The history of nineteenth-century fatherhood really begins in the previous century as a variety of forces after 1750 began to refashion attitudes about family life and children. These new attitudes, in turn, began to transform fatherhood itself. Although the exact nature of these forces remains somewhat obscure, historians suggest that the emergence of individualism and the enlightened religious, political, and economic ideas that gave rise to individualism were at the heart of the transformation. The paternal dominance and evangelical authority that infused Calvinist visions of family life in the seventeenth century eroded in the eighteenth century, as they were slowly replaced by an emphasis on more affective, less instrumental family relationships. Hierarchy and order, the watchwords of older forms of paternal dominance, gave way to a growing emphasis on mutuality, companionship, and personal happiness.[2]

These changing ideas about family life reshaped father-child relations. What was once considered indulgent now became ordinary: parents began purchasing books, toys, and games aimed specifically at children. They adopted naming practices that suggested increasing attention to the individuality of each child—for example, sharing the same first name by fathers and sons or mothers and daughters declined—and parents became more reluctant to foster out their offspring. Even the structure of homes reflected these developments. As material conditions improved and the spartan life of the seventeenth century receded into memory, typical homes now afforded more privacy, including special sleeping areas for children.[3] Among the middle and upper classes, fathers in both the North and the South found their children's antics a constant source of amusement, took pride in their accomplishments, and noted their idiosyncracies.

Underlying many of these new attitudes was a fundamental religious reevaluation of children. Although some evangelicals still clung to older ideas of will-crushing, more moderate views toward children—at least among the literate and genteel—began to emerge in the North and, to a lesser extent, in the South. Gone was the assumption that children were "infant fiends." Beginning in the mid-eighteenth century, evidence suggests that increasing numbers of fathers saw their children as malleable innocents whose character needed shaping, not breaking.[4] In 1746, Isaac Norris of Philadelphia noted, "My little Babes have yet no Characteristick but their innocence." Rearing children was a process of nurture and growth, not a battle between righteousness and depravity. Although children were vulnerable to sin, they were also full of goodness and could be led, with the help of reason and free will, to salvation.[5]

Accompanying such changes was a development with tremendous implications for fathers: as the status of children rose, so, too, did that of mothers. Especially among middle- and upper-class families in commercial seaboard cities or on Southern plantations, mothers—freed from the onerous tasks of home production so common to farm wives—increasingly assumed the care of their children. If children needed guidance and nurture and their character development needed constant tending, who better to do it than nurturing mothers who could devote themselves to such a task? Meanwhile, increasing numbers of fathers were drawn into a commercial economy that took them ever farther from the hearth. Here lay the fault lines of a shift that would reverberate for years to come.

The American Revolution fueled this shift by creating a series of social and ideological changes that politicized motherhood and marginalized fatherhood.[6] The war brought forth a growing sense of female competence and autonomy and a new conception of women's traditional sphere. The prepolitical woman became the republican mother entrusted with the socialization of children, especially her sons, to proper republican adulthood. By serving their families, mothers would serve the state. Women's mundane tasks were elevated and ideologically tied, via the concept of republican motherhood, to the future of the country. Mothers, not fathers, were entrusted with molding the character traits in children on which a free nation depended. Giving women this responsibility, in turn, led to demands for expanded educational opportunities for them and the insistence that their civic responsibilities be recognized. In short, the Revolution accelerated a trend that had been evident at midcentury—a growing recognition that mothers, not fathers, had primary responsibility for child nurture and moral development.

Mothers could learn to fulfill this responsibility with the help of an outpouring of child-rearing advice. Whereas seventeenth- and eighteenth-century literature had generally ignored mothers and directed advice to fathers, late eighteenth-century works did the opposite. Enlightenment rationalists and evangelical Protestants found common ground in their

celebration of motherhood, which prefigured the apotheosis of motherhood in the nineteenth century. Writers of the late eighteenth and early
nineteenth centuries emphasized mothers' crucial role during infancy,
the joys and importance of breast-feeding, the danger of wet nurses,
and the malleability of the child's character.[7] By contrast, writers gave
little attention to fathers or fatherhood.

Industrialization and the Ideology of Breadwinning

Although Revolutionary fervor eventually waned, the growing influence of
motherhood and the relative decline in the significance of fatherhood continued in the nineteenth century. Propelling such change was the decline
of the corporate household economy and the emergence of a commercial-
industrial world in which increasing numbers of men became breadwinners who commuted to work while their wives assumed direction of the
household. In short, the restructuring of American capitalism refashioned
fatherhood, and though regional variations remained, the more important
story is the national impact of industrialization on family life.

At the heart of this change was the decline of the corporate household economy. This system—best exemplified by the family farm or the
small artisan shop—helped promote fathers' influence over their children. With its household production, limited-exchange system, self-
sufficiency, community moral surveillance, and family hierarchy, the
corporate household economy of the seventeenth and eighteenth centuries provided a world in which fathers worked in close proximity to
their children. Men directed the work of the family, introduced their
sons to farming or craft work, and maintained (or at least tried to maintain) harmonious relations within the household. Thus, the home was
not only a center of production but also a system of authority.

This economic system began to erode in the late eighteenth and
early nineteenth centuries. It was replaced first by a proto-industrial
economy and then by a factory-dominated culture. As the corporate
household economy declined, more and more fathers became en-
meshed in the world of competitive capitalism beyond the home. Rising numbers of men became commuters, shuttling between home and
work. For those in the middle class, their destination might be an office
in a bank or a place on the salesroom floor; for men of the working
class, work might be in a small central shop or in a large factory. Regardless, urban and even town residents found that the bond once uniting men with their children had been broken. Increasing numbers of
men now spent their days away from home, engaged in what became

the defining characteristic of manhood for over a century—breadwinning.

These changes ultimately transformed fatherhood. Man the earner, woman the nurturer came to represent the ideal. While some writers urged men to establish closer relationships with their children, the structure of work and the ideology that legitimated it worked against such bonds. This is not to say that some men did not try. E. Anthony Rotundo's analysis of men's letters found that some late nineteenth-century fathers established companionate relationships with their offspring. Frank Kendall was one such man; he played an active role in rearing his sons, offered them advice, cared for them when ill, and followed their development with loving attention. When work took him away, he took pains to stay in contact, and he did not shy away from expressing his affection. Writing to a grown son, Kendall closed his letter with these heartfelt words: "Remember dear boy how much we *think* and *dream* and *pray,* for our beloved son so far and so long away from us, and how everything of interest to him is of interest to us. . . . With much, much, love dear Son, Your affectionate Father B.F.K." George Laflin expressed similar sentiments in a letter to his son, Louis, himself a new father: "You and Josephine must live quite cosily and happily with your new born babe. I know how it is, it recalls our own [happy] experience with our little ones." In another letter he wrote of his "true affection" and "confiding and [unchanging] Love" for Louis.[8]

Men like Kendall and Laflin were not alone. They represented a style of fatherhood congruent with long-developing attitudes about children and in line with the hopes of domestic moralists that men commit emotional energy to their wives and children. But such emotional bonds were difficult to establish and likely uncommon. Structural barriers that undermined father-child bonding were endemic to an economy in which increasing numbers of men earned wages and salaries outside the home. Although many nineteenth-century Northern fathers surely tried to forge emotional, companionate bonds with their children, breadwinning obligations sabotaged such efforts. Fathers' work in stores and factories kept most from meeting the new standards of child care prescribed by the domestic ideal; thus, while moralists hoped to bring fathers and children together, the structure of the economy drove them apart.[9]

Obviously, such was not the case for thousands of farmers who taught their sons how to succeed on the land or for craftsmen who maintained their trade despite the rise of the factory culture. But the general trend was clear. Under the impact of industrialization, fathers' control over their own future and that of their children declined. Even farm fathers found it difficult to maintain generational continuity. The age structure of out-migration and depopulation figures in rural communities suggests that farm children looked elsewhere for economic opportunities. Although farm fathers devised a variety of relatively successful strategies to keep their children nearby, long-range economic and demographic trends worked against them: ultimately farm children became the inhabitants of towns and cities.[10]

Once in factories, fathers found it difficult to maintain craft skills or to pass such skills to their offspring. The skilled cordwainer of today became the deskilled factory hand of tomorrow. While traditional craftsmen in new factory towns faced the most difficulties, men in small rural communities faced similar pressures. Both the number of trades and the men who performed them, for example, declined markedly in Chelsea, Vermont, between 1850 and the end of the century. Where there had been fourteen shoemakers in 1850, there were two in 1900; five tailors plied their trade in 1850, none a half-century later.[11] To make a living, ever more men from both rural and urban communities had to work long hours in central shops and new factories away from home; meanwhile, their children were at the mercy of nineteenth-century industrial capitalism and sought work wherever they could get it. Although some might follow their fathers into the same factory, the transmission of skill from father to son had become ever more difficult.

Men in the middle class faced a different kind of difficulty in establishing close relationships with their children. Breadwinning became ever more important to a class increasingly wedded to consumption. To earn the salaries that purchased the accoutrements of middle-class life, fathers often had to work in distant downtown offices. These were America's first commuters, residents of the streetcar suburbs that began developing even before the Civil War.[12] Their travels between home and work left them little time to spend with their children, and thus their wives dominated child rearing. What these fathers had to offer was something more tangible—money. While their children were young, middle-class fathers provided an impressive standard of living. As their children matured, fathers subsidized sons until they received the necessary training for success in the middle class and daughters until they found an acceptable husband.

Such support could be protracted. Nineteenth-century middle-class children commonly waited until their twenties before they moved out of their parents' household, married, and established their own homes. In Philadelphia, fully one-fifth of young people remained in their parents' home until their late twenties.[13] In Utica, New York, 40 percent of native-born men between fifteen and thirty and over 50 percent of those of that age in the white-collar class lived with their parents at midcentury.[14] Young men in white-collar occupations were especially likely to reside at home up to the age of thirty. In 1860, almost 40 percent of Utica's clerks lived with kin, usually their parents.[15] This sustained financial dependence on fathers coupled with extended schooling and training certainly heightened the importance of male breadwinning. After all, positioning a child for life in the middle class was not easy. The life course of daughters was predictable enough, yet even their educational desires and needs expanded over the century. Finding an occupation in the burgeoning middle class for sons, however, required extended oversight, special training and education, and protracted support of a young man's career preparation. As Mary Ryan put it, "Children of white-collar and professional fathers were the latest to enter the work force, the longest to remain with their parents, probably the most highly educated, and hence the most expensive to rear."[16] With much of their material and psychological care provided by mothers and even sisters, sons remained at home to take advantage of educational and training opportunities. Lacking land or a trade to pass directly to sons, fathers had little to offer but some free advice and some hard-earned money.

In short, the occupational tie between father and son was gradually severed. In mid-nineteenth-century Utica, New York, for example, only 6 percent of middle-aged household heads had white-collar positions, whereas 16 percent of the young men had acquired such standing. By contrast, a substantially smaller percentage of the younger than the older generation worked as artisans.[17] The son of an artisan shoemaker might well become a clerk, accountant, or teacher, all respectable occupations though quite removed from that of the father. In a rapidly changing society, the successful father had to settle for providing his son the education or vocational training required for success in the new middle class.

Men's absence from home also undermined the relationship between fathers and daughters. The simultaneous emergence of industrialization and domesticity in the nineteenth century gave rise to a distinctive world of "female love and ritual." This world's roots lay in the breakup of the corporate household economy and the consequent rise of more rigid gender-role differentiation. These developments created social and psychological spaces in which women established lasting bonds with one another. Brought together by frequent pregnancies and childbirth, nurturing lifelong friendships with impassioned letters and frequent visits, bonding together in reform and church associations, women created a world in which men, fathers included, "made but a shadowy appearance."[18]

This homosocial culture had many dimensions, at the center of which were mother-daughter relationships. "Daughters," Carroll Smith-Rosenberg writes, "were born into a female world. Their mother's life expectations and sympathetic network of friends and relations were among the first realities in the life of the developing child." With few alternatives to wifehood and motherhood, girls automatically followed the lessons of their mothers. A virtual apprenticeship system developed as young girls learned the craft of domesticity and the rituals of female friendship. Over time, this tight relationship between mothers and daughters fostered "mutual emotional dependency" and a high degree of intimacy, sympathy, and understanding. Mothers also connected their daughters to the dense network of female kin and friends that sustained the female world once daughters started their own lives.

Men appear along the edges of this world. How much they were a part of it is still a matter of debate, but it seems likely that fathers were cut off from their daughters and their homosocial bonds. Fathers' frequent absences from home coupled with their daughters' immersion in a female world militated against deep father-daughter relationships.

Southern Variants

Industrialization ultimately redefined American fatherhood, but large numbers of Americans were relatively untouched by it until well into the twentieth century. The experience of white planters in the antebellum South, for example, was both similar to and unlike that of men in the North. Slave fathers and freedmen, in turn, had a different experience altogether. We now turn to these varieties of fatherhood.

Beginning in the second half of the eighteenth century, Southern planter families became increasingly based on emotion and affection. Marriage became less a union of families and more a bond of companionship between two people. These sentiments carried over to father-child relations. With their Northern counterparts, Southern fathers openly expressed affection for their children and grieved deeply at their deaths. Consoling his bereaved brother-in-law, James Baker empathized with his suffering: "I know my dear Brother how to appreciate your feelings. I too have lost fond and affectionate children endeared to me by a thousand infantile ties known to no one but a parent." Moorhead Wright was equally taken by his children and equally sad at the death of his newborn: "[My wife] had been very carefull [sic], and much we both regret [it] for if there is anyone that have a fondness for children I am that individual."[19]

Children who survived the rigors of infancy were quickly recognized by both parents as distinct personalities. Writing to a friend, Isaac Avery made no effort to disguise his pride in his four-month-old son's accomplishments and good looks: "Thomas Lenoir Avery, a young gentleman . . . can sit alone, laugh out loud and cut other smart capers for a fellow of his age and is the handsomest of all [our] . . . children." Such interest in children's antics continued as the youngsters moved beyond infancy. Daniel Blake Smith found that wealthy Southern parents in the years after 1750 took great delight in the innocence and playfulness of their children. Charmed by their offsprings' prattle and liveliness, these parents exhibited none of the anxiety about children's basic natures that so vexed parents in the previous century. Although mothers had primary responsibility for daily child care, fathers wrote and spoke affectionately of their children, lamented separation from them, frequently gave them gifts, worried about their health, delighted in their accomplishments, and even participated with gusto in their play.[20]

When their children reached school age, fathers helped make necessary arrangements, suggested curricula, and stressed the importance of academic success.[21] As to the latter, such advice went to both sons and daughters. George Capehart tried to foster academic competitiveness in his son: "I am in hopes you are improving in all your studies. You must try and keep ahead of all the little boy[s]." Elizabeth and Courtney McPherson received similar advice from their father, Willie: "[W]e should be Glad to here [sic] from you and at the time have some information on your progress in your studies, your examination is coming on and I hope you will remember the advantages it will be to you to acquit yourselves with credit[.] It will be a satisfaction to your preceptors and a pleasure to all your acquaintance." Minerva Cain's father reminded her of the importance of diligence and hard work: "I have so often (in conversation) recommended to you and my other children attention, industry and application to whatever you see[,] hear and are about doing, that I do not mention them now as duties merely; but I point them out to you again and again, as conducive, nay as absolutely necessary to your pleasures, your happiness and your respectability."[22]

This kind of personal evidence suggests Southern planter fathers' continuing interest in their offspring. Fathers listened to their children's desires, respected their sons' career choices, acquiesced in their offsprings' mate selection, and rarely, unlike their eighteenth-century forefathers, withheld land to maintain power over their sons.[23] In short, the Southern gentry shared with Northern middle-class families increasingly child-centered family relations. However, unlike fathers in the North whose experience was being reshaped by industrialization and domestic ideology, Southern white fathers held to a vision of patriarchy predicated upon veneration of forefathers and to child-rearing practices that used shame and humiliation to inculcate a sense of hierarchy and honor.[24] The evidence that Bertram Wyatt-Brown marshals in *Southern Honor* to prove the first point need not be recounted in detail. Suffice it to say that more than Northern families, those in the South paid special attention to family lineage, particularly the achievements of male ancestors. Whereas Northern child-naming practices, for example, signified increasing emphasis on the individuality of each child, those in the South tied children to their father's father and their mother's father. This ancestral linkage of father to father was not without its impact on the child: "The relation of the dutiful child to ancestors and to community," writes Wyatt-Brown, "was thus made clear; one could not easily escape to pursue one's own hopes under such circumstances. Duty to fathers came first. The future, even the present, rested on the past."[25]

This centrality of fathers was also evident in Southern child-rearing practices. While Northern middle-class child nurture became increasingly self-conscious, rational, mother-dominated, and preoccupied with the inculcation of guilt, Southern nurture remained somewhat haphazard and dedicated to the inculcation of honor in sons, a task entrusted in large part to fathers. While Southern fathers, as was true of fathers in the North, took little routine care of small children, they did look for "early signs of manliness in sons and vivacity in girls." And if Southern fathers and mothers of an evangelical persuasion might mirror Northern parents in their emphasis on conscience, guilt, and religious redemption, traditional Southern fathers distrusted feminized child rearing, maternal indulgence, and religious instruction because they believed it sapped male prowess. Male children had to prove their toughness and aggressiveness, their willingness to ride, hunt, fight, even duel. It was the obligation of fathers to see that their sons developed such abilities; after all, male prowess and male honor were inextricably linked. To live without honor, as Alfred Huger of Charleston consoled the father of a son killed in a duel, was not to live at all: "Give me such a One as your Brave Boy, aye, in his winding sheet and Napkin, sooner than another who prefers Existence to *that*, which confers upon Existence its only value."[26]

Racism and Black Fatherhood

The emphasis on honor among Southern fathers was a language of civility among equals and domination of inferiors. The latter part of this discourse defined the place of black fathers in the Southern hierarchy. The fundamental difficulty of black fathers is not hard to understand. In describing his allegedly kind former master, a black father went to the heart of the matter: "I was dat man's slave; and he sold my wife, and he sold my two chill'un. . . . Kind! yes, he gib me corn enough, and he gib me pork enough, and he neber give me one lick wid de whip, but whar's my wife?—whar's my chill'un? Take away de pork, I say; take away de corn, I can work and raise dese for myself, but gib me back de wife of my bosom, and gib me back my poor chill'un as was sold away."[27] This former slave eloquently expressed what separated him from all white fathers: he had no legal control over his children. They were his only at the sufferance of the master, and when it suited the master to sell the children, a slave father could do nothing to stop the transaction.

Of late, historians have emphasized the resiliency of the black slave family and the complexity and importance of slave kin ties. Marriages were remarkably stable and most slave women had their children by the same father. The great majority of slave families were headed by two parents, who usually had blood connections with a host of other slave families. These family relationships provided a crucial resource that helped blacks endure the oppression of slavery.[28] For their part, slave fathers played a vital role in black family life even though their power was tightly circumscribed by their white masters. Although slave fathers were not breadwinners in the same sense that free men were, recent scholarship has demolished the idea that slavery created a "tangle of pathology" that rendered black fathers irrelevant and the black family matriarchal and crippled.[29] Despite the horrors of slavery, including the breakup of roughly 20 percent of slave marriages by sale, most slave children grew up in homes with a slave father and mother. These fathers often named their sons, especially their first-born, after themselves, a practice that symbolically bound the two generations together. On one North Carolina plantation, for example, almost half of slave fathers with at least three children named a son after themselves, and on the Good Hope plantation in South Carolina six of thirteen male children bore their fathers' names. These naming practices, as historian Herbert Gutman has pointed out, defied the masters' assumption that slave fathers were irrelevant: "Parents who named sons for their fathers but not daughters for their mothers contradicted in their behavior the practice of owners who only recognized 'uterine' descent among them. By so dramatically affirming the important cultural role of the slave father, the slaves, once more, showed how their beliefs and practices differed from those of their owners."[30]

Although some slave fathers may have been irresponsible at best and brutal at worst, historian Eugene Genovese is surely correct in concluding that "others, probably a majority, overcame all obstacles and provided a positive male image for their wives and children." Such is certainly the sense of one ex-slave's recollection of his father: "I loved my father. He was such a good man. He was a good carpenter and could do anything." Noting the bond between his father and mother and his father's ability to interpret religious issues, the ex-slave had fond memories of the lessons he learned from his father: "I sometimes think I learned more in my early childhood about how to live than I have learned since."[31] Slave fathers had much to teach. Using skills that their own fathers or other relatives taught them, slave fathers enhanced their families' living standards, often by supplementing meager food allowances with fish or game. Louisa Adams of North Carolina recalled her father's efforts: "My old daddy partly raised his chilluns on game. He caught rabbits, coons an' possums. He would work all day and hunt at night." Slaves took pride in their hunting abilities and sons took pride in their fathers' ability to hunt. When their sons were old enough, fathers passed on their hunting and fishing skills.[32]

The bonds between slave fathers and children, of course, went well beyond teaching survival skills. In a brutal and exploitative world, they gave meaning to men's lives, a point made by fathers forced to cope with the sale of their children. Georgia slave Abream Scriven poignantly revealed his sentiments in a letter to his wife in 1858: "Give my love to my father & mother and tell them good Bye for me. And if we Shall not meet in this world I hope to meet in heaven. My Dear wife for you and my Children my pen cannot Express the griffe I feel to be parted from you all."[33] Other men simply wept, while one expressed his sentiments more brutally: to prevent forced separation from his son, he chopped off his left hand with a hatchet.[34]

These examples of inconsolable grief and self-mutilation starkly reveal the unbridgeable gulf that separated the experience of slave and white fathers. Slave fathers might well teach their sons how to hunt and fish; they could surely enhance their families' food supply and improve their modest quarters; they could give their offspring attention and tie them to the kin network by the careful selection of a name. But the fact remains that slave fathers had little or no control over their progeny's ultimate destiny. Masters separated fathers and children when it suited their financial needs. On large plantations, one in three slave fathers lived apart from their wives and children, and on smaller plantations the percentage was even higher. Those lucky enough to remain with their wives frequently witnessed the sale of their children. As children neared their teenage years, for example, the probability of sale increased dramatically, but even younger children faced the auction block: in New Orleans, the South's largest slave market, 10 percent of all sales were of children under thirteen.[35] One former slave bluntly recalled a painful childhood memory: "Well, dey took us on up dere to Memphis and we was sold jest like cattle. Dey sold me and ma together and dey sold pa and de boys together. Dey was sent to Mississippi and we was sent to Alabama."[36] Fathers were helpless in such situations. When their authority collided with that of the master, it was a foregone conclusion as to who would win.

Historians have also analyzed the black family in the years following slavery, and here, too, the evidence destroys the old argument that slavery left in its wake a dysfunctional matriarchy. Rather, the demographic evidence reveals that the great majority of black children in the postbellum years lived in two-parent households. Despite some variation over time and place, the proportion of two-parent black households was never below 65 percent, and in most studies in either the urban North or the urban or rural South, the figure was 75 to 80 percent.[37] Evidence from Louisville, Kentucky, gives further meaning to these figures. In that city, the percentage of female-headed households was higher in the decade before the Civil War than in the decade after. Such evidence suggests that fathers forced to live apart from their families under slavery reunited with them after emancipation.[38]

This evidence should not obscure an equally important point. Studies confirm that the percentage of black families headed by females in the late nineteenth and early twentieth centuries outstripped that of native-born and immigrant whites. The precise figures vary from time to time and place to place, but the evidence reveals a higher percentage of black than white fathers living apart from their wives and children, particularly in urban areas. The urban environment, in fact, was especially hard on black families in both the North and the South. Driven off the land by the crop-lien system, low agricultural prices, and crop failures, thousands of black men and women who moved to Southern and Northern cities were greeted with persistent discrimination, segregation, and under- or unemployment.[39] In this environment, fathers often found it necessary to leave their families to find work.

Although we later explore in detail the economic difficulties of white and black working-class fathers, here the point is that black fathers invariably encountered greater hardships than white. Denied factory jobs, excluded from unions, routinely paid lower wages than whites, black fathers had extraordinary difficulty supporting their families. In Southern cities, economic opportunities for blacks actually declined between 1850 and 1925. In New Orleans, for example, the number of black carpenters, cigar makers, painters, shoemakers, coopers, tailors, bakers, blacksmiths, and foundry hands dropped sharply in the three decades after 1870. After assessing data from New Orleans and other Southern cities, Herbert Gutman concluded "that Afro-American fathers were not able to pass accumulated skills to their sons at this early date."[40] Many, it appears, were simply unable to support their families at all and had to leave them to find work. Thus black fathers left their families more often than whites not because "slavery had emasculated the Negro males, had made them shiftless and irresponsible" but because agricultural enclosure, racist attitudes, and the class structure of urban, industrial America undermined their ability to support their wives and children.[41]

Farm Fathers and Rural Life

The distinctive class and race system of Southern agriculture was absent in the North. Here the popular, nostalgic image of the farm family had some basis in fact. Although this study cannot treat Northern farm fatherhood at length, it is important to note that competing visions of farm families in the American past helped shape debate in the twentieth century. When moral commentators and social scientists analyzed the critical developments that had shaped modern fatherhood, they invariably cast the "new fatherhood" of the twentieth century against the backdrop of the "old," rural fatherhood. Those who lamented the decline of rural America highlighted the organic unity of the farm family and the fact that farms were household enterprises in which husband, wife, and children worked together to earn a living. By contrast, those more positively inclined toward urban life and modernity underscored the superiority of urban families and children's desire to break away from the world of their fathers. These competing visions—the one emphasizing the economic and generational unity of the farm family, the other its claustrophobia and generational tensions—shaped the thinking about families and fatherhood in the late nineteenth and early twentieth centuries.

The former tradition in the 1920s is best represented by leading rural sociologists Pitirim Sorokin and Carle C. Zimmerman. Against their colleagues who celebrated the individualism and growing segmentation of urban American families, Sorokin and Zimmerman praised the inter-generational unity at the heart of rural life. Rural families were strong, they implied, because fathers had not relinquished their authority and because family members worked together for the good of all. Compared to urban families, those on the farm were more stable, orderly, and economically integrated. Their description underscored the mutual dependence and support that characterized the family farm:

> It has functioned as a real economic unit; its property has been not the property of this or of that member, but of the whole family; the work of the members of the family were not independent works of individuals but those of members of a whole social organism controlled and directed by it; their incomes and expenses were not something determined by their individual efforts, but only shares from the common pot or con-trolled by the family.

Rather than just a collection of individuals, the rural family was a "real social organism in which the individuals have been, so to speak, entirely melted. They have been but only parts of a family collectivity."[42]

This relative lack of individualism troubled most family experts, but Sorokin and Zimmerman saw it as a source of strength because it underlay parental control of children. Although their description of this control was frustratingly abstract—always exercised by "the family," "the parents"—they clearly implied that rural fathers had greater power over the life choices of their offspring than did urban parents: "While the members of the city family have a choice in many of their actions, free from the rigid control of their families, beginning with the economic callings they follow and ending with the choices of mates, in the rural family many of these actions are still under the strong control of the family and 'the freedom' of its members is still more limited." As a result, parental control promoted cohesion and stability among rural families and made them superior in every respect—economically, socially, educationally, even biologically—to city families.[43]

When Sorokin and Zimmerman focused on the specific factors that engendered strong rural families, they again wrote in abstractions, but the importance of fathers to their interpretation is implicit. Thus, the rural family was strong and stable because "its members are engaged in the same work, they are partners in the best sense of the word: their economic interests are identical because all work for the same family unit"; moreover, although urban homes have become little more than "a parking place over night," rural parents and children "are together most of the twenty-four hours in a day. . . . In brief, their direct-face-to-face contact is more incessant, and permanent." This constant contact between parents and children coupled with the relative isolation of the rural family increased parental control: in rural communities, fewer outside agencies vied for the attention of children, fewer extrafamilial "friends," "gangs," and "companions" competed for their affections, fewer commercial establishments satisfied their wants, and fewer vices attracted the interest of the young.[44]

These realities tied rural children to their parental homes and gave them a sense of place. Unlike the lives of more peripatetic urban youth, which frequently lacked "any material traces of the activities of its fathers and forefathers," farm families often lived in "the same house or farm or abode sometimes for several generations," which reinforced family unity and bonded the young with earlier generations. This bond forged by fathers across generations, as Sorokin and Zimmerman's critique of urban life suggested, comprised a "family culture" in which the older and younger generation shared "language, traditions, beliefs, mores, tastes, and what not." In the city, by contrast, the withering of the family's functions and its invasion by a host of outside agencies had broken the generational bond and left only a remnant of paternal power:

> [I]n the city, the parents . . . succeed in retaining only "a weakened and faded paternal authority." This latter is something very meager in comparison with that they have had and to a considerable extent still retain in the rural family.[45]

In a nutshell, Sorokin and Zimmerman believed that American families were at risk. What worried them was the invasion of the family by the state, the decline of the family's functions, the undermining of its unity, and, perhaps most fundamentally, the erosion of parental, particularly paternal, authority. Only among rural families did they see much hope.

Against the march of those praising modern, companionate, and democratic families, Sorokin and Zimmerman's conservative affinity for multifunctional, mutually dependent, patriarchally organized families was out of step.[46] But there was truth in what they said: family farms were (and are) economic enterprises to which all in the family contributed. In a 1930 survey of several hundred youth, rural boys and girls not only outperformed urban youngsters in most routine household tasks, they also did child care, tended gardens, milked cows, fed chickens, gathered eggs, watered stock, canned food, and worked in the fields at rates far surpassing those of city and small-town youth.[47] Common sense would suggest as much; thus, it comes as no real surprise that 76 percent of rural boys but only 6 percent of big-city boys had worked in the fields the previous year, or that 42 percent of the rural girls but less than 10 percent of girls from large cities had canned fruits or vegetables in the previous twelve months.[48] The more important point is that they did so as part of a household economy in which fathers and mothers directed their children in a myriad of economically critical tasks.

But the bonds between parents and children were, of course, more than economic. Rural children spent more time in the company of their fathers (and mothers) than did city youth. While at home, rural youth were more apt to spend time with their parents than with friends or alone; when away from home, the same pattern held. Sixteen percent of rural boys and 17 percent of rural girls spent every evening at home; figures for urban boys and girls were 4 and 5 percent, respectively. By contrast, 14 percent of urban boys but only 5 percent of rural boys spent every evening away from home. (In some Chicago immigrant neighborhoods, over 30 percent of the boys spent every evening away from home.) Family togetherness among rural families extended to religious observation: 74 percent of rural families had either read the Bible, said grace, prayed, or attended church together in the previous month; this was true of only 60 percent of families from large cities.[49]

This evidence confirmed key elements of Sorokin and Zimmerman's analysis. Unfortunately, it shares with them a propensity for abstraction. Boys and girls spend time with "parents," attend church with "parents," even go to movies with "parents." Perhaps such diction reflected more than sociological prejudices. One young farm woman offered this account of rural family life at the 1926 meeting of the National Country Life Conference:

> But to me, the farm home is a picture of family unity. The members of the farm home work together, play together, share equal responsibilities about the home, whether it be the care of the flower garden, vegetable garden, dairy farm or whatnot. They have an equal share in the ownership of the farm. The boy becomes a joint owner with dad. The girl becomes a joint owner in the poultry business with her mother. They develop self-reliance and confidence and that is where we think the farm youth is far ahead of those in the city.[50]

But prejudice or no, behind the abstraction were fathers working side by side with sons and daughters, spending leisure time with them, fulfilling that vision of organic unity so appealing to those troubled by modern urban life.

Or so it seemed. No doubt many fathers fulfilled this vision, but a variety of difficulties in the first third of the twentieth century eroded rural fathers' ability to sustain these bonds; moreover, most sociologists and psychologists argued that farm families were rife with generational tensions and that urban companionate families performed the crucial task of shaping children's "personalities" more effectively than their rural counterparts. Rather than lament the passing of the rural household from cultural prominence, these writers celebrated the shift to modern, child-centered family relations characteristic of urban middle-class life.

Without question, economic problems and the allure of city life made it difficult for farm fathers to sustain the intergenerational bonds of farming. Although many youth stayed in agriculture—a 1934 study of Genesee County, New York, for example, found that four-fifths of the farmers and three-fourths of their wives had been reared on farms—such prospects generally eluded the children of tenants and those from families with more than two children. One estimate from the 1930s stated that less than one-half of rural youth would ultimately find a place on good commercial farms, a warning echoed in 1938 by Secretary of Agriculture Henry A. Wallace, who lamented that "within the next two decades, approximately 7,000,000 farm youths will mature with virtually no prospect of finding land to farm or even steady employment as agricultural laborers." The subsequent migration of farmers and farm youth to urban areas, particularly from the South, bore out Wallace's warning.[51]

The troubles of farm fathers were cultural and generational as well as economic. Although fathers might praise life on the land, their children were drawn to urban amusements. Paul Landis, an expert in rural sociology, described how this developed: "Increasingly as farm youth have contacted town and urban school systems, they have absorbed the pleasure-seeking philosophy and having done so cease to find the enjoyment and spiritual strength in work that their parents claimed to find. At this point there is a clash which often leads to a separation between the old generation and the new." The budding youth culture of rural and small-town schools, Landis argued, allowed children to escape from adult patterns and ultimately undermined fathers' control of their children: "The entrance of farm youth into the high school has probably done more to break down patriarchal patterns in the rural home and to divorce youth from parental domination than any other single influence."[52]

One South Dakota student described just how this process worked. At an early age, his father had integrated him into farm work, and by age ten he plowed corn and took pride in doing a full day's work. But school changed his attitudes: "One of the first things I noticed at school was that my classmates delighted in making fun of farm boys. In order to become popular with his father's town boys, I began to fool myself into believing that the farm was an uninteresting place and that I did not like it." His father noticed the change and "took me out to work on the farm every Saturday, hoping to keep me interested in it. But the work was drudgery for I had lost my former interest in it and was in constant fear that some of my new friends would hear that I worked on a farm and cease associating with me." Only since starting college had he become reconciled to doing farm labor, but now for reasons that had nothing to do with his father's love of agrarian life: "I would probably still have the same attitude were it not for football. Learning that nearly all the good athletes in college kept in shape in the summer months by working on farms, I was able to enjoy farm work." Farm work as a pre-season athletic training camp was a far cry from farming as a way of life, and in a telling, no doubt painful comment to his father's ears, the boy made it clear that working the land was not in his future: "I have no desire to become a farmer."[53]

This youth's dissatisfaction with farm life and the implicit conflict with his father were shared by many other farm youth. Surely many young boys loved farm work and the steady contact with their father that such work afforded, but many others resented it deeply. As one farm boy wrote: "I hated the work on the farm and everything associated with it, and often wished that I had been born to other parents." Admitting that he never dared voice his anger to his father, he confided his resentments to his mother, but she offered little sympathy: "However, Mother took the position that I owed this to her and Dad and as a result most of my childhood was spent at work."[54] A fourteen-year-old farm boy from West Virginia offered his sentiments more bluntly: "I ain't goin' to stay here much longer; I have to work myself to death and don't get nothing out of it; never get to go *nowhurs*. I don't like it and ain't goin' to stay."[55]

This boy's anger belied the image of father and son, mother and daughter contentedly working side by side on the farm for the good of the family. An expert from the Jewish Agricultural Society confirmed the prevalence of these frustrations: "I find that many of the boys are dissatisfied because they don't know what they are working for in so far as money return is concerned. The income all goes into the family pot. . . . [H]e feels dissatisfied that he doesn't know at the end of the week just what his return is going to be for his labor."[56] A survey of three hundred farm youth in Ohio reported that 73 percent had no systematic pay arrangement for their labor, a haphazard policy that left children dependent on the goodwill of their parents: "In most cases the young people were forced to be content with subsistence plus whatever else the parents felt able to give, which frequently was nothing at all." Parents even routinely pocketed the earnings from produce raised by their children for school projects, thereby discouraging their youngsters' participation in future such endeavors.[57] Clearly, the mutual obligations at the heart of the farm economy were not without their fault lines.

In fact, these resentments against fathers and farm life were widely shared. In a study of farm children's autobiographies, Mildred B. Thurow found more tension between fathers and children in rural than urban homes but less tension between mothers and children. A similar study by William Mather came to the same conclusion: rural children resented their fathers' authority and discipline more than urban children and demonstrated less affection toward and confided in them less.[58] A national study discovered that rural white boys and girls were less likely to "almost always" tell their fathers their "joys and troubles" than urban youth, and that the rural and village youth more frequently criticized their fathers than did urban adolescents.[59]

Ultimately, these data are only suggestive. Summarizing the experiences of rural fathers and their offspring is hazardous, given the great diversity of agriculture in the United States. But the evidence suggests generational fissures in the family life of rural Americans. As some experts suggested, perhaps the patriarchal dominance of rural fathers coupled with their constant presence created problems for rural children.[60] Whether it was unrelenting work, boredom, the lure of the cities, their fathers' dominance, or even frequent attendance at movies—almost 45 percent of rural and small-town children attended the movies at least once a week—children found much to criticize about their fathers' lives in particular and rural America in general.[61] Asked what career they wished to follow, only 22 percent of farmers' sons in Missouri wanted to follow in their fathers' footsteps. (Almost 15 percent wanted to become aviators.[62]) Ultimately, many of these rural children moved to the city and left behind much of the world of their fathers.[63]

Fathers, the Law, and the State

Economic change altered fatherhood in the nineteenth century and prompted a renegotiation of men's family responsibilities. To chart the changing course of nineteenth-century fatherhood, however, we must move beyond the economic sphere and explore how other cultural and social changes reshaped the lives of fathers. Legal thinking about parenthood, state intervention in family life, and new attitudes about child rearing all suggest that fatherly authority declined during the nineteenth century, ironically at a time when men's economic responsibilities were never greater.

Legally, fathers most certainly became the "second" parent. Holding that children were the property of fathers, courts had traditionally given fathers custody of children when marital disputes split families. New attitudes toward motherhood and children influenced jurists in antebellum years to move away from this common-law doctrine and argue that the father's right to custody was only presumptive and could be overcome if the child's interests were better served by the mother. Soon courts even abandoned the idea of fathers' presumptive right, arguing that mothers and fathers had equal rights and that custody decisions should be based on the "best interests of the child."[64] The California Supreme Court, for example, decided in 1860 that mothers, not fathers, could better serve those interests: "That a child of the tender age of this," wrote the court, "could be better cared for by the mother, with whom she could be almost constantly, than the father, whose necessary avocations would withdraw him, in a great measure, from personal superintendence and care of her, is plain enough."[65]

The court had neatly condensed into one sentence over a hundred years of family history: children were "tender" and in need of constant care; absent fathers could not supply such attention but mothers could; therefore, mothers should provide the care and nurture of young, innocent offspring. Other courts even argued that the presumptive right of custody ultimately resided with mothers. The Pennsylvania Supreme Court took this position as early as 1840 in granting custody to a woman who refused to live with her husband, a nobleman residing in Switzerland. Although tradition dictated that the father gain custody, the Pennsylvania justices evoked the sentimental language of domesticity to give the mother the presumptive right to custody: "Every instinct of humanity unerringly proclaims that no substitute can supply the place of *her,* whose watchfulness over the sleeping cradle or waking moments of her offspring is prompted by deeper and holier feelings than the most liberal allowance of a nurse's wages could possibly stimulate."[66] The practical effect of this reconceptualization of custody law was that by the closing decades of the nineteenth century, the great majority of custody awards in divorce suits went to women.[67]

The expansion of the state also eroded the formerly preeminent position of fathers. Although the state's impact on fathers is treated in more detail in later chapters, several general points are in order. In the 1830s and 1840s, a variety of public institutions emerged to deal with orphaned, vagrant, and incorrigible children. Faced with a variety of threats to public order—immigration, labor unrest, restless and wayward children—reformers began building asylums to rehabilitate miscreant youth and prepare orphans for entry into the adult world. While the child savers gave lip service to creating family environments within the asylum walls, the institutions they created were a rebuke to the more permissive, child-centered families emerging in antebellum America. By placing a premium on obedience, discipline, and silence, the asylum superintendents not only absorbed a function once performed by mothers and fathers but implicitly chastised them for their loss of authority and control.[68]

Courts even made the case that the long-range interests and expertise of asylum reformers should take precedence over the desires of insensitive or incompetent parents. As a Pennsylvania court explained in an 1838 decision upholding the constitutionality of a young girl's commitment to the Philadelphia House of Refuge, such asylums made their inmates industrious, moral, religious, and capable of earning a living: "To this end, may not the natural parents, when unequal to the task of education, or unworthy of it, be superseded by the *parens patriae,* or common guardian of the community?"[69] Public, not private patriarchy became increasingly evident as justices settled disputes between parents and the state in favor of the latter.

The state's sovereignty over paternal control was even more evident in the growth of public schooling. While the relationship between schooling and fatherhood is also treated at length in later chapters, suffice it to say that although education of the very young remained entrusted to mothers, formal instruction of children over age six shifted away from the family altogether. The common schools assumed the crucial task of educating growing numbers of children for life in a republic. As early as the 1830s, states proposed compulsory attendance laws and insisted that such laws take precedence over parental desires, a philosophy that underlay the spate of such laws passed in the late nineteenth and early twentieth centuries.[70]

These trends toward greater state involvement in family life reached new heights at the turn of the century. The state became increasingly involved with what had once been the family's traditional economic, educational, health, and welfare functions. Convinced that falling birth rates, rising divorce rates, expanding opportunities for women, loosening sexual mores, and restless juveniles threatened the very existence of the family, reformers responded ambitiously to intervene on its behalf. Influenced by educators, reformers, sociologists, psychologists, social workers, physicians, and clergymen, legislators tightened marriage and divorce laws, passed anticontraceptive statutes and restricted abortion, and erected domestic relations courts with special jurisdiction over family problems. To enhance the welfare of the young, reformers pressed for and successfully established a juvenile court system, child labor laws, and compulsory school attendance laws. To improve child rearing, progressives put into place parent education programs in schools and colleges and sponsored special conferences and institutes on parenting.[71]

Behind all these new developments was the assumption that families could not be left to themselves, that fathers and mothers were either so incompetent or so overwhelmed that only professional expertise and government assistance could fulfill their obligations. No longer could fathers be expected to cope with unruly juveniles without assistance from a beneficent juvenile court system; no longer could mothers run efficient, well-managed, healthy homes without the assistance of home economists and health professionals; no longer could parents understand the complex development of their children without information from child-rearing experts. Agents of an increasingly therapeutic culture would answer these needs, in the process transforming power relations within families in complex ways.

These developments had ironic implications for men. The language of science and expertise had been appropriated in ways that left fathers ever more irrelevant to the rearing of their own children. Motherhood was increasingly seen as a science, fatherhood a seldom discussed art. Thus, pioneers in the new field of child study urged mothers to keep careful records of their children's development and to form child study groups to share information about their own and their children's experiences. Writers like G. Stanley Hall and Luther Emmett Holt advised mothers to put child rearing on a scientific basis and to replace instinct and love with reason and routine. Although Holt's emphasis on order and regularity soon yielded to less routinized approaches, he was the leading child expert in the early twentieth century and greatly influenced Mrs. Max West, author of the popular *Infant Care* pamphlets published by the Children's Bureau. Hall, Holt, and West were not, of course, the first experts to advise mothers, but thanks to wide distribution in pamphlets, magazines, and newspapers and to steady dissemination by government agencies, home economists, and social workers, the concept of scientific mothering had never had so wide an audience and so much influence. All this advice assumed that mothers were the primary child rearers and that to fulfill this responsibility they needed knowledge of hygiene, nutrition, child development, and the like. This advice also assumed that men's lives largely existed outside the home and that their chief responsibility lay in earning a living.[72] In short, as the century came to a close, fathers were becoming increasingly marginal within the home itself.

Fatherhood and Breadwinning

Fathers entered the twentieth century divided by class, race, and region, but they were inheritors of historical changes that had redefined fatherhood. Fatherhood had become increasingly identified with breadwinning at a time when men's other functions had been absorbed by an active state and an expansive maternal culture that relegated fathers to a secondary position within the family. Yet breadwinning presented its own problems and pressures. Plagued by un- and under-employment, subject to periodic layoffs and pitifully low wages, working-class fathers maintained a precarious hold on respectability in a society rapidly becoming more materialistic and consumer-oriented. What they offered their children were lessons in mutual support; what they tried to attain was some measure of financial security and a better life for their children; what they found fleeting was their ability to spend sustained time with their offspring.

Middle-class fathers faced pressures of a different kind. Living in growing cities or suburbs, working within the newly emerging, segmented and bureaucratic middle class, these men found that economic security quickly became entangled with ever rising standards of consumption. To be middle class was to consume, and men underwrote the act. Their efforts were more or less successful but fraught with difficulty as constantly changing definitions of the good life required more of fathers' time and energy. Men would give it, and in doing so they gained the status and prerogatives that came with the male monopoly of decent work. But in giving it they wedded themselves to a division of labor and a vision of the good life that made father-child closeness problematic. What men gained in the world of power they may have lost in the world of sentiment. Such was the trade-off at the heart of male breadwinning.

3

Breadwinning on the Margin: Working-Class Fatherhood, 1880–1930

H ANDEL, A THIRTY-FOUR-YEAR-OLD LABORER, FACED AN UNCER-
tain future. Married seven years, the father of a five-year-old boy, he
had once been a successful worker in the Akron, Ohio, rubber industry,
but his wife's poor health and her desire to be with relatives in Pittsburgh prompted a move that proved disastrous. Unable to find steady
work in Pittsburgh in the 1920s, Handel bounced from job to job, each
time "laid off again, not for anything we done but because *they* run out
of work." What was worse, he realized he was not alone and that he was
vulnerable to things over which he had no control: "And there was hundreds of men just like me—dying to work—willing to do anything—
took on as though for a permanent job and then laid off without any
warning or any pay." Handel measured his despair by his family's
wretched living standards—he said they lived "like pigs only with not so
much to eat"—but even more poignantly by his inability to help his
child. Living in the family's damp shed without electricity, heat, gas, or
water, Handel's son, Paul, had gotten pneumonia, a crisis that underscored Handel's own sense of frustration and impotency: "He got a bad
cough that stuck to him all winter and then one specially [sic] bad wet
spell it went right into pneumonia. I pretty near went crazy to see him
lying there so still and hot and me with no money to get a doctor."

Fortunately, the Kingsley House social settlement came to the Handel family's aid, securing treatment for the son and a menial job for the father. Nevertheless, Handel's future was still bleak, buffeted as he was by the vagaries of an uncertain job market. His confidence shattered by eighteen months of unemployment, the laborer was torn between keeping a dead-end but relatively secure janitorial job or finding a higher-paying but risky job in industry. All he knew for sure was that his expenses would continue to rise and the prospects for his son would more than likely dim: "Of course a hundred a month ain't much compared to what I made in Akron and when the kid gets bigger it'll seem less and less. If he ever gets a little brother or sister like he ought to have it'll sure go fast." The caseworker likewise agreed that the son's prospects were none too bright: "At present their child is being brought up in the worst mud-hole in Pittsburgh. Smoke, dirt and dampness greatly impede his physical development and the depressing surroundings must undoubtedly leave their mark." The caseworker, too, realized Handel's dilemma and asserted that the laborer would probably opt for security: "The fear instilled into him by those eighteen months has gone deep . . . and he is more than likely to 'stay put' and keep his family's development curtailed within narrow limits. His experience has hit hard at his courage to face the future."[1]

The experience of Handel was more depressing than that of many, perhaps most men of his class, but his difficulties highlight key features of working-class fatherhood in the early twentieth century. Industrial workers were overwhelmingly dependent wage laborers who found it next to impossible to support their families on their wages alone. Through ruthless underconsumption and the assistance of wives and children, millions of working-class fathers managed to eke out a living in an economy of unpredictability, under- and unemployment, and worker transiency. In so doing, they found that the equation of manhood with fatherhood and male breadwinning came not without its costs and that fatherly authority was difficult to maintain in the face of wage dependence and an uncertain job market.

Working-Class Strategies and Masculine Identity

Men in factories confronted head-on the realities of urban industrial life and the incredible strains it placed on their traditional "duty to provide." For these men, breadwinning meant long hours of work and vulnerability to the vicissitudes of the American economy. While some men maintained craft traditions within factory gates, many more became machine tenders with little control over their work. Industrial capitalism thus transformed breadwinning and fatherhood: fathers and mothers now worked out complicated strategies of survival that relied heavily on child labor. So long as men had work, these strategies insured their dominant place within the family, but when economic downturns left fathers un- or underemployed, their authority became suspect, their confidence waned, and their identity as men might even crumble. To understand working-class fatherhood, then, is to understand the marginal position of men in this class and how their class position shaped their response to their fatherly responsibilities, their ability to nurture and spend time with their children, their aspirations for their children, and the tensions and disappointments they experienced as fathers.

One fact is crucial: most industrial workingmen could not support their families on their wages alone. The vulnerability of the hireling, not the autonomy of the artisan, characterized their lives as breadwinners. Although most skilled workers could manage a decent living, unskilled laborers and machine tenders lived between outright poverty and modest subsistence, their survival dependent upon steady work and the income supplied by their wives and children. Between 1910 and 1920, workers in Chicago's slaughterhouses, for example, earned on the average only 38 percent of the minimum needed to support a family of four; as late as 1922, that figure had climbed to only 48 percent. Italian fathers in Buffalo at the turn of the century encountered the same predicament: they needed some $650 a year to support a family of five, but the average laborer from 1890 to 1916 earned between $360 and $625.[2]

Faced with this predicament, men turned to family strategies for survival.[3] As children came of working age, parents sent them into the work force, and despite the ruthless exploitation of child workers, their earnings spelled the difference between disaster and a small measure of security for their families. In late nineteenth-century Philadelphia, for example, Irish children contributed about 40 percent of the total family income, German children a little over 30 percent, and native-born offspring roughly 30 percent.[4] But how did this dependence on the earnings of children affect fathers? In a culture that defined men as providers, did this family economy shore up or erode fathers' power? How did children respond to fathers' decisions about child labor and wage pooling? Was the family economy a cooperative realm or a world of conflict and divided loyalties? To answer these questions is to recognize that the family economy of industrial wage work both enhanced and undermined the position of fathers.

The family economy certainly had the potential to tighten the bonds between men and their children. Despite their dependence on the supplemental earnings of wives and children, men had the responsibility by custom and law to support their families. Thus, while mothers worked sporadically in the labor force and helped their children prepare for its demands, fathers' identity as breadwinners made them the key emissaries between the home and the working world. Fathers helped prepare their children at an early age to fulfill their obligations to help support the family. In fact, for many children, the home and the mill were virtually inseparable: children lived next to or near the mill, played in its shadow, constantly heard about mill work from kin and neighbors, and frequently visited the workrooms. During these impressionable years, both parents instructed their children in the importance of family sharing and sacrifice and provided role models for the future workers. Geddes Dodson, a Southern textile worker, remembered the tasks assigned him during his daily visits to his father:

> When I was a little fellow, my daddy was a-working in the Poinsett Mill. He was a loom fixer. He'd run the weavers' looms through the dinner hour so they could go eat their dinner. We lived about a mile and a quarter from the mill, and I'd carry his lunch ever day. He'd tell me to come on in the mill, and he made me fill his batteries while he run the weavers' looms—and I was just a little fellow. See, I knew a whole lot about the mill before I ever went in one.[5]

Once their children reached working age, fathers helped them find work, preferably in rooms with kin who acquainted the greenhorns with workroom gossip, shop rituals, and labor shortcuts.[6] This responsibility became quite important as the children, especially sons, reached marriage age; whereas daughters were expected to leave the work force upon marriage and pregnancy, sons would soon become breadwinners and fathers in their own right. Interviews with Polish and Italian workers in Pittsburgh, for example, reveal that fathers often played a critical role in securing work for their sons. Nicholas R. relied on his father's influence to get a job installing streetcar lines for the Pittsburgh Railways. Walter K.'s father found work for Walter and his two brothers at Phoenix Iron and Steel. The father of Joseph D. secured his son an apprenticeship with a housing contractor to learn a trade. Many Poles found work at Armour Meat Company with the help of fathers or close relatives, and at Heppenstall's machine shop most jobs went to the sons of employees. Joseph L. and John S., who followed their fathers into the shop, recalled that Heppenstall's was a "father and son deal where everyone was putting in his own son."[7]

Young workers often entered the labor force not as independent agents but as individuals connected to a family. Such practices could affect workers in both positive and negative ways. "New workers," writes the historian Tamara Hareven, "bore the label of their kin." Such labeling, as Hareven explained, might bestow privileges or create problems: "The status of relatives present in the mill sometimes descended to the shoulders of a new worker. The sins of the fathers were not necessarily visited upon the sons, nor was a worker uniformly treated as an independent agent. In this respect, kinship ties bestowed disadvantages as well as advantages."[8]

Having secured a job, child wage earners generally continued to live at home, where they remained financially dependent on their fathers, who supplied most of the family income and provided the young workers with room and board. By keeping children in a state of semidependence until well into their twenties, this arrangement prolonged fathers' authority over their children. Transitions to adulthood, in fact, proceeded at a slower pace at the turn of the century than later in the twentieth century. Children started work at an earlier age but left home, married, and established independent households at a later date than their mid-twentieth-century counterparts. Thus, a family economy dominated by breadwinning fathers and home-managing mothers decisively shaped the transition to adulthood in early twentieth-century mill towns. As was true for the thousands of young workers at the huge Amoskeag Mills in Manchester, New Hampshire—where over half the young men and women in their early twenties still resided with their parents—independence was slowed by the prolonged financial dependence of young adults upon their fathers.[9]

While children resided at home, parents expected them to relinquish control of their wages, an arrangement that left children, daughters more so than sons, dependent on their fathers and mothers. In the early years of the twentieth century, boys over the age of fifteen in Southern textile mills gave up about 73 percent of their wages to their parents, while girls of the same age handed over almost 90 percent. Children kept even less in Northern textile mills: girls contributed 96.6 percent of their wages to the family, boys 82.4 percent.[10] Mack Duncan, a Southern millworker, remembered turning over his pay to his father: "I weren't any different than anybody else. When I went to work, my daddy always got all my pay. Any money I made went to him automatically."[11]

Many young workers accepted such arrangements as inevitable and necessary; they assented to the authority and power of their fathers and to the postponement of their own goals for those of the family. As Amoskeag worker Richard Laroche remembered, "There was no question. . . . It stands to reason that the father expected, when there was nine or ten children, that they're all gonna start working and pitch in." Marie Proulx, a French-Canadian immigrant in Manchester, New Hampshire, recalled her own sense of responsibility with a combination of resignation, sadness, and pride:

> Papa said: "Well, now, my little girl, we'll no longer be around the house. We'll have to look out so that we'll work." I told him, "I'm going today with my cousin to the mills." My father was never able to support a family of eight children on $1.10 per day. It was miserable at first. Oh, were we miserable! Our old parents worked till their foreheads were sweating to try to have what we get for nothing today. So I had to go work somewhere, and all there was were the mills, there was only Amoskeag. We had to help our father; I was the oldest one. Four dollars and twenty cents per week—I couldn't go far with that.[12]

Fellow Manchester resident Yvonne Dionne accepted her work responsibilities as a matter of course: "We were brought up in a large family—my father was a weaver and loomfixer—and as soon as one girl was old enough, she went to work. That was the way. The oldest one started, and the rest of the family had to follow suit."[13]

Ray La Marca, the son of an Italian immigrant, recalled his own contributions to the family economy: "When you work, you understand, you used to bring your pay home and give it to your parents. And whatever they feel they want to give you, they decide. There was no disagreement. That was their style." Nor would his father accept a boarder's fee from his son, an arrangement that would have given the son some autonomy by allowing him to keep some of his wages: "And don't you dare talk about paying board, especially in my dad's house. If you want to pay board you have to go somewhere else. We never thought of that. We never had it in our mind. There was no such thing." To his father, a boarding fee from one of his own children destroyed his concept of family life: "The minute you wanted to pay board they would throw you out. 'There's no board here,' my father would say. 'This is no boardinghouse. This is a family.' He said to us to bring our pay home and whatever it was, we would make do."[14]

Success on the Margin

The family economy required cooperation that boys like Ray La Marca and girls like Yvonne Dionne willingly gave. Such family reciprocity insured a measure of security for daughters until they married, for sons until they established their own households, and for parents who faced the chronic problem of low wages and layoffs. And security for many breadwinners was the definition of success: for men on the margin, success often meant a steady job and the ownership of their own home. A home, in fact, was a tangible asset and proof of achievement. To own a home meant that a man had gained some success as a breadwinner. It was both a hedge against hard times and the caprices of a landlord and a symbol of success that "could provide a sense of pride in a world where work often denied one feelings of worth."[15] Pittsburgh worker Joe B., whose father came from Russian Poland in 1900, recalled his parents' quest to own a home: "Really it was the prime thing on their mind, the paying off the mortgage, and they did."[16]

Others, especially immigrants, did the same. By 1930 foreign-born whites in Pittsburgh owned their own homes at a rate considerably higher than that of native-born whites.[17] What is more, those immigrants who remained in Pittsburgh between 1910 and 1930 showed impressive gains in homeownership. In 1910 about 18 percent of a sample of Poles owned their own homes; twenty years later 30 percent did so. Italians showed almost exactly the same gains, and although the overall homeowning rates of Northern- and Southern-born blacks were lower than those of immigrants, they too had success in buying homes. In Detroit at the turn of the century, 55 percent of the Germans, 44 percent of the Poles, 46 percent of the Irish, but only 27 percent of the native white Americans owned their own homes.[18] By investing not only his own savings but also those of his wife and children, by building a modest home with the help of fellow workingmen in what Olivier Zunz has called "the informal housing market," these men bought security and a "place" in the immigrant neighborhood for their families. Homeownership, no matter how modest the dwelling, signified some success as a breadwinner and hence some success as a man.

The other sign of success for breadwinners on the margin was occupational mobility, and numerous studies have convincingly shown that working-class fathers found incremental occupational mobility a reality.[19] In dynamic, rapidly growing cities like Atlanta, Los Angeles, and Omaha, about 20 percent of manual workers rose to white-collar positions within ten years, a figure that varied considerably by race and ethnicity. Among Boston men whose work histories could be traced from beginning to end, about a quarter who started their careers as manual workers ended their working lives in the middle class.[20] The meaning of such mobility in relationship to fatherhood is not entirely clear. Given the cultural emphasis on male breadwinning and men's obligation to support their children, upward mobility must have confirmed a father's sense of success. To move upward was to create more options for one's children: child labor could be avoided, schooling extended, special lessons afforded. And even if they could not move up, most men hoped their children could do so. Although Amoskeag fathers sent their children into the mills at an early age, most did not want their children to end up as millworkers. If possible, they wanted to keep their children and wives out of the mills, buy a home, educate their offspring, and attain middle-class occupations, if not for themselves, then for their children.[21] A personnel officer's survey of Amoskeag workers in 1935, for example, found a "very small percentage of the heads of families display any interest in having their children employed in the mills permanently."[22] One worker, Jeanne Hebert, recalled that "my father said we'd never work in the mills. That's one thing that my father didn't want us to do, to work in the mills." Oscar Johanson, the son of a Swedish immigrant, had a similar recollection: "My father said to me: 'No mills for you down there.' So my brother was a postal inspector. I was a cost accountant . . . we went to school."[23]

Thousands of immigrant children replicated Johanson's experience. Although some failed to attain the status of their fathers—in Poughkeepsie, New York, second-generation sons of craftsmen were more likely than their fathers to become factory operatives or to move into low-status trades, an experience duplicated by sons of German craftsmen in Philadelphia—in general, working-class sons outstripped the career achievements of their fathers.[24] Between 30 and 40 percent of boys born into working-class homes in Boston edged their way into middle-class jobs, a figure in line with studies from other cities. Even sons from the bottom of the working-class in Boston showed impressive gains: 40 percent of male youths whose fathers were unskilled workers made the climb to middle-class occupations.[25]

To begin life in poverty, to cobble together a livelihood in extremely trying conditions, and then to see one's children secure a foothold in the expanding American middle class could not help but bring to these fathers a sense of pride that was hard-earned and edged with sacrifice. One writer recalled that he scarcely knew his father. Only a deathbed conversation had provided a hint of the meaning of the old man's life:

> And none of us had ever taken thought that Father wanted anything in this life, except the privilege of working twelve to sixteen hours a day to keep a roof over the heads of the rest of us. . . . It is an inconspicuous part that fathers seem to play in life. Yet how unselfishly, how resolutely they set their faces to the task of building and maintaining homes that families may be raised.[26]

Work and Nurture

Such satisfactions for many working-class men came not without cost. Long hours at work coupled with leisure patterns that took fathers away from the home were not conducive to father-child closeness.[27] Consequently, fathers' time with their children declined relative to that of their wives or to that of men in the middle class. Certainly, what little evidence we have of working-class fathers' involvement in child study suggests as much. John Anderson's examination of three thousand American families in the early 1930s, for example, found that working-class fathers read less about child care than men from the middle and upper classes and showed markedly less tendency to listen to radio programs about child care or to attend child study and parent-teacher association groups.[28]

It comes as no surprise that working-class, especially immigrant, fathers did not have the time, the education, or the inclination to follow advice about child rearing emanating from the middle class. Parent education, however, is not the same as parental involvement, and here the data are even more elusive. Anderson found little systematic difference among fathers of different social classes in regard to their play involvement with their infants.[29] As children grew older, however, class disparities increased. Middle-class fathers, for example, read to or told their offspring more stories than working-class fathers, a disparity, Anderson suggested, that "may be due entirely to the fact that professional class fathers spend more time with their children."[30] Nor did working-class fathers play as active a role in child discipline as middle- and upper-class fathers, evidence that to Anderson "fits in with data from other sections of the report which show that the father takes more part in the care and training of the child in the higher than in the lower classes."[31]

This does not mean that working-class men did not enjoy their children or worry about them, but only that in some sense they were outsiders. Novelist Thomas Bell captured this quality in his description of Mike Dobrejcak, a young Slovak who worked in the steel-mill towns of Pennsylvania. Mike liked his children, especially their babbling in English, but his intimacy with them was limited, in part because he felt unsure of himself around them and in part because there "were definite limits to the intimacy they permitted, and after a few awkward attempts to meet them on their own level, which seemed to embarrass them acutely, he was content to watch and listen." Clearly, he had a strong sense that fathers, like steel bosses, represented authority and that they must maintain some degree of distance from their children: "Joking with them, he discovered, was an unsatisfactory business, curiously like a boss in the mill condescending to joke with one of his men; the man laughed but not comfortably and on the whole would have preferred the boss to keep his place." By contrast, his wife seemed closer to the children, "which was only natural." Unlike him, she addressed the children as equals, and as equals they accepted her, all of which left Mike feeling distant and alienated: "Beside her Mike felt clumsy, and against his own inclination—it was as if they had entered into a conspiracy—he found himself cast in the role of Papa, solemn, preoccupied and not to be lightly bothered."[32]

Dobrejcak was not alone. An immigrants' son remembered his own father in similar terms: "He was a dutiful father, but he never kissed me, never talked to me and had conversations with me. He never hugged me—he never hugged anybody. He could play solitaire for five, six hours. He had affection but he never showed it." The father-child friendship so much a part of the companionate vision of fatherhood had little place in this man's upbringing: "I could never talk to my father. I couldn't talk to him about anything. He never told me any of the things about his life."[33] Such reserve was no doubt largely shaped by their class experience. Long working hours, cramped quarters in the home, and the masculine environment of saloons took many working-class men away from their families for most of every day. After a long day of work at miserably low wages, many men spent a good portion of their leisure time in a sex-segregated world of pubs, billiard halls, bowling alleys, and fraternal organizations. One investigator of working-class households in early twentieth-century New York City observed that "the husband comes home at night, has his dinner, and goes out with the 'men,' or sits at home to read his paper."[34] Many fathers headed for the ubiquitous ethnic saloon for fellowship, news, job information, and gossip. Others did so, as one mechanic put it, to forget their troubles: "Men who get small wages and are in uncertain employment become easily discouraged when they think of the needs at home. . . . They go to the saloon to drown their despondency and trouble."[35]

Vulnerability and Breadlosing

Mr. Moran, a Boston sheet metal worker, certainly had reason to head for the local tavern. He had held a steady job for fourteen years, but when his factory moved to an outlying town, Moran decided to remain in Boston on the supposition that finding work would present few difficulties. Instead, he began five years of chronic underemployment and unemployment characterized by the receipt of public charity, the repossession of the family furniture, and, worst of all, the malnutrition of his five children. These calamities, according to a caseworker, destroyed Moran's self-respect:

> For two and one-half years he has grown discouraged and demoralized by lack of work, loss of self-respect, lack of regular routine, lack of food and the sight of his overworked wife and underfed children. He goes out three days a week to work in the woodyard. The other three working days he goes out to look for work, to reënforce his waning spirit with good drink, and above all to be away from home, and the scene of his failure.[36]

His children were a daily reminder that he had failed at the fundamental task of fatherhood, which left him consumed by guilt and a profound sense of personal inadequacy.

Moran's sense of failure was in keeping with the ideology of breadwinning. After all, mothers reared children, fathers supported them, and while Mrs. Moran had upheld her end of the bargain, her husband had failed miserably to uphold his. But he was not alone, and in an important sense his failure was not personal but rather part of the structure of industrial capitalism. For millions of American breadwinners, steady work was a yearning rather than a reality: in 1900, the frequency of male unemployment was 27.2 percent (the percentage of workers unemployed at some point in a given year), and the average duration of unemployment was over three-and one-half months.[37] A close study of unemployment in Massachusetts reveals that repeated layoffs, wage cuts, and cutbacks characterized the lives of industrial workers in the half-century after 1870.[38]

Nor was economic vulnerability restricted to only a few occupations. In 1922 workers from a wide variety of Massachusetts industries faced annual unemployment rates above 20 percent. Boot and shoe workers, textile loom fixers, quarry workers, boilermakers, iron molders, blacksmiths, bookbinders, and freight handlers all experienced annual unemployment at this rate or higher. This alarming figure paled next to annual unemployment frequencies that ranged as high as 43 percent for freight handlers, 55 percent for boot and shoe lasters, 60 percent for hod carriers and building laborers, and 75 percent for bricklayers and masons.[39] Un- and underemployment plagued the economies of other states as well and thereby undermined the ability of fathers to fulfill their most basic obligation.

Families coped with unemployment in a host of ways. Many wage laborers, especially skilled craftsmen, planned for layoffs; periodic belt-tightening was simply part of being a wage laborer in industrial America. Thousands more of the unemployed left home in search of work, which helps explain the high rate of geographical mobility among working-class Americans.[40] Wives and children entered the labor force, and families moved to cheaper quarters, reduced their clothing and food budgets, and cut recreational expenses to the bone. Other families borrowed from friends and relatives, obtained credit from trusting merchants, depleted their savings, secured assistance from trade union locals, cashed in insurance policies, pawned personal items, or reluctantly, and often as a last resort, turned to a variety of relief agencies for help.[41] Working-class life was unpredictable and often harsh but mutual help, born of necessity, allowed some protection against industrial life. Aid to a neighbor in need came in part out of sympathy and friendship and in part because one might suffer the same fate. William Dean Howells recognized this point in his utopian novel, *A Traveler from Alturia:* "Does it seem strange to you," a poor woman is asked, "that people should found a civilization on the idea of living for one another, instead of each for himself?" "No, indeed," she replied. "Poor people have always had to live that way, or they could not have lived at all."[42]

Reciprocity and mutuality helped working-class families survive the recurrent setbacks they encountered in the early twentieth century. For thousands of men, however, prolonged unemployment could be devastating; children and wives might *supplement* household income, but fathers *supported* families. To be a father was to be a breadwinner, and from this basic assumption grew men's legal and political status and, more fundamentally, their masculine identity. Men's financial responsibility to their children was deeply embedded in the male psyche, and as unemployment and underemployment eroded their ability to provide for their offspring, fathers responded in ways that illuminate the cultural meaning of fatherhood, breadwinning, and ultimately patriarchy itself.

While men might plan for the inevitable slack times and neighborhood institutions might tide workers over, protracted unemployment diminished men's sense of self and charity undermined their manhood. Case reports by social workers in the 1920s reveal that unemployed men found it extraordinarily difficult to rely on public charity because to do so was an admission of failure. An unemployed Cambridge, Massachusetts, truck driver named Estrada, for example, developed "a bitter attitude toward life, feeling that a man willing to work should be able to have it. He resented charity, going to the length of refusing to eat food that came from sources outside the family connection." The social worker did add, however, that he "was not ungrateful for assistance given by other agencies to his wife and children."[43]

Rzepinski, a semiskilled Chicago Pole, likewise found it difficult to ask for outside aid: "Although they suffered considerably, they did not ask for charity and even though they had been referred to the county for help, Mr. Rzepinski's pride would not permit him to accept it."[44] For an Italian immigrant father of five young children, manhood and fatherly obligations also clashed with accepting charity. As a Boston caseworker laconically put it, "No appeal has been made to agencies for assistance because of DiPesa's pride in his ability to take care of his family."[45] Morris Lipski, a Russian Jew who had emigrated to America by way of Constantinople, spoke for thousands of unemployed men when a neighbor suggested the Lipskis seek help from a relief agency: "Charity! We do not want charity! Give me a job so that I can provide for the needs of my family!"[46]

Sadly and inevitably, many fathers found that satisfying their families' needs was beyond them. Plagued by layoffs caused by mechanization, seasonal downturns, advancing age, business vicissitudes, or personal sickness or injury, many unemployed men became depressed, anxious, and embittered, their sense of manhood destroyed by their inability to support their wives and children. Thrown out of work in the mid-1920s because of mechanization, a pipe cutter named De Macio had seen his family's situation steadily deteriorate. After trying unsuccessfully to support his family as a day laborer and a disastrous attempt at running a small grocery store, De Macio had become discouraged: "He is physically below normal weight. He has lost all interest in the home, feels that no effort is worth while and life is not worth living."[47] Twenty-nine-year-old laborer Rocco Casano shared De Macio's discouragement and regretted his inability to do more for his children: "At 13, I was working on the railroad and at 16 did a man's work. I have a wonderful kid, 5 years old. I don't want him to go through what I've had. I think I can make something of him if I can give him a chance. Gee! I can't even give him enough to eat now. All I can take is a pint of milk a day—a pint of milk for him and the baby, too."[48]

Similar feelings vexed Mr. Caretta, an Italian immigrant who had lost his job as a Philadelphia cabinetmaker and had become a common laborer. With their small savings gone, their cherished personal items pawned, and their children suffering "undernourishment," both parents despaired of the future. Although Mrs. Caretta still worried about her five children's health and her inability to provide them with the right foods, Mr. Caretta had reached the breaking point. In the words of his wife, "My husband says, 'Every night he wishes to be dead by morning and the children too.'" His pessimism and his pride as a breadwinner were inextricably bound together. By his own admission he "would rather die than ask for assistance as once you start getting help it gives you a different feeling and is liable to make you lose your initiative."[49] A fellow countryman responded to his own sense of failure in a slightly different way. This father of five, an unemployed laborer and fish peddler, routinely deserted his home when work became slack. Asked why in family court, Mr. Vezanto replied in broken English: "'Cause I could not give the kids to eat!"[50]

Victims of forces beyond their control, many of these men became obsessed by a painful sense of loss, their aspirations dashed by the vagaries of the economy. Until a business slowdown in 1926, New Orleans resident John Schneider, the son of German immigrants, was well on his way to becoming a master carpenter. He, his wife, and their first child lived a comfortable life in a small half-cottage, but all that changed when John lost his steady job and had to give up carpentry for a series of menial temporary positions. Faced with constant unemployment, the Schneiders exhausted their savings, acquired debts, took in a lodger, and accepted assistance from neighbors. For John, memories of yesterday's comforts and the grim reality of his children's current condition were almost too much to bear: "When I look back on those days, and I see what we have come to, I tell you it makes me sick. Nothing but worry and debts and discouragement. And when I look at the kids I just get wild." John's former optimism had evaporated: "Now with Mary half-sick all the time and no steady work, it seems as though nothing mattered. We don't make any more plans. We don't have much hope left."[51]

For these men, the family economy had broken down. A system predicated on the earnings of fathers and the supplemental earnings of other family members became distorted when fathers became dependents. And dependence was the great male fear. Children could augment a father's earnings, but they dare not supplant his primacy, a lesson Gustave Broussard learned to his dismay. A father of ten and a onetime manager of a Louisiana sugar plantation, he had skidded quickly into the working class when the plantation failed. Unable to find permanent work from the mid-1920s on, Broussard had become dependent on the wages of his two eldest sons and the economy of his wife. As a result, he suffered a deep sense of frustration and loss: "He is beginning to feel that because he is no longer a young man [he was 49] he will not be given a chance to prove that he is an excellent worker. He says: 'Look at my boys; they are fine boys, I say it with pride! But they can't give to a job what I can give, yet they get jobs and I am passed up.'"[52] His frustration ultimately blended with shame. Although his wife acknowledged that the family would survive, especially once two

more sons entered the labor force, she also described the psychic costs
of such dependence on her husband: "If these two older boys, and after
a while Hortense, and Joseph, get and keep good jobs, we are going to
get along—but oh, my poor husband! He just can't see them doing
what he ought to do. We both want them to have some young life, their
own life. They just cannot if they are faced with the responsibility of
providing for all of these little ones!"[53]

The sadness and humiliation of these men stemmed from their own
sense of failure but also from the knowledge that their economic
predicament foreclosed their children's options. Men's identities were
tied, in part, to the success of their children, but when fathers lost their
jobs and family survival depended on the premature labor of children,
such aspirations had to be postponed indefinitely. Louisiana resident
Emile LaForge, a father of eight, saw his hopes for his eldest daughter
evaporate when he lost his job as a maintenance man. Odd jobs
brought in little money, and periodic, prolonged unemployment sapped
his self-confidence. Furthermore, depending on the earnings of his eldest daughter, Louise, age sixteen, humiliated him: "He was most unwilling to have Louise go to work. He had wanted her to go to high
school. He felt a keen mortification at having to depend on her at all.
He began drinking when his discouragement became very great."[54]

Joseph Borczak suffered the same fate. Post–World War I cutbacks
had steadily eroded the boilermaker's ability to support his family, and
he, his wife, and his children barely scratched out a living. Facing a
bleak future, the Borczaks realized that "their children will not be able
to go to high school; instead they must go to work when old enough to
leave." Nor would their children's abilities be nurtured: "Joseph, Jr., is
quite talented musically, but lessons are now out of the question."[55] An
unemployed roofer in Philadelphia shared a similar lament about the
fate of his fifteen-year-old son. The family became largely dependent
on the seven dollars per week the child earned as an errand boy, a job
well below his father's aspirations for him. As his mother explained,
"We hated to have Joe go to work because his father wanted him to get
a good trade, but not in the sheet-metal business because their work is
so unsteady." A sporadically employed Romanian immigrant shared his
wife's disappointment that their oldest son, Louis, age thirteen, could
not continue his education beyond the eighth grade. In the words of
the caseworker, "It hurts them keenly not to gratify the children's desires in regard to their educational and cultural development."[56]

Dependence on children not only vexed men but transformed family
relationships. Fatherhood and breadwinning involved a trade-off: men
accepted the responsibility of supporting a family in exchange for the

power, prestige, and joy that came with fatherhood. Fathers headed the family and in return received respect and deference from wives and children. They also received public affirmation of their masculine identity. But in some sense the status was earned; it stemmed from the serious business of making a living in a market economy that took children's wages for granted and masked the economic contributions of wives. But when fathers became "breadlosers" instead of "winners," children were forced to judge their fathers' worth. Some children's confidence in and sympathy for their fathers never wavered. The case records note instances of children rallying around their beleaguered fathers, their respect for their fathers undiminished by troubles in the job market. The offspring of an Italian laborer, for example, had no doubt that their father's problems were beyond his control: "There is no change," wrote the Philadelphia caseworker, "in the attitude of the children toward their parents. They know their father is willing to work when he can get it. The moral standards of the family are high."[57] A fourteen-year-old daughter of an unemployed Russian immigrant expressed outrage and sympathy as she contemplated the fate of her father: "In my estimation it is a crime that a person physically well and seeking work should be so humiliated by not being able to supply the needs of his family."[58]

Yet the record reveals another, sadder story as well. As the pain and humiliation of unemployment worked on men's psyches, they often responded in ways that drove a wedge between themselves and their children. Some men simply became inattentive. The wife of a twenty-eight-year-old roofer noted how her husband's behavior changed once he became unemployed: "He loves them kids and plays with them all the time, except when he's out of work. Then he won't play with them, but just says all the time, 'Don't bother me, don't bother me.' And of course the kids don't understand why he's so different."[59] Others became abusive and turned to drink. The illegitimate power of force and alcohol replaced the legitimate power of breadwinning. A Philadelphia truck and taxi driver found that such behavior could earn the wrath of even very young children. A virtuous and steady man when working, he turned to drink and male companions when laid off, and it was this behavior that caused his four-year-old son, Harry, to lash out at his father. Harry's mother recounted the story:

He [her husband] quit drinking for six months last year, because I told him what Harry said about him when Harry was in the hospital. He is only four, but would you believe it, when I came in to visit him he said, "Say, Mama, is my daddy drunk yet?" I said, "Harry, what did you say that for?" He said, "Because I don't want my daddy to drink. I want him to get a job."

Later Harry's mother noted her shock and sadness when he confronted his father directly: "I felt awful bad the other day when I heard him say to his father, 'You dirty bum you, why don't you get out and get to work?'"[60]

Other men responded similarly to their problems with similar results. An unemployed Boston plumber who once recoiled at the thought of receiving charity ultimately became dependent on it as he slipped into despondency and discouragement. As his family's condition worsened, he began to spend less time at home and more time in saloons. His behavior prompted arguments with his wife and one of his sons, who sided with his mother. Speaking of the son, the caseworker wrote: "The latter was puzzled at first about his father's actions, but as time went on, he began to lose all respect for his father and actually ran to hide at the latter's appearance in the home."[61] An Italian immigrant from Pittsburgh experienced the same problem. Father of seven, he came to America in 1907 and worked steadily as a laborer until 1927, when his employment troubles began. At first he searched relentlessly for work, but as the months rolled by, he became convinced that no work was to be had; instead, he began to drink incessantly and became abusive toward his children. As a result, domestic tensions soared and the children lost all respect for their father: "The children are all conscious of their mother's anger toward their father and they seem very ashamed of him. They are fond of the boarders, who take quite an interest in their home. One of the children said she wished that her father would die so that her mother could marry the boarder, and they'd have things nice!"[62]

In the judgment of welfare workers, the collapse of paternal authority brought on by unemployment could even undermine social order. As social workers surveyed the wreckage of fathers' lives, they saw a connection among fathers' failure, children's disrespect, and juvenile delinquency. While theorists debated the etiology of delinquency and offered a variety of ways to rehabilitate young offenders, social welfare workers on the front lines reported that unemployment and the consequent collapse of fatherly authority often brought in its wake juvenile misbehavior.[63] When the Detroit Dodge factory laid off Paul Lombetti in 1926, for example, he searched gamely for work but ultimately gave up hope. As his optimism dimmed, the Italian immigrant's home life quickly deteriorated and he lost authority over his stepchildren. The caseworker described the family's descent:

The children no longer showed any respect for their parents and were rude and disobedient. We knew of no bootlegging, or gambling—but in juvenile delinquency, two of the boys, within the past two years, have come under the ban of the law. Florentino, the oldest child, is now confined in an industrial school for driving away an auto—his excuse being that he wanted to see the world. Bernie, a boy of nine, a truant from school and given to pilfering, is now on probation to the Juvenile Court. No trouble of this sort occurred in this family up to two and a half years ago.[64]

To the caseworkers, respect for fathers and juvenile discipline went hand in hand, and when unemployment destroyed the former, the latter was difficult to maintain. Discouraged by his inability to find steady work, a thirty-seven-year-old father of five began drinking and abusing his wife and children. Eventually the parents separated and the children lost all respect for their father, referring to him as "the old man." The youngest daughter, age ten, began to "run the streets" and became a discipline problem at home, school, and the settlement house. Her sixteen-year-old brother also became a problem both at home and at school.[65] An out-of-work Italian carpenter had a similar problem with one of his six children. At about the time he became unemployed, his eldest became truant from school and later ran away and joined the army. His mother laid her son's problems at the doorstep of her poor health and her husband's unemployment: "He was always a bit wild,—ever since that first time Mister was out of work and I was sick—seems as if we never could get Louis in hand again after that."[66]

If the experience of Ben Rosario, an Italian fruit peddler, is typical, fathers deeply felt the pain of their children's misbehavior, especially if they traced it to their own economic inadequacy. Thrown out of work by illness, Rosario found it impossible to reestablish his small business and was forced to work when he could as a common laborer. As the material conditions of his family declined precipitously, Ben's children became discipline problems at school, misbehavior the school guidance department attributed to "the effect at home, irregular school attendance, and restlessness, probably due to undernourishment." Despite growing hopelessness and despair, Rosario believed that fathers should support their families, and he accepted aid with a profound sense of shame. Equally troubling was the anguish caused by his oldest son's misbehavior. While Rosario looked for work out of town, his teenage son got into enough trouble that a court sentenced him to the Industrial School for Boys. Although the sentence was suspended, the blow to the father's pride was palpable. As the social worker recounted, "He tells his children,—'I'm a poor man; we are poor; but my name is good and I am trusted. I depend on you to keep it good.'"[67]

The Lives of Black Fathers

In a more extreme way, black working-class fathers shared many of these same problems with white working men. On Southern farms or in Southern and Northern cities, black men occupied the bottom of the occupational hierarchy. Constrained by Jim Crow laws and racist attitudes, most black fathers found it extraordinarily difficult to support their families. In the South, the crop-lien system and the collapse of Reconstruction left black men economically marginalized and politically vulnerable, and these liabilities often dashed their hopes of supporting their families by farming. For instance, whites did all they could to prevent black men from owning farms: inflated prices, exorbitant interest rates, fraud, and, if all else failed, violence kept blacks from purchasing land. In Mississippi, as an example, only 14 percent of black farmers owned their own land in 1920; the other 86 percent were tenants. Moreover, most of the land owned was of poor quality. Other measures ranging from enticement statutes to vagrancy, contract, and false-pretense laws inhibited the mobility of black farmers.[68] When these tactics failed to keep black men in line, plantation owners commonly resorted to the whip to control intractable blacks.[69] Thus, the plantation system survived into the twentieth century and the great mass of black farmers remained propertyless and powerless.

For fathers, the difficulties of this system were enormous. Supporting a family in any degree of comfort was all but impossible, and the labor of wives and children became absolutely necessary. Although many croppers hoped to keep their wives out of the fields—Mississippi resident Pearlee Avant noted that after she and her husband married "I never did work in the field no more. . . . He didn't believe in women going to the field"—such hopes rarely overcame the need for the labor of women and children.[70] Even so, in bad times the family might end a year of toil in debt to exploitative creditors. Nor could many fathers protect their families from racist, vindictive landlords. Backed by sympathetic sheriffs, courts, and public opinion, white landowners used the lash to enforce discipline and to strike fear into the hearts of poor landless blacks. One woman recalled her parents' fear of the riding boss: "It could have been slavery time . . . the way they act, scared of him. . . . You see our parents wuz scared of white folks."[71]

Faced with economic hardship on the land, thousands of black men consequently sought supplemental wage work, a search that inevitably drew them away from home. Some went to Southern cities, there to find work almost exclusively in domestic and manual labor. Pushed out of the skilled trades and into casual day labor and odd jobs, Southern black men in cities often earned less than their wives. For many it was difficult to find any kind of nonagricultural work. In Mississippi, for example, black women in 1940 had more success in finding nonfarm work than black men: while over 70 percent of the black labor force was male, women made up almost half of all black urban workers.[72] The structure of black households also changed in the migration from the rural to the urban South. In rural areas, the percentage of mother-headed households ranged from a low of 11 percent in Edgefield County, South Carolina, in 1870 to a high of 24 percent in Lane's Schoolhouse, Mississippi, in 1880. By contrast, the same figures for Southern cities ranged from a low of 20 percent in Louisville in 1870 to a high of 44 percent in Mobile in 1860.[73]

Racism and economic oppression thus combined to alter the nature of breadwinning for these men. Seeking opportunities in Southern cities, black fathers found opportunities no more inviting there than life on the land. The high rates of female-headedness, in fact, suggest that many men found it impossible to become breadwinners and left their families to find work. Others experienced in the early twentieth century what white working-class and middle-class American men would encounter in large numbers only after World War II: a transformed family economy in which husbands and wives shared breadwinning responsibilities.

Southern cities offered one destination, Northern cities another. Interviews with blacks who arrived in Pittsburgh before 1917 document an ever-widening search for wage labor. These migrants recalled the recurrent departure of their fathers from the home: some left the farm because their white owner cheated them, others left because of crop failure, still others could not resist the lure of good wages in coal mines. Regardless of the reason, these men found it necessary to spend time away from their families, sometimes for months on end.[74] Such absences dramatically reshaped black family life and black fatherhood. Black men who migrated North overwhelmingly went to cities and experienced upheavals similar to those of black men who moved to Southern cities. Upwards of one-third of black wives worked for wages and families were frequently female-headed; moreover, rates of female headedness were higher than in rural Southern communities. In 1880, 15 percent of black households were headed by women in Pittsburgh, 21 percent in Cincinnati, 26 percent in Philadelphia, and 31 percent in Boston among blacks born outside the South.[75]

By themselves, these figures simply tell us that as blacks migrated to cities, the number of households headed by females increased. We also know that the black rate of female-headedness far exceeded that of whites, although when income is held constant the variance declines sharply. Interpreting these data as they relate to black fathers, however, is difficult. The long and sometimes vitriolic debate on the reasons for and the meaning of the high rate of female-headed black families will surely continue, but several points seem clear and several speculations, specifically about black fathers, are in order.

Clearly the argument that slavery destroyed the black family and produced in black males an irresponsible attitude toward family life cannot bear the weight of the evidence to the contrary. Black families after the Civil War were overwhelmingly headed by two parents and, even more telling, former slaves had higher percentages in this regard than free blacks.[76] The evidence also reveals that migration to either Northern or Southern cities produced high rates of female-headedness that outstripped those of white immigrants.[77] What seems apparent is that racism coupled with the structure of the urban economy placed great strains on black marriages. Excluded from most clerical, sales, and factory jobs and relegated to menial work when they could find it, black men found it extraordinarily difficult to support their wives and children in the wage economy of the late nineteenth and early twentieth centuries. In fact, unemployed black males in Boston were far more likely to desert their wives than men with work, and those in menial work (where most black males labored) were almost twice as likely to leave their families as those in nonmenial occupations.[78]

The overwhelming fact remains that far more black than white families were (and still are) female-headed. What this demographic fact has meant for black fathers has been lost amid the debate over the origins and implications of the phenomenon. In the absence of direct evidence, we can only speculate. One point is clear and bears repeating: black fathers left not because they were irresponsible or stunned by the legacy of slavery but because of the wretched conditions they confronted in urban, industrial America. In short, they left not by choice but under duress. Unfortunately, these men disappear from the historical record; therefore, we can only make logical inferences and reasonable speculations about their lives and emotions. One such inference about black fatherhood outweighs all others: in losing their children in the urban environment, black males experienced a profound historical tragedy. Men—who named their sons after themselves, wept when their children were sold, and tramped the roads of the postwar South in a desperate bid for reunion, who migrated with their families to Southern or Northern cities in hopes of finding a better life and sacrificed mightily so that their children could attend school—must have experienced profound pain when racism and economic distress forced them to leave their children and search for work. Such men went from being the heads of their households to being either permanently absent from or itinerant guests within their own homes. It was a displacement of a kind and magnitude experienced by no European immigrant.[79]

Given such difficulties, the influence black fathers had over their children's economic destiny differed from that of European immigrants. In their study of blacks, Italians, and Poles in Pittsburgh from 1900 to 1960, John Bodnar, Robert Simon, and Michael Weber suggested that black parents tried to inculcate a sense of personal resourcefulness in their children. Unlike Italian and Polish fathers who often found work for their children and insisted that children sacrifice their individual goals for those of the family, black parents realized that their children would have to make it on their own. Black fathers seldom had either influence with the factory foreman or secure jobs to pass on to their offspring; instead, they emphasized education and personal achievement. As the authors of the Pittsburgh study put it, "given the nature of class and racial subordination, young blacks emerged from their formative years with a realization that survival would ultimately depend upon their own personal resourcefulness. Rather than emerging as adults fixed to the responsibilities of their families of origin, [black] migrants and their children looked toward a future that they alone would shape." The father of one Pittsburgh black man summed up this philosophy when his son turned twenty-one: "You are your own man and you can go on your own."[80]

Such sentiments would have been uncommon among working-class European immigrants who predicated their survival strategies on mutual support and the sacrifice of individual desires for the good of the family. As we have already seen, in immigrant families the father, as family patriarch, earned the main income and his children augmented it. Among black families in Pittsburgh, by contrast, such a practice was decidedly more rare. Rather than turning over unopened paychecks to their fathers and mothers, black children retained all or most of their earnings.[81] This practice likely limited intergenerational conflict—survey data revealed frequent conflicts between immigrant children and parents over children's earnings and spending money—and helped to create a sense of independence among black youngsters.

Black fathers' attitudes toward schooling also promoted independence among their children. Whereas Italians and Poles did not hesitate to pull their children out of school to enhance family income, black parents reluctantly did so because of their high emphasis on education. Fewer than half of fifteen-year-old immigrant children in Pittsburgh were in school in 1910, while almost two-thirds of black children still attended. Among sixteen-year-olds, the same figures were 30 percent versus 41 percent.[82] To black fathers, such a strategy reflected their own vulnerability in the labor force. Unable to establish secure positions in industry or small business, lacking craft skills that could be passed to sons—as Herbert Gutman has pointed out, artisanal openings for blacks declined in the late nineteenth and early twentieth centuries—black parents placed their faith in education and tried to transfer this faith to their children.[83] Recalling his father's emphasis on education, a farmer's son told why he returned to school after working in a sawmill: "I felt I would be better prepared to land the job I wanted. I figured that a person with enough education would always be able to get a nice easy job."[84]

Working-Class Fathers and the State

The marginal economic position of working-class fathers undermined paternal authority. This erosion was both checked and expedited by an expanding state that tried, on the one hand, to shore up traditional family relationships and, on the other, either inadvertently or intentionally undermined paternal power.[85] Worried about poorly paid, dangerous work for men, rising labor participation rates for women, and substandard housing for families, convinced that the family was undergoing an important transformation as many of its functions withered, advocates of state intervention devised policies for the new age that nevertheless reflected and supported traditional gender relationships. Despite such intentions, many reform efforts paradoxically weakened the power of individual fathers and shifted patriarchy from "the power of men within families to the power of men through the state."[86] In other words, the state both promoted traditional family relationships and simultaneously challenged the authority of individual fathers.

In this context, the seeming contradictions of state intervention in American families and in the lives of American fathers begin to make sense. Such intervention was intended to promote the well-being of private, male-headed, economically viable nuclear families, not to destroy the integrity of families via state "invasion." As Eli Zaretsky has written, "Rather than the state undermining the family, it is difficult to imagine how any form of the family could have survived the enormously destructive uprooting that accompanied industrialization without some intervention from the state. The issue is not whether the welfare state eroded the family, but rather in what form it preserved it."[87]

The chosen form should come as no surprise. Reformers at the turn of the century sought to preserve the family as an economically private unit of breadwinning fathers and home-centered mothers. In short, the image of a state invasion of the family obscures rather than clarifies what took place. The state intervened not to undermine the family but, rather, to foster its economic independence and its functional interdependence. It could not do so, however, without impinging on the power of *individual* husbands and fathers. This can be seen from a variety of angles. For example, protective legislation for women, laws on family desertion and nonsupport, child labor laws, and agitation for the family wage all embodied the assumption that the family was, first and foremost, a private economic entity and should remain so and that this interdependent entity was ideally characterized by wage- or salary-earning fathers, domestic mothers, and nonproductive but highly valued children. Such assumptions shaped Progressive legislation: protective legislation for women, for example, gained legitimacy owing to women's responsibilities as mothers; laws against male desertion stemmed from men's obligations as family breadwinners. Laws against wife-beating embodied assumptions about ideal manhood and womanhood, while child labor laws and the struggle for the family wage signified both a cultural commitment to female domesticity and to the dignity and self-reliance of the male provider. Each of these Progressive-era reforms was an expression of the state's commitment to family life of a "traditional" sort and each sought to accommodate this traditional conception to the reality of the industrial age.

That the notion of a "state assault" on the family was misguided does not mean that working-class fathers were unaffected by increasing state intervention in family life. Quite the contrary: as the target of many Progressive-era laws, working-class men were often forced to yield to the designs of middle-class reformers. If one purpose of Progressive reform was to shore up traditional gender relationships, such was small comfort to individual fathers who found their authority challenged by child labor reformers and juvenile advocates. In each instance, the power of the state could overwhelm the private authority of individual fathers.

As we have already seen, child labor was essential to the family wage economy of urban, industrial workers. By 1900 one child out of six between the ages of ten and fifteen was gainfully employed, and in 1910 the official estimate of working children under the age of fifteen was almost two million—no doubt an undercount. Yet, this upward trajectory would not continue indefinitely: by 1930 the number of child workers under fifteen had fallen to fewer than 670,000, with especially sharp drops registered among children ten to thirteen years old.[88] Behind these statistics was a protracted debate between child labor supporters and their opponents that was fundamentally cultural and moral and focused on the definition of children's economic and sentimental value.[89] Defenders of child labor emphasized both its importance to family survival among the working class and its beneficial impact on the character of working children. As one immigrant father of two laconically put it in defense of children's wage labor within the home, "Keep a kid at home, save shoe leather, make better manners."[90] Nor would parents willingly forfeit their right to place their children at work. A 1909 government report on Southern textile working conditions found great resistance to child labor laws among parents: "The fathers and mothers vehemently declare that the State has no right to interfere, if they wish to 'put their own children to work,' and that it is only fair for the child to 'begin to pay back for his keep.'"[91] Child labor investigators constantly complained that the parents of working children routinely lied when compelled to sign affidavits attesting to the age of their offspring.

These parental attitudes were supported by those who feared that child labor laws undermined parental autonomy. As the *New Republic* put it, "The immemorial right of the parent to train his child in useful tasks . . . is destroyed. The obligation of the child to contribute . . . is destroyed. Parents may still set their children at work; children may still make themselves useful, but it will no longer be by right and obligation, but by default of legislation." An assemblyman from Nevada saw such laws as part of a much broader assault on patriarchal prerogatives: "They have taken our women away from us by constitutional amendments; they have taken our liquor from us; and now they want to take our children."[92]

Despite resistance from working-class parents, Southern mill owners, the National Association of Manufacturers, and conservative ideologues, reformers ultimately succeeded in passing child labor laws, first at the state and then at the national level.[93] Reformers made legislative headway for a variety of reasons, in part because changing technology, rising standards of living, and an influx of cheap foreign labor made the labor of children less necessary, and in part because reformers attacked the motives and morals of parents who sent their children to work. Showing no awareness of the economic reality of working-class families, reformers denounced fathers and mothers "who coin shameful dollars from the bodies and souls of their own flesh and blood." These parents, hardly more than parasites to the reformers, "have no civilization, no decency, no anything but covetousness and who would with pleasure immolate their offspring on the shine of the golden calf."[94] Given their role as breadwinners, fathers received especially sharp rebukes from those fighting against child labor. Anecdotal evidence often passed for analysis. One club woman active in child labor reform reported: "It is but a few weeks since a friend told me of seeing a father who showed no sign of weakness take six of his children to a mill for work—he himself claimed to be too feeble to do regular work—a 'vampire father,' as such men are now called, living upon the money earned by the sapping of the vital forces of his children!"[95]

Such attitudes were indicative of the fundamental gulf separating working-class parents from reformers on the issue of child labor. Working-class fathers and mothers viewed child labor as part of a mutual exchange between parents and children, an obligation children owed the family in return for the support they received from it. It was, as we have seen, a system directed by parents in which fathers introduced their offspring to the working world at an early age while mothers maintained the home. The system depended on filial obedience and mutual support: children handed unopened pay envelopes to their parents and received a small allowance in return.

To reformers, however, such an instrumental view of children ran counter to what Viviana Zelizer has called the "sacralization" of childhood, a view of children emphasizing their economic uselessness and their emotional pricelessness. Reformers denounced children's work in the family economy as a violation of childhood innocence and a degradation of children's sentimental worth. What is important, of course, is that the reformers prevailed; and from perhaps the most important standpoint, the reduction of child labor should be applauded. Many of the reformers' claims were indeed correct: child labor did stunt the intellectual development of children, risked their health, led to callous exploitation, and suppressed wages. All these reasons justified state intervention. But admitting as much, we may still say that reformers misread parents' motives and, in their eagerness to describe the evils of child labor, callously disregarded the economic predicament of working-class parents and undermined the authority and judgment of working-class fathers.

The incursion of the state into traditional patriarchal prerogatives is even more visible in the emergence of the juvenile court system in the early twentieth century. Established by Progressive reformers, this system dealt with youthful offenders, the great majority of whom came from immigrant working-class families: for example, 71 percent of youngsters arraigned before the New York juvenile court in 1925 had foreign-born parents.[96] Reflecting the high status of the modern child and backed by child development specialists, club women, and social welfare workers, this court system focused not so much on the illegal act itself as on the offender's character, home environment, psyche, and soul. Reformers hoped to offer therapy, not justice, to youthful offenders, and by 1920 all but three states had a juvenile court system.[97]

The problems with the juvenile court system have been well documented. Suffused with therapeutic ideas of reform and a desire to make hearings nonadversarial, juvenile courts regularly impinged on the basic legal safeguards of the children caught up in the system. Dominated by judges who functioned as father, friend, and counselor, these courts limited the role of defense lawyers, stretched or even abandoned customary rules regarding the nature of testimony, violated established notions of due process and the right to trial by jury, withdrew the right of appeal, and disregarded provisions for equal protection of the law.[98] Reformers took these steps with the best of intentions, but their effect diminished the power of fathers, especially immigrant fathers, and enhanced that of the state. Although parents themselves sometimes made use of these hearings, these proceedings could still substitute state authority for that of fathers. In fact, reformers often portrayed the state as a benevolent surrogate parent that helped children find security, happiness, and right living when their biological parents proved incapable of doing so.[99] If a father seemed unable to control his child, perhaps a wise, kindly, empathetic judge and probation officer could do so. The young miscreant needed care, not punishment; supervision, not incarceration; guidance, not justice. That such an approach often impinged on the rights and powers of parents was freely admitted: "The juvenile court laws," noted one reformer, "are usually so broad that the State, in its capacity of *parens patriae* . . . will take jurisdiction over practically every significant situation where it appears it should do so in the interests of the child."[100] A Minnesota judge put the issue less abstractly: "I believe in this kind of court. . . . It is to reach the boy and teach him to follow in the correct line . . . and if need be, to take him from an immoral and vicious and criminal environment, *even if it takes him away* from his parents, that he may be saved even though they may be lost."[101]

Parents who tried to prevent the loss of a child to the juvenile justice system found little sympathy in the courts. Several key decisions in the Progressive period affirmed the state's right to commit juveniles to correctional institutions. Although parents might object to lax legal standards that removed their child from their care, courts insisted that rehabilitation, not justice, was at stake. The very fact that juvenile hearings were nonadversarial, that no jury was present, and that traditional standards of testimony were not observed proved to the courts' satisfaction that such hearings and detentions were indeed therapeutic and not criminal in nature. Thus, children and their parents had no need of traditional constitutional safeguards. Saving children, doing them "good," justified the abrogation of their basic rights. A Kentucky appeals court in 1911 captured the odd logic behind such thinking when it noted that thirteen other state high courts had already upheld the constitutionality of the juvenile court system, all "upon the theory that the proceedings are not criminal, but merely the services of the government called into play for the purpose of protecting, training and correcting a class of children who . . . are unable or unwilling to care for themselves."[102] With such reasoning, woe to the immigrant working-class father who sought to maintain control over his intractable son or daughter and in so doing became an obstacle to the state's therapeutic purposes.

In the name of social progress, reformers posed the power of the state against the desires of fathers. The father who needed his children's labor or wanted his troubled son or daughter to remain at home might have his wishes subverted by a state that forced children out of factories and into schools, out of the house and into an institution for delinquents. Against such power, fathers could only scheme and evade, lie and deceive. But the state impinged on the power of working-class fathers even more directly. Nowhere was this clearer than in reforms and laws involving child abuse and desertion, two issues that reveal the paradoxes of Progressive reform and give the lie to theories of state usurpation of "family autonomy." Reformers hoped to reestablish family unity but recognized that to do so the state might have to intercede on behalf of one family member against another.

Although laws regulating violence against children appeared in seventeenth-century New England, child abuse became a social issue only in the 1870s.[103] Inspired by nativism, suspicion of lower-class family mores, and fears of urban social disorder, influenced by an increasingly sentimental conception of children, upper- and middle-class reformers in the late nineteenth century established a host of societies to combat the evils of child abuse. If the Massachusetts Society for the Prevention of Cruelty to Children (MSPCC) was typical, reformers combined a genuine concern for children's well-being with a deeply rooted conviction of cultural superiority when dealing with their overwhelmingly immigrant and working-class clientele.[104] To upper-class child protection officers and their agents, child abuse was overwhelmingly a lower-class problem caused by fatherly drunkenness and, more broadly, cultural inferiority.

Given such attitudes, agents felt free to intervene in the lives of their cultural inferiors. Acting as if they were police, MSPCC agents conducted searches without warrants, issued letters to parents that looked like legal summonses, threatened parents with arrest, gathered evidence from neighbors and relatives, and even confiscated physical evidence from homes (liquor bottles, for example) to be used in court.[105] If the Society decided to press its case legally, it could prosecute a child abuser for assault and battery or neglect. Usually accepting the Society's recommendations, judges might fine or incarcerate parents or grant custody of the children in question to the Society itself. It also had the power to arrange adoptions, trusteeships, and custody.[106]

Reformers justified this aggressive intervention in working-class family life by denigrating working-class fathers. In the minds of child reformers, traditional patriarchal relations—in which fathers had control over all other family members within the context of a family economy—had become an anachronism, a system out of line with new restrictions on paternal power, new standards of child rearing, new conceptions of domesticity and motherhood, and new ideas about child labor and male breadwinning.[107] To these early defenders of abused children, the drunken immigrant father—the characteristic villain of the Society's reports—violated all standards of manhood and fatherly decency. He was drunk when he should have been sober; impatient when he should have been understanding; harsh when he should have been kind; economically marginal when he should have been financially secure. His attitudes and behavior were illegitimate, his manly bearing lamentable. Consequently, reformers felt no compunction about intervening in the family affairs of such men.

After the turn of the century, fathers became less central in the battle against child abuse. An increasingly professionalized staff of reformers now emphasized maternal neglect when assessing the etiology of child abuse and argued that prevention, not punishment, should be at the center of child-saving efforts.[108] A medical model came to the forefront: child neglect was symptomatic of family pathology, specifically excessive individualism by mothers and inadequate discipline by fathers. The former, however, was the more important factor: fathers receded into the background, their former preeminence replaced by a focus on mothers' domestic shortcomings. The "sacralization" of children and the growing emphasis on child psychology and "educated motherhood" meant that mothers had become the central focus of child abuse experts.[109]

The emphasis on mothers' failures, however, did not mean that other kinds of fatherly abuse went unexamined. In the late 1890s, middle-class reformers began drawing attention to the growing problem of male desertion and nonsupport. An 1895 survey of 800 charitable agencies by Reverend E. P. Savage, superintendent of Minnesota's Children

Home Society, documented over 7,000 cases of deserted children, two-thirds of whom had been abandoned by their fathers. From these figures, Savage estimated that over 25,000 children had been deserted nationwide, findings that prompted reformers to lament the ineffectiveness of old laws. Savage concluded that the deserting father usually escaped penalty because "there is no one with money enough or interest enough to bring him to justice" and that uniform legislation was needed to cope with the growing problem.[110] Some proposals were bizarre—one reformer wanted to sterilize convicted deserters—but all agreed that the public should be informed of the problem, men reminded of their obligation to support their dependents, and offenders apprehended and punished.

The targets of such proposals were working-class husbands and fathers who needed reminding, by force if necessary, of their breadwinning obligations. Such men, reformers insisted, did not need the dole; it would only sap what little initiative they already possessed. Deserters left their families because they lacked character, not capital. Whereas Progressives increasingly viewed the unemployed as victims of the system, no such sympathy was extended to the deserter. He was a moral failure, more to be condemned than pitied. Lilian Brandt's 1905 study of over five hundred deserters concluded that "the most constant element is the irresponsible, ease-loving man who acts on the theory that when hard times of any sort come he is justified in making arrangements for his own comfort which do not include his wife and children."[111] The ideal man, by contrast, was the frugal, thrifty, industrious, "self-supporting, self-respecting, able-bodied" workingman, the "*natural* wage-earner, whose place cannot be filled, even temporarily, by the wife."[112]

Given these assumptions about male breadwinning, reformers first tried to reconcile the man and his family, even if that meant returning a cruel and insensitive husband to his wife and children. If that proved impossible or only temporarily successful, reformers put forth legislative proposals that challenged male irresponsibility. By campaigning for stricter punishment, greater police involvement, the right to extradite offenders, and the power to compel men to make support payments, reformers urged the state to challenge husbands' and fathers' avoidance of their breadwinning responsibilities. Such agitation soon began to bear fruit: in the first decade of the new century, eleven states made desertion or nonsupport of destitute families a felony; eighteen increased the fine and/or the length of imprisonment for these crimes; others allowed third parties to bring suits, permitted wives to testify against husbands, and granted probation agents the power to apprehend the deserter and oversee his conduct. By 1920 a third of the nation's states and territories had taken steps to insure that men fulfilled their half of the family bargain.[113] After all, the desertion of wives was bad enough, but to leave one's children not only increased demand on relief agencies but violated all canons of masculine decency.

The disciplinary approach to male desertion reached its peak between 1910 and 1915, thereafter giving way to more therapeutic remedies. Rather than fines and jails, wayward husbands and fathers after 1915 increasingly encountered probation officers, social workers, guidance counselors, and paternalistic judges. Nor were these agents of the state encountered in criminal courts; instead, state after state established special domestic relations courts dedicated to the principle of family reconciliation. First appearing in 1909, domestic relations courts (with the help of probation officers) tried to rebuild the character of deserting fathers, reconcile them to their families, and secure support for destitute dependents. Probation officers freely intervened in the family affairs of deserted families, including the collection and distribution of court-ordered weekly payments from men to their wives and children.

These courts increasingly downplayed the depravity of deserters and nonsupporters; instead, by the 1920s the focus was on their psychological maladjustment. Such men were less bad than troubled: sexual dysfunction, emotional tension, even a lack of recreation might account for male desertion. The point was not to punish men but to rehabilitate them: state intervention would reduce family dependence and enhance family unity. But to accomplish this goal, probation officers and domestic court officials now had to explore some of the most private dimensions of family life.[114] The state's interest in insuring that men met their obligations as husbands and fathers superseded deserters' right to privacy; more generally, the desire of men to break free of family obligations ran headlong into the state's intention to enforce them. In essence, the state shifted the balance of power within families, however slightly, toward its weaker members. Without abandoning a traditional vision of family life, reformers and legislatures nevertheless took steps that undermined the power of some working-class fathers and husbands.

Ironically, these steps were taken within the context of Progressive concern about the "decline of the family," a fear historian Linda Gordon rightfully sees as a backlash against women's and children's rising autonomy.[115] Meeting the problem of child neglect required a reassertion of fathers' traditional obligation to support their wives and children. Reformers believed fathers had successfully fulfilled that obligation in rural America but were too often evading it in industrial cities. To child abuse reformers imbued with such bucolic prejudices, the sine qua non of good family life—privacy and economic independence— rested squarely on the shoulders of men: without self-support, none of the other virtues of good family life could develop; with it, deviance and vice could be avoided.

In leaving their wives and children in dire need, men disregarded their masculine responsibility as breadwinners. Yet, danger lay in grant- ing aid to wives and mothers because such aid might destroy the inde- pendence of the family and erode the authority of the male breadwin- ner.[116] Better that an agency force a husband and father to support his family—even if the agency collected money from the deserter and allo- cated it to his wife and children—than that the family become depen- dent on the state. The Massachusetts Society for the Prevention of Cru- elty to Children, for example, became a virtual collection agency as its agents wrung money out of deserting and nonsupporting husbands and fathers and dispensed it to needy women and children.[117]

The Society also frowned upon mothers' working for wages, even if their husbands were disabled, unemployed, or irresponsible. In the judgment of Society officials, working mothers created neglected chil- dren and irresponsible fathers, an assumption that also informed the Society's opposition to mothers' pensions. These state-funded pensions went to single mothers and made good sense, but many child welfare reformers feared that such aid might well invite male irresponsibility. Realizing that the state would support their families even if they did not, lazy and dissolute fathers might simply walk away from their manly responsibilities. Such positions and policies added up to a profound dis- trust of female-headed families and an equally profound commitment to the importance of male breadwinning and female economic depen- dence.[118] In this they were like other policies of the state that affected working-class life in the early twentieth century. The state did become more active in family life: the family was, in a sense, invaded by outside agencies. Schools, child labor reforms, juvenile courts, societies for the prevention of cruelty to children, and reforms dealing with male deser- tion and nonsupport did impinge on the prerogatives of working-class fathers. But this invasion often came at the request of weaker members within families. Abused wives and children wanted state intervention; so, too, did poor and deserted wives. Such intervention might well di- minish the relative power of fathers as the state put its weight on the side of less powerful members in the family.

But this is not to say the state destroyed or even diminished "family autonomy," an abstraction with virtually no meaning. It is a phrase that obscures the fact that families are comprised of individuals with relative degrees of power. State intervention certainly worked at the fault lines of the generational and gender cleavages that characterize family life, but to equate this process with an "invasion of family autonomy" is to misunderstand the reality of family life. Families have never been autonomous in any meaningful sense: relatives, neighbors, churches, and courts have always interceded in the affairs of family. In the early twentieth century, the source and focus of this intervention simply shifted: the state took a more active role in regulating family life on behalf of weaker members.[119]

Nevertheless, state intervention was meant to strengthen and modernize families and to reinforce the importance of fatherly breadwinning and family privacy. Neither reformers nor the state ever backed away from a vision of male-supported, economically independent families. To achieve this goal, however, fathers might have to change their cultural habits, take their children out of the work force, send them to school, and generally adopt, or at least try to approach, middle-class conceptions of family life. Such were the costs to working-class fathers as patriarchal power increasingly came to lodge in the public rather than the private domain. But not all was lost to these men: the result remained a conception of fatherhood predicated upon female economic subordination and male dominance.

Breadwinning and the Meaning of Working-Class Men's Lives

Life on the margin was difficult for working-class fathers. An increasingly activist state eroded their authority directly, by passing child labor laws and creating a juvenile court system, or obliquely, by passing laws against child abuse and desertion that upheld the breadwinner ideal but undercut the power of irresponsible fathers. Nor was success in the economic realm any easier. Fathers' triumphs as breadwinners were small victories—a cheap home, a slight rise up the occupational scale— whereas their defeats undermined their identity. This latter point is crucial. The vicissitudes of industrial wage labor played havoc with the demands of breadwinning and left working-class fathers vulnerable to forces they could scarcely comprehend, let alone alter. Staking so much on breadwinning invited enormous risk. An unexpected layoff coupled with an unsuccessful search for work could bring on depression and loss of self-respect. While wives and children might initially offer sympathy and support, this too could fade as unemployment dragged on. Over time, such men became more depressed, irritable, and disengaged, their wives and children more needy and contemptuous. With luck, perseverance, and a rebounding economy, jobs might eventually appear, and these men could begin to regain their self-respect. But the vulnerability remained, and what breadwinning could give, breadlosing could take away.

4

Fatherhood, Immigration, and American Culture, 1880–1930

WHEN LEONARD COVELLO BROUGHT HIS REPORT CARD HOME, HIS Italian immigrant father reacted with horror: "'What is this?' he said. 'Leonard Covello! What happened to the *i* in Coviello? . . . From Leonardo to Leonard I can follow, . . . a perfectly natural process. In America anything can happen and does happen. But you don't change a family name. A name is a name. What happened to the *i*?'" Leonard explained that his teacher, Mrs. Cutter, "took out the *i*. That way it's easier for everybody. . . . What difference does it make? . . . It's more American. The *i* doesn't help anything." With bitterness and resignation, Leonard's father bowed to the inevitable and signed the report card. Leonard's mother, however, made one last effort to impress upon her son the significance of what the teacher had done: "A person's life and his honor is in his name. He never changes it. A name is not a shirt or a piece of underwear." Her argument fell on deaf ears: "The *i* is out," said her son, "and Mrs. Cutter made it Covello. You just don't understand!" Leonard's mother responded with what must have been the lament of thousands of immigrant fathers and mothers: "Will you stop saying that! I don't understand. I don't understand. What is there to understand? Now that you have become Americanized you understand everything and I understand nothing."[1]

Covello's father was right to worry. Immigrant fathers were liminal figures, suspended between an old culture and a new, children of European fathers, fathers of American children. With different intentions and varying degrees of success, they tried to maintain their prerogatives in a culture that relentlessly undercut the foundations of traditional paternal authority. In the streets, at school, or on the job, their offspring encountered a set of values, a way of looking at the world—in a word, a culture—often at odds with the Old World assumptions of their fathers. In essence, the meaning of America to fathers and children differed: whereas fathers held on to the Old World even as they moved to the New, their children more often than not had no such ambivalence. Their parents' European world was not without impact, but immigrant children would have American lives. The generational battles within families were heightened by reformers' efforts to Americanize immigrant children and immigrant parents' struggle to resist such efforts.

Fatherhood and Cultural Strain

Cut off from their cultural moorings in Europe, spending hours on end away from their children, living on or below the margin, immigrant fathers maintained with difficulty their authority over their children. Some resorted to bombast and exaggerated displays of male authority, a fact Robert Orsi noted in describing the Italian Harlem community as a public patriarchy in which "its residents helped to create and present a public image of their fathers as stern authoritarian figures, demanding and frequently harsh." Insisting upon elaborate, sometimes theatrical displays of respect from children and wives alike, these men liked to appear as "blustering, loud and angry disciplinarians."[2] For better or worse, they often succeeded: "At the time," recalled one man of his youth, "to be reprimanded by my father in the street was like having a knife pierced through my heart." And yet this posturing came not without cost. For these children looking back, their father was less a real person than an abstraction—"The Father"—whose image seemed distant and indistinct.[3]

In the formal, patriarchal home, life was especially difficult for daughters. Many found their mothers more flexible than their fathers, less suspicious of American ways, more tolerant of their social lives, and far less demanding of elaborate displays of deference.[4] Recalling her childhood and adolescence, Marie Concilio resented the mission of Italian daughters to "help the mother in spoiling the father and the brother by waiting on them and by making them helpless around the house."[5] An Italian-American woman recounted to Leonard Covello a searing experience with such prejudices while visiting a bedridden neighbor who had just returned home after a serious operation: "Her father happened to call at the same time. She greeted him in a casual, matter of fact way and the old man was highly insulted. She should have kissed his hand as a sign of respect for him."[6] Such formal, rather distant relationships were not without long-range and troubling consequences. One woman explained to Covello the authority structure as she knew it and what it meant for father-child relationships: "In the majority of Italian homes the father is the dominating force in the family. He is the one who says what must be done and what must not be done." Wives and children even had to ask his permission to go somewhere, but such deference, she noted, often stemmed from fear rather than love. "In order to maintain this reverence he goes about with a countenance of severity and because of this fails to develop the love and friendship of his offspring."[7]

Jewish children, especially daughters, had similar memories of the patriarchal hold. Elisabeth Stern began her autobiography with these remarkable words: "I remember looking down at the face of my father, beautiful and still in death, and for a brief, terrible moment feeling my heart rise up—surely it was in a strange, suffocating relief?—as the realization came to me: 'Now I am free!'" Her bondage had lasted for almost three decades: "All my life, for twenty-nine years, he had stood like an image of fine-carved stone, immovable, unbending, demanding that I submit my will and my thought, my every act in life, to the creed he represented."[8] In her semiautobiographical novel *The Bread Givers*, Anzia Yezierska painted a similar portrait of Reb Smolinsky, a character based on her own father. Consumed with the study of the Torah, Smolinsky lived off the earnings of his daughters and lamented that he had no sons who could pray for him after he died. His daughter Sarah, the main character, placed his lament, and hers, in wider perspective: "The prayers of his daughters didn't count because God didn't listen to women. Heaven and the next world were only for men. Women could get into Heaven because they were wives and daughters of men." Nevertheless, they did have a critical function to perform: "Women had no brains for the study of God's Torah, but they could be the servants of men who studied the Torah. Only if they cooked for the men, and washed for the men, and didn't nag or curse the men out of their homes; only if they let the men study the Torah in peace, then, maybe, they could push themselves into Heaven with the men, to wait on them there."[9]

Men like Smolinsky grimly held on to the old ways. Their children rebelled in every manner conceivable, often with the tacit help of their mothers, who many times served as a buffer between the children and the father.[10] But the hold was powerful. Yezierska tried to explain just how powerful to Samuel Goldwyn when his studio began shooting the film adaptation of her novel *Hungry Hearts*. Asked about the story line for her next novel, Yezierska told Goldwyn that it was about "the expiation of guilt." As the movie mogul stared at her, no doubt pondering how such a theme would play in Hollywood, she groped for an explanation: "I had to break away from my mother's cursing and my father's preaching to live my life; but without them I had no life. When you deny your parents, you deny the ground under your feet, the sky over your head. You become an outlaw, a pariah."[11] This sentiment appeared again at the end of *Bread Givers*, but now with a sharper focus on the power of the patriarchal hold. After years of conflict with a father she considered "a tyrant more terrible than the Tsar from Russia," after fulfilling her dreams by rejecting his, Sarah ultimately decided to take the elderly widower into her own home. In the end she was drawn back to old ways and responsibilities: "In a world where all is changed, he alone remained unchanged—as tragically isolate as the rocks. All that he had left of life was his fanatical adherence to his traditions. It was within my power to keep lighted the flickering candle of his life for him. Could I deny him this poor service?" She could not. For all she hated about her father, he remained an elemental force in her life: "It wasn't just my father, but the generations who made my father whose weight was still upon me."[12]

Yezierska brilliantly captured the ambiguous position of immigrant fathers. Their powerful hold on their children was rooted deeply in the history and culture of their native societies. Nevertheless, men could feel their grip beginning to weaken under the corrosive influences of American culture. Whether on the streets or at the movies, in stores or at school, immigrant children began to assume the trappings of a culture very different from that of their fathers. How quickly and to what extent depended, among other things, on the size and strength of the immigrant enclave, the age of the child and the number of years spent in the Old Country, and the attitude of both fathers and mothers to assimilation. Nevertheless, observers and immigrants themselves believed that immigrant children were being pulled steadily away from their parents' culture. Many writers have described this process, among them Hutchins Hapgood in his 1902 book, *The Spirit of the Ghetto:*

In America, even before he begins to go to our public schools, the little Jewish boy finds himself in contact with a new world which stands in violent contrast with the orthodox environment of his first few years. Insensibly—at the beginning—from his playmates in the streets, from his older brother or sister, he picks up a little English, a little American slang, hears older boys boast of prize-fighter Bernstein, and learns vaguely to feel that there is a strange and fascinating life on the street.[13]

Inexorably, the religion of their fathers lost power for the Jewish boys who, Hapgood noted, "gradually quit going to synagogue, give up 'chaider' promptly when they are thirteen years old, avoid the Yiddish theaters, seek the uptown places of amusement, dress in the latest American fashion, and have a keen eye for the right thing in neckties. They even refuse sometimes to be present at supper on Friday evenings. Then, indeed, the sway of the old people is broken."[14] Nourishing such rebellion by the young was the sense that their parents were out of step with modernity: "The growing sense of superiority on the part of the boy to the Hebraic part of his environment," wrote Hapgood, "extends itself soon to the home. He learns to feel that his parents, too, are 'greenhorns.'"[15]

Nor could home life compete with the lure of the street. "He runs away from the supper table to join his gang on the Bowery, where he is quick to pick up the very latest slang; where his talent for caricature is developed often at the expense of his parents, his race, and all 'foreigners'; for he is an American, he is 'the people,' and like his glorious countrymen in general, he is quick to ridicule the stanger." This intolerance could even be turned against his own community. The Americanized Jewish youth might well laugh "at the foreign Jew with as much heartiness as at the 'dago'; for he feels that he himself is almost as remote from the one as from the other." Faced with such rebellion, fathers could only cry out in frustration, "Amerikane kinder, Amerikane kinder!"[16]

Lincoln Steffens, another astute observer of New York City's Jewish East Side, described the generational split in the ghetto as "an abyss of many generations; it was between parents out of the Middle Ages, sometimes out of the Old Testament days hundreds of years B.C., and the children of the streets of New York today." This abyss could create contempt on the part of the young toward their fathers that Steffens described as ubiquitous:

We saw it everywhere all the time. . . . We would pass a synagogue where a score or more of boys were sitting hatless in their old clothes, smoking cigarettes on the steps outside, and their fathers, all dressed in black, with their high hats, uncut beards, and temple curls, were going into the synagogues, tearing their hair and rending their garments. . . . It was a revolution. Their sons were rebels against the law of Moses; they were lost souls, lost to God, the family, and to Israel of old.[17]

Jewish fathers and sons sometimes even came to blows: "If there was a fight—and sometimes the fathers did lay hands on their sons, and the tough boys did biff their fathers in the eye," police would be called, indiscriminate clubbing would ensue, and blood would be shed. "I used to feel that the blood did not hurt, but the tears did, the weeping and gnashing of teeth of the old Jews who were doomed and knew it. Two, three thousand years of continuous devotion, courage, and suffering for a cause lost in a generation."[18]

Alienation of immigrant children from their fathers came from every quarter, so much so that "the fear of losing the children haunts the older generation, . . . a vague uneasiness that a delicate network of precious traditions is being ruthlessly torn asunder, that a whole world of ideals is crashing into ruins."[19] Paternal anxieties about this crash could come suddenly and without warning. Rose Cohen's father feared that his daughter spent too much time with gentiles and that his son was being seduced by the gentile world. When his son found the word *Christ* in a library book, the discovery prompted Cohen's father to throw the book out the window. Rose was incredulous: "When I looked out and saw the covers torn off and the pages lying scattered in the yard I . . . wept aloud that I had a right to know, to learn, to understand . . . that I was horribly ignorant; that I had been put into the world but had been denied a chance to learn."[20]

Popular amusements might divide the generations. In a letter to the *Jewish Daily Forward,* one father expressed concern about his son's love of baseball and suggested that a chasm separated first-generation fathers from second-generation sons:

It makes sense to teach a child to play dominoes or chess. But what is the point of a crazy game like baseball? The children can get crippled. When I was a boy we played rabbit, chasing each other, hide-and-seek. Later we stopped. If a grown boy played rabbit in Russia they would think he has lost his mind. Here in educated America adults play baseball. They run after a leather ball like children. I want my boy to grow up to be a *mensh,* not a wild American runner. But he cries my head off.

Despite admitting that most Jewish fathers considered baseball "a wild and silly game," the editors nevertheless resigned themselves to the inevitable and counseled the troubled fathers to "let your boys play baseball and play it well, as long as it does not interfere with their education or get them into bad company. Half the parents in the Jewish quarter have this problem."[21]

Even food could become an object of contention. The effort of school authorities to change Italian dietary practices, for example, incensed the father of Leonard Covello: "[O]nce at the Soup School I remember the teacher gave each child a bag of oatmeal to take home. This food was supposed to make you big and strong. You ate it for breakfast." His father, however, had little use for such nonsense. "My father examined the stuff, tested it with his fingers. To him it was the kind of bran that we gave to pigs in Avigliano. 'What kind of a school is this?' he shouted. 'They give us the food of animals to eat and send it home to us with our children. What are we coming to next?'"[22] But the senior Covello could do little more than protest. The world of Avigliano was but a hazy memory for the boy.

The problem, of course, went a good deal deeper than books, baseball, and breakfast food. At stake was the future, and the shape of the future was rapidly escaping the guiding hand of fathers. Yezierska's Reb Smolinsky saw it as a simple matter of respect: "Blood-and-iron! . . . What's the world coming to in this wild America? No respect for fathers. No fear of God."[23] But it was more complicated than this. The world that had nurtured the respect so desired by Reb Smolinsky no longer prevailed. Exposed to a new American culture in the streets and at school, children were quick to absorb its language and mores as they moved steadily away from the values of their parents. But they did more than this. As they embraced the new culture, the young became sources of authority, cultural guides and mediators for parents bewildered by the strange institutions and customs of America. It would be too much to say that the child became father to the man, but sometimes the strange new position of children seemingly inverted authority relationships within families. When tenement reformer Lawrence Veiller, for example, decided to provide tuberculosis information for Italian immigrants, he originally intended to print it in Italian. After learning that most adult Italian immigrants read neither Italian nor English, Veiller took Dr. Antonio Stella's advice and printed the information in English, confident, as Stella put it, that "the children will then read it and translate it for their parents."[24]

Day-to-day transactions might require a child's intercession. One Jewish daughter always accompanied her father to the doctor as his translator and took pride that her parents "really depended on me." Another young woman realized that language was power: "I was the one who conquered the language, so I became the emissary. Whatever had to be done, like getting a license or being a translator, it was I." Although she no doubt exaggerated the influence this ability brought her—"I became the head of the family"—her sentiment suggested awareness of the unstable nature of family relationships.[25] Hapgood saw the same process at work among Jewish boys. In Russia the father provided for the educational and material needs of his children, but in America fathers found economic success elusive and an understanding of the outside world difficult. Thus, children often were the family's ambassador to the outside world: "As he [the child] speaks English, and his parents do not, he is commonly the interpreter in business transactions, and tends generally to take things into his own hands. There is a tendency, therefore, for the father to respect the son."[26]

But this respect could go only so far and was bounded by the competing cultural tensions within the hearts of immigrant fathers. These men, after all, had chosen to leave the Old World to start a new life. Understandably, some took pride in and did all they could to foster their children's Americanization. The father of one German girl required that all her books be in English and threatened to burn those that were not, while an immigrant daughter recalled "that much as they clung to their habits and restrictions from the Old Country, they were delighted with any of their children who became Americanized."[27] But this delight came not without cost, a point made by Mary Antin, who recognized that the Americanization of the young had revolutionary implications: "My parents knew only that they desired us to be like American children; and seeing how their neighbors gave their children boundless liberty, they turned us also loose, never doubting but that the American way was the best way." Yet, her parents had neither standards by which to judge proper American behavior nor, and more important, any authority to do so: "In their bewilderment and uncertainty they needs [sic] must trust us children to learn from such models as the tenements afforded. More than this, they must step down from their throne of parental authority, and take the law from their children's mouths; for they had no other means of finding out what was good American form."[28]

Although Antin averred that the immigrant father "forgets exile and homesickness and ridicule and loss and estrangement, when he beholds his sons and daughters moving as Americans among Americans," many fathers feared that success in America too often came at the expense of deeper values.[29] In Budd Schulberg's *What Makes Sammy Run*, Sammy's father, "struggling to maintain his last shred of authority, the patriarchy of his own home, demanded to know why he was not at cheder." The reason was simple: "Sammy hated cheder. Three hours a day in a stinking back room with a sour-faced old Reb who taught you a lot of crap about the Hebrew laws." Instead, Sammy had used the time to make money, a decision that earned a stiff rebuke from his father. "'Sammy!' his father bellowed. 'Touching money on the Sabbath! God should strike you dead!'" His father then snatched the money and threw it down the stairs. Unrepentant, Sammy snapped back: "'You big dope!' Sammy screamed at him, his voice shrill with rage. 'You lazy son-of-a-bitch.'" His father did not respond, however, but retreated to an older, more stable world: "His eyes were closed and his lips were moving. He looked as if he had had a stroke. He was praying."[30]

Such conflicts were not confined to fathers and sons. A young Jewish woman remembered what happened when she took a job that required her to work on Saturdays: "My father would not take my money when I brought it home. He said it was tainted. My father did not speak to me for one whole year!" She had not taken the job to be rebellious but because "I felt I couldn't live in Europe. I had to live in the United States."[31] In her "autobiography," Yezierska vividly captured the cultural clash between father and daughter over the meaning of success. Her father insisted that her "first duty to God is to serve your father," then added with bitterness, "But what's an old father to an *Amerikanerin,* a daughter of Babylon?" Defending herself, Yezierska reminded her father that she had given him one hundred dollars she had earned as a writer. Unsatisfied, he lashed out: "Can your money make up for your duty as a daughter? In America, money takes the place of God." Hoping that her father might take pride in her success, she began to tell him of the ten thousand dollars she had received for the motion picture rights to her book but his stinging rebuke interrupted her: "Can you touch pitch without being defiled? Neither can you hold on to all that money without losing your soul."[32]

Other men shared such fears. In a letter to the *Jewish Daily Forward,* a man described meeting a shabbily dressed cookie seller who, he found out, had three successful children. Asked why he lived so poorly when he had offspring who might help him, the elderly Jew explained at some length the cultural gulf between him and his children. His children, he said, lived only for money: "I cannot live among machines. I am a live man and have a soul, despite my age. They are machines. They work all day and come home at night. What do they do? Nothing." Their intellectual and spiritual lives had withered, to be replaced by a crabbed emphasis on money: "Books have nothing in common with them; Jewish troubles have nothing in common with them; the whole world has nothing in common with them." His children found his desire for intellectual discussion a quaint relic of a foreign land: "When I first came here I used to speak and argue with them. But they did not understand. They would ask: Why this and that? This country is not Russia. Here everybody does as he likes." The father decided that his values and those of his children had nothing in common: "They make money and live for that purpose. When I grasped this situation a terror possessed me and I did not believe these were my children. I could not stand it to be there; I was being choked; I could not tolerate their behavior and I went away."[33]

Fatherhood and the Youth Culture

American culture changed immigrant children, but immigrant children changed American culture as well. On the streets, in schools, and at work, working-class children established a distinctive group identity—a youth-and-work culture—that played a critical role in pulling immigrant children out of the orbit of their parents' traditional culture. Thus, the American culture that so troubled many immigrant fathers was, ironically, created in part by their own children. The structural basis of this culture developed at the turn of the century as immigrant children's participation in schools and the industrial work force became important features of their lives.

Schooling brought immigrant children into a new environment where, as Hutchins Hapgood described it, "the little fellow runs plump against a system of education and a set of influences which are at total variance with those traditional to his race and with his home life."[34] Packed in overcrowded classrooms with students of widely varying ages, subject to the hostility of teachers who made fun of their names and customs, targets of aggressive Americanization campaigns intended to root out their heritage, immigrant children nevertheless found in schools a social space free from parental influence where they could mix elements of the old culture with those of the new.

High schools played an especially important role in this process as thousands of working-class youths began enrolling after the turn of the century. Although attendance rates differed by ethnic group and gender—many more girls than boys graduated between 1900 and 1920— high schools increased the significance of the peer group and heightened children's independence from adults.[35] A variety of school organizations and a host of extracurricular activities kept students away from home for many hours each day. Students could spend this time forging peer bonds beyond the reach of either their parents or school authorities. In fraternities, sororities, and a host of social clubs and athletic organizations, students sought the approval of fellow classmates and became "highly conscious of their personalities and styles of social interaction," in the process helping to transfer "emotional ties from the family to the peer group."[36] School pranks, rebellious and unconventional behavior, or athletic success could all be used to win approval from the peer group; conversely, one's own behavior underwent constant scrutiny by classmates. The result of this process, as Reed Ueda has argued, was the definition of "preferred modes of self-preservation and personality distinctive of the high school peer society."[37] These modes likely transcended ethnic divisions and made the high school youth culture a melting pot "that facilitated cultural exchange and social bonding between students of different ethnic and class backgrounds. In extracurricular clubs, in student government, on sports teams, and in the classroom, popularity and attractiveness among peers counted more than the occupation of one's father."[38]

The peer culture also took shape on the shop floor. Young men and women, drawn into the work force to supplement their fathers' inadequate income, increasingly labored not in domestic or small-shop isolation but in the large factories, offices, and department stores of the expanding corporate economy.[39] Here young men and women staked out a measure of personal and generational autonomy for themselves. In part, this autonomy came as young workers resisted the routinization of labor by enforcing informal work rules, adhering to the "stint," and socializing new workers to the culture of the shop floor. It also came less obviously through the gossip, jokes, slang, clothing, hairstyles, songs, and social rituals that distinctively marked the work culture of the young. Such seeming epiphenomena offered young workers an identity forged in the heat of class and generational resistance that was distinct from that of their bosses but also from that of their parents.

On the job or at the close of the working day, the young affirmed their allegiance to the fads, styles, and habits of their co-workers and their interest in the romantic entanglements of their fellow employees.[40] While their parents endured grinding poverty, girls like garment worker Sadie Frowne, for example, might have other thoughts about money: "A girl must have clothes if she is to go into high society at Ulmer Park or Coney Island or the theater." Another young woman echoed these sentiments: "If you want to get any notion took of you, you gotta have some style about you."[41] (And how better to find out about style than at the movies, where young women learned that the right combination of makeup, clothes, and personality might lead to marrying "up."[42]) Frank discussions of sexuality, spiced with ribald jokes and sexual advice, punctuated the conversations of young women in ways that would have appalled their parents. One observer of female restaurant workers could not conceal her shock: "They were putting on their aprons, combing their hair, powdering their noses, . . . all the while tossing back and forth to each other, apparently in a spirit of good-natured comradeship, the most vile epithets that I had ever heard emerge from the lips of a human being."[43] An observer at Macy's decried the sexual emphasis of the employees' conversations: "[T]here was enough indecent talk to ruin any girl in her teens who might be put at work on that floor."[44]

Try as they might, fathers found it difficult to counter the growing importance of peer relationships. Surely the loose talk of the shop floor was more inviting and exciting than the sage advice or misguided exhortations of one's father. Nor was the peer culture restricted to the factory, office, or department store. Unlike their fathers, who spent much of their leisure time in saloons and fraternal organizations, or their mothers, whose leisure was oriented to the home and kin, working-class youth were drawn to heterosexual, pleasure-oriented commercial amusements. After a hard day of work, girls put on their finery and promenaded in the streets or headed for movie theaters or the ubiquitous dance halls to engage in "tough dancing" with boys of their class.[45] One middle-class observer offered a view of this culture that no doubt would have troubled the dancers' fathers:

> I saw one of the women smoking cigarettes, most of the younger couples were hugging and kissing, there was a general mingling of men and women at the different tables, almost every one seemed to know one another and spoke to each other across the room, also saw both men and women leave their tables and join couples at different tables, they were all singing and carrying on, they kept running around the room and acted like a mob of lunatics let lo[o]se.[46]

More exciting still was a trip to Coney Island and the amusement park rides that literally threw young men and women together. For poorly paid working girls, all these activities were underwritten by the system of treating: boys paid for the cost of the evening's entertainment in exchange for companionship and sexual favors.

This nascent youth culture was not without inequality—girls remained economically dependent on boys and ran the risk of pregnancy—but this world was in many ways beyond the reach of parents. Relentlessly heterosexual, shaped by commercialized recreation and the burgeoning culture of consumption, the culture of the young eroded paternal prerogatives and the influence of traditional immigrant cultures. City streets, dance halls, amusement parks, and movie theaters all offered immigrant youth social space for sexual experimentation, personal assertion, and the renegotiation of cultural mores. Compared with the excitement of a sexually charged dance hall with its "promiscuous interaction of strangers," its ribald language, and its general bawdiness, a quiet night at home with parents or a chaperoned evening with a beau seemed impossibly old-fashioned to the working girl just off a ten-hour shift.[47]

In short, fathers found it difficult to shelter their children from the corrosive impact of this new culture. Appeals to Old World values, religious guilt, or the honor owed parents could not withstand the power of a new sexual culture in the making. Because their own economic vulnerability made them dependent on their children's earnings, fathers lost control not only of their children's social world but, in part, of their children as well. Although some children dutifully handed unopened wage envelopes to parents, others insisted that contributions to the family income came not without cost. The culture of the young might anger and alarm fathers, but an employed child could press her advantage: "[T]he costume in which she steps out so triumphantly," wrote a social investigator of one young immigrant girl, "has cost many bitter moments at home. She has gotten it by force, with the threat of throwing up her job."[48] Other girls might go even further and pay board to their parents while keeping the remainder of their wages or, like Mashah Smolinsky in Yezierska's *The Bread Givers,* blithely spend part of their wages on whatever caught their fancy.[49] Abraham Bisno, an organizer for the International Ladies' Garment Workers' Union, described the implications of this arrangement: "This change in their lives which allowed them the right to do whatever they pleased with their own money, and gave them standing and authority because of their earnings and contributions, was for them a very significant item in their lives. They acquired the *right to a personality* which they had not ever possessed in the old country."[50]

This "right" and the emerging culture of the young generated conflict between immigrant parents, especially fathers, and children. Children fought with their parents over hairstyles, curfews, and courting and sometimes resented their fathers' backwardness or lowly economic position. Leonard Covello concluded that Italian-American boys wanted to be "pals" with their fathers but at a deeper level realized such hopes were ridiculous; the gulf between their culture and that of their fathers was too great. Thus, Covello's effort to organize a father-son dinner at his high school flopped, a failure he attributed to the sons' shame at being seen with their fathers outside Italian Harlem.[51] Milton Meltzer's memoir records similar sentiments. Once, in the company of his middle-class girlfriend whom he had met at school, Meltzer saw his father washing windows and, ashamed, hurried by with barely a hello. The girl chided him for not introducing her.

> "And why didn't you introduce me? You just rushed past."
> I could feel how hot my face was getting. "It's easy for you to act so superior. Your father doesn't have to clean up other people's dirt."
> "But he's your father! You think a man's what he does for a living, only that, nothing more? He's as good as anybody else!"
> "Easy for people to say, but do they really mean it? Look, my pa's a window cleaner, yours is a newspaper editor. Do people see them the same?"

Meltzer remembered, too, that although the girl had already suggested more than once that she meet his parents, "I managed never to arrange it. And now she'd met Pa. She was appalled by my attempt to avoid it. And I was ashamed."[52]

Alfred Kazin's recollections suggest that shame was not a monopoly of the young. As Kazin thought about his own grim struggle to achieve in school, he realized "how little my parents thought of their own lives. It was not for myself alone that I was expected to shine, but for them— to redeem the constant anxiety of their existence. I was the first American child, their offering to the strange new God; I was to be the monument of their liberation from the shame of being—what they were. And that there was shame in this was a fact that everyone seemed to believe as a matter of course."[53]

Immigrant Fathers and American Schools

The marginal economic position of fathers, the emerging work culture of the young, and the clash of cultures between immigrant youth and their parents all undermined paternal authority. Compulsory school attendance laws, which pitted the power of the state against the economic needs and the decision-making powers of parents, did the same. Certainly many immigrant fathers and mothers sacrificed mightily to secure an education for their offspring, but the privilege came with a cost. A child at school was not a child at work. Confronted with evidence of his daughter's truancy, one immigrant father minced no words in revealing his understanding of this relationship: "He stated emphatically that the only conditions under which he would send Lily to school would be if the city contributed to his family income the same amount that his wife earns so that his children (nine) could have what he considers the necessities of life and his wife could stay home and take care of them."[54]

The state's commitment to compulsory schooling clashed not only with the economic needs of parents but with their culture as well. As immigrant children entered public schools in great numbers after 1900—among students in 37 American cities in 1908, almost 60 percent had foreign-born fathers—school officials aggressively sought ways to Americanize them. Health inspections, patriotic lessons, history classes, Protestant prayers, flag ceremonies, derogation of immigrant customs, and pageants were all put to the task.[55] Even primers played their part. One Slovenian woman recalled that after a steady diet of the "Dick and Jane" series, she "became ashamed that my parents spoke 'funny'; that we laughed too loud; that we drank homemade wine; that our walls were papered in flower patterns; that we grew our own vegetables; that my father raised chickens in the garage."[56]

On one side stood school officials confident of their ability to mold foreign students into American citizens; on the other, immigrant parents clung to the old culture while gingerly approaching the new. In the middle were the children, sometimes bored and exasperated with school life, sometimes eager to adopt the customs, styles, and mores promoted by school officials. Immigrant parents thus found themselves in an awkward situation. Many, perhaps most, equated schooling with increased opportunity for their offspring. Enrollment figures certainly suggest as much, as immigrant youth flooded urban school systems and the immigrant press relentlessly emphasized the importance of education to immigrant success. In 1909 the percentage of foreign-born schoolchildren ages five to fourteen outdistanced the percentage of native white youth, evidence confirming immigrants' faith in the importance of schooling.[57]

But this faith in education masked deeper tensions between the culture of immigrant parents and that of school men and women. School officials saw education as the great engine of Americanization. William H. Maxwell, superintendent of New York City schools, put the matter squarely: "[T]he majority of the people who now come to us have little akin to our language; they have little akin to our mode of thought; they have little akin to our customs; and they have little akin to our traditions. They come here and are planted in an environment totally different from that to which they have been accustomed. It is a great business of the department of education in this city—I shall not say its greatest business—to train the immigrant child from the shores of the Mediterranean Sea to become a good American citizen."[58] Educators agreed that if immigrant children were to be successful, they must become Americanized, even if that created a gulf between parents and children. As longtime educator Julia Richman remarked, the more successfully schools Americanized the immigrant child, "the more it is weaned away from the standards and traditions of its home. The parents remain foreign; the children become American. There is thus created an almost unbridgeable gulf between the two."[59] The state's interest in acculturation thus clashed with the parents' fidelity to their native culture, but it was the parents who were to yield: "They must be made to realize," wrote Richman, "that in forsaking the land of their birth, they were also forsaking the customs and the traditions of that land; and they must be made to realize an obligation, in adopting a new country, to adopt the language and customs of that country."[60]

To this end, schools began a broad-based effort to Americanize immigrant youth. Maxwell described just how wide-ranging this effort should be: "In the first place we must teach him [the immigrant child] to take care of his health, so that he may become physically strong and vigorous. In the second place we must give him the power of using the English language. In the third place we should give him as good an intellectual education as his limited time will permit." He concluded with an odd juxtaposition of two further goals: "Then we must teach him how to play, and we ought to teach him the rights and duties of an American citizen."[61] Guided by such goals, schools sought to transform the culture of their immigrant charges. Geography, English, music, manual training, and even cooking classes were all turned to the task of inculcating American values.[62]

Such efforts were not lost on the students. In fact, the entire world of schooling could seem at odds with the culture of the students' parents. Some students took home practical lessons in American living for their parents—"I came home and made hot chocolate and corn bread and showed [my mother] how to make it"—while others remembered the celebration of American heroes and heroines and the emphasis on patriotism and the glories of the American past: "We learned about the Revolutionary War, the Civil War, and our founding fathers." School calendars honored Christian holidays, Bible readings occurred frequently, and little or no regard was paid to Jewish dietary practices. Oral history interviews suggest that perhaps the teachers themselves had the greatest impact on reshaping the culture of the young. One immigrant recalled that the "manners and clothes, speech and point of view of our teachers extorted our respect and reflected upon the shabbiness, foreignness and crudities of our folks and homes." An immigrant elaborated on his teachers' impact years before when he had been in school: "By virtue of their speech, their attitude, their manners, their dress, they set a model. This meant being an American. They didn't say 'Emulate us because we're Americans,' but they became synonymous and perhaps because they did not say they were Americans, and because they sort of breathed Americanism all over you, you absorbed it."[63]

Such efforts, school leaders acknowledged, drove a wedge between immigrant children and parents. District Superintendent Henry E. Jenkins described how the process worked: "You know, that the City of New York takes the children away from their parents for purposes of education. It says to the parents: 'you must not send your child to work. . . .' What does the city return to the parent? It gives the child a complete education and teaches him reverence for the law and the flag."[64] But as Leonard Covello explained, it taught something else as well: "In fact, throughout my whole elementary school career, I do not recall one mention of Italy or the Italian language or what famous Italians had done in the world, with the possible exception of Columbus, who was pretty popular in America." This omission had a profound impact on the impressionable boy: "We soon got the idea that 'Italian' meant something inferior, and a barrier was erected between children of Italian origin and their parents." This barrier dealt a terrible blow to parent-child relations: "We were becoming Americans by learning how to be ashamed of our parents."[65]

While social workers and educators might cheerfully acknowledge "that the authority of the parents is weakened by those influences with which the younger generation comes into contact" and that public schooling "undoubtedly breaks the shackles of parental control," immigrant fathers felt otherwise.[66] These men were torn between their commitment to education and their realization that schooling pulled their children into a new world. Their ambivalence increased as compulsory school laws began to be enforced in the first two decades of the twentieth century.[67] Responses varied. To help perpetuate cultural traditions and language, some immigrants built separate school systems while others held special classes after public school hours. Slavic-Americans put little faith in schooling in general. They introduced their sons to the working world at an early age and often found them their first job. In Pennsylvania, for example, fathers took their sons out of school and into the mines or factories, a move that made sense to a group that put family security ahead of individual mobility.[68]

Many immigrant fathers, in fact, considered extended schooling a waste of time, particularly for daughters. Novelist Jerre Mangione noted the combination of forces that worked against prolonged schooling for Italian girls: "To give a daughter more education than that required by law was considered an extravagant waste of time and money. . . . But everyone also knew that a man was not interested in a girl who knew much more than he did."[69] Leonard Covello recalled how one Italian father lamented the ambition that schooling had kindled in his daughter: "In fact, the father always cursed the day he came to America, because if he had stayed in Italy, no daughter of his would have the desire to become a teacher. She would have to work on the farm or in the house."[70] Another young Italian girl accepted her father's restrictions on her education but noted that her sister did not:

> My sister got disgusted with shop work and told my father that she wouldn't let him prevent her from educating herself as he had with me. She told him she would go to night school and work during the day. My father didn't like it much. He didn't want her coming home late and he thought school and work was too much of a burden. But she did it anyway. She had to work because the family needed her wages.

She reported that her sister ultimately became a high school teacher and, perhaps equally important, that her sister's strength had bent her father's will: "She put him in his place completely, and he changed his attitude."[71]

Immigrant sons also encountered obstacles to education. The reasons might vary. Many Italian-American fathers, who put high stock in manual labor, doubted whether extended schooling, the white-collar jobs such schooling would bring, and masculinity were compatible.[72] More common was simple economic need. Jimmie Capasso, the American-born son of an Italian immigrant laborer, had hoped to continue his education, but his father insisted that he find a job. Dutifully but with great sadness, the bookish teenager searched for work, aware that he, the smartest boy in his class, was only one of two who was not going on to high school. As his search for work continued to be fruitless, his father became more severe and impatient: "What's the matter you, Jimmie? Your mother all the time cry. Antoinette no got shoes. You eat, sleep, no can find work. All the time read book. You good-for-nothing bum." Ashamed and depressed by his father's rebuke, convinced that he would never find work and thus please his father, Jimmie finally shot himself but still had no respite from his father's criticisms. At the hospital his father could not hide his exasperation: "You Jimmie, why you kill yourself? Everything I do for you. Today I no work, I lose t'ree dollars."

Jimmie apparently died from his self-inflicted wound, but in a more important sense he died because his father's allegiance to the family economy undermined his son's dreams for an education. Nor did Jimmie's death change his father's belief that children owed the family financial support. Bemoaning his family's current condition, Jimmie's father looked to a younger son for help:

> All the time I work pick and shovel, got no one to help me. My girl, fif-
> teen, she died, sick a de chest. Jimmie, fifteen, he die. Other man he fill
> his belly with chicken; every day me fill belly with bread and beans. No
> chicken, no spaghetti, no wine. Mother she all time cry. Children no got
> shoes, no clothes, sometimes go to bed hungry. Who going to help me?
> Next boy, Ralph, he still too young. Wait 'nother year before he get
> through school and go get job.

His father's faith in Ralph was evidently well placed. In the presence of his father, Ralph had once denounced his older brother's intentions to continue his education:

> Graduatin' don't get him nothin'—he got to get a job first. And he don't
> want to work, neither. I bet when I get through that darned old school
> you don't ketch me goin' on to high school![73]

Ralph was willing to fulfill his father's vision of filial obligations, the more sensitive Jimmie was not. It is fruitless to speculate on which was the more common response. Children's emotional and psychological re-actions to paternal demands surely resist such simple categorization: guilt, devotion, shame, duty, love, sacrifice, and selfishness were hope-lessly entangled as the young responded to parental expectations. Yet, it is fair to say that the conflicting pull of school and home created ten-sions between the generations.

Most immigrant fathers no doubt confronted the public school system with profound ambivalence.[74] They realized that the child who walked into the school would not be the same one who walked out. Schooling was an opportunity but also a threat. Fathers could only watch their children "go into the kindergarten as little Poles or Italians or Finns," wrote the sociolo-gist John Daniels in 1920, "babbling in the tongues of their parents, and at the end of half a dozen years or more he sees them emerge, looking, talk-ing, thinking, and behaving generally like full-fledged 'Americans.'"[75] Con-trol over the cultural destiny of children was passing inexorably from fa-thers and mothers to the schools, the streets, and the state.

Immigrant Fathers and American Culture

Summarizing the experience of immigrant fathers may well be impossi-ble. It depended upon a host of variables, shaped in turn, by many other variables. The experiences of an Italian and a Slav surely differed but so did the experiences of big-city and small-town Italians. An immigrant's economic success or, more broadly, his class position affected his experience as a father, but perhaps no more so than the strength of his community's ethnic institutions. These factors that shaped men's expectations and behaviors, moreover, were subject to endless idiosyncratic personality differences. The Americanization program that prompted one father to send a child to parochial school might well have been welcomed by another. One Polish father might shrug off a daughter's date with a non-Pole while another might respond with rage.

Bearing in mind the caveat that generalizations must be made with caution, we can say that immigrant men were liminal figures, neither fully a part of the old culture nor of the new. Success as breadwinners and patriarchs was elusive. Their wages were low, their work unpredictable, and yet in great numbers they managed to buy homes, secure stable livelihoods, and rear families. Their hold on the culture was even more tenuous and fraught with contradiction. Men could leave Europe, but Europe seldom left men. The same man who left the Old Country and embraced the opportunities America afforded lamented that his children lacked respect for traditional ways. Conversely, the same man who grumbled about the attenuation of ethnic life in the old neighborhood might take pride in a son's or daughter's move to a new working- or middle-class suburb.

In essence, these first-generation fathers confronted an unmanageable dilemma. They were Poles or Italians who lived in America, but their children were Polish-Americans or Italian-Americans who knew more of Washington and Lincoln than of Pilsudski or Garibaldi. Their liminal status as transitional figures brought with it an inevitable sense of loss. Even when they succeeded, they failed. In a piece by Walter Weyl, a fictive Polish miner put it this way: "America is a wonderful land, but it is a land of forgetfulness. My children are not my children, for my children have forgotten that they are Poles."[76] "Forgotten" may be too strong, but by the 1920s second-generation immigrants were moving beyond the enclave, taking more tolerant attitudes toward ethnic intermarriage, and identifying themselves as Americans.[77] Parents tried to counter these trends through parochial schools, recreational programs, and ethnic cultural revivals, but the forces undermining the old culture were too strong. The traditional ethnic culture would not disappear completely, but the Old World ways of immigrant fathers would recede under the powerful influences of consumerism, residential change, education, an activist state, and, most of all, time.

5

The Invention of the New Fatherhood, 1920–1940

IN THE MAY 2, 1925, EDITION OF THE *SATURDAY EVENING POST,* FOR-
mer boxing great Gentleman Jim Corbett contributed a piece titled "If
I Had a Son." He began by lamenting that he and his wife had never
had children and then suggested what kind of father he would have
been had he had a son. In his judgment, affection, commitment, and
companionship made up the essence of good fathering: fathers must
become involved with their sons and try to enter their world of play. As
the bond between father and son grew stronger, the two should share
confidences: "By all means in your power," wrote Corbett, "get him to
feel that he can always talk to you about things that trouble him, as man
to man, and not in a shamefaced way." Ultimately, Corbett hoped, the
tie would become so close that even the most personal matters could
be discussed: "[I]f he has learned that he can talk freely and frankly
with his dad maybe he will also bring his problems of the body to you.
And he should be able to learn about them from you with greater safety
than he can from the boys at the corner."[1]

Corbett was not alone in his call for a closer, more personal bond between fathers and children. In the closing decades of the nineteenth
century, a new conception of masculinity called men to the home and
to child rearing. Influenced by the emergence of more companionate
family relations and new assumptions about manhood, as well as by

changing class and residential patterns, middle-class men at the turn of the century increasingly sought meaning in the private realm. In burgeoning suburbs, thousands of men finally had the income and the leisure to construct a new conception of fatherhood that reflected the values of a therapeutic culture dedicated to growth, personality, and self-realization. As providers men underwrote a consumer culture that equated the purchase of goods with happiness and self-expression; as nurturers, men tried, albeit with mixed success and considerable ambivalence, to become more involved in the development of their offspring's personalities and individual growth.

This new mode of masculinity and fatherhood—"masculine domesticity," as one historian called it—had great implications for twentieth-century manhood and family life. It reshaped patriarchal relations and revitalized and redefined domestic life; it became a key element in the creation of "compulsive heterosexuality"; it helped to delineate class boundaries; and it became part of the therapeutic management of interpersonal relations.[2] Although inspired by liberal assumptions and democratic impulses, the "new fatherhood" paradoxically had a conservative impact on twentieth-century family life. Until challenged in the 1970s and 1980s from both the left and the right, this reigning orthodoxy helped to modernize, redefine, and legitimate male dominance and a gender-based division of labor among the American middle class.

Middle-Class Masculinity in Crisis

In the half-century after 1880, the cultural meaning of fatherhood changed as the white-collar sector took shape as a class out of the shared experiences of work, consumption, residential location, and family life.[3] White-collar occupations grew rapidly after 1880 and with them men with secure incomes who could purchase a cornucopia of goods that promised to enhance well-being and social standing.[4] Consumption thus became the hallmark of the new middle class: in residential enclaves that ringed the cities, white-collar men and their families affirmed their new class identity by their purchasing power, the homogeneity of their surroundings, and their social and physical distance from the working class.[5]

Class identity also came from new family values. For middle-class males, family relationships underwent a process of renegotiation. It was the middle class that forged the modern companionate family, characterized by romance, companionship, sexual fulfillment, mutual respect, and emotional satisfaction.[6] The result of a host of complex factors, the companionate family—though predicated upon a strict division of labor—represented a shift in the nature of patriarchy from an emphasis on sexual repression, male authority, and hierarchical organization to an emphasis on sexual satisfaction and mutual rights and responsibilities. Central to this new vision of domestic life was an emphasis on fatherly nurture. Unlike thousands of mid-nineteenth-century middle-class men whose participation in arcane and lengthy fraternal rituals took them away from home night after night, the new fathers of the twentieth-century middle class ideally took a more active role in their children's development.[7] In part, this emphasis grew out of the cultural emphasis on family companionship in general, in part out of concern that boys needed a manly presence to escape becoming overly feminized. Regardless of the impulse behind the advice, commentators urged men to play with their children and to form close, affectionate bonds with them. The emphasis was on mutual companionship, growth, and enrichment: men would learn the joys of nurture, children the joys of fatherly solicitude and good cheer. Friendship and play, not obedience and discipline, would define the ideal paternal relationship with children.[8]

This new vision of middle-class fatherhood emerged when older sources of male identity were disintegrating and a "crisis in masculinity" was at hand. The many sources of this crisis reflected a century of social change. Men who had once known the pleasures of face-to-face relationships on farms and in small towns now lived in cities and suburbs that fostered a sense of anonymity and insignificance.[9] Men who had once worked as artisans or farmers now labored among the ranks of the white collar, an increasingly segmented and specialized domain in which the worker was less dependent on his character than on his "personality."[10] Men who had once found meaning in religion and the stern injunctions of Puritan forefathers now heard only platitudes of good cheer, a rhetoric of "evasive banalities" that impoverished the ability of religion to give meaning to life.[11] Nor could men find stability in gender relationships. Since the mid-nineteenth century, domestic moralists and feminists alike had attacked male prerogatives, prompting a few intrepid men to espouse feminist principles but even more to worry about a seemingly overcivilized, excessively domesticated culture and to call for a retoughening of American boyhood.[12]

For most middle-class men, however, the answer to the crisis in manhood, to the decline of the autonomous self, to feelings of fragmentation and emptiness, lay neither with feminism nor antifeminism but with a redefined conception of fatherhood, breadwinning, and consumption. Middle-class men would become increasingly concerned about the quality of their private lives and about their lives as fathers, ironically at a time when work took them outside the home for most of the day. Such concern was part of a new cultural emphasis on "growth," "personality," and the pursuit of material well-being.[13] Psychologists, self-help advisers, and popular literati promoted these ideals and even religion accommodated to the times as ministers highlighted "the inward shrine of man's personality," emphasized "the potentiality of human life," and hailed Christianity as "the greatest of all therapeutic agents."[14]

For middle-class men, fatherhood became part of this growing emphasis on personal life. Men could find meaning in the private realm as fathers, a task elevated and shaped intellectually by an increasingly self-conscious group of family professionals drawn from social work, sociology, psychology, home economics, and psychiatry. The emergence of these professionals gave intellectual coherence to fathers' place in the therapeutic culture. These were the men and women who analyzed modern fatherhood, examined the connection between fathers and personality formation, set new standards for fatherly behavior, and explored the relationship between that behavior and class identity. The research and prescriptions for change promoted by this group shaped the discourse on fatherhood for the next several decades.[15]

The New Fatherhood

It was family experts in the 1920s and 1930s who first explored the complex, sometimes contradictory relationships among fatherhood, the new middle class, companionate family relations, and therapeutic ideals. Central to their analysis was the belief that family life and fatherhood were in transition, perhaps even in crisis. In the past, the family had been a multifunctional institution entrusted with a variety of tasks including economic support, education, religious training, recreation, and health and welfare responsibilities.[16] Fathers and mothers had had mutually supportive and complementary obligations whose fulfillment brought strength and considerable independence to families. Over time, however, these functions had been absorbed by society, and the result, according to the experts, was to weaken the family.

To leading family thinkers like Ernest Groves and Ernest Mowrer, the family was "drifting," buffeted by urbanization, materialism, individualism, oversexualization, and changing gender relationships.[17] All these forces promoted the self at the expense of the family, thereby undermining the spirit of sacrifice necessary to establish strong family bonds. Childless couples faced special risks: "With only sex and comfort as motives, and no functioning of parental love," warned Groves in 1926, "there is little to protect restless couples from divorce."[18] But couples with children had their own difficulties. Married women's desire for work, children's immersion in a nascent youth culture, new patterns of recreation that "tempt each member of the family to follow his own desire or join friends in the spending of free time" evidenced a weakening of family bonds.[19]

In the judgment of family researchers, family bonds were not only weakened but distorted, especially because the shrinkage of parental functions had left fathers with very little family role. Their responsibilities as religious guides, educators, welfare workers, counselors, and disciplinarians had all been usurped; consequently, the balance of power had shifted within families and fathers who hoped to regain traditional authority only courted disappointment: "If the father tries to build up an atmosphere of the old sort by which he can suppress the child's desire," wrote Ernest and Gladys Groves in 1928, "he finds he has lost the family, to the extent that he has been successful. When this happens the child too often comes to think of the family only as a necessary evil to be temporarily endured until he is able to free himself."[20]

Children could no longer be dominated by fatherly power, reasoned the experts, because fathers had little power at their disposal. Although middle-class men had at one time assumed many responsibilities, their traditional educational, recreational, and protective obligations were increasingly fulfilled by agencies outside the family. The state quickly absorbed what parents too readily gave up. "The desire of parents to escape responsibility," cautioned Ernest Groves, "has been met by a menacing eagerness of institutions to take up what fathers and mothers are all too glad to drop."[21] This exchange reduced fathers to breadwinners, a status that many seemed happy to adopt. The illusion that bread-winning fulfilled a man's parental responsibilities troubled the experts: "When one catalogues the fathers of one's acquaintance, one soon discovers how few of them give influence or time to their home. Indeed, a code of behavior has become acceptable which requires mostly of the father that he be kind and a good provider: as long as he keeps the pocketbook replenished, he is regarded as having met his obligations."[22]

Given these developments, what role should fathers play in this era of transformed family relations? In a seminal article published in 1926, Ernest Burgess suggested an answer. Impressed by the family's loss of functions and troubled by the stresses it faced in the urban environment, Burgess redefined the family as a process or network of interaction. For him, the family was "a unity of interacting personalities," less a thing or a structure than a process that changed over time as the individuals within it changed.[23] Individual adjustment and personality formation became the sine qua non of successful family life, tasks best accomplished in tolerant, nonauthoritarian families that enhanced the emotional fulfillment and psychological security of each member.[24]

The implications of this view of family life for fathers was profound. If psychological adjustment, individual happiness, and ultimately social order depended on the quality of familial interaction, then fathers could no longer rest content as breadwinners. Fathers were now also entrusted with important affective and psychological responsibilities. Such demands were not entirely new. In the mid-nineteenth century, female authors praised domesticated, nurturing men and condemned those who eschewed the pleasures of home. By the turn of the century, middle-class fathers participated in family leisure activities by making good use of the country clubs, parks, and social groups that had become part of the new suburban communities ringing older cities. These fathers, too, delighted in their offspring's mental and physical development, worried about their health, and offered testimonials on the psychological rewards for men who spent time with their children.[25]

Not until the 1920s, however, did the call for fatherly involvement become fully linked to theories of psychological development and social order. Inspired by Burgess's assumptions, family experts argued that fathers provided a different but essential perspective to the development of their children's personalities. Appearing to their offspring "as a mysterious traveler into the outer world," nurturing fathers brought "a different set of contacts from those furnished by the mother," thereby enabling children to profit from the unique perspective offered by each parent. Fathers were especially important in carrying "the child's thought consciously away from babyhood toward the hard-won delights of growing up into independence."[26]

As children matured, fathers provided much needed role models for both boys and girls. "The boy," wrote one expert, "is building from infancy his conception of manhood, making little models in his thoughts of how he must behave to be a man. How false his models must be when they are based on brief, superficial glimpses of his father."[27] Girls, too, needed fatherly attention. Their image of the ideal man began with their own fathers, and their selection of a mate—for good or ill—was shaped most significantly by their father's example. As the *Ladies Home Journal* put it, "The daughter who has had the love and companionship of her father is apt to pick out the right kind of man for her husband, for she tends to pattern her ideal of a man upon the example her father has put before her, instead of collecting all her ideas of manhood from the movie sheik."[28] Such fatherly engagement also engendered healthy personality development by helping to prevent both boys and girls from becoming unduly fixated on their mothers.[29]

The New Fatherhood and Sex-Role Identity

Such concerns prompted sociologists and popular writers in the 1930s to work out a theory of sex-role identity that persisted more or less unchanged until challenged by feminism in the 1970s. The theory had several critical components, all of which had appeared incipiently in the previous decade. These writers shared with their colleagues in the 1920s the belief that traditional family authority had withered under the impact of industrialization, the division of labor, and individualism. These social changes had brought sharp reductions in the family's functions as schools, factories, hospitals, welfare agencies, and juvenile courts took over tasks that were once managed by mothers and fathers. This transfer of functions undermined traditional patriarchal power and family solidarity, a problem exacerbated by the tremendous amount of time children, particularly boys, spent with mothers and with women in general.

The implications of these assumptions were profound as well as troubling. If the family's functions were truly narrowing and paternal authority was on the wane, what vital role could fathers and the family play in the social order? The answer to this fundamental question was simple and endlessly elaborated over the next several decades: fathers and families had a new and different role to play in the modern world. Rejecting instinct theory and drawing instead on Burgess's theory of the "unity of interacting personalities," family thinkers in the 1930s emphasized interpersonal relations and sex-role socialization.[30] Rather than bemoaning the transfer of functions to other agencies, sociologists applauded the change: what family members did best was to provide emotional support and affection for one another; what fathers did best was to be sex-role models for their sons and daughters.[31]

Serving as a proper sex-role model was no minor task. By the 1930s, fears of overfeminization were a steady refrain in both academic and popular literature. Although the fully embroidered theory of "momism" would not appear until the following decade, writers in the 1930s regularly decried mothers' excessive role in the lives of children. The roots of the problem, the experts agreed, lay with the rise of industrialization: "There was a time," wrote Robert Foster in a lead editorial in *Child*

Study, "when the boys of the family were virtually apprentices working with their father in his trade or craft. . . . Fathers and sons were in constant contact from earliest infancy to adulthood." Urban industrial life, however, had broken these generational bonds: "In modern city life fathers are often hardly more than visitors in the home. The result is that children are growing up with little or no masculine influence in their lives; and many fathers are anxious to find some way by which they can achieve a closer relationship with their children."[32]

Other experts made the same analysis and expressed similar concerns. James Hymes, Jr., looked back with fondness to a simpler age: "Not very long ago, father ate breakfast with the whole family; he came home for lunch and was back at home shortly after the workday, with ample time for chores or fun with the children before their bedtime. . . . There were fewer of these mysterious 'offices' to which Dad departs now on the 7:59, and from which he returns—fatigued and tense—an hour or two after the workday." This pastoral simplicity had been destroyed by industrialization and urbanization, twin forces that took fathers "out of the home [and] transformed them into commuting office and factory workers."[33] A writer in *American Home* complained that family life had reached the point where "fathers are supposed to be seen and not heard" and where they "feel themselves less and less necessary to anyone in particular—except on the first of the month." *Parents' Magazine* was more blunt in its assessment of the crucial problem facing the American family: "It is fatherless."[34]

Motherly domination had unfortunate results for fathers and, in the opinion of experts, for children as well. Fathers' frequent absences from home undermined their ability to become effective sex-role models for their children, a point borne out by a Los Angeles study that found that mothers served as models for their children more frequently than fathers. Although boys accepted their mothers as models at about the same rate that girls accepted their fathers, "the degree to which girls accept their mothers exceeds the degree to which boys accept their fathers as models by 22.6 per cent."[35] This sociological concern with modeling was part of a wider analysis in the 1930s of the family's role in inculcating proper sex-role identity. Convinced that masculinity was at risk because of long- and short-range social changes, psychologists in the mid-1930s, as Joseph Pleck has explained, sought answers to one overriding question: "What makes men less masculine than they should be, and what can we do about it?"[36] Lurking behind this question was the assumption that "for each sex there is a psychologically normative or ideal configuration of traits, attitudes, and interests that members of that sex demonstrate to varying degrees." How well one adhered to these sex-appropriate traits was the measure of one's personality adjustment.[37] That masculine and feminine traits were simply defined as a compilation of "those characteristics that one sex said they had more often than the other sex did" in no way slowed down the pursuit of "masculinity-femininity" testing or the incorporation of such testing into a variety of personality inventory scales.[38]

Acquiring proper sex-role traits required exposure to those who already exhibited them, and where better to attain masculine and feminine values than from one's parents. Of elegant simplicity, the theory of sex-role identity explicitly encouraged fathers to become models for their children. The task could not start too early, especially because all too many "girls frequently find it difficult to adjust to masculine relationships and boys show submissive attitudes due to the domination of mothers and women teachers."[39] From birth, wrote one expert, "the father should begin to make his presence felt. From the time a father first holds his child in his arms and talks to him, the child senses that he is being handled and talked to in a manner different from that of the mother." Doubtful at first, the baby soon enjoys the difference and ultimately comes to idolize his father: "The child begins to worship his father; he imitates him, and gradually absorbs his attitudes. That is why it is so essential that a father make his stature heroic in his small child's eye."[40]

Such sustained fatherly contact and admiration promoted good personality development. Well-adjusted children in one Rhode Island community, for example, grew up in "close-knit, cooperative, affectionate" households. By contrast, shy and retiring children in the study lived in homes dominated by mothers who overprotected their offspring. Fathers in these latter households were either easygoing and submissive or absent.[41] Other researchers found that the consequences of poor fathering might be considerably more serious. Speaking in Chicago before the American Orthopsychiatric Association, Martha Wilson MacDonald declared that delinquent juveniles came from homes with aggressive, masculine mothers and submissive fathers. Although she examined only eight files from Chicago Guidance Clinics, Wilson MacDonald saw a pattern in the cases. The mothers of the boys were aggressive, hostile, and rejecting, while the fathers were "depressed, submissive," and little interested either in their own lives or in those of their children. Nor were the sons' problems restricted to their delinquent behavior; they tended to be "sissies" who showed a marked preference for feminine diversions like sewing, cooking, and doll play.[42]

As children approached adolescence, a father became ever more important. As the intermediary between home and the outside world, a father bore chief responsibility "for the child's ideals of social conduct and his major aspirations and ambitions toward the social world."[43] This worldliness, moreover, could counteract overdomestication: "Fathers sometimes forget that without them the small child lives in a woman's world and absorbs women's attitudes. If these attitudes are not balanced by a man's point of view, the child will lack a rounded view of life when he reaches adolescence."[44] This masculine perspective could be passed on to children in simple ways. One father described the great lessons of manhood he passed to his son on fishing trips. Where better to learn patience, control, courage, and humility than at the end of a fishing pole? Another insisted that the time he spent with his son building model boats taught the boy accuracy, patience, and resourceful-ness.[45] Girls, too, profited from a close relationship with their fathers. In addition to passing on useful experiences and knowledge, fathers introduced daughters to the world of men.[46] In a nascent culture of "compulsive heterosexuality," this introduction was of no small importance. With psychological fulfillment for women defined in terms of wifehood and motherhood, fathers helped daughters navigate the difficult psychological shift of affection from one sex to another. Unlike boys, whose earliest love object was of the opposite sex, girls' first love was of the same sex. The psychologist Lewis Leary described the difficulty for girls: "But the girl whose infantile emotions likewise center in her mother, must find the fullest satisfactions of her adult life in her husband, who is a man."[47]

To make this transition, girls needed their fathers. One writer in *Parents' Magazine* succinctly described the role fathers played in the seasons of their daughters' lives: "But this shift can be made naturally and safely, if the girl is able first to transfer her emotional focus from her mother to her father as an intermediate step preparatory to its final resting in her husband."[48] This transference of emotion, warned one expert, must begin when the child is quite young: "If her later adjustment is to be healthy, she must make the transition to her father at an early age."[49] Thus, inattentive and absent fathers put their daughters—even more than their sons, in the judgment of Caroline Zachary—at considerable risk: "The girl has suffered even more, because her development as a woman and her future attitude toward marriage depend largely on having a satisfactory rapport with her father."[50] From this odd perspective, a father became the husband to the child, a masculine paragon who could help his daughter "discern for herself qualities valuable in a future husband."[51]

Good Fathering

The theory of sex-role identification of the 1930s simply reaffirmed and gave some small measure of psychological sophistication to ideas about modern fatherhood discussed in the previous decade. The same might be said regarding popular advice on good fathering. The family advisers of the 1930s persistently invoked the same recommendations offered by their counterparts ten years earlier. Likewise, the same laments appeared. Too many fathers did not spend time with their children; slaves to the commuter trains and to their jobs, these middle-class men became strangers to their children. "Accuse the average father of not really knowing his children," wrote one father, "and he will deny the charge vehemently. Yet the fact remains that the usual mode of urban or suburban domestic life today brings about this lamentable condition. Definite steps must be taken to correct it—immediate steps lest you waken some fine day to realize that your sons or daughters are practically strangers to you."[52]

Despite the recognition that modern life split fathers from their children, child advisers held fathers accountable for father-child estrangement. The problem was personal, not social. Even the busiest, most successful men could make time for their children if they so chose: "A few courageous fathers have done this very thing," wrote one adviser, "overcoming obstacles for the sake of sharing mutual interests with their sons; the vast majority, on the contrary, no matter how much assurance they may display in business or social circles, seem to be utterly indifferent to or ignorant of the needs and interests of their boys."[53]

And so little was required to rectify the situation. Fathers simply had to become pals to their offspring. The popular literature of the 1930s relentlessly reiterated this point. Almost any issue of *Parents' Magazine*, for example, had at least one article from an expert or one testimonial from a father extolling the wonders of father-child companionship. If only fathers would take time from their busy schedules to engage in sports, hobbies, and other diversions with their children, mutual companionship, affection, and trust would follow. But the writers conceded that such results came only with effort and planning. The busy middle-class father had little time for children; commuter trains had to be caught and business deals transacted, and somehow time had to be made for boat building, kite flying, nature hiking, and stamp collecting with one's children.[54] No wonder child advisers applauded a group of fathers in White Plains, New York, who started a Girl Scout support group. In addition to raising money for the Scouts, the men taught their daughters a variety of skills, took them on outings, and discovered that they "enlarge their own horizons and enjoy, above all, growth in companionship with their daughters."[55]

This vision of father as entertainer came unencumbered with irony. In the popular literature, the ideal father seemingly presided over an after work Romper Room: "In this part of the day Dad should reign. During these companionable sessions Mother should be careful that there are no admonitions of: 'Hurry up, the dinner will be cold.' This spoils the importance of the occasion."[56] Sometimes the popular literature went beyond this simplistic vision of father-child relationships, but not willingly and not for long. In a letter to the magazine *Child Study*, for example, a mother admitted she now felt "somewhat differently" about her "physically mature" twelve-year-old-daughter "sitting on her father's lap, patting his face, begging him to kiss her and obviously wanting him to play with her in a manner involving a lot of physical contact." The experts at *Child Study* reassured her that her concerns were legitimate, that the sexuality of children must not be denied, but that although such activity "should not be directly rebuffed, it must be discouraged by her father and diverted into other kinds of activity— playing games together, making things, reading, going places, and anything else which leads to work or pleasures shared."[57] Apparently, the problem of intrafamily sexuality was nothing that a round of croquet or a trip to the park could not fix.

Not surprisingly, the idea of fathers as buddies clashed with traditional views of patriarchal authority, but the error was on the side of tradition, not modernity: "The patriarchal tradition has always sanctioned this role," wrote Lawrence Frank, "but fathers are slow, if not reluctant, to realize how destructive this stern parental discipline and rigorous punishment may be to the child's adult life." Such misplaced discipline indelibly marked the child: "It is destructive because it so often creates a persistent resentment against all authority and arouses those strong feelings of aggression and desire for retaliation which undermine the child's socialization."[58]

Overcoming such anachronistic visions of fatherhood became the mission of a host of writers in the 1930s. The modern middle-class father was now seen as a kindly, nurturing democrat who shared rather than monopolized power. When not collecting stamps or building backyard playhouses with his offspring, the modern father organized family meetings to deal with issues of the moment. When disciplinary problems arose, he dealt with them dispassionately, fairly, and, above all, rationally. One father described his approach in these terms: "I mean I'm bigger than Freddie and I know and he knows that I can physically force him to do what I command. Instead of asserting my authority, I like to let him think things out for himself—when I have the patience to do it." The man's approach won the admiration of a friend: "Fred attempts to treat Freddie as a person, not as his own appendage. Basically, he tries to get Freddie to arrive at his own conclusions, within sane limits."[59] Denouncing his own onetime "temperamental, imperious, [and] straight-laced" approach to child rearing, another father rejected the weight of ancient teachings: "I would throw all traditional patriarchal interpretations of the Fifth Commandment overboard and base my claim to honor and obedience on something other than thunder on Mount Sinai."[60]

Other testimonials applauded the same values. Fathers needed to blend rational, imaginative discipline with empathy, respect, compassion, and love. Joint family counsels, not paternal edicts, made for strong, happy families.[61] A 1935 quiz to determine "How Good a Father Are You?" defined "goodness" in terms of fatherly companionship, solicitude, and respect for the needs of children.[62] A survey of two hundred Cornell University students suggested that these values shaped children's desires about family life. The students spoke warmly of family counsels and joint decision making and averred that these approaches to family governance increased their willingness to confide in their parents.[63] Likewise, eight hundred high school students lauded a father for "respecting his children's opinions."[64]

The implications of this celebration of affection and individualism went largely unexplored. In fact, instead of worrying about the impact of individualism on family life, progressive ideologues and their supporters in the 1930s applauded the process. Still under the sway of Burgess's theory of "interacting personalities" and convinced that the rise of the "companionate family" had only positive implications, family experts celebrated the fact that fathers' authority now hung by the gossamer threads of good feelings, playtime, and family counsels.[65] And although a few conservative sociologists like Carle Zimmerman challenged this orthodoxy, such doubts evaporated as World War II came to Europe and the "democratic" family became part of the battle against fascism.[66] As leading child expert Lawrence Frank put it in 1939, the greatest threat to democracy came from "unhappy, distorted, frustrated personalities," from people who "have never learned to accept themselves or to manage their feelings." Rebelling against the autocratic behavior of their own fathers, these people "have a lifelong resentment of authority." For Frank, fathers had mighty responsibilities: "Democracy, like charity, begins at home, where the fundamental patterns of human relationships are developed that will govern the child's subsequent adult conduct and social adjustment. The father in the family carries the major responsibility for these developments and by his attitudes and actions he is deciding the fate of our democracy."[67]

Because of the war, Frank's pronouncements were unusually heady and grave, but he shared with other sociologists, child psychologists, and popular writers of the 1920s and 1930s similar assumptions about fatherhood and sex-role development.[68] Without challenging the gender-based division of labor and the ideology of male breadwinning, these writers staked out a vision of fatherhood that would prevail until the late 1960s. At its core, this vision asked more of men without fundamentally challenging gender relations. Men were to give more of themselves, but their gift entailed little sacrifice and was intended to shore up traditional visions of masculinity and femininity. The new fatherhood hoped to compensate for mothers' preponderant role in child rearing by transforming a bill-paying outsider into a parent. The problem, as Ernest and Gladys Groves noted, was not so much maternal excess as paternal neglect: "In many cases where we say the child has been spoiled by too much mother, the actual fact is not that the child has been hurt by the over-abundant love of the mother, but by too little affection from the father."[69]

Thus, love and involvement, not discipline and authority, were the hallmarks of the modern father. Family sociologists and popular writers realized that the traditional sources of paternal authority had forever eroded.[70] Now fathers needed to foster companionship and personal growth, and to realize their child was "a new individual who must have his own way of living."[71] Lincoln Steffens described his son in just these terms: "Pete was an individuality from the start, a regular fellow, and when he came, he was so self-sufficient that the nurse chucked him on a cot to look out for himself while she and the doctor took care of his mother. And that's how I first saw him, lying alone, patiently waiting his turn, independent, self-reliant, an equal, as he has been ever since."[72]

Fathers' recognition of such individuality would ultimately lead, as one father explained, to egalitarian relationships within families: "We are a gang. And I don't insist on being the leader of the gang more than my share of the time. . . . We don't have any heavy father and subservient son stuff. No sirree, not in *our* family."[73] Children, counseled the experts, needed more fathers like this one; otherwise, fathers and children soon grew apart and men became little more than sources of sustenance and spending money for their offspring. As one father put it, "This new generation of fathers has a chance to help their boys and girls to get hold of life by the right handle. They can try to be something more than a sort of animated tin bank out of which you shake pennies, or perhaps dollars, if it happens to be a bank that yields big money."[74] Above all, fatherhood required commitment: "If you don't want to be disturbed," admonished one father, "don't have a son. If you have a son, don't scold him for being one."[75]

For those willing to be disturbed, the rewards were indeed great. Close father-child relationships would enhance the psychological well-being of each. Access to fathers promoted the child's self-confidence, maturity, and judgment: "Two persons to learn from are better than one, in learning to think. . . . Two persons are better than one for assuring the child of his security; two persons are better than one for preventing unhealthy emotional fixations."[76] For fathers, the benefits were equally therapeutic: "Once a father discovers the charm of his child he uncovers a source of joy second to none in life; children inspire, instruct, draw out the fever of competitive life, and add to the zest of living. We can never find more profitable or more loyal comrades than our own children, once a genuine fellowship is established between us."[77] One father recalled with great fondness a heart-to-heart talk with his son: "That talk with my son that evening was a red-letter day for me. My boy and I were always good friends, thank God, there wasn't much distance between us, but now we are pals. He awakened me."[78] Ultimately, the emotional bond between fathers and children would give meaning to men's lives. As a man aged and reflected upon his life, suggested Edward Bok, "the more does he realize that his children are all that he has; they are his hopes; in them lies the perpetuation that is so close to every man."[79]

Thus, fatherhood would become a significant realm of meaning for the modern middle-class man. An account in a popular magazine of one man's life dramatically captured the implications of these assumptions. Barton Alexander had spent his life building a successful business but had ignored his five children, whom he found annoying and a constant source of interruption. One by one the children grew up and moved away until only Barton, Jr., remained at home, but no sooner did the father begin to show some interest in the boy than the child was struck and killed by a truck. Devastated by the accident, Barton, Sr., lost interest in his work: "It didn't take the old man long to discover that without children he didn't have a home at all." All the grieving father could do was build a new house that he and his wife had once dreamed of as a place for their growing family. But with his family gone, the new home became a sad monument to the father's inability to enjoy his children when they had been at home. When his wife finally died, Barton forlornly visited the school yard every day, there "to watch the little folks and try to coax their love with his pieces of candy."[80]

The Reality of the New Fatherhood

Barton Alexander had come to the new culture too late. Expecting to find meaning in the world of work, he had wagered his happiness on the building of a business, only to find belatedly that private relations held the key to personal satisfaction. But others who did not make his mistake sought to balance the demands of breadwinning with those of the new fatherhood. These pioneers were transitional figures between the Victorian age and modernity. Their numbers would multiply in the post–World War II era, but as early as the 1920s sizable numbers of middle-class men began wrestling with the twin responsibilities of breadwinning and modern child rearing.

That the middle class led the way seems clear. In a study undertaken at the close of the 1920s, scholars began a comprehensive survey of the conditions of children in three thousand representative American families. Impressed with the importance of parental education, the investigators sought information on parents' efforts to acquaint themselves with trends in child development. They found that middle-class parents, fathers included, were the most likely to read literature related to child rearing, to listen to radio talk shows on child care, and to attend child study groups and parent-teacher association meetings. For example, middle-class parents owned and read more newspaper articles, magazines, and books about child care than their working-class counterparts: 91 percent of mothers and 65 percent of fathers in the professional class read articles in newspapers and magazines about child care, whereas only 34.5 percent of mothers and 12 percent of fathers in the day-laboring class did so.[81] The same general pattern held for listening to radio shows about child care and for attending child study groups and parent-teacher association meetings.[82]

Fathers who attended PTA meetings and child study groups were also more likely to read or tell stories to their children than men from lower classes. Although the proportion of mothers reading or telling stories to their children differed very little class by class, great variance by class existed among fathers. Six percent of children from professional homes had heard stories by only their father the day before the interview, an experience shared by just 2.5 percent of the children of day laborers. More significantly, over a quarter of children in the upper two classes had listened to stories by both parents the day before the interview; the figure for the lower two classes was between 5 and 6 percent.[83] Anderson and his associates easily explained these differences: "The greater number of stories told the children in the upper classes may be due entirely to the fact that professional class fathers spend more time with their children."[84]

Paternal participation in the discipline of children also revealed class variations. Whereas in the lower classes 30 to 45 percent of the mothers did all the punishing, in the higher classes, less than 20 percent did so. Roughly 80 percent of both fathers and mothers disciplined children in the upper two classes; by contrast, only 50 to 60 percent of both parents meted out punishment among poorer parents.[85] It also appears likely that upper-class fathers used disciplinary methods recommended by child experts more frequently than did fathers from lower classes. Since the mid-nineteenth century, child advisers had urged parents to abandon corporal punishment and to discipline children by appeals to reason, and though the White House study did not differentiate between the kinds of punishment used by fathers and mothers, the evidence reveals that middle-class parents more frequently adhered to "progressive" assumptions about child discipline than parents from lower social classes. Middle-class parents less often resorted to spanking and more frequently relied on reasoning to deal with misbehavior.[86] Summarizing the data, Anderson bluntly assessed its meaning: "In general, the upper socio-economic classes use better methods for disciplining their children."[87] Or as another writer put it, "It's give and take between father and son, just as between husband and wife. The days when Father demanded everything and gave nothing but bed and board and the razor strap are passed."[88]

Anderson's survey data did not explore the relationship between fatherly involvement and personality development. This connection, however, did not go unexamined. In a massive study involving thousands of youth, Ernest Burgess, the scholar who conceptualized the family as "a unity of interacting personalities," sought to uncover the relationship between home environment and personality formation. In doing so, he examined the new fatherhood at work and found it commendable and well-established. Basing his evidence on autobiographical accounts provided by youth and questionnaires filled out by adolescents and their teachers, Burgess concluded that tolerant, flexible, and affectionate family relations engendered healthier personality development than parental domination and emotional reserve. A corollary to this conclusion was that what went on within the family was more important than what went on outside it. Unlike Anderson, who systematically explored class variables in family life, Burgess insisted that personality—his crucial focus—was shaped by "subtler and more intangible aspects of family life, such as affectionate behavior, relations of confidence, inculcation of regularity in health habits and reactions to the illness or nervousness of parents."[89] Burgess also concluded that urban children had better personality adjustment than rural youth, evidence that validated "the assertion that the loss of certain economic and other functions from the home makes possible the more harmonious organization of family life upon a cultural and affectional basis."[90]

In pursuing his themes, Burgess examined the father's role in personality formation and discovered a connection between father-child closeness and well-adjusted personality development. Among urban white boys of American fathers, only 33 percent of those who "almost never" confided in their fathers had good personality development, while 18 percent had poor development; by contrast, among boys who "almost always" confided in their fathers, 52 percent had good personality adjustment, only 7 percent poor. Figures for girls were similar. Of those who confided in their fathers, 65 percent had well-adjusted personalities, only 4 percent poorly adjusted. The same relationship held for the child's "moral habit" rating; boys and girls who confided in their fathers (and mothers) had better moral habits than those who did not.[91]

Children identified as well adjusted invariably characterized their own families as cooperative and harmonious. As to their fathers per se, young men and women drew attention to their involvement, fairness, and nurture. One student recalled that "his father has been a great companion to us. He has always appreciated and realized a child's desires, and he has done everything for us—though not so lavishly as to make us unappreciative of it. He built toboggans for us in the winter, hung up swings and hammocks in the summer, and was always contriving some new and fascinating toy. He gave us everything he could."[92] Others drew similar attention to their closeness and companionship with their fathers, their fathers' interest in their activities and recreation, and their security in being able to confide in their fathers and mothers. As one student remembered, "Mother, father and I always have confided in one another and I find now when I do really have problems that the old feeling of wanting to tell mother and father is a blessing."[93]

Other students were not nearly so successful in establishing close ties with their parents, but their negative testimony confirms the importance young people placed on fatherly empathy and understanding. These youth invariably described their fathers as distant, unaffectionate, disapproving, cruel in punishment, unreasonable and arbitrary in discipline, cold, stern, or unsympathetic. Clearly Burgess included such evidence not only to reveal children's longings for paternal empathy but also to suggest the despair engendered by paternal neglect. One college woman admitted, for example, that her parents provided well for her but "they have never given me the affection I always wanted. I have never confided in my mother, and only since I entered college have I talked seriously with my father." Although she had of late learned to love and respect her father, his overbearing qualities when she was young made it difficult to establish close bonds: "My strongest feeling toward my parents was that of respect, and perhaps fear of my father. I have always felt very much misunderstood by my whole family. . . . I objected to my father's swearing, punishment of us, and stubbornness." Her despair and sense of loss were, at times, nearly overwhelming; when she visited families full of love and companionship, she wished she were dead.[94] She was not alone. A young woman's memories of her father centered upon his harsh discipline and her reaction to it. "I used to plan all sorts of revenge and even went so far as to think of committing suicide."[95] Another young woman in a similar situation decried her father's aloof, harsh, suspicious manner: "He makes no effort whatsoever to understand either my brother or me. . . . He was forbidding and harsh as far back as I remember, though I really think that he is rather proud of us when he's talking with other people."[96]

In the best of families, according to the White House study, the frontiers of father-child confidentiality extended into the realm of sexuality. Here lay a true test of parent-child companionship and understanding; here, too, lay a rigorous test of parental commitment to enlightened child rearing. The data again confirmed the general theory: families characterized by a high degree of companionship were likely to provide good sex education for their offspring. Among boys who seldom confided in their fathers, only 25 percent received their first sex education at home; among those who frequently confided in their fathers, close to 50 percent did so. College youth reported the same connection between parent-child intimacy and sex education. Among college boys who confided in their fathers "very much," 73 percent received sex education within the family; among boys who confided "very little," only 38 percent received sexual instruction at home.[97]

Sex education fostered companionship between parents and children and, in fact, adolescents clearly wanted it from their parents. Asked what changes they would make in rearing their own children, college girls listed, in order of frequency, more companionship between parents and children, better sex education, and less punishment. For boys, a desire for sex education was even more prominent. They listed it first, followed by more companionship and less punishment.[98] The key was openness. In Burgess's judgment, children must be able to go repeatedly to their parents for sexual information and advice, a point he illustrated with one young man's narrative: "I loved to talk confidentially with my father," wrote the college student, "because he seemed to know so much and because of the wholesome easy manner in which he explained things." No topic was taboo: "When I was in the eighth grade," the young man continued, "I was first troubled with masturbation. I went to Dad and told him. He did not frighten me in the least, but explained why it was wrong and how it could create a desire that would be difficult to curb. He told me always to come to him with my problems no matter what they were. I have always done so and I'm glad that I have."[99]

Although we may today disagree with the substance of the advice, the father's willingness to counsel his son, to talk frankly and openly about such personal matters, was what mattered. Here, indeed, was a "new father." By contrast, those fathers who because of ignorance, embarrassment, and outmoded values refused to discuss sexuality with their offspring came in for special criticism. Their children too often learned about sex from unreliable, sometimes objectionable sources. As one young man lamented, "I never received any sex education at home. Because my parents have always evaded my questions on sex I have learned it in a very undesirable way from the corner gang and as a result got a very distorted view of sex."[100] Another young woman expressed similar disappointment: "Sex was one question that was simply left out of our home altogether. Mother is mid-Victorian and shy about it and dad wouldn't think of talking to a daughter about it. It was the one big gap in my training. I gained my knowledge from companions who had a none too wholesome aspect on the situation, and as a result I have had a rather warped view of the whole thing."[101] The source of one college man's befuddlement about sex lay closer to home but was not too difficult to trace: "The only education that my father gave me was to tell me always to have the same respect for other girls that I had for my mother. He also told me that if I thought too much about matters pertaining to sex I might go crazy, for a very large percentage of the inmates in feeble-minded institutions were there for that reason."[102] Parental reticence on such matters, warned the White House study, could be costly: "The failure of the parent to instruct his son or daughter often leads to a further withdrawal of the child from the parent." Ultimately the results could be disastrous: "The parents who have not broken down the barrier between themselves and their children on the subject of sex information have often quite effectively cut their children off from all counsel in the whole realm of sexual conduct, friendships with the opposite sex and adolescent love affairs."[103]

To the White House researchers, the narratives and statistical evidence confirmed their beliefs about parenthood and family life. Dictatorial authority—most often wielded by fathers—undermined family unity; so, too, did discipline without reason. Sympathy, understanding, rational discipline, and a willingness to discuss the most sensitive matters, by contrast, enhanced it. Summarizing his data, Burgess concluded "that the home which incorporates the child into a unified family circle, with confidential relationships between parents and child, contributes most both to the happiness and to the well balanced adjustment of the child."[104] Fortunately, the study had found, thousands of American fathers were playing their part in creating such homes.

The Patri Papers and the New Fatherhood

The large social surveys of Anderson and Burgess suggest that some fathers had embraced the new fatherhood. Not content to restrict themselves to breadwinning, these men instructed and counseled their children, listened to their problems, and even gave advice on sexual matters. Some even looked for guidance from child-rearing experts, a new group of professionals and semiprofessionals who helped to reshape the rearing of children in the years after 1920. In letters to Angelo Patri, an Italian-born educator, New York City junior high school principal, and author of a nationally circulated newspaper advice column on child rearing entitled "Our Children," American parents from throughout the country looked for help from this well-respected, award-winning pioneer of liberal education. Not surprisingly, the great majority of letters came from mothers, but fathers likewise took advantage of Patri's invitation to write to him personally. Although the ironies of the child expert are analyzed in the next chapter—particularly the differential impact of such expertise on mothers' and fathers' power within the family—the letters do reveal the range of some fathers' involvement with their children.[105] If the Patri correspondence suggests the subtle coercion and dependence that developed when fathers sought the advice of a well-known expert, it also offers important access to the fatherly feelings and concerns of middle-class men in the 1920s and early 1930s.

Judging from the stationery letterhead or explicit mention of the fathers' occupation within the letters themselves, it is clear that most of the men who wrote Patri were middle-class businessmen or professionals. By and large, these men were highly self-conscious about fatherhood; their letters related concerns and anxieties that ran from simple questions (do you think children should read comics?), to the mundane (what should one do with a child who dawdles?), to the psychologically complex (what can a father do about a son who is a "sissy"?). The most

common set of questions involved anxieties about the school performance of offspring.[106] Regardless of their specific concern, these men
were the "new fathers" who had likely read articles on child rearing—in
fact, many letters began by noting that the correspondent regularly read
Patri's columns and/or listened to his radio show on child rearing—who
may have attended a child study group, who had enough doubts about
their own abilities and enough faith in those of experts to seek outside
advice. These men sought, like a father from Boston, to establish companionate relationships with their children: "Without forcing our society
upon him, we have given him freely of our time, trying to establish an
intimate companionship with the boy, showing him that we are interested in the childish things which mean so much to him, seeking to be
real pals with our son."[107] And they wanted wide-ranging advice from
Patri. Some simply focused on practical matters. What do you do about
a child's fallen arches? Is the *Book of Knowledge* better than *Compton's
Encyclopedia?* Are private violin lessons more or less effective than
group lessons? Should six-year-olds do homework every night? Is *War
Nurse* an appropriate movie for young children to see? What kind of
household tasks can a boy of eight be assigned? What do you do when a
child has too many material possessions? When and how should sex education begin? What books on child rearing are especially good?

Other men sought advice on behavioral problems. A New Hampshire father worried about his eleven-year-old son's bed-wetting, and a
father from Washington, D.C., asked how to prevent his son from stealing.[108] A Hastings, Minnesota, man asked Patri what to do with a son
experiencing a textbook case of the "terrible twos," a problem he
shared with a Florida father who lamented the "mulish" nature of his
three-year-old daughter.[109] The tall tales of one four-year-old boy
prompted another Minnesota father to seek Patri's advice on the difference between imagination and lies.[110] Noting that his son's behavior
caused him great discouragement, a New York City father described his
child as "a wild boy" and asked Patri whether a boarding school might
not be in order.[111] A Chicago railway worker had much the same complaint. Gone from home much of the time, he feared his wife was "not
stern enough with the children" and that they ruled her instead of vice
versa. He closed with a simple request for "a few words of advice to a
well meaning Dad."[112] Another well-meaning father wrote Patri after
discovering that his ten-year-old son knew the facts of life, had tried
cigarettes, and had apparently engaged in some sort of sex play with
children in the neighborhood.[113]

Many men expressed similar concerns about the sexuality of their
children. Some simply wanted advice on how to tell their children the

facts of life or worried about their children's sexual curiosity, but others had more complicated problems.[114] An officer with the Chicago Urban League was concerned about his three-year-old's erections, and several requested advice on stopping their children's masturbatory behavior. One father, for example, could not disguise his alarm upon discovery "that our dear child is a victim of this vicious habit. . . . She is our only child and means so much to us that we just cannot see such a perfect bud blighted by this vile pest." In Indiana the father of a teenager warned his son that masturbation likely led to insanity and wasted one's energy, and he asked Patri how he might become "a real pal to his child" and help his son "over-come this bad habit."[115] A New Jersey father of a five-year-old expressed concern about his son's interest "in the underwear of his mother," and the father of a young teenager worried about the dangers in Chicago, where "the Serpent of Evil lurks about everywhere, in stores, factories and homes" and where the young have "Petting and Cuddling . . . uppermost in thier [sic] minds."[116]

Concerns about sexuality and sexual development made up part of fathers' more general anxieties about their children's social and psychological development or, in the vernacular of the 1920s and 1930s, their "personality." Such anxieties became and were to remain one of the hallmarks of the new fatherhood. Many fathers asked for advice on coping with children's irrational fears: one man asked Patri what to do about his son's fear of elevators; a father from Cleveland wanted to know how to deal with his two-year-old son's newly developed "fear of wind and rain either with or without thunder and lightning"; and a Brooklyn father worried about his daughter's nervousness and her over-attachment to her mother.[117] A Louisville father described his four-year-old as healthy but "a little nervous," but lamented that "he insists on sitting on the toilet to urinate." Despite his parents' insistence, the preschooler would not relent and in desperation the father wrote Patri looking for suggestions.[118] The anxiety of a Chicago father was easier to understand. His "high strung, emotional and sensitive" eight-year-old son had suddenly developed a variety of fears. Although the parents used up-to-date child-rearing methods—"He is a child we can and do reason with as you would with a grown person"—such a modern, approved approach did little good and brought forth a plaintive reply from the child: "I know Daddy. I shouldn't be afraid, but I just can't seem to help it. I'll try so hard to overcome it."[119]

Several men worried about their sons' masculine development. In a culture that extolled athleticism, masculine prowess, and the combativeness of economic life, such anxieties were understandable. Sons who lacked masculine bearing and seemed unwilling to stand up to other boys troubled fathers who found in such qualities a key to success. Noting that his son's playmates "simply run over him yet he won't fight back," a man from West Virginia requested advice on instilling "in him that old fighting spirit because I know it will be a great benefactor to him in the future."[120] A father from Washington, D.C., had a similar problem with his nine-year-old son: "He would rather play with the girls than the boys, is looked upon by all the boys his own age and older as a sissy [a characterization with which the father agreed] and is the target for the neighborhood teasing. His lack of physical strength, as well as his disinclination to fight, makes him the butt all the time and his journeys to and from school are usually to the tune of his own wailings for he is a great crybaby." His son's petulance, insistence on having his own way, even his excessive bookishness worried the father who feared that his boy's problems might be "entirely mental and the forerunner of some desperately serious future condition."[121] Another man bluntly asked Patri how "to make my son tough. . . . I want my little fellow, who is three and a third years old, to stand right up to the other 'kids' and be able to 'sock 'em in the nose,' before they do it to him; and to push the other boy in the face and take his toy, before it is done to my boy." With little success, he had tried to teach his thirty-eight-pound bantamweight to make a fist and to punch, and he hoped that Patri would pass on information that would help the boy become "athletic and strong." Despite admitting that his letter might seem like "the ravings of a foolish father," he assured Patri that he had the child's long-range interests in mind: "Today, it is 'every man for himself.' Be polite and self effacing, and you are stepped on; be tough and aggressive, and you receive respect, and incidently a whole skin."[122]

These fathers' worries about personality development reflected concern about their children's individual competence and future success. With little to offer their offspring except properly formed psyches and access to education, some middle-class fathers joined mothers in monitoring every step of their children's development. In doing so, they demonstrated their allegiance to the new fatherhood. Such concern could start extremely early. The father of a boy not yet three wrote Patri that the child was "balky" and unwilling "to try to learn things that are very simple and that we wish him to learn." As evidence, the father described his son's unwillingness to use the pedals on a "kiddy car" when his boy was one-and-a-half; instead, the child stubbornly walked the new toy despite his parents' best efforts to instruct him in the use of the pedals. What was worse, the boy was immune to peer pressure, a point the father made with great emphasis to Patri: "He saw all his playmates pedal it around, but *he would not try.*" Nor was the youngster any better at playing ball. Although he could roll the ball, throw it, and chase it, he would not catch it, nor would he "hold his hands so that he can catch it. He sees others do it, we try to show him, but no; when it comes to catching it he quits." The boy's failures did not stop with pedaling and catching; he would not climb out of bed, blow a whistle, or find things that he had misplaced, a litany of shortcomings that prompted the father to ask Patri if "you know of away [sic] to get around that peculiarity."[123]

This focus on children's competence was especially evident when fathers expressed concern about their children's education. Lawyers, doctors, academics, corporate businessmen, and engineers gained class security by virtue of their special training, knowledge, and expertise, but these qualities and abilities could not be handed directly to their offspring. Mothers and fathers could only inculcate the right values, engender the required personality traits, and provide all-important encouragement for academic work so that their children, too, might join the ranks of the middle class. Consequently, the social reproduction of the middle class required an intensive focus on schooling. Entry into primary school was the first of many academic steps that enabled middle-class children to consolidate their own class position, and by the 1920s, extended schooling for the middle class was a fact of life. Given its importance, many men kept a watchful eye on their offsprings' scholarly performance. In fact, fathers continually requested advice from Patri about improving their children's school performance, evidence suggesting that fathers—as breadwinners—took a special interest in the one facet of a child's life that was indirectly, if not directly, tied to the world of work.

Vexing educational questions could crop up even before the child outgrew diapers. The proud but cautious father of a two-and-a-half-year-old wrote Patri for advice on how to proceed now that he had taught the toddler the alphabet: "I taught him his letters at the rate of three or four a week in the form of a game and it was great fun for him. I am afraid to proceed any further without expert advice."[124] A father who deliberately refrained from teaching his daughter nursery rhymes could not shake his doubts about his and his wife's decision: "Are we right in not burdening a three year old child's memory with nursery rhymes—and does the mere fact that a child at three can recite from memory mean that it is gifted intellectually."[125] Once formal schooling began, fathers worried if their children did not want to attend—one Brooklyn seven-year-old simply collapsed on the sidewalk and refused to budge when his father tried to take him to school—but more common were anxieties about their offsprings' academic achievement.[126] A typical letter from a Denver businessman noted his eight-year-old son's daydreaming while doing homework and another from a Rochester, New York, businessman admitted that his young son "is very slow at grasping things taught him at school. . . . His memory isn't bad, because he remembers things very well, but is very slow in learning to read and write."[127] A six-year-old daughter's "mental inertness" was the target of a Boston lawyer's anxiety: "She is very fond of her imaginative play, that she is a fairy, a bride, the owner of a menagerie, etc. etc., and is much absorbed in her fancies. We have the greatest difficulty in fixing her mind on a concrete question." Her reveries apparently carried over to school: "Her teacher has put her in the second division of her class, saying that while she reads well and is earnest in her work, she does not apply herself well when left alone at her desk,—that she is 'slow.'"[128] A New Jersey father did all he could for his son, age ten, who simply could not understand numbers: "Arithmetic is the subject which gives him the most trouble. I am satisfied he is trying his best, and both his mother and I have worked faithfully with him night after night. . . . In spite of this, he continues to have the greatest difficulty, some days getting a grade of zero on his arithmetic paper."[129]

A subtext of many of these letters were paternal fears about their children's ultimate success in life. If children failed to succeed or if schools failed to challenge, parents could expect only the worst for their offsprings' futures. A father of a fourteen-year-old Texas boy, for example, worried that the onetime honor student now took little interest in school or in his future, a fact that caused the boy's father and mother considerable distress: "He is the only child we have and we are very ambitious for him."[130] Another father with high ambitions worried that his son's habit of doing homework with the radio on might sabotage his college prospects.[131] A father of four described his disgust with the lax standards in New York City public schools and the dire consequences of such frivolity: "There is no sense of seriousness instilled into their heads and the sense of duty and responsibility is utterly suppressed. But what could be more important where this world of ours is cold to sentiment and demands work, duty, seriousness and responsibility."[132]

Properly organized, schools should demand of students what the world would ultimately require of them. If so, success in the former would promote success in the latter; conversely, failure in school might indicate an absence of the character traits required for success in life. A Weehawken, New Jersey, father put the matter squarely: his nine-year-old son concentrated poorly, had a weak memory, needed constant help from his parents in completing homework assignments, and, in his father's judgment, "does too much talking and star gazing while in the classroom." Although neighbors found the boy intelligent and articulate, his father had grave doubts about his son's future: "However, I feel that his ability to absorb things in school is most important; and dread to think that he may be unable to hold his own in the business world in time to come." To forestall such failure, fathers could worry, help with homework assignments, cajole and hector, talk with school authorities, demand early bedtimes, and if all else failed, consult an outside authority for assistance. The stakes were nothing less than securing a middle-class position for one's offspring.[133]

Thus, the new fatherhood had much to offer, but its rewards came not without pain and the risk of failure. That such was the case became clearer as children reached high school. Fathers writing about adolescent children exhibited anger, urgency, and frustration. Setbacks in the primary grades could be rectified, but what was a father to do, for example, when his son attended a school staffed by incompetent teachers who caused his child to lose "all confidence in himself or his ability to do anything"?[134] What could a father do when his son—ambitious, hardworking, attentive—continued to get Bs and Cs despite the father's conviction that his son "is getting much more real education out of his high school than his play mates." Given his son's aspirations for college and then medical school, the father could not help but worry about his son's future prospects: "His marks would look as if he could not do college work and I think he can."[135]

More common, however, were fatherly complaints about their adolescents' lack of ambition, laziness, and emotional imbalance. In broken English, an Italian real estate agent described the problems of his sixteen-year-old son: "In June, last year, he flung [sic] in Latin and Algebra. . . . He has no ambition and therefore is a very poor student, ready to drop going to school, to do anything else. I think that a person without ambition cannot have success in changing one career for another." An Idaho father registered a similar complaint. His fourteen-year-old high school son "gets a grade of C in everything on his report card and a list of Xs for annoying others, whispering too much, wasting time, capable of doing better etc." To the father, the problem was obvious—his son was "too full of play" and "monkeyshines"—and though he had taken steps to remedy the problem, he hoped Patri would offer ideas on how to cope with an underachiever.[136] A Massachusetts dentist even tried to bribe his daughter with money and music lessons if she would improve her marks, all to no avail.[137]

In one sense, the fathers who wrote Patri were exceptional. Most middle-class men did not write to him or anyone else about their children's problems. Yet, in another way they expressed interests and anxieties shared by the new middle class. Gone from home most of the day, these men nevertheless took an acute interest in their children's personality development and school performance. Without the former, success in the latter would be difficult, and without success at school, children could hardly hope to succeed in the new class structure emerging in the opening decades of this century. Breadwinners by day, psychologists, counselors, academic helpers, and pals by night and weekend, these men were, indeed, the "new fathers."

The New Fatherhood and American Culture

The men who wrote Patri, attended the child study clubs, and treated their children as "pals" fulfilled the hopes of the experts who called for a less authoritarian, more companionate style of child rearing. In so doing, they helped forge a modern conception of fatherhood. Assessing the meaning of the new fatherhood, however, is not easy. At one level, Patri and his correspondents appear humane, progressive, and attuned to the needs of children. These fathers took the time to read about child development, to worry about their youngsters' school performance, and to ponder how they might enhance their offsprings' mental or physical development. Not content to leave such matters to their wives, these men actively engaged in the upbringing of their children and were the forerunners of today's enlightened, new father.

But the superficial should not obscure the complex. In history, timing is everything, and the new fatherhood arose at the historical moment when masculinity and domesticity were both in crisis. Traditional sources of male identity in work, religion, and community had evaporated during the second half of the nineteenth century; consequently, many middle-class men, as we have already seen, increasingly sought meaning in the private realm. Concurrently, feminists and the "new woman" directly and indirectly challenged Victorian assumptions. The certainties of separate spheres no longer prevailed: many women experimented with new living arrangements, thousands made use of divorce courts, and the best educated spurned marriage altogether. Feminists went further and denounced the once hallowed home as a barrier to progress and a breeding ground for "social idiot[s]."[138]

These developments sparked concern about the future of gender relationships. Some called for a toughening of American manhood and a return to the masculine virtues that had settled a continent. Clerks applied to be scoutmasters and alumni flocked to football stadiums. Boys needed woodlore and the challenge of athletic competition lest they become effete. Women were a source of worry as well. Physicians attacked female education, and a host of writers lamented women's rejection of men, marriage, and motherhood. More vitriolic commentators even suggested that unmarried career women had forfeited their claim to womanhood and were an "intermediate sex" or, worse, "Mannish Lesbians." By the 1920s, such charges had become a common way to discredit female professionals, educators, and their institutions.[139]

These attacks put independent women and feminists on the defensive, but such alarms could not alone revitalize the domestic sphere. Nor was it possible to restore the frontier manliness of a bygone era. Only so many men could be scoutmasters, let alone cattle ropers à la Teddy Roosevelt. A modern conception of marriage and the home was needed to give meaning to men's lives and contain women's desires for autonomy and independence. In the 1920s, just such a reformulation took place as sociologists, psychologists, doctors, counselors, and liberal reformers modernized domestic ideology and redefined the meaning of both female freedom and fatherhood. Freedom for women now meant marriage, birth control, greater sexual expression, increased emotional commitment from husbands, and new conceptions of parenthood. Those who rejected such freedom were denounced as infantile, unfulfilled, unnatural, frigid, and deviant.[140]

The new fatherhood emerged within this context. It helped to redefine the meaning of the domestic sphere. Just as women were to find meaning within the home, so too, in part, were men. If the family had lost its historical functions, then new ones would have to be found. Helped by the new science of child development, fathers were to play a key role in the manufacture of their offsprings' personalities. Enriched by the knowledge of experts, fathers would prove that commitment to growth, tolerance, and flexibility produced well-adjusted, happy children. Yet, such seemingly progressive attitudes masked conservative consequences. In helping to revitalize the domestic sphere, fathers were to join mothers in elevating the cultural importance of heterosexual family relations and the domestic sphere. Family therapists, moralists, and researchers invited women to find satisfaction and identity as wives and mothers, albeit in a family now dedicated to emotional intimacy, sexual satisfaction, and enlightened child-rearing practices. Those who accepted this invitation were praised for the wisdom of their choice; those who did not were denounced as either backward or unwomanly. By becoming a crucial element in this redefinition of family relationships, the new fatherhood helped to enlarge the cultural significance of the domestic sphere at a time when it was under attack from a variety of quarters. From this perspective, the new fatherhood's progressive rhetoric obscured its conservative consequences.

Masculine domesticity and the new fatherhood were conservative in other ways as well. The new fatherhood rarely if ever questioned the traditional gender-based division of labor. Men would spend more time in the domestic sphere, but it remained women's domain. Evidence from the 1920s and 1930s certainly belies any great male commitment to domestic work. Fathers' involvement with children was not about work but play, hobbies, and excursions, about listening to radio programs, reading child-care articles, and attending PTA meetings and child study groups.[141] Neither the popular nor the social scientific literatures had much to say about fathers assuming the more onerous, boring, or vexing aspects of child rearing.[142] Fathers' jobs were to foster creativity, individualism, and proper sex-role identification, not to do children's laundry, pick up their rooms, cook their food, nurse them, or chauffer them. Men considered such labor "woman's work" and therefore unmanly and beneath them. Lincoln Steffens's young wife highlighted such prejudices in describing the advantages of being married to a sixty-year-old first-time father:

> The old father does not know it is "unmanly" for a man to bother with a baby; he does not know that centuries of tradition have made infant-care a woman's job only; he sees in the baby not only a squalling, ugly, red-faced bundle that has to have physical attentions and that makes a disturbing noise; he sees his own immortality; he sees the "biologically most advanced human being" on earth. He will carry it about, wheel its pram, watch it in the bath, even scald its milk bottles, with the feeling that he is serving, perhaps, a genius—in any case a fellow human being. And he wants to take his share of bringing it up. Older fathers really want to "get their hands on the baby."[143]

Few mothers, of course, had the good fortune to be married to a much older man, let alone a Lincoln Steffens. Most labored on, their working hours shortened neither by technology nor by their husbands' domestic contributions.[144]

The new fatherhood thus helped to reassert the importance of the domestic sphere and redefine patriarchy at a critical historical moment. With women's traditional place under attack from feminists and "new women" and men's identity shaken by a crisis in masculinity long in the making, the new fatherhood of the interwar era helped to provide a rethinking of the meaning of gender relationships. The patriarchy of the eighteenth and nineteenth centuries—grounded in a world of independent household producers—was no longer viable; therefore, patriarchy in the twentieth century had to draw its legitimacy from another source. That source was social science and a therapeutic ethos that equated good families with "growth" and proper manhood with companionship and cooperation. The standards for the new fatherhood were psychological and emotional. They were set by outside experts who rarely exhibited self-doubt despite obvious limitations in their theoretical understanding, empirical evidence, or therapeutic recommendations. Confident, university-trained, convinced that only their brand of parent education and mental hygiene could assure satisfactory personality development, these writers gave the imprimatur of science to a new vision of fatherhood that took shape in the early twentieth century and persisted, more or less unchallenged, until the 1960s.[145] We now turn to the contradictions, limitations, and ironies of the new fatherhood.

6

The Cultural Contradictions of the New
Fatherhood, 1920–1940

IN OCTOBER 1924, A BROOKLYN FATHER WROTE TO ANGELO PATRI
for advice about his seven-year-old boy. After first noting that he read
Patri's regular newspaper column "with much interest," he detailed the
problems he was having with his son. Although the child had gone to
school the previous year without incident, he now resisted all efforts to
get him to attend. One day the boy might walk to school with his
mother or father but then refuse to go to class; the next, he might collapse on the sidewalk in front of his house, immovable and inconsolable. Cajolery and punishment would not do the trick. Nor would
calm discussions, assurance, isolation, and even "a sound licking" get
the boy to school. The father had gone to a friend and to the principal
of his son's school for advice, but neither offered anything helpful. The
principal, in fact, told the father to keep the boy out of school until he
"made up his own mind to go." Hearing of the father's problem, a doctor volunteered that the boy "was suffering from an exaggerated case of
hysteria," but the doctor offered no practical solution either.

Whatever the reason for the trouble, the father was at an impasse: "I
certainly am up against a blank wall and need the advice of wiser heads
than mine." If he kept the child out of school, he feared violating New
York's compulsory education law; if he made him attend, it would be by
force. All he knew was that he felt terribly sorry for himself, his wife,
and the child. His wife was at the point "of almost nervous collapse her-

self over it and I was not much better, . . . [and] if there is anyway I can help the youngster I want to do it for I pity him." In a sensitive, sad conclusion to a long letter, he hoped Patri might somehow help him and the boy: "If you can give me any such advice you certainly would be doing a great service, not only to me but to the child as well, for I am sure that the trouble is something that troubles him almost as much as it does me for I know he is not happy and there is something that he can't quite understand about it himself."

In the kindly and reassuring tone characteristic of his replies, Patri tried to put the father's fears to rest by noting that the boy's problem was not unusual: "I have met your little boy many times in my school career. I meet him and his sister every term opening." Nor was it difficult to solve: "We just take him and put him in his seat and see that he stays there until he discovers that school is not a bad place at all but actualy [sic] holds happiness for him, when he forgets his fear and forges ahead."[1] Thus, what was perplexing and soul-shattering for the father was a simple matter of school management and discipline for Patri. Incompetence met competence, the amateur met the expert.

This father's difficulty should be read in two ways. On its most straightforward level, it reveals a compassionate, sympathetic, and committed man who was not ashamed to seek help to give his child the best care he could. Yet, at a deeper level, the account gives evidence of contradictions at the heart of the new fatherhood. This father clearly played an active role in his child's life, yet, for whatever reasons, had lost the power to control the youngster's behavior. Having lost that power, the father asked a self-proclaimed child expert for guidance. Such an appeal for help suggests one of the central ironies of the new fatherhood. Becoming a new father increased one's dependence on the very experts who had first mapped this new paternal terrain; moreover, men's responsibilities as breadwinners coupled with the ironies of parent education, children's attachment to their mothers, changes in the nature of breadwinning, and the emergence of a distinctive, school-centered peer culture worked to make outsiders of men. In short, the new fatherhood emerged within a culture none too congenial to its basic assumptions. Men might try to be new fathers, but a variety of factors either subverted or obstructed their good intentions.

Fathers and Experts

Obviously, not all men shared the Brooklyn father's inability to deal with such problems nor would most have written to an advice columnist looking for guidance. Nevertheless, this letter and others like it suggest some of the difficulties of middle-class fatherhood within a therapeutic culture that could simultaneously bestow privilege and promote dependence. Men who sought to become more nurturing, who rejected the equation of fatherhood with breadwinning and joined their wives in seeking specialized knowledge on child care, found that experts could dispense useful information. But if one examines the relationship among fathers, children, and experts more closely, one also sees, ironically, that there was a gulf between these men and their children that Patri and other experts filled.

The men who wrote Patri were highly self-conscious about their responsibilities and questioned him in ways that suggested their own intense involvement with their children's emotional, psychological, and intellectual development. They were, in short, new fathers, men sufficiently concerned to seek help from outside experts. Yet their admission to the world of modernity came at a cost. Rather than trust their own judgment and sense of paternal responsibilities and obligations, they looked for expert assistance. Their concern for their children was not matched by any sense of competency about how to rear them. Common sense and received wisdom were not enough; child rearing required assistance and mediation from outside the home. Such assistance came from counselors, educators, and therapists—experts with their own language, agenda, and assumptions—who substituted professional expertise for the knowledge that had traditionally come from family lore, community mores, religious teachings, and the like. To the extent fathers relied on experts to handle problems they once would have solved or at least muddled through on their own, a relocation of authority had taken place.

Thus, the men advised by Patri gained a modern vocabulary and approach for dealing with children at the expense of their autonomy and self-confidence. Their empathy, concern, and understanding was evident, but so was their dependence, ineptitude, and frustration. In this sense, they were early explorers in the thickets of a nascent therapeutic culture. A few examples make the point. These fathers—many of whom were highly educated professionals or businessmen—often requested advice about the simplest issues. What should a man do when his wife takes the children to a movie of which he disapproves? How can a father get a slowpoke moving in the morning? Is there any way to overcome a child's fear of elevators? What should a father do about a child with too many material possessions? (One father vexed by this problem sent Patri a photograph of his son surrounded by all his toys.) What do you do with a boy who is reluctant to catch a ball or ride a bike? What about a four-year-old who lies? Should a father permit his sister-in-law to "dance and jump around the floor" with his nine-month-old baby daughter? Are private violin lessons preferable to group lessons? "Is it or is it not good educationall [sic] procedure to have a child in the first grade, age six years, assigned homework each night?" Will forcing a boy to eat and write with his right hand instead of his left cause speech defects and eye watering?[2]

From one perspective, these questions seem fatuous, simpleminded, and hardly worthy of the attention of a nationally syndicated child rearing expert. Yet, the lack of confidence and competence that prompted these queries stemmed from the logic of modern child rearing and the therapeutic culture itself. Children were complex psychological beings that required educated parental monitoring, nurture, and guidance; the family was a "unity of interacting personalities," and personality development was too complicated to leave to old wives' tales and common sense.[3] After all, a child's unwillingness to ride a bicycle might be evidence of more basic personality problems; forcing a child to eat with her right hand might cause stuttering.

Maneuvering through such dangers presupposed a competence that few parents, particularly fathers, could possibly have; hence experts filled the void. As the examples above make clear, Patri's range of competence was as broad as his subscribers' was narrow: he dispensed advice on everything from movies to music, eating to elevators, Santa Claus to sleeping, diet to death. His tone was kindly and reassuring, but he left little doubt that he had the expertise to solve the problem at hand. Where the fathers exhibited weakness, he showed strength; where they evidenced confusion, he demonstrated clarity; where they gave up in frustration, he offered an answer. His answers, in fact, often assumed that fathers did not understand their own children. Upset by his eleven-year-old son's petty thievery, a Saint Paul man hoped that Patri could help "in our time of great sorrow over the boys [sic] misdeeds." Patri responded by first chastising the parents—"First of all I would beg you to stop whipping and scolding and threatening the boy because this will not help"—and then provided a much needed lesson in child psychology: "The lad is going through his boyhood stage, on the verge of adolescence and cannot be expected to have much moral sense or ethical appreciation. He is beset by experiences that are new and strange." The source of the boy's wrongdoing undoubtedly lay with a sense of inadequacy, but such feelings were common in many boys his age. Patri then launched into a long list of suggestions for dealing with the youth, most of which ran counter to those tried by his father. Rather than scolding and whipping, the boy needed his father's attention and devotion: "Father needs to stand by and help the boy, take him with him on excursions, work with him, no matter how much he gets in the way at first. Boys like this need their father's good word, his hearty good will, his laughs and his strengths." Patri also urged the parents to monitor their child's friendships and to take him to "a child specialist who thoroughly understands the growth of adolescent boys." Finally, if the youngster was to become more responsible, dependable, and mature, the parents needed "to treat the boy more as a grown up than as a child."[4]

This exchange was just one of many in which Patri offered fathers quick lessons in child psychology, implying that he understood children better than they did. When a Chicago father plagued by his son's insolence turned to Patri for help, Patri's seven-page response outlined his views of the youth's troubles. From the evidence, he assumed the boy's "expressions of defiance, his impudence, his threats, are the gestures of the thwarted adolescent." Even the youngster's handwriting showed "a lack of co-ordination, a lack of rhythm, a great instability." But, Patri reassured the father, the boy's behavior was not all that unusual: "An adolescent is the most uncertain, most disconerting [sic] boy imaginable." Nevertheless, if this father were to succeed as a parent, he would have to realize that boys pass through stages of psychological growth: "To-day [sic] he is in one stage of growth and by after noon [sic] he may be in another. His savage period may last a week, a day, a year or so or it may continue indefinitely and the child become fixed at this stage. That is the great catastrophe." To prevent such unhappiness, parents must "allow each stage to develop naturally and spend itself as soon as may be."

But there was more. Patri discerned that the child felt less helpless around his mother than his father, not unusual in that "this sort of lad always has a feeling of superiority over women." By contrast, the boy likely felt insignificant in light of his father's stature: "You are far and above and beyond him and his pride rebels at his weakness." In this situation, the father must neither misunderstand the boy's sentiments nor mistake the simple for the complex: "When he tells you how little he cares he is caring and suffering the most. This boy is suffering. Don't believe for an instant he is not." Nor should the father misinterpret the boy's complaints. They, too, were deeply rooted in psychological needs: "He believes himself ill used, but that is but the defensive gestures of his eager praise-mad self." At the end of his long reply, Patri posed six questions for the father to consider, ranging from overcoming the boy's "feeling of inferiority" to enhancing his "self expression."[5] Heady stuff for a busy breadwinner, but part and parcel of the therapeutic assumptions behind the new fatherhood.

Nor was one expert always enough. Time and again Patri offered advice but suggested the parent also consult a doctor, psychologist, or educator. Child rearing had evidently become so complicated that a battery of specialists were now at the disposal of beleaguered parents. A bank cashier, for example, wrote to Patri in 1925 about his seventeen-year-old son. In his father's eyes, the boy lacked academic abilities but had a good mechanical mind and could "fill a place in the world pursuing some trade, so the question is, what is the best trade for him to take up, or where is there the right kind of a trade school for him to enter to get a good training." Patri replied that such a decision required specialized assistance: "Have you had the lad examined by a vocational expert? These are men and women who test a youth to see whether or not he should have a technical education or a cultural one."[6]

More commonly, Patri suggested that fathers consult medical and psychological specialists. The proposed solution for overcoming the timidity of a four-year-old boy, for example, required medical intervention. As Patri advised, "I would not take anyone's word for his physical fitness but would have him carefully gone over by and [sic] expert and make sure too, that eyes and ears and nose were functioning perfectly. You know a pair of eyes that do not focus will make cowards of the best and bravest."[7] Patri instructed the father of an eight-year-old boy afflicted with a variety of fears to seek psychological help: "The great difficulty lies in the fact that this sort of child buries the fear in his unconscious mind. Often he does not know himself what it is he fears. An expert psychologist ought to be able to help you locate his fear and treat it. In the meantime be very gentle with him and do not force him against his will."[8]

Ultimately, reliance on such specialists might well relegate fathers to bystanders. A father who wrote Patri about his son's slow academic progress was advised to do little more than coordinate information gleaned by experts of one sort or another. "You will need the information about the child's physical examination for the psychologist," wrote Patri. "It would shed some light on what the school situation was. He would need the doctor's report and the teacher's report in detail and any more facts that the school could give him. . . . Should these records not be available then I would go [see] the psychologist, explain the situation to him and he will know the best doctor to help him on the case. But the school records are needed if the experts are to discover why the child cannot get on there. I am sure they will help you when they understand."[9] Likewise, Patri counseled a father whose son would not go to school, "It would be advisable to have some good doctor and a good psychologist examine him and some good schoolman, or perhaps the psychologist could tell you of the right school for him."[10]

The involvement of these men with their children would have warmed the heart of family ideologues who found in close father-child relations an important source of strong personality development. Yet, experts left many fathers without confidence in their own judgment. Men who believed in fatherly nurture, sought and trusted expert advice, and refused to adopt more authoritarian styles of control had difficulty maintaining their authority in a culture dedicated to liberal, therapeutic values and specialized knowledge. In fact, an undercurrent of doubt and paternal self-blame runs through the correspondence. Such doubts could start early. The father of a fussy nine-month-old boy wondered whether "the whole difficulty is too much attention in the past," and a man with five boys worried that he and his wife might be "derelict as parents."[11] Another worried that he and his wife had spoiled their only child: "Frankly Mr. Patri, we are very much worried about this situation. We believe that we have our own selves to blame partially, because we have given the child everything he desires."[12] The father of a five-year-old groped to explain his son's poor school performance and settled, in part, on his own behavior: "The teacher is not at fault as far as I can see nor do I blame the boy entirely. I feel that possibly I am the one who needs correction."[13]

Older children likewise sparked pangs of self-doubt. A North Carolina father admitted he had failed to build a close relationship with his now disobedient eleven-year-old son: "All of these thing are are [sic] heart-breaking to me as I always imagined myself and son as chums, but as it is I do not know him. I know that it is probably my fault, but I do not know what to do about it."[14] Another father likewise criticized himself and his wife for their inability to deal with a volatile teenage daughter: "On the other hand, we apparently are at fault, since she so aggravates us, at times, that we say things we shouldn't. We do not contend that she is always in the wrong." They even invited criticism from Patri: "It is quite a trial for us to know just what to do. We are about at our wit's end and would appreciate any suggestions or comments you might be able to offer. In your suggestions you are at liberty to be free to criticize us, if you feel we deserve it, since we do not claim that we have handled the situation perfectly by any means." Patri offered no direct criticisms but suggested the couple might profit by sending their child to a skilled child specialist: "Fathers and mothers get so close to the children, so emotionally involved in their difficulties," wrote Patri, "that it becomes hard for them to help the children, and it is then that the stranger, the skilled specialist can be of so much assistance."[15]

Faced with the bewildering complexity of modern child rearing and apparently bereft of independent standards for rearing children, fathers who approached the therapeutic culture frequently expressed doubts about their own abilities. They displayed a readiness to defer to the specialized knowledge of doctors, psychologists, and educators whose expertise had become increasingly segmented and separate from everyday experience. Perhaps the outer limit of the new fatherhood was, as one father demonstrated, the abdication of paternal responsibility altogether. Thus, an articulate, obviously educated father literally demanded that Patri decide whether his son attend a public or private school: "This is a very serious problem for us to decide, and we want you to make the decision for us. Please do not tell us to 'do what is best for the child.' We want you to tell us what is best. You have sufficient experience with children, and can solve this problem for us."[16] Patri made a choice, suggesting in doing so that the therapeutic culture masked coercive, albeit in this case benign, forces embedded within itself.

Fatherhood and the Ironies of Parent Education

The men who wrote Patri, attended child study classes, and tuned their radios to programs on child care were in a double bind. If they joined the therapeutic culture by becoming new fathers, they were in step with modern thinking but subject to the consequences discussed above; if they remained outside it, chose to rely on folk knowledge, and concentrated on breadwinning, they found themselves relegated to the status of the second parent. Either way, men lost. Modernity had its price, but so did tradition. To understand more fully both these prices, we must know something about the history of the new culture of specialists. The critical point for our purposes is that this culture was not built by experts alone but by mothers and experts together. Consequently, women's involvement with the therapeutic culture differed markedly from that of men. For men it represented a loss of authority; for women, both a loss and a gain. Fathers were the outsiders, women the insiders. Consequently, most men concentrated on breadwinning but in so doing heightened their own alienation from their offspring. Thus, men could not win for losing. To appeal to an expert was to enter a world fathers had little hand in creating and to concede, at some level, their own incompetence; to rely on folk knowledge and concentrate on breadwinning was to invite criticism and threaten father-child intimacy.

Most men chose the second course and remained outsiders. To understand why and with what implications requires a brief look at the history of the parent education movement in the United States. To repeat a critical point: from the late nineteenth century until the present time, mothers, not fathers, have played the critical role in establishing ties with child specialists. The modernization of parenthood has been largely the modernization of motherhood. True, fathers have made connections with the movements, but from the very beginning, experts directed their advice to mothers and considered mothers the "first" parent. Writing in 1920, Frank Ward O'Malley noted this fact: "Sometimes I catch myself wondering why men of the high-powered scientific caliber of Dr. L. Emmett Holt, Dr. Roger Dennett, Dr. Crozier Griffith and other specialists who have given so much intelligent thought to the borning and breaking of children never seemed to have worked back to the discovery that there can be no children without fathers. Do you ever remember having seen the word 'father' used once, even once, in all the best-selling baby books written by Dennett or Griffith or Holt? Neither do I."[17]

The secondary position of fathers was evident right from the start when some thirty New York City mothers formed the Society for the Study of Child Nature in 1890. Soon after, other chapters emerged. These chapters in turn gave birth in 1908 to the Federation for Child Study, and by 1919 the federation was in contact with over thirty other child study groups that sent speakers to inform organizations about developments in the field of child study. Meanwhile, in 1897 prominent educators, clergymen, and politicians joined with a group of mothers to form the National Congress of Mothers, publisher of the journal *Child Welfare* and advocate of parent-teacher associations. By 1908 these efforts had resulted in the formation of the National Congress of Mothers and Parent-Teacher Associations, whose membership sooned reached 100,000 with branches in every state.[18]

By the 1920s child study and parent education had come of age. In 1924 the Federation for Child Study became the Child Study Association of America and, with financial help from the Laura Spelman Rockefeller Memorial Foundation, it emerged as a leader in the parent education movement. During the 1920s, the foundation spent over seven million dollars to set up institutes and research stations at universities across the country to investigate child development and child rearing. The Child Study Association also used Rockefeller money to organize and supervise parent education groups and to train home economists and teachers to become "parent educators." In addition, it enlarged its magazine, *Child Study,* for a national audience and offered lectures, conferences, and publications on various aspects of child rearing, child psychology, children's literature, and other issues of interest to parents.[19] With the cooperation of the association, Teachers College at Columbia University also offered a program for students preparing for careers in parent education.

Other organizations also began emphasizing parent education programs in the 1920s, but the shapers and targets of parent education remained overwhelmingly mothers, not fathers. Starting in 1923, the American Association of University Women (AAUW) inaugurated a child study program for its thirty-five thousand members to provide "a more scientific understanding of children from birth through adolescence, and to help improve methods of dealing with children in homes and in schools." Within one year, 124 child study groups had been organized among university women, and by the end of the decade there were more than 500 such groups meeting under AAUW auspices.[20] In a similar vein, the American Home Economics Association began emphasizing parent education in the mid-1920s for mothers interested in becoming more knowledgeable child rearers, and in 1930 the American Social Hygiene Association formed a Division of Family Relations whose goal was "to minimize the number of broken homes; to increase intelligent application of knowledge to practical family life."[21] State-funded programs enhanced these private efforts, but here, too, the experts, specialists, and state legislators who funded the programs assumed that motherhood and parenthood were virtually synonymous. "Mothercraft classes" started in Oklahoma in 1921, and in the following year Nebraska offered "mother training courses."[22]

The rise of the child expert and the parent education movement's focus on mothers had complex, ironic implications for fathers. The call for fatherly involvement in the family was not matched by any sustained effort to bring fathers into the modern world of child rearing. Fathers remained ignorant outsiders in the land of the educated. And if, as we have seen, the knowledge of specialists could create dependence *among* parents, it could also create privilege *between* them. Mothers and experts together built the parent education wing of the therapeutic culture in ways that isolated many middle-class fathers from child rearing. Women worked in the research stations, staffed the child-rearing organizations, and spread the word; moreover, middle-class mothers wanted, even demanded information about child rearing. Rather than passive partners, mothers actively participated in shaping parent education. They led the child study groups, PTA associations, special programs, conferences, and seminars on child rearing; they attended these same conferences and enrolled in the correspondence courses on better parenting; they wrote the majority of letters to experts soliciting—even demanding—answers to their pressing questions. Some middle-class mothers no doubt blindly followed the experts' advice, but most more than likely accepted what worked, reinterpreted or rejected what did not, and continued to try to expand their knowledge about child development, psychology, and physiology.

Meanwhile, most fathers continued to concentrate on breadwinning. The disparity of mothers' and fathers' involvement with the parent education movement is evident from data gathered in the late 1920s. Although middle-class men paid some attention to the experts, mothers were the overwhelming targets and consumers of expert information. The White House Conference study, *The Young Child in the Home*, demonstrated this imbalance rather dramatically. Among all social classes, mothers were far more likely than fathers to read child-rearing literature: overall, fully 73.9 percent of mothers but only 36.7 percent of fathers sought child-rearing guidance in newspapers and magazines.[23] Mothers were also more likely than fathers to listen to radio programs about child rearing and to attend a child study group or belong to a parent-teacher association group.[24] An investigation of the clientele of parent education programs in Minnesota revealed the limits of fathers' involvement in parent education even more dramatically. The 1927 study found that of the 540 people attending child study groups and another 750 enrolled in a correspondence course on child rearing, all participants, *with one exception,* were women.[25]

In short, women dominated parent education and men concentrated on earning a living. If rearing children was a science that required knowledge of physiology, hygiene, nutrition, child psychology, and personality formation, the question as to which parent would acquire such knowledge was settled by default. Fathers might occasionally read a newspaper article on child rearing, some might even attend a child study class, but it was middle-class mothers who had the time and the inclination to acquaint themselves with the barrage of literature that comprised parent education in the 1920s and 1930s. Most men either remained ignorant or depended on their wives' insight. Either way, men's relative separation from the parent education movement helped relegate them to a secondary status within their own homes. Put differently, if parent education could create dependence—a point made by most scholars of the subject—it could also create privilege by equipping one parent with knowledge the other lacked.[26] So long as fathers relied on common sense and folklore, they were at a relative disadvantage as parents. By contrast, mothers, who understood the specialized knowledge and language of the family ideologues, had the advantage.

By being connected to the therapeutic community, they were, by definition, modern; without such connections, most fathers were, by contrast, premodern and lacked "scientific" understanding.[27]

In this new culture, fathers were on the defensive. How much so is evident in a 1928 study of sixty "motherless families" that found men virtually incapable of rearing their children without assistance. Obviously, men's absence from home to make a living was the key problem, but their ignorance was another. Bereft of mothers' specialized knowledge, these fathers were especially poor household consumers, often wasting money owing to inexperience. Many did little better as housekeepers and disciplinarians. "Motherless families," asserted the study's author, tended to show "a lack of recreation in the home, a drifting from church influence, a decidedly irregular school attendance, authority ruthlessly dictatorial and futile—or pathetically absent—promiscuous sex relations, or malnourishment." Such deterioration might well prompt and require the dissolution of the family, "many times a hard thing to achieve if the man makes a sentimental plea to keep his family together."

But sentiment, the author concluded, had no place when fatherly ignorance and neglect jeopardized the welfare of the young: "In spite of the sentimental pleas of keeping the family together, the most successful plans are those which involve a breaking up of the family unless the children are few in number, old enough to assume the responsibility, and there is good history and sufficient income." If the welfare agency decided to keep the family together, it must compensate for fatherly ineptitude and ignorance: "Many duties which in other families the visitor quite properly assumes indirectly through the mother become the immediate job of the agency. It is not enough to plan for the buying and preparing of meals, and keeping the house clean, but health, sex education, recreation must all be kept in mind. Some of these can be delegated to relatives, but it is too much to ask the father to be both mother and father in the short hours he is at home."[28] Fathers without wives thus faced hard choices: remarry, forfeit their children, or find help from the state in rearing their offspring.

These recommendations point toward another of the great ironies of the new fatherhood. The same culture that called men to the home recognized that their responsibilities as breadwinners limited their capacity to nurture children. The new fatherhood functioned best in homes where mothers, with the help of specialists, reared the children and men provided for and spent what time they could nurturing them. This arrangement, particularly the union of mothers and child experts, could leave fathers feeling like outsiders. That such might be the case is clear in a humorous yet pointed 1920 essay by Frank Ward O'Malley that captured with poignancy and bitterness one man's frustrations with the new culture. Despite the lighthearted but grumpy tone of the article, O'Malley profoundly recognized how the union of women and experts had relegated fathers to the sidelines. He began by lamenting men's exclusion from the birth room by female relatives and medical personnel. Such exclusion continued through the child's infancy, a time when the father was made to feel superfluous and stupid: "At best he is made to realize that in knowledge of handling infants, in the matter of intelligence in general, he has far to go intellectually before he can hope to match wits with a baby that at least knows enough not to offer fool suggestions." Finally, when the baby is about a year, "the young father is first graciously recognized as being vaguely related to the baby." Still, the father is kept at bay "by entire regiments of rank outsiders who don't know enough to mind their own darned business. It's a conspiracy."

Particularly intrusive, in O'Malley's view, were doctors and child experts: "Even the family doctor himself, who starts in by daring to bar a man from his own wife's bedroom and gets away with it, works hand in hand with the rest of the outfit. Then while the baby is being nourished up to the progressive point where it can get croup and mumps and everything, along comes the modern child specialist and further encourages the deviltry." These specialists could make fathers feel like interlopers in their own homes: "The nearest I ever came to getting a glance of recognition from the baby specialist who comes to our house was one day when I had the effrontery to step into the nursery, whereupon he looked me over coldly for a second and then intimated to the nurse that he could not go on with whatever it was he had to say to her until the room had become less crowded." Ultimately, the medical profession bore the brunt of O'Malley's attack, for it was doctors who forged the alliance with mothers and who kept fathers in unnecessary ignorance:

> If the medical profession could only be made to see that fathers will always perforce remain a scorned institution just so long as the doctor himself is the arch conspirator in the propaganda to shove fathers into the outer darkness of ignorance, then perhaps the male parent could be led into his own. If the children specialists would turn out between mother books just one volume or one series of snappy articles for the Sunday newspapers or the lay magazines on the general subject of What Every Young Father Should Know, and written in English instead of Medicoese, maybe the outcast father would begin to get somewhere.

Despite the humor of the article, O'Malley was aware that his comments about child specialists in general and doctors in particular were petulant: "If a note of bitterness seems to creep into these remarks, reader, pray bear with me. In recent months of parenthood I've been mixed up with these lads sufficiently to get their number; that is all."[29]

For fathers, the parent education movement was rife with irony. On the one hand, it shored up the patriarchal structure of the family by heightening women's identification with the home and child rearing and by justifying men's relative uninvolvement with the sometimes vexing and onerous task of rearing children. Although some fathers joined their wives in reading child-rearing literature and others consulted specialists about their offsprings' emotional and intellectual development, most middle-class men deferred to their wives on such issues and found more reward in an extra hour at the office than in a child study group. If some men made a concerted effort to spend time with their offspring, for many more, breadwinning seemed to offer more certain, surely more tangible rewards.

On the other hand, men's gains in the working world may have been fathers' losses in the home. If a gender-based division of labor redounded to men's overall benefit, it did separate fathers from their children. One might argue that fathers simply saw children when they chose to and cleverly left the boring child-rearing tasks to their wives. The previous chapter suggested as much by arguing that even the new fatherhood was more about play than about work and that it shored up patriarchy by emphasizing the cultural saliency of the home at a critical moment when the domestic sphere was being challenged by feminists and the new woman. And yet to stop here misses an equally important point: what men may have gained as a gender, fathers lost as parents. The structure of the parent education movement—the fact that mothers, not fathers, were its targets—only confirmed and gave the imprimatur of science to men's secondary place in the world of their children. Their status as such can be seen by investigating the surveys of parental preference that dotted the social science literature in the 1920s and 1930s.

"I Like Mom Better"

Mothers who followed the advice of the experts in the nurture of their children, understood their psychological needs and developmental stages, planned their diet and exercise, cared for them when ill, read them books, and listened to their problems developed the kind of parent-child bonds that the specialists applauded. Fathers, by contrast, who earned the family income and managed to read an occasional story or play a game of catch now and then, did not have the same degree of success. In interviews with five hundred schoolchildren ranging in age from five to nine years old, Margarete Simpson recorded an "overwhelming mother-preference" that grew in strength as the children aged. By age nine, 12 percent of the boys and girls preferred their father, 72 percent their mother. They even dreamed more and more favorably about their mothers. Children were considerably more likely to dream about receiving gifts from their mothers, taking trips with them, and perhaps most important, receiving physical affection from them than from their fathers.[30] In another study of 1,600 children, those youngsters who recorded a preference strongly preferred their mothers. Even among ten- to twelve-year-old boys—an age range when identification with fathers would likely be strong—only 10 percent listed their father as their favorite person in the home, while 18 percent accorded their mother this status. Less surprisingly, between 3 and 4 percent of girls of this age listed their fathers as their favorite compared with 16 percent who listed their mothers.[31]

This preference for mothers over fathers was also evident when investigators studied the patterns of children's jealousy. Children reported being the most jealous when affection was shown by their mothers to another child. Half the children reporting jealousy noted that it occurred in this context. Although most youngsters at this age never reported being jealous, of those who did 14 percent of the boys and 21 percent of the girls mentioned being jealous when their mothers showed affection for another child. In contrast, only 9 percent of the boys and 14 percent of the girls felt such jealousy when their fathers showed affection for a sibling, a finding in keeping with children's preference for mothers in general.[32]

By the time children reached adolescence, these preferences shaped the parent-child contact. Asked the degree "to which they tell their mother and father their joys and troubles," eighth- through tenth-grade boys and girls made it clear that they far more often confided in their mothers than their fathers. Forty-one percent of urban white boys and 62 percent of urban white girls "almost always" confided in their mothers. By contrast, only 27 percent of the boys and 23 percent of the girls "almost always" confided in their fathers. Among rural youth, the disparities were similar save for rural white boys, who seldom confided on a regular basis with either their mothers or fathers.[33] This pattern of maternal preference continued among young adults. A 1928 study of almost 3,000 men and women in their late teens and twenties (1,336 males and the same number of females) found that only one-half as many sons and one-fifth as many daughters confided as completely in their fathers as in their mothers. Sixty percent of the sons confided "certain things only" with their fathers and 6 percent confided nothing at all. More remarkable was that 45 percent of the young men noted that they would willingly attend a place of amusement with their mothers, but only 31 percent would do so with their fathers. This evidence led the study's author to argue that "the fathers of this study enjoy the companionship of their children,—so far as common, willing attendance at places of amusement is concerned,—rarely or not at all."[34]

To the social scientists who authored these studies, the evidence underscored the importance of studying mother-child rather than father-child relationships. Ernest Burgess, for example, explained the differential focus in his study of adolescents in the following terms: "For both boys and girls the key to a confidential relation with the children lies in the hands of the mother. For this reason, the relation of mother and child was studied more intensively than that of father and child."[35] Fathers were certainly important—after all, good personality adjustment correlated with father-child intimacy—but they were of secondary significance compared with mothers.[36] The social scientists, as did the children, voted with their feet and flocked to the side of mothers.

"Buy It for Me, Dad"

Given the sexual division of labor and the union of mothers and child specialists, it is not especially surprising that children preferred their mothers over their fathers. But the evidence is important and reflects a degree of alienation between children and fathers made sharper by changes in the structure of middle-class breadwinning itself. Put differently, the bond between fathers and children of the old "middling class" had been broken by major transformations in the structure of the American economy. In an economy dominated by household production, fathers and children worked in close proximity; moreover, fathers passed family land to sons, small proprietors handed the shop over to their offspring, and skilled artisans entrusted the secrets of their craft to the next generation.[37] As we have already seen, this system declined over time as land shortage and agricultural modernization limited the ability of farmers' sons to assume the work of their fathers; so, too, the relative decline of the household economy and the rise of an industrial economy eroded the ability of artisans to pass craft skills to their offspring. Finally, the growth of corporate capitalism and recurrent recessions that took their toll on small businesses reduced the percentage of young men who could expect to inherit a father's business. By the turn of the century, fewer and fewer Americans were self-employed, and more and more earned their livelihood from wages and salaries.

The new fatherhood was, in part, a response to the attenuation of occupational bonds between fathers and children. If fathers and children could no longer work together, at least they could play together. But here, too, developments undercut fathers' ability to achieve such results. Historically, fathers had had primary responsibility for the support of their families, but in the early twentieth century an emerging culture of consumption gave new meaning to this obligation and put middle-class fathers to the test. Material goods promised not just sustenance but vitality, experience, "personal growth," and life itself, and it was up to middle-class fathers to make these goods available to their families.[38] Young men understood the implications of this new vision even before they were married. Asked by a social scientist how many children he wanted to have once he married, a nineteen-year-old college student replied: "I should like to have two children, to be a boy and girl. I feel that I should not be married until I could adequately support a wife nor should I have any children until I could be able to support them in some luxury." Another was more laconic: "The size of family depends on my income."[39]

This new emphasis on consumption had important implications for American family life. If family experts clamored for fathers' times, their wives, children, and the wider culture clamored for their time and money. It was, as Robert Lynd put it, a key element in "the increasing secularization of spending and the growing pleasure basis of living," part of "a new gospel which encourages liberal spending to make the wheels of industry turn as a duty of the citizen."[40] Americans wanted to live "in the here and now, utilizing instalment credit and other devices to telescope the future into the present." Belt-tightening held little attraction; rather than squaring expenses with income, Americans increasingly sought to expand their income to meet their growing consumer desires. Ultimately, Lynd argued, America was undergoing a seismic shift: the older values of thrift, saving, hard work, and struggle were being replaced by an emphasis on leisure, consumption, and, in the last analysis, money. As Lynd put it, faced with "the increasingly baffling conflict between living and making money in order to buy a living," Americans showed "the tendency, public and private, to simplify this issue by concentration on the making of money."[41]

Lynd wrote of "individuals," but within middle-class families "individuals" translated into fathers. In a culture increasingly marked by consumerism, the breadwinning responsibilities of fathers changed. Meeting new standards of health, comfort, cleanliness, and child rearing required money; so, too, did growing interest in leisure, travel, and personal attractiveness.[42] Children's needs expanded right along with those of the rest of the middle class, and it fell to fathers to satisfy these new subjective wants and to meet these new markers of middle-class respectability.[43] Some did so with evident pride. A New Hampshire father writing to Angelo Patri noted that his son had "a large library, a pianola, victrola, and [a] good radio receiving set," and other men wrote of their children's music lessons, sporting endeavors, horses, toys, books, and automobiles.[44] That such expenditures might cause anxiety was also evident. A Boston lawyer disapproved of his son's many possessions and expressed anxiety about the impact of such materialism on the child: "[W]ithin a week after Bruce got his electric train, in three different gusts of vexation, he used the train and tracks as the object on which to vent his displeasure. My belief is that such a thing is a radically false moulding of the child's character."[45]

Another man displayed the same uneasiness. Although he had provided the money for his child's material wants, he worried about the long-range effects. The Memphis businessman acknowledged that he had sent his son to private school, helped to finance the boy's dates, and did not want "to forbid him privileges and opportunities enjoyed by his friends." Yet, the "keeping up with the Jones' problem" troubled him: "On the other hand I can see distinct signs of his developing in the present formative period of his life a certain lack of appreciation of the realities of life." Acknowledging the power of the peer culture, yet uneasy about the message his son received from it, the man groped for direction: "Disliking to put him in a different position from his contemporaries I still feel sometimes that even though it is his vacation, I should require him to do some work and have some definite responsibilities as well as a sense of earning at least some of the money which he desires for amusements."[46]

Despite this man's ambivalence, fathers increasingly tried to "buy life" for their families, a simple fact that caused Robert and Helen Lynd to ask of Middletown residents, "Why Do They Work So Hard?" The Lynds answered their own question by suggesting that as work became more mechanized, routine, and alienating, a focus on consumption and money-making became more dominant: "For both working and business class no other accompaniment of getting a living approaches in importance the money received for their work. It is more this future, instrumental aspect of work, rather than the intrinsic satisfactions involved, that keeps Middletown working so hard as more and more of the activities of living are coming to be strained through the bars of the dollar sign."[47] After examining wage and salary trends against cost-of-living increases, the Lynds concluded that Middletown residents, despite making real gains, suffered nonetheless: "[B]oth business men and working men seem to be running for dear life in this business of making the money they earn keep pace with the even more rapid growth of their subjective wants."[48]

For many men, satisfying such wants became the definition of fatherhood. But this world of transformed breadwinning, as a San Francisco father put it, was not without its psychic costs: "My work, cogenial as work goes, has involved a large element of drudgery. It is a mistake for women to assume that men have no share of this. Even if it be a kind master, the job enslaved me. For the sake of those economically dependent upon me, independence, desires, and sometimes ideals must be put in the discard. I find my enthusiasms dimming, my objectives disappearing, my interests dying." Despite a yearning to recapture a zest for life—including a desire for a passionate love affair, perhaps the reason he chose not to sign his letter to the editor—he had scant hope that such would come to pass: "Instead I commute daily to the city. I should like to stop earning a living and engage in scientific research with an old pal of mine. Actually the field of research is limited to the discovery of a way to secure a more adequate income for the growing family."[49] Breadwinning and consumption had their rewards, but the palpable weariness of this man suggests they also had their price.

If the new middle-class culture centered on money and material goods, equally significant was that purchasing became increasingly individuated. Robert Lynd's description of this development was apt: "A rising standard of living, coupled with new ideas as to equality of marital partners and in parent-child relationships, and an increased degree of mobility and independence among women and children have all operated apparently to distribute the family's spending money more generally through the several members of the family. Merchants testify that children are buying more things today unassisted by their parents."[50] Although the full dimensions of the youth market would become evident only in the prosperous years following World War II, Lynd had rightfully drawn attention to a major development in American life. Fathers might underwrite the consumption of the family, but the process itself was becoming ever more divided, the youth segment ever more important.

Lynd had uncovered an irony of modern family relations. The encouragement of independence and egalitarianism in interpersonal relationships was meant to enhance family unity and personality development. In the economic realm, however, these same values reduced the control of middle-class fathers over family consumption. Advertisers pitched their promises of vitality, "real life," happiness, and sensual delight not so much to families but to fathers, mothers, husbands, wives, teenagers, and children. Family members consumed, at least in part, to fulfill these promises and, in so doing, enhance their own sense of well-being.[51] Authority was thus reconstituted outside the family by agencies that continually invaded and reshaped its desires.[52]

Fathers were thus pulled in two directions: whereas experts advised them to spend time with their children, advertisers urged them to spend money on their families. Many middle-class fathers found it hard to do both and put their energies into the pursuit of the latter rather than the former. After all, work and money brought men status and some measure of power; time with children brought intangible satisfactions and unpredictable rewards. In a nation that measured success by the size of one's house and the brand of one's car, that equated vitality and the good life with the consumption of a seemingly endless variety of goods, most middle-class fathers dedicated themselves to breadwinning.

If consumption did little to bring fathers and children together, neither did leisure. Despite shorter hours in most fields of work, leisure time within middle-class families—particularly those with adolescent children—became increasingly individuated. Suburban fathers in the twenties had about seven and a half hours of leisure per day at their disposal, most of which was spent, when at home, eating, reading, visiting, gardening, and listening to the radio and, when away from home, visiting, eating, playing or watching sports, and motoring. Suburban children spent less of their leisure time at home than either their fathers or mothers, and when at home they read, studied, or listened to the radio a substantial part of the time—all solitary activities.[53] Increased leisure did not, therefore, necessarily translate into greater father-child contact. After examining the pattern of leisure among American families, Burgess concluded, "Social interaction between members of the family during almost the only time when the entire family is at home together is limited to whatever casual conversation interrupts the reading and studying carried on by the children."[54]

Fathers and children might spend considerable time in the home and yet scarcely see one another. As one young suburban daughter remarked, "Oh, yes, I've been home, and so has Father, but I haven't seen him for three days." Her experience was not atypical: out of some 800 suburban girls, only 37 percent interacted with any family member during a typical day. Nor did meal times offer much chance for family togetherness; only 16 of every 100 suburban families ate three meals a day together. By contrast, 38 of 100 families managed to squeeze in just one meal together per day. The crucial variables were the income of the father and whether he commuted. Those with higher incomes who commuted to the city spent considerably less time at meals than fathers who did not. Many commuting fathers, in fact, left for work before their children were awake and returned from the city after they were in bed. For these men, the call of the new fatherhood became lost in their commute.[55]

The leisure of both parents and children was reshaped in directions that tended to separate rather than unite the generations. Ernest and Gladys Groves noted that public transportation, telephones, automobiles, and good roads "tempt each member of the family to follow his own desire or join friends in the spending of free time."[56] Such temptations, Angelo Patri found, could create real problems for parents. One Chicago father wrote that he had to watch his son with great care: "The moment I am not watching him he gets on the elevated train and goes down-town [sic] to a show and does not come home until two or three o'clock in the morning."[57] The automobile figured centrally in these trends, and though some Americans believed cars promoted family unity—one Middletown mother cheerfully remarked, "I never feel as close to my family as when we are all together in the car"—most were less sanguine. Automobiles appeared to be a "decentralizing agent" within families and a frequent source of conflict between parents and children. Parents lamented that "joining a crowd motoring over to dance in a town twenty miles away may be a matter of a moment's decision, with no one's permission asked," while roughly one-third of high school boys and girls cited the family automobile as a source of disagreement between them and their parents.[58] The father of a twenty-year-old college dropout had little doubt as to what caused some of his son's problems: "That Packard acted on that boy just like a drug. As soon as he got in that Packard it was just as if he had taken cocaine."[59]

Youth often piled into automobiles to go to the movies, a new and dominant form of entertainment that further separated fathers and children. Children attended movies far more often without their parents than with them, perhaps largely because the films that attracted the young—*Flaming Youth,* for example, promised "neckers, petters, white kisses, red kisses, pleasure-mad daughters, sensation-craving mothers, by an author who didn't dare sign his name; the truth bold, naked, sensational"—upset the moral sensibilities of their fathers and mothers.[60] Whether such movies actually altered the moral values of the young remains unknown, but Middletown schoolteachers insisted that films brought about early sophistication and a relaxation of sexual mores in the young. A juvenile court judge even saw a clear connection between movie attendance and juvenile delinquency.[61]

Autos and youth, movies and youth, sexuality and youth all added up to the emergence of a distinctive heterosexual youth culture that undermined the authority of fathers. The erosion of fatherly influence over the romantic life of children had been long in the making. As early as the eighteenth century, children gained increasing control over courtship, mate selection, and ultimately marriage.[62] Nevertheless, middle-class parents remained centrally involved in the courtship rituals of the young throughout the nineteenth century. Generally, young middle-class boys "called" on girls under the watchful eye of fathers, mothers, or community members, and it was the rituals of these social "calls" that affirmed one's class standing and established the boundaries of propriety between young men and women.[63]

As the twentieth-century began, calling gave way to dating, a new system that undermined parental involvement in courtship. Originating among lower-class youth whose families lacked the private space and financial wherewithal to support the calling system, dating became firmly entrenched within the middle class by the 1920s.[64] What made dating so different was that it occurred beyond adult supervision, often in public places of amusement, and that its rituals and meanings were shaped by the young themselves. The controls fathers and mothers once exercised under the old system fell away, replaced by a competitive system of courtship that took shape within a budding youth culture. Dating in the new system was not about adulthood and marriage—the traditional concerns of parents—but about the ineffable qualities of popularity and status, which only the young themselves could define.[65] It was also about sex. Taking advantage of the privacy afforded by automobiles and movie theaters, youth found it increasingly easy to get beyond the reach of their parents and into the reaches of each other: 48 percent of high school boys and 51 percent of high school girls in Middletown marked as "true" the statement, "Nine out of every ten boys and girls of high school age have 'petting parties.'"[66] Most apparently answered from experience: 88 percent of the boys and 78 percent of the girls responded that they had participated in a "petting party."[67]

Dating was also about money. Gone were the days when "one could sit on the davenport at home with one's 'best girl' and be perfectly contented. . . . You can't have a date nowadays . . . without making a big hole in a five-dollar bill."[68] To date was to spend, a fact that created conflicts among fathers, mothers, and children. Almost 40 percent of high school boys (and 29 percent of high school girls) listed differences about spending money as a source of disagreement between them and their parents. Many boys took steps to reduce their financial dependence on their fathers' often grudging largess. Almost 40 percent of the boys earned their own spending money, 9 percent earned money to supplement their allowances, and 31 percent supplemented earnings other than by an allowance.[69]

Drawing on both the money and the time of adolescents, the youth culture of the 1920s and 1930s—based on expanding high school and college populations—pulled children away from their fathers' influence and toward peer associations.[70] In fact, few adolescents even spent much time at home. Fifty-five percent of Middletown high school boys and 44 percent of girls were home three evenings per week or fewer. Almost 20 percent of the high school boys spent not even one evening per week at home. Fathers and mothers often resented this mass exodus of their children: both high school boys and girls listed disputes about how often they went out on school nights as the leading cause of friction between themselves and their parents.[71] Nor were adolescents likely to give up their time away from home. Asked to recall their most enjoyable occasion during the preceding year, only 5 percent of high school boys and 17 percent of high school girls cited an incident or experience that took place in their family home; moreover, what they enjoyed—sports, outdoor activities, parties, dancing—were done in the company of other young people, not parents.[72]

The Alienation of Fathers

In the opening decades of the twentieth century, middle-class men faced a host of ironies. Their very success as breadwinners meant that their children were no longer part of the family economy; instead, they were part of a growing youth culture with standards and values often at odds with those of their parents. The lives of these children were marked by segmented leisure, prolonged schooling, peer associations, the ubiquitous automobile, and consumerism. All were artifacts of the new middle class, all depended on the earnings of fathers for existence, all helped to separate men from their offspring. This separation, manifest in the parental preference surveys and in more impressionistic evidence, was traceable to the structure of the new middle class itself.

Thus, despite widespread calls that fathers spend more time with their children, contradictory forces within the new fatherhood drew fathers and children apart. The same therapeutic assumptions that called men to the home, for example, extolled the liberating potentiality of consumption; the same experts who emphasized the importance of fatherly nurture assumed that such nurture needed constant professional attention and instruction; the same culture that lauded parent-child togetherness praised the fostering of adolescent independence. If these contradictions alienated fathers and children, what is the meaning of this separation? The answer depends on whether one looks at the family as an arena of power or sentiment. In an arena of power, the quality of father-child bonds may be irrelevant—male domination is founded on power, not affection—or a perfect expression of patriarchy at work. So long as fathers identified themselves as breadwinners and focused on the public dimensions of their lives, being the second parent in the eyes of their children was of little consequence. It only confirmed the cultural significance of contemporary gender ideology: mothers dominated the affective dimensions of family life, fathers the instrumental.

This argument is not without merit. The relative weakness of the father-child bond undoubtedly heightened the identification of children with women, an identification that simultaneously entrenched men's standing as breadwinners. Yet, the story is surely more complicated. The family is not only an arena of power but also of sentiment, affection, and love. And here men encountered difficulties as they watched children establish closer bonds with mothers than fathers. This disparity of affection occurred, moreover, at a time when middle-class men as well as family ideologues were singing the praises of fathers willing to commit the time and energy necessary to establish companionate relationships with their offspring. They had to make this commitment and at the same time honor their obligation to earn the family bread. And it was just this dual responsibility that put fathers at a disadvantage. Children needed and wanted both love and money; mothers supplied healthy doses of the former, but middle-class fathers by and large were the sole suppliers of the latter. Consequently, children looked to their mothers as emotional caretakers and to their fathers as combination playmates and bankers. Without major changes in family life, without a major challenge to the gender-based division of labor at the core of modern economic life, children would remain in many ways alienated from their fathers. Men could be either breadwinners or companions in the new culture, but they would and still do find it hard to be both. The transformation of middle-class breadwinning in the opening decades of this century had established the preconditions for "the psychological or physical absence of fathers from their families," a development that the psychologist Samuel Osherson has called "one of the great underestimated tragedies of our times."[73]

7

Fathers in Crisis: The 1930s

IN 1934 A TEXAS FATHER WROTE TO PRESIDENT FRANKLIN ROOsevelt: "I have done all I could to pay the note and have failed on everything I've tried. I fell short on my crop this time and he didn't allow me even one nickle [sic] out of it to feed myself while I was gathering it and now winter is here and I have a wife and three (3) little children, haven't got clothes enough to hardly keep them from freezing. . . . My little children talking about Santa Claus and I hate to see Xmas come this time because I know it will be one of the dullest Xmas they ever witnessed."[1] An even more desperate New Jersey man spoke of his own fatherly guilt: "I haven't had a steady job in more than two years. Sometimes I feel like a murderer. What's wrong with me that I can't protect my children?"[2]

The despair of these men at their failure to fulfill a father's most basic obligation is palpable. Theirs is not the only story of the 1930s, but it is the most important. Millions of American men saw only a marginal decline in income in these years; and researchers continued their studies of the father's role in personality and sex-role development. But such continuities pale next to the crushing blow to breadwinners of the Great Depression.[3] For the millions of fathers who lost their jobs, farms, and income because of the Depression, the thirties were a nightmare that destroyed their sense of manhood and personal identity. Faced with the loss of their jobs, their homes, and all too often their self-respect, these men left a sad record of the devastation's effect on them as fathers. Their words confirm the importance of family bread-winning and fatherhood to male identity and ultimately to patriarchy. Thus, it should come as no surprise that New Deal policies sought to revitalize men's and especially father's breadwinning abilities, for a pa-triarchal order based on male breadwinning, fatherly responsibilities, and female economic dependence hung in the balance.

The Collapse of Breadwinning

A great deal of discussion about sex-role and personality development took place during the Great Depression, and most issues of *Parents' Magazine* and scores of sociological and psychological articles hardly mentioned the devastating impact of unemployment on the identity of millions of men. Perhaps such neglect is understandable; at the nadir of the Depression, three-fourths of those seeking work still had jobs. Mil-lions of men had enough financial security to question, as one father did, whether Sunday was a day to spend with the children or a day "to sleep late, play golf, and generally do as I please."[4] Others undoubtedly had no greater problem than the father who wrote Angelo Patri in 1932 about his son's "sulky" personality, or the man who worried about his daughter's "stubborn temper," or the one who asked if "a child two months old that occasionally goes into a tantrum if he is placed in his bed instead of being held be allowed to cry it out if by merely picking him up he becomes contented and goes to sleep within a reasonable time?"[5] But devastation there was, and it struck at the core of men's self-worth. Over the course of more than a century, to provide had be-come synonymous with manhood. Breadwinning conferred status, power, and self-assurance, and to fail at this task was to fail as a man: "Since everything depended on his success as provider," wrote Jessie Bernard in her analysis of the breadwinner role, "everything was at stake. The good provider played an all-or-nothing game."[6]

Obviously, fathers had played this game before the Great Depres-sion. As we have seen, men in previous decades had felt the sting of un-employment and knew what it meant to fail as providers. What was new in the 1930s was the magnitude of the failure, the number of breadwin-ners who lost their jobs. From the peak of prosperity in 1929 to the depths of the crisis in 1933, the unemployment rate climbed from 3.2 to 24.9 percent.[7] One survey found that for every four Detroit, Pitts-burgh, and Birmingham families in 1929 earning less than $1,200, there were eleven such families in 1932.[8] Such grim statistics need no elaboration here. Suffice it to say that the United States faced its gravest crisis since the Civil War, and at the heart of the crisis was the problem of men's unemployment.

The travail of the unemployed man and his family did not lack for investigators. Popular writers, academics, and government officials probed the subject, some focusing on men's self-esteem, others on intrafamily dynamics. Although a few asserted that breadwinners' unemployment had actually brought families closer together—"Never have I seen such a demonstration of the power of family life," said John Elliot of the Hudson Guild—most emphasized its destructive impact.[9] Regardless, they shared the belief that strong, flexible, and adaptable families formed the foundation of American culture. After at least three decades of ferment about gender roles, the Depression reaffirmed the importance of both the new fatherhood and male breadwinning to men's identity and social order.[10]

There were researchers who found the silver lining: economic hardship in some cases actually prompted fathers to become closer to their children. Robert Angell described a new relationship one such man established with his children after calamitous setbacks to his business interests: "He has made his paternal love more than an abstraction. He has taken a very definite interest in the children's interests and in the mother's activities. In turn he has shared his confidences and his cares, thus bringing the rest of the family more closely in alliance with him and with each other."[11] An engineer named Pike had the same experience. After losing his job and seeing his income fall from $4,400 to less than $600 per year, the sporadically employed day laborer had every reason to be bitter and humiliated. Despite his economic setbacks, however, "Mr. Pike has managed to keep up his morale remarkably in the face of disaster and a complete change in his position as the family's sole support." He had also changed the way he spent his time: "His occasional jobs as a laborer take up very little of his time. The balance he spends helping at home and doing professional reading. He is much closer to his children than before."[12] So, too, with a hard-pressed, small businessman who had once dominated his family but had become far more "kindly and sympathetic" to his wife and children after a substantial decline in his income.[13]

In the judgment of experts, the men most likely to weather unemployment and retain the love and respect of their children exhibited the "modern" traits that comprised the new fatherhood. Men whose authority rested on love, nurture, and admiration maintained their status despite their job loss far better than those whose authority derived from instrumental grounds or fear.[14] Cold-blooded breadwinning might suffice as a source of authority in flush times, but the true test of filial

devotion came when a father lost his job:[15] "Loss of the father's status
in the outside world, loss of money as means of control," wrote Mirra
Komarovsky, "was not fraught with danger for the father because of his
success in personal contacts with his children."[16]

The Depression and Male Identity

It was one thing to make the commonsense observation that highly unified families endured the crisis better than highly fragmented ones and
quite another to recognize that the Depression shattered the identities
of millions of men as fathers and breadwinners.[17] The first fit well with
then current debates about the importance of "personality adjustment"
and "role complimentarity" to "successful family life"; the second probed
the very core of patriarchal power. Observers in the 1930s discovered
that the unemployed father might become morose, depressed, abusive,
or suicidal over his inability to support his family; meanwhile, his children grew nervous with worry or angry with resentment. Some researchers feared that social order itself might be at risk as fathers fled
their homes in disgrace while their delinquent children gathered on
street corners looking for trouble.

Men expressed their anxiety and sense of failure as fathers in many
ways but none more poignantly than the thousands who wrote to President Franklin Roosevelt and other government officials seeking a job,
relief, advice, a change in policy, or just reassurance. Their sentiments
ranged from simple requests for help to agonized admissions of failure.
Facing foreclosure on his home, one father of five pleaded for help:
"Gentlemen, this is *all* I have in the *world* my home and family. . . . If
they are allowed to take away my little home I don't know what I'll do
[sic]."[18] A Tennessee man with five children told his congressman of his
children's desperate straits: "I am a ruptured man my family is bar-
footed and naked and an suferns and we all are a goin to purish if I cannot get some help some way [sic]."[19] A West Virginia man with a similar
problem described to a United States senator the consequences of his
children's clothing shortage: "My family needs some clothes for they
are about naked i have four boys going to school and this makes the
second week they have stay home for they do not have any clothes or
shoes to wear [sic]."[20] The same senator received this letter from another constituent: "I am riting you this letter to tell you they wont give
me no work on the relief and my children have not got no shoes and
clothing to go to school with and we havent got enough of bed clothes
to keep us warm [sic]."[21] Finally, this sad, barely literate plea from an

Alabama father: "Mr. Roose Velt Sor Please Sor tell Miss Davis [a welfare worker in Mobile] Please mam Give me Sume thing to Eat my Chrildren are hongre my Wife are Ded [sic]."[22]

Such desperation generated self-pity, bewilderment, and guilt. Some fathers turned in on themselves; others became abusive. Some became irritable and self-centered, others cringing and sickly. Komarovsky explained the centrality of work to men in the 1930s and the meaning of its absence: in America "work is apparently the sole organizing principle and the only means of self-expression. The other interests that existed in the lives of these men—active sports, hobbies, political and civic interests, personal and social relations—turned out to be too weak and insignificant for their personalities to furnish any meaning to their lives. Work, the chief, and in many cases only, outlet was closed to the men, and they faced complete emptiness."[23]

This emptiness, however, came not solely because of the lack of work but because without work men could not provide for their families. And such provision, as one mental health worker explained, defined manhood: "It is fair to assume that the average American wage earner is an individual with ideas and ideals. He has a purpose and goal in life which is built, to a very large extent, around the welfare of his family and the securing for his children of opportunities that will permit them to lift themselves to a higher social and economic level than he has been able to enjoy."[24] When unemployment thwarted such goals, a man's identity as a husband and father, as Komarovsky explained, suffered a severe setback: "He experiences a sense of deep frustration because in his own estimation he fails to fulfill what is the central duty of his life, the very touchstone of his manhood—the role of family provider. The man appears bewildered and humiliated. It is as if the ground had gone out from under his feet." Almost as an afterthought, she suggested the connections among fatherhood, breadwinning, and patriarchal power: "He must have derived a profound sense of stability from having the family dependent upon him."[25]

With the responsibilities of breadwinning came the rewards of seeming indispensability. The dependency of children and wives conferred power on men, and when they lost their jobs, they lost much of their power. No wonder that observers at the time noted the personality disintegration of so many of the unemployed. One study of unemployed men described how a "father cried almost continuously, showing evidences of *depression mania* as he told how their 'little boy missed things' that they could no longer buy" and how his son "can't understand why daddy is out of work."[26] Worry and nervousness became all-consuming: "The father and mother could not sleep at night. Sometimes the father did not go to bed but moved from chair to chair all night long." Another father "'nearly went crazy' in the interval between his loss of work and the time when he began to receive relief. He became nervous and brooded."[27] Some developed psychosomatic illnesses like those of an Illinois man: "The father maintained a surface calmness, but his feeling of insecurity found outlet in great fears of bodily illness. He developed headaches and had spots on his body that 'burned.' He believed he had cancer and went from clinic to clinic, to be told in each that his only difficulty was nervousness."[28] Others contemplated truly desperate measures. In a letter to a New Deal agency, an unemployed Pennsylvania policeman and father of six expressed utter hopelessness: "We cannot go along this way. They have shut the water supply from us. No means of sanitation. We cannot keep the children clean and tidy as they should be. They are all 6 in school but will soon haft to take them out if something is not done." His request was simple—"I want work and money enough to support this family"—and his question morbid: "Can you be so kind as to advise me as to which would be the most human way to dispose of my self and family, as this is about the only thing that I see left to do. No home, no work, no money."[29]

The sadness, despondency, and hopelessness stemmed from the frustration of prolonged unemployment coupled with overwhelming concern about one's dependents. But children's responses to the Depression also shaped fathers' anxieties in the 1930s. Children's deep concern about their fathers' predicament could only fuel fathers' sense of failure. In a letter to President Roosevelt, a boy of twelve noted his family's fear of the landlord, their dependence on credit, and their inability to obtain relief, but he also sketched a moving picture of his own and his father's anxieties: "My father he staying home. All the time he's crying because he can't find work. I told him why are you crying daddy, and daddy said why shouldn't I cry when there is nothing in the house. I feel sorry for him. That night I couldn't sleep."[30] The eleven-year-old daughter of an underemployed laborer, to take another example, attended a "fresh air" camp in upstate New York where she played in a lake and took her first motor- and sailboat ride, but when she wrote home, her terse letter left no doubt where her thoughts resided: "Dear Mother: Did father bring home all his pay?" A young boy with an unemployed father refused to tell his teacher that his family could not afford to pay his locker fee at school. His mother gave some indication of the depth of his pride: "I think he will leave school before he will tell anyone that his parents have to receive charity."[31]

The responses of these youngsters illustrate a point made by one family expert: "Children in the homes of the unemployed lose their sense of security. They cease to feel that they can depend on their parents." This loss translated into "bewilderment and mental confusion, a loss of assurance and a sense of futility and inferiority."[32] Adolescents seemed to suffer the most. The unemployment of a father could be a catastrophe for adolescents, deeply influenced as they were by a peer culture shaped by consumerism. The daughter of a middle-class professional immediately experienced problems in school when her father became unemployed: "The financial condition of the family had so upset her that it was impossible for her to study or to concentrate on anything. The child lost weight and became extremely nervous."[33] The high school daughter of an unemployed salesman felt crushed by her family's forced move to a tiny apartment and "deeply humiliated by the plight of the family."[34]

This humiliation could develop into indifference, hostility, or even resentment toward the father. The unemployed father's constant presence in the house, for example, could undermine the "paternal mystique." One researcher described the lament of an Italian father whose children now treated him with indifference: "As for the children, they used to meet him in the evening with a glad welcome, and now that he is at home all day they don't pay any attention to him. Now when he comes in, they sometimes call out, 'Hi, Dad,' and again they may not even do that." Even worse, the father's constant presence could breed disputes about child rearing. "Now that the husband is at home all the differences in the attitudes of the couple come to the foreground. The disagreements might be over the eating habits of the children; whether or not the daughter should help with the housework; whether the baby should be taken out of the crib when she cries; whether the boy should be locked out of the house when he is naughty; how late the children should be allowed to play out of doors—and so on."[35]

Fathers who suffered the indifference of their children were ahead of those who aroused resentment. But their children's confusion often led to just such an attitude. As one academic explained, "Where the father was unemployed, while the next-door neighbor continued on the job, children could not grasp the social reason. The father, not social conditions, was to blame. He was a failure, whereas society had taught respect only for success."[36] As the following examples culled from interview data attest, unemployed fathers expressed both sadness and bitterness as they reflected upon their children's resentments:

"I am afraid the children don't think as much of me now that I am unemployed. . . . "

"The children act cold toward me. They used to come and hug me, but now I seldom hear a pleasant word from them. . . . "

"If I only had money, I could make the girl do things for me. Now that I cannot offer her a nickel for helping her mother with the dishes, there is no way of getting her to do it. . . . "

"It's only natural that the unemployed father should lose authority with the children. . . . "

"Children's love must be bought. . . . "

"It's inevitable that the children will begin to wonder why their old man can't get a job. . . . "

"It is the father's job to provide for the family. The children can't help but resent it if he fails in his duty. . . . "[37]

Perhaps the experience of a Mr. Scott can sum up the impact of unemployment on millions of fathers. As his joblessness continued and his frustration mounted, Mr. Scott withdrew from his children and became increasingly irritable. He explained his behavior as follows: "Before the depression, I wore the pants in this family, and rightly so. During the depression, I lost something. Maybe you call it self-respect, but in losing it I also lost the respect of my children, and I am afraid I am losing my wife."[38]

Unemployment brought more than a severing of affective bonds and a blow to paternal respect. It could breed outright rebellion in children as well. As many fathers lost the ability to provide for their children, they also lost their ability to control them. Noting this dynamic among his young clients, the director of a child guidance clinic understood the development perfectly: "Is it any wonder that many children in this situation rebelled and became disagreeable, disobedient, and sullen toward their parents?"[39] To many observers, the Depression increased the relative independence of adolescents, made them less indebted to their parents but especially their fathers, and prompted various forms of rebelliousness.

At the heart of this rebellion was the sine qua non of consumer culture—money. As one out-of-work father troubled by the increasing disrespect and disobedience of his three sons put it: "Our hands are tied without money." One of his children had taken up with an unsavory companion, yet he understood why he was powerless to do anything about it: "I know that if I had the money, I could think up some ways of inducing him not to play with that boy." Money conferred power, and its absence brought weakness, a point made by the seventeen-year-old son of a father on relief. Although the boy had once deferred to his father, the youth's position as the only breadwinner dramatically changed the balance of power within the family. When his father asked him to save his money rather than spend it on a date, the boy quickly clarified their relative positions in the family: "It's none of your business how much money I spend. It's mine. You keep your nose out of it." The boy reflected on the source of his new-found power: "Nobody can tell me what to do or how to spend my money. Working makes you feel independent. I remind them who makes the money. They don't say much. They just take it, that's all. I'm not the one on relief. I can't help feeling that way." The source of this feeling did not escape the adolescent: "He is not the same father, that's all. You can't help not looking up to him like we used to. None of us is afraid of him like we used to be. That's natural, isn't it?"[40]

Indeed it was. The boy's older brother remarked that such disobedience would have been at one time inconceivable—his father would have "killed him" if he had made such remarks before the Depression. But the Depression had destroyed the father's authority, and although the older brother did not share his sibling's hostility, he did admit that his attitude had changed: "I don't know that I have lost respect for the old man the way Henry has. I guess I sort of pity him. I feel like I want to help him. I'll tell you how it is. I feel he is more my equal than he used to be."[41] One son's anger was thus another's pity, just two of a wide range of sentiments that came to the fore when the Depression destabilized paternal authority within American families. Investigators continually noted shifts of power as wives and adolescents assumed influence forfeited by unemployed breadwinners.[42] Such role reversals humiliated men and robbed them of their identity. Describing the "mental perils of unemployment," R. O. Beckman noted how devastating the loss of work could be: "A single fact—the loss of his work—has swept away most of his accustomed opportunities for self-assertion, for domination, for business rivalry, for purposeful activity along the lines to which he has become habituated."[43] Such a man had become virtually powerless, "a citizen without courage, a husband without the moral support of his wife, a father without control over his children."[44]

Fatherhood, Unemployment, and Social Order

For some fathers, flight seemed the only recourse. Although divorce rates declined during the 1930s, rates of marital separation went up. The director of the Emergency Work and Relief Bureau of New York City reported that the number of men arraigned for abandoning their wives and children in New York City was 134 percent higher in 1931 than in 1928.[45] Vagabond fathers might well be joined by adolescents, all driven by the same logic. As one young wanderer described his decision: "There was nothing else I could do. There is no income in the home, and I figured that there will be one mouth less to feed. . . . My father has had no work in months, and there is not a square meal in sight. It could not be worse on the road. . . . I am sick and tired listening to the complaints of the old folks and the squalling of the young ones. . . . I will live as I can and no questions asked."[46]

But it could, indeed, be worse on the road. Cut loose from the authority of their fathers and from stable family environments, these young itinerants became the focus of those who worried about crime, especially juvenile delinquency. As thousands of young men hit the road—a three-day survey in 1933 in Los Angeles, for example, found 1,666 homeless boys—concerned citizens feared that the young migrants would fall under the influence of men with "no stake or interest in normal life." Bereft of a father's guidance, a boy might well associate instead with a stranger "who scoffs at those ideals that society values. . . . He derides honesty, hard steady work, and sobriety." The stranger may even advocate "the most extreme 'isms.' He laughs at law and order. The boy in the jungle is subjected to this."[47]

These boys, as well as those who remained at loose ends in their hometown, contributed to the rising incidence of juvenile delinquency. With so many fathers stripped of their ability to support and control their children, some of their offspring began engaging in both minor and major crimes. Case records from welfare agencies suggest they might have done so in a desperate attempt to compensate for the failure of fathers. The son of a long-time unemployed father grew desperate when he lost his job and hence his ability to help support his family: "One day in a public place he saw a coat hanging on a wall. Under a sudden impulse he searched the pockets and took $10. He was arrested and jailed. With help he paid back the money and was put on probation and later got a temporary job. What he needed was a job, not jail."[48] Others committed crimes out of a misplaced sense of need:

> Ernest Hill is a very bright fellow with no record of delinquency until the depression. During the long unemployment he could not have the clothing he used to have, wanted a sweater, broke into the Y.M.C.A. to steal one and while in there took some money also. He was not a selfish type and would not have stolen had he not thought he needed a sweater. He did not really need it.[49]

Regrettably, others stole out of pure greed: "Ralph Emmons is very selfish. His attitude is that, if his family need [sic] to get along without what they have had, at least he will not. He will have as good things as he has had in the past. So he stole various articles of clothing he did not need."[50]

The experiences of these three boys were part of a wider pattern analyzed by William H. Mathews, director of the Emergency Work and Relief Bureau of New York City, who found a connection among unemployment, fatherly abandonment, and juvenile crime. According to Mathews, the sharp rise in the number of men who had abandoned their children helped explain the troubling fact that youth under twenty committed 44 percent of all burglaries and 46 percent of all larcenies in New York City in 1931. With their fathers gone, these youth had "become demoralized as a result of extended unemployment. Their families have been broken up and they are thus deprived of the steadying influence of normal family and neighborhood associations."[51] Welfare workers even attributed sexual misconduct to fathers' unemployment. The sexual order, so went the argument, depended in part on family stability, and when unemployment eroded that stability, sexual misconduct of the young followed. Teachers noticed this moral devolution in the lives of young girls whose fathers' had lost their jobs: "As a girl's sense of inferiority increases because of poor clothes and the drop in the social position of the family, her impulse for recovery inclines her to an extreme use of the means of sex attraction within her reach. Girls become more extreme in their sex abandon with boys."[52]

Not all girls, however, were driven by status anxieties. Some found sex a means of survival. The case of Evelyn Gordon exemplifies the sad connection between a father's job loss and his daughter's sexual impropriety. When her father became unemployed, he and Evelyn began a fruitless search for work. In desperation, Evelyn finally left home and found work as a hired dance partner. The report describes what happened next: "She got five cents a dance and danced from eight P.M. to three A.M. She was not allowed to sit during this time. She must solicit any man who entered." But the meager earnings from the endless dancing were not enough: "She earned about $4.85 a week from the dancing and what she could get from the sale of her tired body after three. . . . After awhile she contracted a venereal disease and was thrown out." Sadly, her sacrifice had been in vain: "Meanwhile her family had lost its place in the community. Father, mother and children ceased going to church. Their clothes were unfit."[53]

Perhaps the real fear of welfare officials and social commentators was simple. By disrupting family life, and undermining the patriarchal order, the Depression heightened an already dangerous trend. James Williams examined case records from a host of welfare agencies and concluded, "What the depression has done is to accelerate this sexual individualism, a revolt that was coming anyway but more slowly and in a fashion that could more readily have been handled constructively than now, forced on us as it is by this harsh, resistless pressure of economic need, despair, cynicism."[54] The apparent sexual anarchy of the young and all the problems in its wake—promiscuity, pregnancy, prostitution, venereal disease—had been held in check by strong family values and, it seems, the earnings of fathers. But when economic failure beset these men, they could not hold back the tide of permissiveness.

Behind all these concerns was an unarticulated assumption: male identity and social stability depended on a gender-based division of labor, a patriarchal order in which breadwinning husbands supported dependent wives and children. Fathers without work were men without power; if men's power stemmed from wage and salary earning, joblessness undermined not only male identity but the entire patriarchal order as well. New Deal reformers noted this fact and shored up traditional gender relationships by emphasizing work relief and passing legislation that either assumed or promoted the economic dependence of women on men.

New Deal Work Relief and Fatherhood

Convinced that men wanted and needed employment, not charity, American social workers in the 1930s successfully campaigned for work relief programs. Although a complete history of New Deal work relief is beyond the scope of this chapter, a brief analysis of the ideological assumptions underlying the programs is revealing.[55] Most obviously, New Dealers targeted the work programs at men, most of the beneficiaries were men, and most of the programs discriminated in favor of men. Moreover, programs discriminated against women while reforms on their behalf emphasized skills for domestic work. Thus, a quarter of the National Recovery Administration wage codes discriminated against women, and arbitrary job classifications did the same. At no point during the short life of the Civilian Works Administration did more than 7 percent of the jobs go to women. In the Works Progress Administration (WPA), only one worker per family could be employed, and that worker had to demonstrate breadwinning status. Louisiana left no doubt as to which spouse held such status by mandating that "a woman with an employable husband is not eligible for referral, as her husband is the logical head of the family."[56] Male workers in the WPA received five dollars a day, female workers only three, but even that was better than the record of the Civilian Conservation Corps, which excluded women altogether. Women lucky enough to find work on WPA rolls inevitably worked at sewing, that most traditional of all female labors.[57]

Such discrimination, coupled with the simple fact that men monopolized the work relief opportunities, suggests that the question was not unemployment but male unemployment. Moreover, as Harry Hopkins and others pointed out, the programs involved far more than simply finding work for men. They were also meant to shore up men's psychological well-being. Hopkins, who directed the massive Works Progress Administration, made the case for work relief by emphasizing the connections among work, manhood, and respect. In his judgment, men without work "actually go to pieces. They lose the respect of their wives, sons and daughters because they lose respect for themselves, even though they have broken no laws and even though their deportment as fathers and neighbors continues to be above reproach."[58] Nor was direct relief the answer. Echoing others, Hopkins lamented the psychological damage caused by direct relief: "America has a tradition that a man should work. Direct relief for an able-bodied man is hard on his morale. His status in the community is destroyed, together with the respect of his family and his own self-respect." This loss of respect could have long-range and dire consequences: "After a time he gets the idea there is no need for him to work, at least many do. Then he becomes a public charge, not only for the present, but for all time."[59] Homer Folks, a leading New York welfare reformer, made much the same point: "The receipt of relief without work by an able-bodied person is inevitably humiliating, terribly distressing, and idleness coupled with dependence [upon public charity] is a thoroughly abnormal experience and strongly tends to demoralization."[60]

The danger of direct relief, in a nutshell, was that it undermined independence and promoted laziness. It also flew in the face of accepted ideas of manhood and womanhood, of what it meant to be a father and a mother. As Hopkins put it, "the majority of people have associated the chance to earn their living with self-respect." But the chance to earn a living was not randomly distributed among the population: "Most of our family habits and customs," Hopkins continued, "are constructed around the central fact that the father is the breadwinner. He must be respected. The mother is the domestic guardian. She can be looked to for protection, but she, too—at least this is the traditional notion— should be protected."[61]

Men needed work, but in Hopkins's judgment, not just any work would do: "You can't fool these people on the value of what they are doing. Unless you give them real jobs with real public value you are not doing anything to keep up their self-respect."[62] As relief administrator

Aubrey Williams declared: "The only kind of relief which has validity is that which enables the jobless to regain their independence."[63] And the only kind of relief that would restore independence was relief free from an investigator's questions, free from payment in kind, and free from well-intentioned but misguided advice about how to run a family. Such was the promise of work relief: real work paid for with real wages. But work relief promised even more. Beyond simply meeting the material needs of family members, it would meet their psychological needs by reconstructing families along traditional patterns, a development that would redound to the benefit of both fathers and children. To Hopkins and others, one key virtue of work relief was that it restored the respect of fathers in the eyes of their children. Reflecting on the achievements to date of the WPA, Hopkins remarked in 1936: "To the extent that the work program has centered once more in the father the authority and prestige which he has lost when out of work, and to the extent that the family need has been diminished, WPA has helped the young person."[64]

Fatherhood and Female Employment

In practice the WPA fell short of these goals and succumbed to a variety of contradictions endemic to public welfare.[65] But the vision behind the program reflected the gender ideology whose roots were deep in the American past. The same could be said for those laws and programs in the 1930s that related to female employment. Just as the WPA and other work programs tried to shore up men's place as breadwinners, other legislation simultaneously discriminated against working women. In fact, the two developments shared the view that men were obligated to support their families, and if women threatened this obligation, remedial legislation was in order. And the threat was real. As men lost their jobs, wives and daughters became increasingly important to family survival; moreover, because of the segmented labor force and the fact that the Depression hit "male" occupations harder than "female" occupations, it was easier for women to find work. Inevitably, some men charged that women eroded male job opportunities, and thus a spate of legislation was passed that restricted married women's access to jobs. The message was clear: the obligation and the right to support families resided with men, not women, with fathers, not mothers.

Although opposition to working wives had been present in the 1920s, the Depression intensified such sentiment. At the heart of the matter, as historian Alice Kessler-Harris has written, was the ironic fact that although the economic need of families propelled women into the work force, public sentiment and public policy "fostered a public stance that encouraged family unity and urged women, in the interest of jobs for men, to avoid paid work themselves."[66] As breadlines lengthened, women became scapegoats for male misery and family upheaval. If wives would remain in the home, they would neither take jobs from men nor neglect their children. They could, instead, focus on the one crucial task that had not been usurped by outside agencies—the care and nurture of the young. Meanwhile, men would then have access to the jobs vacated by women and could again assume their rightful role as family providers. A 1939 proposal revealed the simplistic logic of such thinking: "There are approximately 10,000,000 people out of work in the United States today," wrote Norman Cousins; "there are also 10,000,000 or more women, married and single, who are jobholders. Simply fire the women, who shouldn't be working anyway, and hire the men. Presto! No unemployment. No relief rolls. No depression."[67]

The breathtaking simplicity (and naïveté) of this proposal ignored the segmentation of the labor force—as one feminist asked, do men "pine to slave in somebody's kitchen, to work in beauty salons?"—but reflected the view that women stole jobs from men, that family bread-winning resided with fathers, and that women's ultimate responsibility was home maintenance and child nurture. Working mothers in families with unemployed fathers, critics feared, inverted the social order and laid the basis for a problem "vastly more terrifying than the economic wolves howling at the apartment door." Fathers stood to lose their sense of manhood, women their femininity, children the desperately needed care that only a mother could provide.[68]

These cultural concerns would be of passing interest had not they provoked legislation at all levels of government that blatantly discriminated against women in favor of breadwinning men. Whereas state and city governments worked as early as 1930 to remove married women from the civil service—New York assemblyman Arthur Swartz, for example, denounced the employment of married women and urged "our federal, state and local governments [to] cooperate to remove these undeserving 'parasites'"—the most famous piece of legislation was Section 213 of the federal government's Federal Economy Act of 1932.[69] It mandated that whenever the executive branch made cuts in personnel, married persons with a spouse who also worked for the government were to be discharged first. Although the section did not single out women per se, the intent was to remove wives, not husbands, and this is precisely what occurred. From the Federal Farm Board to the Office of the Adjutant General, to the War, Navy, and Veterans Administration departments, to small-town post office clerks and substitute rural mail carriers, married women employees found themselves out of work. Within a year, more than 1,600 females had lost their government jobs.[70]

Nor was Section 213 unpopular. Despite immediate opposition from a host of women's groups, the discriminatory law remained in effect until repealed in 1937. This reflected the fact that throughout the Depression, public opinion overwhelmingly opposed the employment of married women. Asked in 1936, "Should a married woman earn money if she has a husband capable of supporting her?" over 80 percent of the sample said no. Two years later, Americans responded to a similar question in an almost identical fashion. This latter survey did show that women had a slightly greater tendency than men to approve of wives working in spite of husbandly support, but the fact remains that both overwhelmingly believed women belonged in the home and that men were the rightful breadwinners of the family.[71] Such sentiments bolstered local and state attempts to restrict the employment opportunities of married women. Despite the repeal of Section 213, efforts continued throughout the decade to restrict female employment. Although some colleges and universities refused to hire married women and others replaced married women with men or with single women, the nation's school systems exhibited the most pervasive discrimination against wives. Almost 80 percent of the country's school systems refused to hire married women and half dismissed teachers who married.[72] Nor did legislative activity abate. In the last year of the decade, legislators in twenty-six states considered some form of "married persons" law whose intent was to restrict the employment of wives.

Although such efforts ultimately failed in all but one state—and in Louisiana the bill remained on the books for only six months—the fight against them shored up the traditional view of fathers as primary breadwinners and mothers as nurturers. To defend the interests of working women against such legislation, women's groups abandoned earlier arguments of the 1920s and early 1930s that wives had a right to work, that work enhanced personal fulfillment, and that employment opportunities should be increased wherever possible and replaced them by an emphasis on the necessity of wives' labor for family survival. Fathers were the rightful breadwinners; if married women worked, they did so not because they wanted to but because they had to. A Business and Professional Women's study concluded that wives worked "only because their families needed the money they earned. They preferred not to work outside the home."[73] Thus, even traditional defenders of working women adopted the rhetoric of their opponents and in so doing tightened the linkage between breadwinning and manhood.

The Depression and American Fatherhood

Historians of the battle over Section 213 have concentrated on the experience of women, and properly so. Attempts to exclude married women from the labor force reveal a host of assumptions about the structure of patriarchy in the 1930s. When Margaret Worrell, president of the League of American Civil Service, testified before Congress on behalf of 213, for example, she told a story about a couple who both worked for the government. One day they returned home and beat their child because the youngster used language picked up in the streets. Whose fault was it? Worrell had no doubt: "It was the fault of the mother and father. It was the fault of the mother particularly, because she was not home to attend to her duty. The duty that God imposed upon her when He gave her the child."[74] Although the implications of her statement for women were clear enough, their meanings for men and fatherhood were not immediately evident, in large part because the issue of fatherhood were part of the subtext, a historical given seemingly in no need of explication. But if the subtext is read, certain assumptions become clear. The "married persons' clause" represented one of many efforts to respond to a crisis in gender relations caused by the Depression. The Depression had laid bare the relationship among breadwinning, fatherhood, and male identity. Men who feared for the economic well-being of their wives and children responded in a multitude of ways, but investigators were especially struck by their anger and frustration and their unsettling sense of powerlessness. Their very manhood was at stake, and the public policies of the 1930s recognized as much. From gigantic New Deal work relief programs to local ordinances against married women schoolteachers, the unspoken assumption remained the same: men gained their identity from breadwinning. Working wives, by contrast, allegedly worked for "pin money," took jobs from men, ignored their God-given role, and usurped men's responsibilities. Fathers needed to work, mothers needed to rear children. The crisis could be met by the restoration of a traditional division of labor within the home.

From this perspective, the Depression had a conservative impact on American fatherhood. And yet the story is more complicated. One central irony of the Depression is that because of the economic crisis, increasing numbers of older, married women entered the work force. In 1930, slightly under 30 percent of all wage-earning women were married; ten years later, that figure stood at 35 percent.[75] Caused by a variety of both short- and long-term changes, this surge of married women into the labor force would accelerate during World War II and continue throughout the postwar years. Thus, the Depression and, as we shall see, the war years set in motion forces that would ultimately have a profound impact on fatherhood, the structure of families, and male identity.

8

Fatherhood, Foxholes, and Fascism, 1940–1950

THE 1944 PICTURE IS STARK. TEN MEN, ALL MOVING IN THE SAME DI-
rection, are at an elevated railroad platform. From their dress, they appear to be from a variety of social classes. Some carry briefcases, others
satchels. One is in uniform. None smile. Below the picture in large letters is the message, "I'm no hero." The text then explains why: "I never
had any illusions that this war was going to be a pushover. I knew the
day would come when they'd have to call even us—the pre-Pearl Harbor fathers. Well, I've been called. I don't like leaving my wife and kids.
But I'm in and, while I'm in, I won't be seeing much of my family. . . .
But whatever I'm asked to do, I'm going to be the best damn soldier I
know how to be. I'm no hero. . . . *I just want to get home as soon as I
can.* That's what you folks want, too. Want all of us home."[1]

This war bond advertisement graphically portrays some elemental
truths. World War II was, indeed, no pushover; its very scope did ren-
der men anonymous; it did ultimately require fathers to be called up;
and the struggle in many ways was about getting home. But the ad does
not show what the war did do for American fatherhood: after the difficulties experienced by so many breadwinners in the 1930s, the World
War II years not only restored men's breadwinning abilities but reaffirmed fathers' critical role in the health of the republic. For some,

the war underscored the importance of fathers to social order; for others, the connections between fatherhood and democracy; for those more psychologically inclined, the crucial connections among fatherhood, proper sex-role identity, and the emotional health of children. Together, they asserted the centrality of fatherhood to the economic, political, and emotional well-being of the nation in ways that were ultimately conservative. The war became not only a war against fascism but, more fundamentally, a war in defense of the American home and its traditional division of labor.

War, Democracy, and Fatherhood

For most American men, the problems of the Depression vanished with the advent of war, and from 1940 to 1945 a variety of developments reinvigorated paternal influence. Most obviously, the war brought full employment, indeed, a labor shortage. Fathers who went begging for work in the 1930s now had a variety of high-paying jobs from which to choose, and with work men gained a new sense of manhood.[2] The sociological focus on the unemployed man and his family disappeared. Instead, a new set of concerns came to the fore. Now the focus was on strong, democratic families capable of meeting the fascist threat. The family became vital to the nation's survival, both as a symbol of democracy and as a counterpoint to the autocratic families of the Third Reich. The good health of the American family was what the war was really about, and almost all family experts agreed that the traditional family, with its homebound mother and wage-earning father, would best maintain the domestic stability needed to win the war.[3]

This vision appeared even before the United States entered the war. As totalitarian governments began to threaten freedom, the American family became an important symbol of democratic values and national strength. Only strong families, social scientists insisted, could provide the order and stability necessary for the inculcation of the fundamental values at the heart of democratic life—individualism, freedom, tolerance.[4] The ideal home should become a classroom for democracy, where children learned to make thoughtful decisions based on respect for others. Out of this experience, wholesome families would produce children capable of defending the nation against the totalitarian onslaught.[5]

Once war actually came, these themes became even more powerful. The family became both a symbol of American values and the incubator for them. To some, in fact, the family was what the war was all about, or as the editors of *Better Homes and Gardens* put it, "the status of the home [was] the supreme issue in this titanic struggle."[6] And the desired "status" was an odd combination of liberal sentiment and conservative ideology. The sentiment was clear: American families may not be perfect democracies, but American parents had little in common with their authoritarian counterparts in Germany and Japan. As spouses, Americans treated each other with mutual respect, and as parents they listened to the opinions and wishes of their offspring. Ernest Burgess went so far as to say that "the concept of the family as a companionship embodies the ideals for the preservation of which we are waging this war—of democracy as the way of life, of the equality of men and women, and of personality as the highest human value."[7] By contrast, family life in fascist countries simply mirrored the authoritarian nature of fascism itself and lacked any semblance of equality, let alone companionate relations.

But the conservative ideology behind the liberal sentiment was equally clear. Family experts described the American family as democratic against the backdrop of German families, not in light of any sustained analysis of its actual democratic nature. Democracy in American families meant a propensity for discussion, nurture, mutual respect, perhaps family councils. It also meant resistance to state encroachment in family life, a position that led American Roman Catholic periodicals to attack Planned Parenthood as a "home grown species of Hitlerism."[8] It did not mean any intention or desire to alter the basic structure of American families. Throughout the war, most commentators insisted that ideal families had breadwinning fathers and stay-at-home mothers.

This commitment to a traditional division of labor persisted despite the massive movement of women into the labor force. Although a few liberals applauded this development on feminist grounds, most experts and policymakers were unwilling to admit that women's (especially mothers') wage work was anything more than a temporary necessity. The Children's Bureau, for its part, called for income support to fathers, housing subsidies for families, and government health care for children, all with the hope that such programs would allow mothers to stay at home. Likewise, the Commission on Children in Wartime hoped to shore up traditional family arrangements through higher pay for servicemen, increased income for fathers, and expanded Social Security benefits and cheap housing for families. What is more, the arrival of full employment made this vision increasingly possible for millions of American men. Fathers were now at work; with a little help from the government, they could become the sole breadwinners and claim the privileges and power that came with that status.[9]

The insistence that women's and mothers' war work was temporary, and the desire to shore up fathers' breadwinning abilities with government aid if necessary, grew out of basic assumptions about the war, the family, and social order. For most the war had less to do with high ideals than it did about personal matters. American men, as Robert Westbrook has explained, "were not called upon to conceive of their obligation to participate in the war effort as a *political* obligation to work, fight, or die for their country" but rather "to defend *private* interests and discharge *private* obligations."[10] This was the message of Norman Rockwell's enormously popular *Saturday Evening Post* illustrations of President Roosevelt's "Four Freedoms," particularly the freedoms from fear and want. Images of family life dominate both illustrations. In the former, a mother and father look in on their sleeping children; the mother tucks them in while the father, standing slightly back, holds a newspaper with news of London bombing horrors. In the latter, a grandmother serves a three-generation family a huge Thanksgiving turkey while her husband serenely stands at the head of the table, ready to carve the bird. The illustration simultaneously suggests the success of men in providing such fare and of women in preparing it.[11]

The popular iconography of the war years likewise offered personal, familial answers to the question, Why do we fight? In wartime advertising, the American state and private corporations interpreted the obligations of Americans to support the war effort, as Westbrook explains, "as a duty owed to the family in which they were raised, the family they were themselves raising, the family they would some day raise, and/or, somewhat more abstractly, to the family as a social institution."[12] Given such aims, messages about father and fatherhood made up an important part of this iconography. Some ads, for example, depicted the wartime bond between fathers and their fighting sons. The Studebaker Corporation ran a series of advertisements with this theme. One example pictures an obviously proud, middle-aged father with his arm around his uniformed son. The caption reads, "When the Marines got Lukavich they took a good man. But his team-mate father still builds Cyclone engines at Studebaker." In the text we learn that the two men used to work together, but like "many other Studebaker father-and-son teams have parted company for the duration."[13] So, too, with the Kowalskis who had once worked at Studebaker. Now the son operates a radio in India, but "the two have continued to 'work together' for victory because the father has been busy building Wright Cyclone engines for the Flying Fortress in a Studebaker Aviation Division plant."[14]

Images of fathers in wartime were not restricted to middle-aged, home-front men like Lukavich and Kowalski. Fathers at war provided the perfect vehicle for expressing the essentially private goals of the war effort. Some ads made a simple point: the war was about protection and security. A Studebaker-sponsored war bond ad depicted a soldier, just back from the Far East, greeting his small son at the yard gate. The caption suggests the sacrifices of war: "Are you my daddy?" the boy asks, and his father replies, "Yes, sonny boy, I'm your daddy—the daddy you don't remember because you were just a few months old when I left for war. War is heartless, little man. It doesn't give much heed to family ties. But along with millions of other men and women in uniform, your daddy is certainly doing everything he can to keep another war from starting when you're grown up and have children of your own."[15] An ad for bed sheets pictured a mother and her two children on a bed. While the little boy slept, the mother and daughter eagerly read a letter from the father. The text left no doubt as to why this man fought: "A gentle young wife. Two tousle-headed kiddies. This Dresden-china trio is the dynamo that powers the toughest Marine in the outfit."[16]

Other ads combined images of children with postwar hopes for the good life. A 1945 Nash Motors advertisement pictured a happily reflective American soldier at the wheel. The text, written in verse, was maudlin but also illustrative:

The tick of the clock in the hall . . .
The feel of clean, fresh sheets . . .
A dog's bark and a boy's clear call . . .
The touch of a hand on my cheek . . .
They're all in my dreams of tomorrow.

After three stanzas extolling the pleasure of driving a Nash with "the girl and the boy and the dog by my side, and the laughter and joy of being alive," the "poem" ended with the soldier summing up his postwar dreams:

The girl I love, my boy, my dog, my car . . .
All the things I long for, all the things I dream of . . .
These things will be mine again, in my tomorrow.[17]

The advertisement mixed men's affective and material desires, implying that the two were inextricably linked. A man's postwar happiness would come from home, children, and, of course, a new automobile.

Not all advertisements were so devoid of a broader political vision of the war's purpose, but even those that mentioned the stakes of the war linked them with domestic themes. Again, an automobile advertisement from 1945 serves as an example. In this ad, a combat-hardened but forlorn GI in the South Pacific reflects on postwar life. He ruminates first about what it would be like to return to his wife and children. After the exquisite pleasure of reunion with his wife—"and the world stands still for a while"—he will go to meet his children: "I'm walking into a room with the biggest and brightest tree in the world and the kids look up from their toys and jump to their feet and come running to meet me and their voices are sweet in my ears, and I duck down quick and hold them tight." The war then abruptly breaks his reverie and prompts a less domestic, more political thought on why it must be fought: "I'll go home sure no kids of mine will ever spend *their* Christmases in jungles, in foxholes, or on beachheads. When I go home, I want it understood the victories we've won . . . the peace we have secured . . . will be meaningless to us unless all our strength, all our power to destroy can be the power to create." The advertisement concludes with the hope that out of war can come peace, out of bondage, freedom.[18]

But even ads that combined domestic visions with more abstract war aims often saw the latter in highly personal terms. A North American Aviation advertisement pictured a wife with her arm around her husband. The father held their small son aloft, and in the boy's hand was a Santa Claus figurine. It was the very picture of a blissful reunion. The text set the scene: "Christmas furlough, 1943 . . . a little fellow he's never seen . . . such a lot of living to be crowded into a few precious days, then off again." The ad continued: "Ask this man, *any* man, what he's fighting for. . . . Conquest? . . . New Order? No, it's bigger—and simpler—than that. It's families and homes and hobbies. It's jobs that can grow with a man's ambitions. It's the right to think, to vote, to worship as a man chooses. It's the heart of America."[19]

Ultimately, many of the advertisements were about the hope that out of war could come a secure, comfortable family life. An advertisement for Bendix Aviation showed a soldier in a foxhole; behind him, bombs exploded and airplanes crashed as GIs attacked a Pacific island. Cutting into this image was the same man after the war, now kneeling with his daughter as the two of them planted a garden. Behind the two was a radiant young wife and mother and a beautiful home. The advertisement was captioned, "The Good Earth," and the text read that "someday it will be Springtime . . . in a garden . . . with loved faces beside him, and a loved home beyond." Such men, the ad insisted, had the right to dream: "For they who have crouched behind ramparts of alien earth have a right to earn a share of their own good land . . . a right to the rewards of free enterprise, and all the blessings it brings. To make that dream come true is the first obligation of all Americans."[20]

Fatherhood, Domestic Disruption, and the Draft

Fatherhood and family life gave meaning to the brutality of the front lines, but wartime problems on the home front worried child experts who reemphasized the indispensability of fathers to social order.[21] Their concerns were not without foundation, because the war brought great disruption to American families. Migration, changing work patterns, hasty marriages, housing shortages, rising rates of juvenile delinquency, sexual promiscuity, and unwanted pregnancies created great consternation during the war.[22] Although all these problems received their fair share of attention, those associated with moral behavior, particularly of the young, seemed especially troubling. Leading child experts focused special attention on the sexual promiscuity of young females, whose behavior was responsible for the disproportionate rise in female delinquency during the war.[23] J. Edgar Hoover of the FBI repeatedly warned of the dangers of juvenile delinquency, and a widely screened *Time/Life* newsreel blamed the rising tide of crime on the war and parental neglect of children.[24]

When congressional hearings in late 1943 took up the issue of juvenile delinquency, considerable attention focused on parental neglect of children. Working mothers received disproportionate blame—Father Flanagan of Boys Town recommended to Congress that the mother should remain in her kitchen "where she belongs. She is the queen of the kitchen, that is where she should reign, not in defense plants"—but authorities agreed that the problem went beyond maternal neglect and that wartime disruptions of fatherly responsibilities played a role as well.[25] When Katharine Lenroot, head of the Children's Bureau, listed the key factors responsible for the rise in wartime juvenile delinquency, number one on her list was the following: "Fathers are separated from their families because they are serving in the armed forces or working in distant war industries."[26] Michael J. Scott, a St. Louis juvenile court judge, likewise warned of the dangers of drafting fathers and the probable impact on the home: "In many instances taking the father away will naturally take his influence away, but by taking him away you may also make it necessary for the mother to be out of that home."[27]

Although witnesses listed a host of agencies, clinics, programs, and approaches to enlist in the fight against juvenile delinquency, most commentators agreed that stable, traditional families were the first line of defense.[28] Fathers capable of supporting their families without help from either their wives or older children and full-time mothers able to devote time to the nurture and supervision of children created optimum conditions for the prevention of delinquency.[29] The father provided an excellent sex-role model for his sons, the mother for her daughters. Moreover, both parents needed to be involved with their children, a point taken to heart by several thousand Memphis, Tennessee, fathers who signed a promissory note pledging to spend a specified number of hours per week with their children. Sponsored by the Memphis Youth Service Council, sixty-five thousand copies of the note were distributed throughout the city, an effort that one early supporter insisted had already cut the delinquency rate substantially.[30]

The relationship between fatherhood and social order became even clearer when congressional hearings on the drafting of fathers affirmed, in a national forum, the significance of fathers to home-front and battlefront morale and to capitalism, democracy, and even the eugenic future of the country. In September 1943 the Senate Committee on Military Affairs held hearings on a bill, sponsored by Montana Senator Burton Wheeler, to exempt fathers from the draft. The debate pitted military officials against Wheeler and his friendly witnesses. The military's position was straightforward: wartime exigencies required the drafting of fathers. The issue, according to Secretary of War Henry Stimson, was whether "the war effort can suffer without serious impairment the withdrawal of 6,000,000 men who are eligible for training and service from the national pool of manpower. Plainly, it cannot."[31] General Joseph E. McNarney seconded Stimson's argument and warned that if fathers received exemptions as a class, they might avoid any contribution whatsoever to the war effort. Even now, McNarney suggested, "There is, I know, a sufficient number of men in the father pool, who, if they were properly employed and were not working in department stores and others places, would be sufficient to fulfill the immediate manpower needs of the entire United States." But, he continued, if you exempt fathers as a class, that "particular class then is not required to furnish any effort for the successful completion of the war. If they see fit they can still dress women's hair."[32]

For Wheeler and his supporters, the issues were far more complex. As did many Americans, Wheeler complained about the misuse of labor power. He repeatedly attacked the squandering of men in industry and the army. Why draft fathers, he asked, when able-bodied single men loaf on street corners, fit young men gain exemptions for specious medical reasons or fail intelligence tests because the standards are too high, and government bureaucracies shelter a host of potential unmarried fighting recruits? And what about the soldiers guarding bridges in Washington, D.C., or recruits ferried from one camp to another without leaving the country? The very idea of drafting fathers exasperated the Montana senator: "In my opinion," said Wheeler, "the drafting of fathers is the most idiotic plan that has been proposed by the government. It is not necessary and cannot be shown to be necessary."[33] In Wheeler's judgment, war and industrial needs could be met if the army and the government would simply straighten out the labor power mess.

If they did not and fathers were drafted, Wheeler and his backers predicted dire consequences. The alarming rise in juvenile delinquency would most certainly continue. Quoting liberally from a report by J. Edgar Hoover, Wheeler feared there was a "complete breaking down of the morale and the morals of the boys and girls in this country" and that the situation would only worsen if fathers were drafted.[34] Social order required a wage-earning father and an at-home mother. Otherwise, he implied, drafted fathers would simply contribute to the already pervasive sense of disorder in American society: "Go to Los Angeles or to any other place, to these large cities, where you have camps," Wheeler challenged, "and see what your conditions are. You take the married men away from their families, and it is breaking down morale."[35] The glaring contrast of fathers trudging off to war while young single men worked for high wages in defense industries could only create profound resentment: "[N]ow you come along and you take married men away from their families, breaking up their homes, making their wives go to work, seeing that their children probably have to be put in institutions, part of the time at least, that certainly creates a very bad psychological situation in the United States of America."[36]

Ultimately, Wheeler feared, drafting fathers would undermine the American way of life. In Wheeler's and his followers' judgment, fathers had an essential role to play both practically and symbolically. Practically, such men should not be dragooned into defense industries or into the military itself. It was far more important that they run businesses and maintain the distribution of goods and services in the nation.[37] Symbolically, fathers who ran small businesses represented the American ideal. As Wheeler put it, "this has been a middle-class country, and it is a middle-class country that preserves its democracy, and if you drive them all into big industry [by the draft or by forcing men into large defense industries to avoid the draft] and put the little industries out of business, you don't have a democratic republic."[38]

Wheeler's vision of the threat that drafting fathers posed lacked precision, but its essential elements were clear enough. The draft had hurt small businesses as men shifted to war industries for better wages and to avoid conscription. The threatened draft of fathers would simply exacerbate this process. In fact, Wheeler at one point argued that drafting fathers was actually an effort to force them into essential war work, that is, into big industry.[39] Such a course, Wheeler warned, threatened the very heart of the nation: "[I]f you put out of business the little business man and simply turn over everything into the war industry and the Army, you are going to do away with a democratic republic in the United States, and the tendency is the little business man, as Senator after Senator has stated, is being put out of business during this war and that is the tendency all over the country."[40]

All these fears meant trouble for the nation. Their exact import was somewhat murky, but their general implications were certainly troubling. Drafted fathers could not assume their rightful position within families nor could they continue to run their small businesses. Consequently, the middle class was at risk. An insecure middle class, in turn, would further weaken family life, and without strong families, the nation and its democratic government would fall, replaced by some variant of totalitarianism. Wheeler's rhetorical question to Admiral King summed up the dangers ahead: "After all, Admiral King, the home is the backbone of a democratic republic, is it not? . . . If you destroy the home, you destroy your country, you destroy America?"[41]

The collapse of democracy would be speeded by the dysgenic effects of drafting fathers, particularly white middle-class fathers. Although Wheeler could understand why the army would prefer to draft whites rather than blacks, native-born rather than immigrants, literates rather than illiterates, he worried about the long-range impact of such choices. A policymaker must think in terms of "what is going to happen to the population of the United States if we kill off all the supermen in the country and leave the drones and the illiterates in the United States, and he ought to think on the moral effect it is going to have on the people of this country if the fathers are taken and the children are left to be raised in institutions."[42] Later, Wheeler reiterated this argument, insisting that single men be drafted first "because we don't want to raise a lot of morons in the United States by exempting all illiterates and defectives."[43]

If Wheeler's views on drafting fathers were his alone, they would hardly bear mention, but the senator had strong public support. Although his bill finally went down to defeat, thousands of Americans shared his opinions about the drafting of fathers. A Gallup poll in the fall of 1943, for example, found that the great majority of Americans preferred drafting single women for noncombat jobs over drafting fathers for the same military work. Moreover, 68 percent favored drafting

single men who worked in *essential* war industries before drafting
fathers, even if they worked in *nonessential* industries.[44] Even the
American Legion opposed drafting fathers. Approximately one thousand delegates to a state legion meeting in Maryland approved a resolution opposing the drafting of pre-Pearl Harbor fathers.[45]

Correspondence to Wheeler's office reflected such sentiments. The
senator testified that he had received over two thousand letters and
telegrams on the draft issue, and over 90 percent of them supported his
position.[46] Some expressed general concern. In one letter, the president of the National Policy Association noted widespread opposition to
drafting fathers and worried about its impact: "My correspondence
from all over America," wrote Thomas G. Greene, "convinces me that
the vast majority of the people feel that the drafting of fathers of small
children is a very real danger to the future of our country and must not
be permitted."[47] Other letters expressed resentment. A mother of two,
for example, vented her frustration when her husband received his
draft notice: "There are hundreds of draft dodgers, single men and
married men, since Pearl Harbor walking the streets of Butte, but I
guess the draft boards don't want to induct them."[48] Many cited instances of featherbedding, malingering, and unwarranted deferments
among single men, including a biting letter from United Auto Workers
Local 659 in Flint, Michigan, complaining that "sons of Chevrolet superintendents and other high officials" were appointed foremen "for
the sole pupose [sic] of enabling them to evade being inducted into the
armed services. . . . We ask that the necessary steps be taken to insure
that the induction of fathers be halted until these draft dodgers are inducted."[49] Protests also came from draft board members who resigned
rather than participate in the drafting of fathers.[50]

Religious leaders added their voices to the dissent. "In God's plan," a
leading Roman Catholic newspaper editorialized, "every child is provided with a mother and a father. Both are needed." The article praised
fathers who eschewed work in defense industries and, instead, worked
closer to home, and it lamented that such men "are to be penalized for
the very qualities which support a Nation's fabric—industry, prudence,
loyalty to sacramental promises." Worst of all, drafting fathers would
drive women into wage work—thereby increasing delinquency among
the young—and heighten dependence of families on the government.
To these religious leaders, sinister intentions lurked behind the drafting
of fathers: "Can it possibly be that some of our officials, for doctrinaire
reasons of their own, prefer the Government nursery to the home?"[51]

Wheeler even enlisted the Harvard sociologist Pitirim Sorokin in the
fight against drafting fathers. In an article for United Press, Sorokin

cataloged the dangers of drafting fathers, a list Wheeler entered into the record of the hearings. In Sorokin's judgment, drafting fathers would hurt the family biologically, psychologically, economically, and morally. Birth rates would likely decline and deterioration of the health of the young would increase; "sadness, sorrow, anxiety, and insecurity" would produce a variety of psychoneuroses; standards of living would fall while the work burden of mothers and children would increase; finally, moral and religious values of weak families would more than likely decline.[52]

In the end, such support could not save Wheeler's bill. After all, who was to deny the generals the men they needed to fight the Germans and the Japanese?[53] But by asserting the indispensability of fathers to family happiness, social stability, proper eugenic development, and, ultimately, the future of democracy, the debate on the drafting of fathers did reconfirm traditional assumptions about fatherhood and family life at a time of national crisis. The exigencies of war might require fathers to serve, but Wheeler and his followers left no doubt that fathers played a vital role in maintaining social order and securing the nation's democratic future. The irony, moreover, is that although Wheeler believed exempting fathers from the draft would preserve home, family, and community, his opponents believed drafting them would help to do precisely the same. It was a debate about means, not ends.

Fathers at War

Once fathers actually went to war, the discussion about them took a new turn. Now attention centered on their psychological indispensability to family life, particularly to sex-role development and early father-child bonding. Beginning in the mid-1930s, psychologists had begun to focus on the formation of sex-role identity, and during the war years such concerns reached the level of popular discussion.[54] Absent fathers heightened fears of "maternal overprotection" and "momism" and prompted popular writers to urge mothers to find proper father substitutes lest their children, especially their sons, develop damaged psyches.

Even before Philip Wylie maliciously coined the term "momism" in 1942, writers began warning of the dangers of excessive maternal influence in a world at war. Martial times called for a martial spirit, and who better to instill the necessary toughness than fathers? In September 1940, *Harper's* magazine worried that American men "have been maneuvered into a position where it is impossible for them to think of anything but women and their wants between the end of each day's work and its beginning the following morning." Americans needed to break from their "softness," their penchant for security, their addiction to luxury and easy living, their indulgence of their children. America's "over-solicitous maternalism" toward the young had to end if democracy were to survive: "In a world of power the gracious, the genteel, the sheltered life has of itself no force. It has no vital consequence. Couple democracy to those ideals, and you marry it to death."[55]

Two years later Philip Wylie launched his splenetic attack on mothers and the effeminacy of American culture. Mothers had become parasites, destroyers of men, "the bride at every funeral and the corpse at every wedding." Mothers crushed boys' ambitions, smashed their dreams of adventure, and left them content to take "a stockroom job in the hairpin factory and try to work up to the vice-presidency." Such "men" remained forever immature, denied by overprotective mothers the necessary battle with their fathers that would bring real independence. Instead, mothers interceded on behalf of their sons, muted essential father-son conflict, and destroyed their sons' manhood in the bargain: "Thus the sixteen-year-old who tells his indignant dad that he, not dad, is going to have the car that night and takes it—while mom looks on, dewy-eyed and anxious—has sold his soul to mom and made himself into a lifelong sucking-egg."[56]

Wylie had virtually nothing to say about fathers, but those who shared something of his views—if not his withering sarcasm and vitriol—fleshed out the implications for fatherhood. Psychiatrist David Levy warned of the psychological dangers of "maternal overprotection" and paternal passivity, while the *Ladies Home Journal* called for more active fatherly involvement lest young boys become homosexual.[57] But it was left to Edward Strecker, a psychiatric consultant to the army and navy, to draw the connections among momism, fatherly neglect, and national survival. According to Strecker, the military rejected at induction over 1.8 million American men because of neuropsychiatric disorders and released another 600,000 for the same reason.[58] His wartime experience on the neuropsychiatric wards of army and navy hospitals had convinced him that thousands of these men suffered from maternal overprotection and fatherly neglect that had rendered them "immature."

Although mothers clearly shouldered most of Strecker's blame, fatherly indifference and weakness helped promote such immaturity. Men who curried favor with their children, never punished them, could not make decisions or deal with life's complexities, acted childlike when sick, or failed to tell their sons the "facts of life" all helped foster the pathology that afflicted so many thousands of young men during the war.[59] What these boys needed were real fathers, not affable but ineffectual "pops." One key was fatherly involvement. Strecker chided those men "who do not wish to be disturbed in their masculine pursuits by participating in the psychological development of their children." Father-child contact was absolutely crucial: "No man, whether he be the executive of a huge corporation or a humble laborer, has the right to evade his plain duty toward his children and his participation with his wife in the performance of that duty."[60] The stakes in all this were very high. Only "mature" children free of maternal domination could maintain democracy in the troubling years ahead: "Only if peace is handled by mature people will it succeed; only if nations as nations reflect maturity can the peace endure."[61]

Millions of Americans apparently shared these fears. Articles and testimonials abound on the subject. While some experts counseled home-front fathers to develop close emotional relationships with their children and to become models for their psychosocial development, others worried about fathers at war and how best to mitigate the potentially harmful impact of their absence. One way, endlessly repeated by child advisers, was for wives to remind their children constantly of their father. One mother kept her husband's presence alive for their two children by refusing to put away his personal effects, thus preserving "some of the masculinity in the household."[62] Another seemed confidant that her efforts to acquaint her daughter with her absent father had succeeded: "I was amazed at how many opportunities present themselves for talking about Daddy, for making him a part of our lives. And I know that when he comes home Debbie will experience no shock, for he will be no stranger to her."[63] Looking back, a veteran testified that his wife's efforts, along with those of many other wives as well, had been successful in this regard: "I, like many other men who had never seen their children," wrote John Waldman, "used to receive letter after letter that was meant to prepare me for parenthood. My wife, like many other wives, tried determinedly to teach her husband the joys and responsibilities of being a father—by correspondence."[64]

Variations on these themes appeared repeatedly, but many child specialists feared such efforts might be insufficient. Wartime absences reaffirmed the importance of fathers to the formation of sex-role identity; thus advisers urged mothers to provide surrogate fathers for their children. Boys in particular needed "masculine companionship and influence"; accordingly, "stray uncles or cousins" were urged to be masculine role models for their young relatives.[65] Columnist Catherine Mackenzie bluntly summed up such ideas: boys "need a man who will take them to do 'men's things' in a 'man's way.'"[66] Nor would just any man do. Psychologist Ada Hart Arlitt hoped that the father surrogates would come from the ranks of Boy Scout and YMCA leaders or from among outstanding male church workers, all worthy models for the five- to eight-year olds who inevitably shift affection from mother to father: "The process of transferring from the mother to the father is essential for emotional development since the girl has to love and respect some man early in life if she is to grow up to marry one and the boy needs to have some male ideal if he is to wish to grow up to be a high type of man."[67]

Try as they might, however, surrogates could not do the job. A father's presence in the family was simply too important to be left to part-time substitutes. Uncles, neighbors, and scout leaders might do what they could, but the absence of fathers in wartime reconfirmed their importance to personality development, sex-role identity, and family emotional health. As sociologists and psychologists assessed the impact on families of fathers' departure for war, their focus inevitably turned to children's personality formation. In keeping with larger cultural developments affecting the family, twentieth-century fathers' claims to indispensability—or claims made on their behalf—would ultimately be psychological.

Reports on the psychological indispensability of fathers appeared from many quarters. Case reports from psychologists, child guidance experts, social workers, and other mental health professionals noted a host of problems caused by the departure of fathers. Some boys became aggressive and unmanageable; others established seductive relationships with their mothers; some children became spoiled, others lonely and withdrawn; some children fell apart at school, others became tyrants in the home. Mother-child conflicts kept in check by the father's presence often flared when he departed. The psychiatrist David Levy, for example, described a boy of six who had become "very domineering toward his mother since his father's departure for the Army. He tells her to shut up, uses filthy language, and is beyond her control." Another child all but deserted his home: "A boy of 7 had been truanting from school and staying away from home overnight, sleeping under porches even in winter. This behavior began after his father, to whom he was much attached, went to the Army."[68] Some children became self-destructive. One four-year-old said little about his father's departure but later drove a rusty nail into his foot. Although soon healed, he refused to walk: "Despite all his mother's pleas and artful wiles, the boy remained on all fours until the day daddy came home. On that day he walked again, and there was no more trouble of that kind!"[69]

A father's departure could create severe depression in a child. One woman worried about the impact of her husband's departure on her son: "It seems as if his [her husband's] going would be the end of John. He is so terribly important to the child, especially now that he has come to feel proud of him and more like a father to him."[70] Reuben Hill's analysis of 135 Iowa families with absent fathers included one in which the man's departure "was no great sorrow" to his wife, "but her daughter did not share her attitude and moped constantly for daddy. She brooded alone for hours and became unresponsive and uncooperative, in spite of mother's insistence that they got along fine."[71] Amelia Igel reported on several such cases where the father's departure exacerbated preexisting problems, including one about a nine-year-old boy who "even strove to deny that the father was actually away and sought to find him in places where the father had been before—the railroad station, the paternal grandmother's home, the other woman's home. His security, centered in the father, was so threatened at the father's leaving that he turned to delinquent behavior." Other boys became uncontrollable, reverted to infantile mischief, or, if older, tried to assume a position of masculine dominance within their families. Families with strong fathers and weak mothers were especially hard hit by the men's departure for the service. Such women could scarcely maintain their homes when their husbands left for war; consequently, Igel wrote, "war deprives these children not of one parent but of both parents."[72]

Back at Home

As the war came to a close, family counselors tried to prepare both the GIs and their wives and children for the coming reunion. *Parents' Magazine* warned women that their husbands might find it difficult to adjust or readjust to the presence of children and that the GIs might resent the time their wives spent with the baby. Counselors advised fathers to be aware of their children's developmental stages and to avoid harboring unrealistic expectations of their toddlers. Perhaps even more important, fathers certainly must avoid meeting all child-rearing problems with more and harsher discipline, a predictable approach with harmful repercussions for the future: "This is the most unwise attitude Father can possibly adopt. He is meeting a critical phase in his relationship to junior which will fundamentally determine whether or not his son will learn to love and accept him or feel that Father is a threatening rival whom he can't love but must distrust and hate." Instead, the returning soldier must help his offspring discover that "it's fun to have a father, that any loss of Mother entailed is more than compensated for by having a kind, friendly man called Father around the house." To foster father-child togetherness, the experts advised the GIs not to be "too much the authoritative father in relation to your son." Because the boy may have acted as the "man of the house" in his father's absence, fathers must recognize the transformed nature of the father-son relationship: "A talk between equals who respect each other will do wonders."[73]

Such homely advice was not enough. Men's induction into the service and their subsequent return, child experts concluded, created profound psychological problems for their offspring. Although some sociological studies minimized father-child wartime difficulties and stressed the ability of families to cope with such tensions, those in the field of child psychology were far less sanguine.[74] In a series of studies involving first-time fathers away at war, psychologists concluded that the fathers' absence had undermined, in almost every conceivable way, the establishment of an affectionate, sympathetic, and loving relationship between the men and their children.[75]

Whether compared with their wives or with fathers who did not go off to war, these soldier-fathers simply did not measure up as parents. Their troubles began even before they arrived at home. For men at the front, the news of their first child's birth was welcome but somehow unconnected to their present lives. As one remembered, "As far as my reactions to having a son when I was overseas, I don't remember—oh, I had a certain amount of mild elation, but it wasn't real. My son didn't mean too much to me. In fact, he didn't mean a great deal for quite a long while after I came home."[76] Upon their return, veterans faced the threefold difficulty of becoming breadwinners, husbands, and fathers—imposing responsibilities that left the GIs feeling tense and inadequate. Under such conditions, the new fathers were often awkward and severe around their children, feelings heightened by their children's shyness and unresponsiveness to this stranger in the house. One GI recalled, "I can remember at the time I didn't seem to have any particular emotion one way or the other. I wasn't tremendously thrilled with the idea of seeing her [his daughter] and I didn't feel that she was any blight in my life either. I was just sort of noncommittal about the whole thing." Another had a similar reaction but was even more unresponsive to his daughter: "I will never forget the night I arrived home. . . . I remember feeling cold toward Ann. I didn't pick her up. She began crying. I was much more interested in my wife."[77]

Many veterans found it difficult to see their children as anything but a burden. Army psychologists reported that some men who already had children considered induction "a socially acceptable excuse for desert-ing their families" and welcomed army life "as a sort of return to bache-lor freedom and displayed only face-saving reluctance in accepting Uncle Sam's invitation to shed the mantle of 'family man' for a military uniform."[78] For many soldiers, the first child was an intruder who sym-bolized responsibilities they were unready to shoulder. One young fa-ther expressed his frustration: "My desire was to get away from it all— away from restrictions. . . . Any restrictions when I came back irritated me. We had to get up at 5:00 A.M. for the baby. I looked forward to spending a lot of time on the beach. But we had to take the baby. Then we had to bring him back for lunch and a nap. We never could enjoy the beach."[79]

This man was not alone. In one study of veterans, about half the sample of wartime fathers believed their baby came between them and their wife. As one GI remarked: "I was anxious to be with my wife every minute. I soon found there was very little privacy." The bedroom was no sanctuary. "Even in our room, the little girl was always busting in. She never let us alone a minute. . . . Every time I sat down beside my wife, our daughter would want something and my wife would get up and leave me and do it."[80] An element of the tragicomic slipped into some of the GIs' recollections: "Our daughter slept in the room with us. She would crawl out of bed when she wet it and get in bed with us." But the little girl had an even more annoying trait: "She used to wake up more than by chance when we were having intercourse. We'd have to move very quickly. . . . I'd get mad as hell. It was very frustrating."[81]

If fathers felt awkward around their children, children often were uncomfortable around their fathers, a feeling the men recalled as they looked back on painful meetings with toddlers they had never known. One father believed this early estrangement had affected his subse-quent relationship with his son: "Don was 14 months old on my return. I remember I took him and pretty soon he was just hollering. He just wouldn't come near me. I was upset but didn't know what to do about it . . . I don't think he ever took to me. There was something there." This father saw himself as an interloper. "I was just an unnecessary addition as far as he was concerned. . . . It's always been hard for me." Another sadly remembered feeling like an intruder: "My balloon burst very soon. I, a stranger, was interference with her and her mummy. . . . She cried because I was in the same room . . . she was unresponsive." This wariness could last for a long time: "For a good many weeks or even months after I got home, Fran and I were not very close. She was suspi-cious of me. She usually kept her distance; she didn't receive my affec-tions very well . . . as time went on it got me down a little." Or as another father remarked with some bitterness, "Even when he was two or three years old he just wouldn't let me come close to him. I didn't like it, I didn't like it a bit." All but two of the ex-soldiers in the Stolz sample believed their war-born children continued to be closer to their mothers, a sentiment foreign to the nonseparated fathers, who tended to describe the child as equally close to mother and father.[82]

What unfolded among these men and their offspring was a family drama that revealed only too well the importance of early father-child contact. Deprived of early involvement with their infants and confronting a difficult social and family situation, returning fathers often criticized their children's behavior and their wives' child-rearing practices. Most commonly, the veterans believed their wives had spoiled their children, a complaint made by sixteen of nineteen fathers in the Stolz study. One GI had sharp words for both his wife and his son: "My wife was more like Allen's servant than his mother. . . . I thought he was spoiled. I thought my wife couldn't handle him. He would have temper tantrums. He lacked proper respect." Another tried to discuss his concerns with his wife but made little headway: "I talked to my wife about how spoiled Mary was and my wife was hurt. She couldn't see it. She kept saying, 'She's such a little girl. She isn't naughty. She doesn't know any better.' But I didn't agree. . . . She had to be the center of everything. She monopolized mealtimes." Another father worried that his wife undermined his son's self-reliance: "She did everything for Dan. If he wanted to be rocked, he'd cry, and she'd rock him. He got so demanding she didn't do anything but wait on him. He couldn't do anything for himself. . . . If she's always cuddling him, always doing this and that and the other thing for him, he doesn't have to have any self-reliance."[83]

Intrusive grandparents exacerbated such problems. With husbands gone, thousands of mothers with infants went to live with the babies' grandparents, especially those on the mothers' side. Not surprisingly, grandmothers and grandfathers often played an active role in rearing the infant-toddler, an arrangement that could create difficulties when fathers returned from the war. Over half the fathers in Stolz's study disapproved of the grandparents' relation to their child, including one man who declared, "It made me just furious when my wife said she wanted to talk to her mother about what to do with our daughter. It cut pretty deep." In almost every instance, fathers found grandparents too lenient in their child rearings. "I felt the grand parents spoiled our daughter," said one vet, "and I began to feel they resented me. When I'd correct her, they'd always have an excuse for her. Sometimes they would even tell me I shouldn't talk that way to my daughter." He had walked into the situation as an outsider, and there he remained: "Sometimes I felt they all would have been happier if I hadn't come home. I felt out of things, as if I didn't belong. They all seemed a tight little family with me on the outside."[84] Or as another recalled as he watched his son playing with his grandfather, "I wondered how long it would take me to convince Peter that, after all, I am his real father and that his grandfather commands a position of only historic significance."[85]

Conflicts about child rearing were by no means restricted to grandparents. The great majority of veterans in the Stolz study complained about their wives' tendency to spoil the child. As one ex-soldier tersely put it, "When Kate came to visit me at camp, I thought she was spoiled. I felt she needed disciplining and I spanked her several times."[86] Once reunited, the veterans assumed the role of disciplinarian and were generally more authoritarian and harsh with their children than their wives had been. A man described how he got his finicky, stubborn son to eat: "If you tell him to eat something, he'll do everything under the sun. Finally you grab him and open his mouth and put it in and tell him 'Now keep it there!'"[87] Such harshness could create marital discord. As another father recalled: "We almost separated over the fact that we didn't agree on how to raise children. If the boy and I got in an argument over how to eat, she'd stand up for him, right in front of him. We had many severe arguments every day."[88]

Although the men felt inadequate to care for their child's daily needs, almost all considered themselves more capable than their wives of disciplining their offspring. As one told an investigator, "I thought he was very spoiled and I realized immediately I'd have to straighten him out because his mother wouldn't."[89] Another had no doubt about the efficacy of his methods: "The only way to make Joe behave was to discipline him. I decided I had better take over. If it was my time to put him to bed, I slapped him—then later I spanked him." The method worked to the father's satisfaction and seemed to prove that the boy needed the strong hand of a father: "That seemed to work; that was what he needed—someone strong to make him mind. Joe was really a hard child for my wife to bring up. Between two and one-half and four I took over and spanked him hard—it had amazing results."[90] Veterans, in fact, used harsher discipline than fathers who had not been at war; whereas the latter more often reasoned, compromised, and used other progressive means of discipline, the veterans turned to scolding, threats, and, most often of all, spankings to enforce their will.[91]

Many also feared their sons had become sissies under their mothers' guidance. Twice as many war-separated as nonseparated fathers complained about the gender-appropriateness of their war-born child's behavior. Said one, "Allen likes to play with girls. . . . I've talked to Allen about being a sissy. I don't want to have anybody picking on him. I want him to fight back if he has to." Another ex-serviceman complained that his son had "very little spunk" and admitted that he "had a feeling that Ray was a 'sissy.'" A third father worried that his son "has played with more little girls than boys. . . . If a boy pushes Ken, he will never fight back, he'll come home." A father with a son of a similar disposition worried about his boy's future: "Have you ever seen Bruce fight anybody? He can be attacked. . . . Someone will come up and swing on him and he won't fight back. . . . Where's the old drive? Where's the old preservation? Is he just going to be an organism to be molded any way anybody wants him to go?" One man explained the root of such passivity as he reflected on his own son's unwillingness to fight with other boys: "I think this may be due to the fact that I was away at war and Don was in a feminine, protected environment."[92]

Inappropriate gender-role behavior was only part of the problem. Returning fathers also found more fault with their child's eating, sleeping, bed-wetting, whining, and thumb-sucking behavior than those fathers who had remained at home. They also tended to be more critical of their child's social behavior, as illustrated by one man who said of his son, "He's the most bossy kid I ever saw. He's always got somebody in tow. Has to run the whole thing." Said another of his boy, "He always wants to be *it*. He sometimes exploits kids—always being pulled in the wagon, never pulling."[93] Unlike the patience and tolerance exhibited by nonseparated fathers, former soldiers often became exasperated with their children's behavior. One father, for example, found his daughter's bedtime behavior intolerable: "When I first came home Kate was spoiled, she would not go to sleep without being rocked, a habit her grandmother had instilled. I felt she needed discipline and spanked her several times . . . I didn't approve of her taking toys to bed with her. She used to take a blanket to bed with her and I didn't think that was necessary. . . . We often had difficulty with her at nap time. Kate always made a fuss and I would spank her." Overall, war-separated fathers mentioned half as many positive and twice as many negative traits in their war-born offspring as fathers who did not go to war.[94]

Such tensions translated into relatively distant relationships between these fathers and their war-born children. The ex-GIs overwhelmingly felt that their war-born children were closer to their mothers, whereas fathers who did not go off to war pictured the war-born child as equally close to both parents.[95] One father rather sadly concluded that things had changed very little since the war: "My wife is the main one in his life. I don't think he's ever really accepted me." Said another, "His mother has been closer to Albert than I will ever be."[96]

Given this situation, war-separated fathers consistently had closer relationships with their second children than with their first. Of the sixteen war-separated fathers who had another child after the war, fourteen felt closer to this second child, a disparity of sentiment not evident among men who had remained on the home front. An ex-soldier voiced such favoritism rather plainly: "In my mind, Edward is my baby. I often call him Babe, my baby, see? . . . My wife says that the younger boy is *my* child." So, too, did another who said of his children, "I don't feel the same affinity for Rick as I do for the other children. The wife often asks me whether I love him. I *do* . . . but other kids are more loveable." Such favoritism could even overcome fathers' traditional affinity for sons over daughters:

> I missed Don when he was one to fourteen months, and I just didn't know how a baby looked, so when Maria was born I showed more concern, more interest with her. All the little things that she was learning which were not new to my wife but new to me. . . . Maybe I did try a little harder to play up to her because I was a little afraid I had lost my Don. And Maria when she became "socialized," when she got out of her crib to look around and become a member of the family, I was there— and she adjusted to me and I had adjusted to her.[97]

In the judgment of the psychologists conducting these studies, the separation between the GIs and their war-born children had a lasting and negative impact. The war-separated firstborns appeared to have more serious problems in eating, sleeping, and elimination. They were also less independent, more prone to unfounded fears, and less successful in making friends with other children. Among other children, they spent considerable time "as onlookers and fringers"—*of* the group but not *in* it—and though somewhat less aggressive as a rule than the nonseparated children, when they did assert themselves, they became more hostile than the nonseparated children.[98] Their relationships with adults mirrored their relationships with other children: "It seems that the war-separated children do not feel free with adults and cannot act naturally and easily in interpersonal relations with them."[99] In short, the wartime separation of children and fathers had left lasting psychological scars on both parties.

War and American Fatherhood

The crisis of war forced Americans to consider fatherhood from new perspectives. Should fathers fight, for example, and if so, did the benefits outweigh the costs? If they had to fight, was their sacrifice best conceived by appeals to abstract and lofty ideals or by emphasis on their obligation to protect their families? And what problems did their absence from and reunion with children pose? The answers to these questions underscored the importance of the domestic and the psychological. As to the former, the popular iconography suggested that men fought the war to get back to a pleasant home with a wife, children, and a Nash Rambler.[100] As to the latter, the war affirmed the importance of fathers to the psychological well-being of children. After all, as a scholar worried about the wartime absence of fathers wrote, a man taught his daughter "to understand and appreciate masculine interests . . . [and] saves his young son from restricting himself to effeminate interests."[101]

It may be too much to say the war succeeded in reestablishing the centrality of fathers to the American family. Yet, much of the discussion of the previous decade had focused on the marginality of fathers, on the material and psychological setbacks they had experienced as the Depression took its toll. The war years ended that focus. Fathers were either back at work supporting families or they had entered the armed services and were, with other GIs, grimly struggling to "get the goddam thing over and get home."[102] Getting back home was the war's purpose, but home for men would mean more than breadwinning. Fatherhood was also about nurture, companionship, and personality development. The war, in fact, had confirmed that children really did need the type of fathers who had been summoned by psychologists over two decades before: nurturant, sensitive, companionate fathers secure in their own identity who could help to shape the personalities of their children. Paternal commitment and understanding held the key; their forced absence during the war had proven as much. As one veteran told a psychologist: "Alma and I had a hard time. Now I can see it. I get a perspective I never had before. It was so different with Pauline [second child]. I saw her from the beginning. If you want to put it in a nutshell, you could say it like this. I was never home with Alma when she was little and helpless. I never felt she needed to be cuddled and protected. . . . I feel I don't give Alma the affection I give the other children. I try to, especially lately I try. She really is getting to be a very nice child."[103]

This man's confession and lament presaged developments that would dominate the discourse on family life in the late 1940s and 1950s. In restoring fatherhood to a central place in the analysis of the family, the war years set the stage for the conservative family ideology of the postwar years. By emphasizing the contributions of fathers to social order, democracy, middle-class capitalism, eugenic trends, personality development, and psychological health, family researchers, politicians, and ideologues reemphasized the importance of fatherhood after its decline in the 1930s. But they did so without challenging a sex-based division of labor that relegated women to the home and left men in control of political, economic, and social affairs. War and its aftermath had made Alma's father aware of his shortcomings and more sensitive to his children's needs, but it had also laid a conservative foundation for the domestic structures of the next decade.

9

Fatherhood and the Great American Barbecue, 1945–1965

IN THE 1955 MOVIE *REBEL WITHOUT A CAUSE*, JIM, JUDY, AND PLATO—the three main characters—personify troubled youth of the 1950s. Jim drinks, smokes, fights, drives suicidally, and is a seething mass of adolescent angst. His girlfriend, Judy, represents the female side of youth rebellion as she struggles with her own inner demons. Plato, the most troubled of them all, is a lonesome, psychologically scarred boy who temporarily finds a measure of security with Jim and Judy in an abandoned Los Angeles mansion. These unlikely rebels at first flush have no reason to rebel against a society that promises so much. They have nice homes, cars, and clothes. What they do not have, however, are nice families. In particular, they all have dysfunctional fathers who embody three distinct cultural anxieties about fatherhood in the 1950s. Plato's father is simply absent, and Judy's father is an overbearing, strict, unsympathetic man unnerved by his adolescent daughter's budding sexuality. Jim's father, by contrast, is kind, understanding, henpecked, and sympathetic to a fault; his son can neither identify with nor respect him. Throughout the movie, Jim begs his father to be a man, to stand up for himself, "to knock his mother cold, just once," to become the kind of father Jim so desperately needs.

But just how was a father to behave? Clearly, adequate breadwinning was not enough: Jim's and Judy's fathers occupied secure if undefined niches in the middle class of postwar Los Angeles, and Plato appeared to come from an even wealthier background. Rebellious without tangible cause, these troublemakers emerged not from the ranks of the poor but from families who possessed an endless array of consumer goods. Instead of grinding poverty, adolescents like Jim, Judy, and Plato were surrounded by cars, cosmetics, and clothes. Their fathers provided everything the children could materially need, so what caused their rebellion? If material comfort could not bring happiness, what did these young people want?

Hollywood provided few answers. Only the police detective who first muscled then befriended Jim seemed to have the right blend of masculine sympathy and manly toughness. Quite clearly, Jim's father was no proper model. Nor could Judy's father offer any guidance.. He was too authoritarian and repressed to be of help. Plato's father was the most useless of all; he and his estranged wife had left their son in the care of a kindly, well-meaning maid. Faced with such alternatives, the three teenagers tried to establish a surrogate family in the empty mansion rather than suffer the indignities and disappointments of home.

Hollywood was on to something here. The movie unfolds in Los Angeles, the symbol of postwar affluence and suburbanization, and the fathers in *Rebel without a Cause* had more than fulfilled their breadwinning obligations. But cars and hi-fi's were not enough. Affluence could induce conformity, emasculation, and, as the movie suggested, a hollowness at which the young would aimlessly rebel. To avoid such a fate, fathers had to be more than feckless money changers. Breadwinning remained critical, but experts in the 1950s and early 1960s insisted that fathers imbued with a democratic, permissive, nurturing sensibility could produce well-adjusted offspring capable of resisting the new dangers of the age—authoritarianism, juvenile delinquency, schizophrenia, and homosexuality. The 1950s and early 1960s, in fact, represent the last hurrah of the first phase of the new fatherhood. The postwar world of rising affluence and rapid suburbanization was an ideal environment for emphasizing fatherly responsibilities. To support children financially while fostering their sex-role adjustment became the essence of "maturity," "responsibility," and manhood itself. To do so in material comfort signified the superiority of the "American way"; to do so without becoming a drone represented one of the main challenges of the age.

None of this should be confused with the second phase of the new fatherhood that arose with the advent of changing work patterns and feminism. Family togetherness and paternal engagement was not a feminist ideology. It did not challenge the assumption that men's primary responsibility was breadwinning while mothers' was child rearing; it simply enlarged the significance of fatherhood while leaving intact the patriarchal assumptions underlying a gender-based division of labor.

Fatherhood in the 1950s did more than reaffirm the importance of the personal, familial dimensions of people's lives. It also helped delineate class boundaries: nonauthoritarian child rearing, fatherly involvement with children, and male interest in domestic life became key markers of middle-class respectability in the postwar world. In a nation in which blue-collar aristocrats were assuming some of the material prerogatives of white-collar bureaucrats, styles of parenting became one way to reestablish class boundaries. If consumption was declining as an effective barometer of class standing, child rearing could become a new index of middle-class sensibility. And where better to realize the key assumptions of masculine domesticity than in the burgeoning middle-class suburbs of the postwar era? Here middle-class men had the job security, financial wherewithal, education, and leisure to practice a style of child rearing that underscored private rather than public life and solidified the social standing of middle-class men imbued with status anxieties.[1]

Breadwinning and the Baby Boom

Soldiers returning from World War II faced an uncertain future. With memories of the Depression still fresh and with experts predicting a resumption of high unemployment, men worried about finding a job.[2] Those who were already fathers had families to support, and those who hoped to become so could hardly risk starting a family without secure employment. Moreover, despite a massive influx of women into the wartime labor force, the general assumption persisted that the responsibility of breadwinning lay with husbands and fathers. Consequently, despite working women's documented desire to keep their wartime jobs, layoffs became their lot.[3]

The insistence that women relinquish their wartime jobs came from many quarters. Some argued that working women neglected their children and risked the future of the home. Others laid the rising wartime rate of juvenile delinquency at the feet of working women. Fearing that women had gotten "out of hand" during the war, the Barnard sociologist Willard Waller worried about the future of the family and called for a restoration of traditional patriarchal relationships: "Women must bear and rear children; husbands must support them."[4] Union leaders, workingmen, politicians, business leaders, and the public generally agreed: women must step aside and make room for the returning veterans lest male unemployment rise and family tranquility decline. A *Fortune* magazine survey of 1946 reflected such views. Twenty-eight percent of male and 17 percent of female respondents believed a "man should have preference over all women for any job that he can fill satisfactorily," and 46 percent of men and 49.5 percent of women believed that "only women who have to support themselves should have an equal chance with men for jobs in business and industry." The same survey also reported that both men and women believed homemaking was a full-time job and that homemakers had more interesting jobs than working women.[5]

Caught in an ideological bind that emphasized female domesticity and male providing, women found that such sentiments overwhelmed their desires to retain their jobs. As war plants reconverted to peacetime production or simply shut down, women workers faced layoff rates 75 percent higher than men's. Other companies revised their age requirements to discriminate against older women, and some large corporations reinstituted restrictions against hiring wives.[6] Although such policies only temporarily affected rates of female employment—as we shall see, women continued to enter the labor force in unprecedented numbers even in the domestic 1950s—they illustrated the pervasive belief that men supported families and women maintained them.[7]

For millions of American families, however, female wage labor was beside the point. Whereas older, married women made significant gains in employment in the 1940s and 1950s, the most significant cultural story of the two decades actually lay elsewhere—in maternity wards, to be exact. The baby boom of the postwar years has already received extensive attention from demographers and, more recently, historians, but its meaning for fathers has been largely unexamined. Why did men and women who had steadily reduced their fertility for approximately one hundred and fifty years suddenly take a new turn? What cultural forces impelled men to propagate and support the army of infants that arrived in America from 1947 to 1964?

To answer such questions, one must first jettison the "happy days" image cultivated by network television and Hollywood productions. Although optimism generated by a booming economy, expanding suburbs, and readily available housing loans no doubt played a critical part, a recent analysis of the 1940s characterized its culture as "the age of doubt," and a study of family life in the 1940s and 1950s highlighted the anxieties and fears that drove people homeward to find security.[8] Thus, understanding why young men marched to the altar at a younger age than their own parents and grandparents and why they seemed so eager to assume the responsibilities of fatherhood involves issues of male identity and cultural anxieties in the postwar era. Or as Barbara Ehrenreich has suggested, the rush to fatherhood came in no small part because to do otherwise courted suspicion about one's sexual identity and maturity. To marry and sire children was "mature," "responsible," a sign of adulthood; to remain a bachelor signified immaturity, irresponsibility, and perhaps even worse, homosexuality.[9]

In short, the willingness to shoulder the responsibilities of fatherhood and breadwinning was the hallmark of mature manhood in the 1950s. In *Death of a Salesman,* Biff Loman expresses this yearning to his brother, Hap, as he reflects on the aimlessness of his own life:

> And whenever spring comes to where I am, I suddenly get the feeling, my God, I'm not gettin' anywhere! What the hell am I doing, playing around with horses, twenty-eight dollars a week! I'm thirty-four years old, I oughta be makin' my future.

But neither Biff nor Hap could ever grow up; they remain adolescents at heart. In one scene, Hap becomes wildly enthusiastic when he fantasizes about the sporting goods business he and his brother might someday operate: "Wait! We form two basketball teams, see? Two waterpolo teams. We play each other. It's a million dollars worth of publicity. Two brothers, see? The Loman Brothers." Warming to his own enthusiasm, Hap underscores the appeal of such a venture: "And the beauty of it is, Biff, it wouldn't be like a business. We'd be playin' ball again."[10]

What had left Biff and Hap boy-men was their failure to pass through the "developmental tasks of early adulthood," including finding a spouse, rearing children, and starting an occupation.[11] To reject marriage invited doubt about a man's masculinity and sparked suspicions that the poor soul suffered some infantile neurosis, some pitiful and hopeless attachment to his mother. At best, such men were escapist; at worst, homosexual. As Ehrenreich makes clear, even literary figures did not escape indictment. One psychologist characterized Rip Van Winkle's long sleep as a way to avoid "the hateful responsibilities of work and marriage" and Henry Thoreau's solitary move to Walden as evidence that Thoreau could not adjust to the "quietly desperate world of work and marriage."[12]

But there were even stronger sanctions against men unwilling to shoulder the burdens of maturity. Men who neither married nor assumed the responsibilities of fatherhood and breadwinning, so went the argument, began a precipitous slide toward homosexuality. As late as

1969, psychiatrist Lionel Ovesey described how men who failed in some aspect of the normative male role might lose confidence in their heterosexual identity and take on that of the homosexual. Any sexual, social, or vocational failure that beset men, wrote Ovesey, "may be perceived as a failure in the masculine role and, which is worse, may be symbolically extended through an equation that is calculated only to intensify the anxiety incident to the failure." This equation was one of ruthless logic: "I am a failure = I am castrated = I am not a man = I am a woman = I am a homosexual."[13] Overt homosexuality soon followed unless the man overcame his adaptive failures, presumably by getting married, having children, and becoming a successful breadwinner. It is difficult to know how much to make of this analysis. The average twenty-three-year-old male in 1954 did not wake up one morning and decide to marry and support a wife and child lest the neighbors in the next tract house think him a homosexual. Sanctions against deviance are more tacit and subtle, more embedded within unspoken assumptions, more a part of the accepted logic of everyday life.

What Ehrenreich is suggesting and what others have affirmed is that a "reproductive consensus" did exist in the postwar era.[14] During the baby boom, most Americans assumed that marriage was the ideal adult state, that parenthood was preferable to nonparenthood, and that having at least two children was superior to having only one.[15] This "procreation ethic," as Landon Jones has termed it, fueled the baby boom, but the boom also came in response to deeper cultural anxieties. As Elaine Tyler May has explained in her book on Cold War families, "the joys of raising children would compensate for the thwarted expectations in other areas of their lives. For men who were frustrated at work, for women who were bored at home, and for both who were dissatisfied with the unfulfilled promise of sexual excitement, children might fill the void." And fill it they did. Surveys suggest that fathers found fatherhood highly satisfying. In a 1957 study, 63 percent of some 850 fathers had a positive attitude toward parenting, but perhaps more significantly, the same figure for mothers was only 54 percent. Moreover, fathers tended to view parenthood as less restrictive than did mothers, a result likely stemming from women's greater child-rearing obligations.[16] Although men were not without complaints—the 1957 evidence, for example, implied that men wanted to be psychologically closer to their children—most seemed to find fatherhood an important source of self-identity.[17]

Testimonials from fathers about the joys and importance of fatherhood certainly suggest as much. As one father noted, "I know it's just as important for our daughter to know her father and for me to know our daughter as it is for me to be able to supply her with the necessities and an occasional luxury of life." Another was less surprised by his daughter's rapid motor development than by "the sense of excitement that came from watching her and the immense pleasure she communicated."[18] When a researcher asked eighty-five New York City fathers from a variety of backgrounds what satisfactions they received from fatherhood, 76 percent mentioned companionship and almost half, the simple fact of having children. Fathers recorded not merely the fun they had with their offspring but their happiness "in being appreciated, the new sense of values, the new purpose which life has, and their stake in perpetuating the species." Ruth Tasch concluded that fatherhood was an important part of male identity, no doubt because it was so multifunctional: "[F]ather is a companion, child rearer, guide and teacher, disciplinarian, example of masculinity, and economic provider. In a creative sense, father is a contributor to the species and its advancement."[19]

Movies and especially the new medium of television promoted this equation of manhood and fatherhood. "Particularly on television, the home entertainment," Elaine May writes, "fatherhood became the center of a man's identity."[20] Work was ancillary at best to the television fathers, whose real life existed within suburban living rooms. The occupations of men like Ward Cleaver and Ozzie Nelson were either vaguely defined or unknown. They forged their screen identities as fathers, not workers. Secure in their suburban homes, untouched by financial problems, marital discord, or political passions of any kind, these men's "work" was the resolution of the minor crises that beset their children. Only men like Ed Norton, the feckless and childless sewer worker in the "Honeymooners," or Sergeant Ernie Bilko, whose "children" were the buffoons and oddballs in his platoon, made much mention of their occupation.[21]

Driven by a variety of forces, apparently undaunted by the enormous emotional and financial responsibilities of fatherhood, middleclass men of the 1950s accepted the challenge of fatherhood with remarkable aplomb. This point was evidenced by fathers interviewed by Robert Sears and his staff in the late 1950s. In lengthy discussions with some forty fathers associated with Stanford University, Sears's research staff explored a host of questions, including fathers' attitudes about breadwinning and fatherly responsibilities. It is striking how clearly the men saw breadwinning as a male obligation and how casually they accepted the responsibilities of fatherhood in general. Almost to a man, for example, they were happy that they were the sole breadwinners and that their wives did not work for wages. Asked whether he wanted his

wife to return to work, one man replied, "Well, I don't think it's necessary for her to," and another responded more bluntly, "No I'd just as
soon she didn't as a matter of fact, although I would never object to it."
Such an objection was unlikely in any event: "But I don't think she has
particularly ever been anxious to be the career woman or anything."[22]
Several fathers' answers were close to the heart of functionalist sociology. As one man put it, "She's pretty much—and I agree—held to the
philosophy that until the child's school age that mothers [sic] time
should be at least in large part, spent with the child, although I don't
think that if she has other interests and activities she should become
completely tied to him." Said another, "If we didn't have children, that
would be another thing—but since we do I would prefer that she didn't
as long as I'm able to provide—satisfactorily."[23]

Although a physician noted that his wife's earlier career as a psychiatric social worker helped to push him toward a specialization in psychiatry and that he "did have some feeling about her not having outside
interests," his concern did not extend to the resumption of her career:
"No, I don't think I would like her to work now—or at any time, I
don't—I don't even, even after our children are fully grown and out of
the house, I still don't think I'd want her to return."[24] Perhaps he
shared the sentiments of another man who conceded that his wife's permanent departure from the work force when she was five months'
pregnant hurt the family's financial situation. Nevertheless, the personal benefits he reaped from this decision clearly outweighed the loss
of income: "Rather have her home than working—make it easier on me
that . . . uh, she is not working. Then there are certain things I don't
have to do around the house."[25]

Certain they knew where woman's place was, these same men were
hardly weighed down by the responsibilities of fatherhood. One father,
for example, spoke for many when he described his casual approach to
having children: "I don't think I ever gave any thought to . . . a . . . most
certainly I never gave any thought to financial responsibilities, because
that wasn't a problem, and I don't . . . I don't really think I gave much
thought to—'you're a father now.'"[26] Another worried far more about
succeeding in graduate school than about becoming a father, largely because he viewed the latter as "natural": "Well, I mean, I'm all in favor of
fatherhood (laughs). I think I was probably more worried about succeeding at Stanford in my studies than I was about—to me that was a
bigger responsibility—trying to succeed there than having Petey. I
mean, children are a rather natural thing, when it comes right down to
it."[27] Other men also gave evidence that they had given the responsibilities of fatherhood little thought. A father of an adopted girl admitted

he had been caught off guard by the demands of parenthood: "Well, I would say primarily, it was we realized that prior to this time we had been rather free with our, our . . . plans. If we decided that we wanted to do something we just did it and all of a sudden we realized well now wait a minute, we have some new responsibility here and we just can't do this—sort of spur of the moment."[28] A father who recalled that news of his wife's unplanned pregnancy left him in shock—"I thought the world had come to an end"—had no qualms about the responsibilities of fatherhood: "Didn't bother me, uh, at all—I . . . just after a while, just like anything else. And that . . . this is perhaps because I worked since I was . . . fairly young."[29]

For one man, becoming a father was just one more addition to an already busy life: "Well, I think there were an awful lot of—many, many new things going on (yeah) and this was one more new thing and uh, I don't think I ever—well, I had no passionate or strong feelings of being a father really until after he was oh a year or two old that (yes)."[30] Two men felt well prepared for the duties of fatherhood, thanks to their experience in the military: "I guess I'd gotten used to responsibility in the Navy, because I was responsible for about a fifteen-man minesweep detail, who could mangle themselves pretty easily, or get out of hand, so . . . I didn't even think about it."[31] A second veteran attributed his equanimity about becoming a father to his military experience and his general maturity: "I don't believe I changed much. I had looked forward to it. I believe I'm older than most fathers when they first have children, let's see I was—35 I believe when David was born and . . . I think I was more mature in many ways having been through the war—the responsibility of going to school while I was married. I think all of these things prepared me pretty well so it wasn't a shock or a great added responsibility at all."[32] Although one man confessed he did not like night feedings, his positive feelings outweighed the negative and his sense of responsibility was mixed with pride: "Um . . . and from this standpoint, the feeling of responsibility was an important one—it was a good feeling for me. Uh, . . . a feeling of pride, a feeling of his having my name."[33] Finally, a father of two encapsulated the sentiments at the heart of the baby boom. Asked about the responsibilities of fatherhood, he replied: "I kind of . . . in a way, I looked forward to it. It . . . a . . . oh, I think I was ready for it at that time." He even admitted that he might have been a bit overconfident but that his confidence was well placed: "I probably thought I was more ready for it than I really was, but . . . a . . . oh, we planned for it, and kind of centered everything around it at the time—it was a lot of fun."[34]

"Fun" was the operative word. Evidence on the sharing of child rearing and household tasks suggests that fathers in the 1950s continued to profit from the gender-based division of labor so central to the structure of twentieth-century family relationships. Despite bold claims that "today's young husband isn't ashamed to be caught wearing an apron" and that "there is no longer any sharp dividing line between man's work and woman's," systematic analyses suggest otherwise.[35] A study of over one thousand Florida families in 1953 documented men's small role in household tasks. Fewer than 4 percent of fathers made beds, only about 5 percent cleaned and dusted, and fewer than 2 percent did any ironing. As to child rearing, fathers did a minimum of day-to-day care: fewer than 6 percent tended to their children's clothing and fewer than one-fourth got their children up on time. Although three-fourths of the fathers taught their children right from wrong, 92 percent of mothers did so, and though about 40 percent of fathers cared for their sick children, over 95 percent of mothers assumed this responsibility.[36] In another study, a high percentage of fathers recorded doing some kind of daily care—although the frequency of such care was not reported—but far more men considered such work a burden rather than a pleasure. In fact, routine child care ranked first as a source of problems and fifteenth as a source of satisfaction among the eighty-five fathers in this study.[37]

Quite clearly fatherly responsibilities had little to do with the day-to-day care of children or home upkeep. Men's belief in the sanctity of the division of labor and the ideology of male breadwinning precluded sustained involvement in daily housework and the less appealing aspects of child care. And though theorists of expressive, permissive, and democratic perspectives on child rearing sometimes called fathers to the diaper pail and the changing table, their basic hope was that men would play a more central role in the overall psychological development of their children.[38] As the child expert Dorothy Koehring put it, father had a special place in the nursery, "not necessarily that of cook and bottle washer, unless there is an emergency or unless he particularly enjoys these routine activities" but as a model of responsibility, faithfulness, and, more simply, "a well-loved presence."[39]

The fathers in the Sears study certainly viewed their parental role in these terms. Most of the men admitted they took little daily care of their young children: "Ah . . . I don't think I changed him [that is, diapers] much. Oh, within the first year I guess I did some—I did take care of him a little bit, when my wife was out or something, to do shopping and things of this sort, but . . . certainly didn't do very much."[40] Another man explained that his work schedule prohibited him from doing much child care: "Um—well—what kind of care—let's see, you feed him, and clean him—what else can you do in the first year? I used to take him for walks about the end of the eighth month, and I always used to do things like that, but . . . I was travelling—oh, gee, at least half the time, I was on this coast, or South, or something." He also had low regard for child care: "So . . . a . . . as far as any—I mean—do I know how to do it? Heck, yeh, nothing to it. Does it bother me? No, uh, just a mechanical task—like Public Sanitation or something. I didn't do it very often—I wasn't there, or I just didn't do it."[41] Two fathers defended their uninvolvement in terms that would have made sense to functionalist sociologists. Asked how much care he gave his infant daughter, the father laughingly replied, "I did as little as possible. The baby was breast fed and I had nothing to do with that—and I would on *rare* occasions change her." He explained his lack of involvement in simple but telling terms: "I think it was more the wife's duty than mine."[42] Much the same response came from a graduate student who explained why he did not do more direct child care: "I'm kind of against that sort of thing. I figure the mother can take care of the child and let the father worry about other things."[43]

Breadwinning, Consumption, and Conformity

For most of these men, "other things" involved breadwinning and the psychological and intellectual development of their children. The consumer culture of the 1920s had been derailed by the Depression and the shortages of World War II. But after the war, Americans enjoyed high levels of personal consumption supported by the earnings of baby boom fathers. Simultaneously, the postwar culture pressed fathers to foster their children's heterosexual identity while adopting modes of child rearing that would promote companionship, democracy, mental health, and social order.

In the postwar years, Americans purchased staggering numbers of homes, cars, clothes, toys, and diapers. The exact figures need not detain us—1.5 billion cans of baby food in 1953, $50 million in diapers in 1957—but the cultural significance of these purchases is important.[44] In one survey from the early 1950s of eighty-five New York City fathers, Ruth Tasch found that breadwinning was the second-most-cited responsibility, just barely trailing "guide and teacher." To these men, father was "'the guy who pays the bill,' the one 'to see that children are clothed and fed,' the 'someone (who) has to bring in money,' who is 'a good meal ticket.'"[45] Such self-perceptions should come as no surprise: fathers made most of the money that bought the new goods filling homes in the expanding suburbs. But the cultural meaning they attributed to this unprecedented consumption remains unexplored.

Part of the explanation lies in the larger meaning of consumption. Not until the 1920s did a full-blown consumer culture emerge that promised to enhance personal vitality, "real life," and happiness and to fill the void created by deep-rooted changes in residential patterns, work, religion, and gender relationships.[46] These assumptions lost a good deal of their cultural saliency during the Depression and the war years, but they reemerged after World War II as consumption, especially domestic consumption, defined the good life and male maturity and responsibility. In the postwar era, to be a man was to be a father, and to be a father required providing a world of goods for wife and children. In the Tasch study, twenty-six of the eighty-five fathers explicitly mentioned providing more for their families than immediate necessities. Caught up in an ever-changing middle-class standard of living, these men now sought comfortable suburban homes and music lessons, sporting goods, summer camps, and finally a college education for their offspring.[47] With VA and FHA loans in hand, they set off for the new suburbs and soon filled their tract houses with washing machines, clothes dryers, furniture, vacuum cleaners, stoves, refrigerators, automobiles, and, perhaps most significantly, television sets.

Television became the consumer item par excellence, both a product of consumption and, thanks to broadcast advertising, the great engine of consumption that helped the postwar baby boomers become "the first generation of children to be isolated by Madison Avenue as an identifiable market."[48] And *isolated* is the critical word. Television played the key role in the segmentation of family consumption, in separating the "needs" of children from those of parents. Whether marketing coonskin caps, Hula Hoops, or Barbie dolls, television helped transform an army of babies into an army of buyers. The fathers who made this buying possible by readily taking on the responsibilities of breadwinning thus found themselves in a difficult position. Television, the "third parent," continually interceded between children and their parents by creating special demands that could be satisfied only by spending money. Thus, the successful breadwinner outfitted his home not only with necessities but also with a host of goods demanded by his children. In this way, television advertising intruded upon and distorted father-child relationships. Worried that advertising mystified the real effort involved in earning a living, Bruno Bettelheim made the point: "They [advertisements] harass the child with how desirable it is to have a new car or dishwasher and how easy these are to get."[49]

Bettelheim's utilitarianism belied him here. Children were less interested in dishwashers than in records, clothes, and cosmetics. The children and teenage market soared in the postwar years, some of it underwritten by baby-sitting and lawn-mowing earnings, most of it by the earnings of fathers. If, as the Lynds observed, consumption was becoming increasingly individuated in the 1920s, children's purchases became one of the hallmarks of the consumer culture after 1950. In 1956, Elvis Presley had five gold records, and within a few years Dick Clark's "American Bandstand" pulled in twenty million weekday viewers, popularizing one song after another between commercial breaks for Clearasil. Record sales rose from $182 million in 1954 to $521 million in 1960. In 1964 the nation's twenty-two million teenagers, armed with weekly allowances that averaged six dollars for boys and four dollars for girls, descended on the drugstores and record shops of America to deposit some $12 billion per year. Coupled with the $13 billion their parents spent on them, the $25 billion youth market was truly staggering.[50] Cars, phones, televisions, cosmetics, records, fast food, and clothes all became vital elements of this new youth market, a sure sign that breadwinning had taken on new meaning. Television's relentless huckstering compelled fathers to satisfy the ever-changing, seemingly endless wants of their children. Yet, how could fathers compete with Elvis? Better to buy "Love Me Tender" and avoid a fight than to take a stand and incur the hostility of a forever wronged teenager.

Such purchases, however, did more than temporarily satisfy the insatiable. Men's ability to satisfy their families' endless consumer wants became the measure of American success in the Cold War. As Elaine May explains in her recent book on American families in the Cold War, the suburban ranch home with its breadwinning father, stay-at-home mother, and well-clad children symbolized the superiority of free enterprise over Soviet communism. The real race, as Vice President Nixon implied in the famous 1959 kitchen debate with Soviet Premier Nikita Khrushchev, was not the arms race or the space race but the consumer race.[51] To Nixon, the ability of both middle- and working-class American men to provide so many goods represented the real strength of the American system. "The family home," May writes, "would be the place where a man could display his success through the accumulation of consumer goods. Women, in turn, would reap rewards for domesticity by surrounding themselves with commodities." And children, May might have added, would reflect the achievements of their fathers by the clothes they wore, the activities they could afford, and the growing number of consumer goods they could purchase.[52]

Postwar consumption in the suburbs thus reasserted and reshaped the primacy of the traditional breadwinning role. As millions of men moved with their families to the suburbs after World War II, they entered a new world of goods that refashioned traditional conceptions of male obligation.[53] A survey of middle-class American men in the 1950s found that consumerism inspired them in the workplace and that they worked less for personal satisfaction and more for a secure and affluent family life. Asked by the psychologist E. Lowell Kelly what marriage had brought them, men responded predictably by first listing love and children, but a sizable number noted that marriage had given them a sense of purpose and responsibility. As one man put it, "Being somewhat lazy to begin with, the family and my wife's ambition have made me more eager to succeed businesswise and financially." Another responded that marriage had brought "stability, a family which I very much admire and enjoy doing my best to provide for." A wife and mother expressed just what success meant in the heady days of the 1950s:

> One fortunate thing which is important in our marriage is our fortunate change in income bracket. When we were married my husband earned $30 a week. . . . Now we have five children and an income of over $25,000 a year. We own our 8 room house—also a nice house on a lake. We have a sailboat, a Cris Craft [sic], several small boats. We own our own riding horse which we keep at home. Our oldest child goes to a prep school. We have a Hammond organ in our home. . . . Unless some disaster hits us, we see our way clear to educate all our children thru prep school and college.

But even financial success was no guarantee of marital bliss. The wife so happy with her lake cottage, Chris Craft motorboat, Hammond Organ, and prep school also criticized her husband for his acquisitiveness and, more significantly, his tendency to commodify personal relationships: "He has terrific drive and aggressiveness, and I feel he tries to own all of us in the family too much." In his own defense, this husband might well have shared the lament of another who resented that his wife seemed to take consumer goods for granted: "[T]he chief weakness of our marriage seems to be her failure to feel any . . . accomplishment from mutual efforts—particularly the family increases in net worth—house and car, furniture, insurance and bank accounts."[54] In turn, the family expert David Mace worried that such a man tried to replace love and commitment with consumer goods: "The prevailing standards often deceive him into the belief that providing bicycles and television sets, with an occasional spree thrown in, is an adequate substitute for getting to know his children and sharing their lives in a vital way."[55]

With domestic consumption now imbued with international significance and the "standard of living" undergoing constant upward revision, the significance of male breadwinning grew but so, too, did the potential for trouble. Men marched off to work to underwrite family consumption but in ways that increasingly worried social scientists and psychologists of the postwar era. The buzzword was "conformity," a plague that infected middle-class men. Gore Vidal put the matter with characteristic acerbity:

> The thing that makes an economic system like ours work is to maintain control over people and make them do jobs they hate. To do this, you fill their heads with biblical nonsense about fornication of every variety. Make sure they marry young, make sure they have a wife and children very early. Once a man has a wife and two young children, he will do what you tell him to. He will obey you. And that is the aim of the entire masculine role.[56]

Vidal may have stretched matters somewhat, but a generation of young men did marry young and have at least two children, and a generation of writers and social scientists did worry that such men had become slaves to conformity, "other-directed" bureaucrats and businessmen who had forfeited real individuality for the security of middle-class society.[57]

From the tragic Willy Loman of Arthur Miller's *Death of a Salesman* to the ironic Frank Wheeler of Richard Yates's *Revolutionary Road,* writers worried about the impact of postwar culture on men's lives. Miller's dark portrait of Loman's failure as breadwinner and father includes a scene in which Loman explains to his sons Biff and Happy why their neighbor Bernard, a boy who will one day grow up to argue a case before the Supreme Court, cannot begin to compete with the two Loman boys:

WILLY: Bernard is not well liked, is he?

BIFF: He's liked, but he's not well liked.

HAPPY: That's right, Pop.

WILLY: That's just what I mean. Bernard can get the best marks in school, y'understand, but when he gets out in the business world, y'understand, you are going to be five times ahead of him. That's why I thank Almighty God you're both built like Adonises. Because the man who makes an appearance in the business world, the man who creates personal interest, is the man who gets ahead. Be liked and you will never want.

Willy later instructs Biff on how to behave before Biff embarks on what ends as a pathetic attempt to borrow money from a former employer: "Walk in with a big laugh. Don't look worried. Start off with a couple of your good stories to lighten things up. It's not what you say, it's how you say it—because personality always wins the day."[58]

In the end, Willy's hopes for himself and his boys come to naught, and he kills himself in the sad hope that the insurance money can give his family a new start. He has failed as a father and done little better as a breadwinner. Having pledged his allegiance to the power of personality and lost, Willy spent his last days veering between hopeless confusion and crazed optimism. Ultimately, as Biff says at the end, Willy failed because "the man didn't know who he was."[59] Willy's modest dream of a home, a car, and a successful life for his two boys came to nothing because Willy traded his true talents as a carpenter for a precarious but somewhat more prestigious life as a salesman in the lower middle class. The price of the trade, as Miller made clear, was high indeed.

Willy's life was fraught with alienation and despair, but Willy himself had little sense of irony. Not so with Yates's Frank Wheeler. After a day of working at a white-collar job he hated, Wheeler returned to his tract home to denounce his deadening life: "Let's have a whole bunch of cute little winding roads and cute little houses painted white and pink and baby blue; let's all be good consumers and have a whole lot of Togetherness and bring our children up in a bath of sentimentality—Daddy's a great man because he makes a living, Mummy's a great woman because she's stuck by Daddy all these years."[60] (*Life* magazine's report that 1.4 million power lawn mowers had been purchased in 1953, up from 10,000 in 1945, would hardly have cheered the embittered Wheeler.[61])

But Frank's sarcasm gave way under the influence of an extra highball to a fear that conformity destroyed not only men's individuality but their masculinity as well:

> And I mean is it any wonder all the men end up emasculated? Because that *is* what happens; that *is* what's reflected in all this bleating about "adjustment" and "security" and "togetherness"—and I mean Christ, you see it everywhere: all this television crap where every joke is built on the premise that Daddy's an idiot and Mother's always on him.[62]

As Barbara Ehrenreich notes in her analysis of Yates's novel, Wheeler was unwilling to act on his convictions. Just hours before his revelation about emasculation, he had accepted a promotion at his company. All that Wheeler had left, Ehrenreich wrote, was his ironic sensibility: "He will make more money, drink more highballs, and cultivate the ironic sensibility his dignity depends on: He knows he is being destroyed as a man, but at least he knows."[63]

A decade before Wheeler's struggle with middle-class angst, the sociologist David Riesman had explored its roots in *The Lonely Crowd*. American men, in Riesman's judgment, had become "other-directed." No longer driven by an inner voice of conscience instilled by strong parents, no longer hard-edged, strong-minded, and full of righteous beliefs, the "other-directed" man was affable and flexible, attuned to the social and intellectual cues of his friends and neighbors, a team player whose convictions floated on a tide of peer approval. These were the men who filled the commuter trains and clogged the new beltways, the men whose success on the job depended on "personality" and "conformity."[64] What is more, as William Whyte made clear in his trenchant analysis of postwar suburbia, the psychology of the workplace and the home melded together. The rootless office worker became the peripatetic suburban dweller; the man who relied on "personality" in the office utilized the same qualities in neighborhood associations; the pal at work became the pal at home. Affability, flexibility, teamwork, adjustment—these watchwords of the workplace became part of the vocabulary of suburban living, family life, and the psychology of fatherhood.[65]

Prescriptive literature directed at fathers certainly spoke in such terms. Popular writers, physicians, and social scientists had little to say about paternal power in general—let alone respect and deference for patriarchal rule—and instead underscored the character traits that made for good fathering. Writing in 1951, psychiatrist O. Spurgeon English and his associate Constance J. Foster titled their book, *Fathers Are Parents Too*, and offered a "constructive guide to successful fatherhood." To be a successful father, the authors counseled cooperation, friendliness, respect, understanding, and teamwork, precisely the attributes that made for success in the white-collar workplace. In fact, their list of the critical factors that made for "emotional maturity" and good fathering might well have instructed the middle manager on becoming a success at the office:

1. He has a sense of reality and makes judgments according to situations as they are, not as he wishes they were. He accepts the unavoidable in life and makes the best of it. But he does not rationalize his failures and mistakes by blaming others, nor does he use escape mechanisms such as drinking to forget or ignore problems.
2. He has the capacity to stand disappointment and unavoidable frustra-

tion without sulking, getting angry, or feeling that he is being imposed upon or unfairly treated.

3. He is consistently engaged in doing something worth while to pull his share of the load. He refuses to be "carried by others" unless he is incapacitated by illness or accident.

4. He uses his abilities with interest, enthusiasm, and satisfaction. He does not ask only for happiness or money as a reward for his efforts. He gets fun out of the effort.

5. He gets along and co-operates with others. He considers their needs, interests, and feelings as well as his own.

6. He has the capacity to love someone other than himself.

7. He is willing to surrender present advantages for the sake of long-range goals. He can be patient and wait where the greater good for himself and others is concerned.[66]

English's and Foster's list of fatherly attributes bore uncanny similarity to the character traits of the "organization man" analyzed by William Whyte and other critics of the new corporate order. Others had somewhat different emphases but none drifted too far from the idea of father as pal, buddy, and confidant. Especially suspect were those men who harkened back to older ideas of father as outside judge and executioner, a misconception that called on fathers "to act like more omnipotent and omniscient beings than they really are."[67] Nor should fatherly tenderness, in the judgment of experts, be equated with femininity:

> Tenderness, gentleness, a capacity to empathize with others, a capacity to respond emotionally and to rationalize at leisure, to value a love object more than the self, and to find a living experience in the experiences of others is not the prerogative of women alone; it is a human characteristic.[68]

When fathers were no longer seen "as mothers' little helpers or powerful ogres," when they no longer disguised "gentler feelings in a preoccupation with community welfare, political activities and pseudoprofound answers to international problems," when they played an active role in rearing properly "adjusted" children, only then would men find real meaning as fathers.[69]

As the decade came to a close, family professionals continued to speak the language of good cheer, affability, and personality. Recognizing fathers' breadwinning obligations, David Mace, a professor of human relations at Drew University, made an early pitch for the importance of "quality time": "But your influence in another person's life depends less on the amount of time spent with that person than on the quality of relationship you have established." Indeed, Mace suggested that a father's "very detachment from the daily routine of the children's lives enables Father to bring a fresh approach and a new perspective that Mother is quite unable to provide." Mace was one of many who celebrated fathers' involvement with children's games and sports, who tended to see fathers as playmates and wise counselors who dispensed information about the outside world: "Junior often dreams of that big world to which one day he will go forth. Between the dream and the distant reality stands Father, uniting the functions of interpreter and guide."[70]

Family experts Gunnar Dybwad and Helen Puner emphasized "the mutualness, the reciprocalness between Mother and Father" and defended fathers who refused to adopt an authoritarian posture toward their children. The new father was a team player: "Father doesn't see himself, by and large, as the figure of authority he once was; he no longer wants to be that figure of authority. He prefers to be a participator in his family's life."[71] In as clear an iteration of such assumptions as one could hope to find, the two authors insisted that the modern father "derives enjoyment from his change of status from a breadwinning, bacon-bringing figure of authority to a sharing, helping, present member of the family." Given the complexity of modern life, fathers no longer could be the source of all knowledge or authority within the family, nor did they want to be: "To *insist* that he knows best, to guard jealously his status and prestige as Big Chief Final Resort of the family would mean, in the kind of society we live in today, not only unrealistic attitude-striking, but the kind of father-child relationship few modern fathers want."[72] In short, new fathers did not struggle to maintain their authority; instead they willingly gave it up.

But did the men who lived on Revolutionary Road with Frank Wheeler respond to such assumptions? Clearly many fathers did so in ways congruent with the therapeutic assumptions that pervaded both the working world and the home and in ways that left the basic gender-based division of labor in place. Although most fathers in surveys reported "helping out" their wives with daily household care, we have already seen that they did little sustained child maintenance; instead, they concentrated on guiding and befriending their children and on enhancing their offsprings' personality development.[73] Ruth Tasch, for example, found that New York City fathers saw themselves first and foremost as "guides and teachers" who got their children "ready for life." In this regard, fathers noted their responsibility to teach their children "the deeper values of life," to offer them the "right ideals," to teach them "the difference between right and wrong," and to "bring up sons so that they can fit in successfully." Almost 40 percent of the fathers emphasized their importance as role models for their children, as "someone to look up to," of "being what you want your children to be."[74]

To be a guide and teacher, however, required that one abandon outmoded visions of patriarchal authority. Although some of the New York City fathers criticized men for abandoning patriarchal prerogatives, the majority underscored the importance of "treating children as individuals," of "giving children reasons why things should be done," of offering "guided development—not imposition."[75] Nor could guidance and instruction develop in an atmosphere characterized by father-child separation. Sixty-two percent of the New York City fathers underscored the importance of father-child companionship, but when fathers evaluated themselves, they ranked it as the most important consideration. And when men criticized their failures in this regard, they singled out specific shortcomings that other men did not seem to have. One man, for example, wanted "to be more ingenious in making up games"; another wished he were "more athletic for [the] boy's sake"; a third admired a father who "is a hunter, fisherman, gamester—all the things I can't do."[76]

Men interviewed by Stanford psychologists at the end of the decade revealed many of the same attitudes. Although most of the fathers avoided daily domestic work, many emphasized their desire to spend time with their children and their intention to be more affectionate than their fathers had been with them. A young salesman, for example, pledged to do things differently: "I don't think, perhaps I had quite the feeling of closeness with my father as I realized I would have liked to have. I, at least, I have been influenced to the point where I am going to make a definite effort to have my son feel as close as he possibly can." Similarly, a surgeon recorded that his parents had shown him little affection but that "I take a much more active part in the family than I can remember my father taking."[77] The son of a baker felt saddened that his father's long working hours prevented the two from knowing each other well: "I feel this is not the way it should be, and so I purposely attempt to spend time with the children."[78]

The emphasis on affection and companionship transformed visions of paternal authority. The diffuse authority of the corporate workplace would have its counterpoint at home. Many of the men interviewed by the Stanford psychologists, for example, indicated that they were more lenient with their children than their parents had been with them. One man said his own parents had been relatively easygoing but then noted, in his halting fashion, that he intended to be even more so: "I hope that we aren't doing things to Jim—I thought a lot of times that my parents were doing—I've mentioned—uh standing on their rights as adults—I thought a lot of times that they were quite unreasonable about this: that they actually didn't reason or—or consider a lot of other facts. I—I hope we can avoid that."[79] Looking back, another man ascribed his own father's strictness to the latter's Victorian views: "My father was—and is—rather a difficult individual to live with. He has his own code of living, which you might describe as Victorian perhaps. . . . I think that because of this, I—don't resent my father anymore, but he's a hard man to understand—uh, I haven't taken the stand that he has, in regard to . . . well, you mentioned table manners, and many other things—social behavior and so on."[80]

Fathers emphasized not only their relative permissiveness but their efforts to mold their offsprings' character. Almost three-fourths of the fathers interviewed by Tasch took an active interest in the development of their children's "social standards, conduct, and control." Tasch's subcategories under this general heading included a wide variety of paternal involvement, much of it involving the development of children's personalities and their ability to interact with other children and adults. In fact, "personality" led the fathers' list of children's virtues.[81] Here fathers recorded their efforts to help their children relate to the adult world, respect others' property, and inculcate manners and approved ways of interacting with other children. Approximately 40 percent of the fathers noted they took actions that would enhance the emotional health of their children, and 30 percent explicitly noted activities they undertook to help promote their offsprings' personality development.[82] When Tasch broke down these categories by gender, she found that fathers mentioned doing daily care, going to places of recreation, and fostering the emotional development of daughters more frequently than sons; conversely, fathers recorded more involvement with their sons' intellectual and motor development than with their daughters'.

Presaging the behavior of new fathers in the 1970s, 1980s, and 1990s, some men actually joined discussion groups on how to become more effective parents. Their concerns mirrored the general cultural focus on psychological development and personality formation. Although expectant fathers in New York City in the 1950s worried about how to help their wives through labor—"We might as well assume, I think, that our wives will be excited and won't remember what they've learned"—fathers of preschoolers focused on their children's physical, psychological, and social development.[83] One man commented about the psychological dimension of sleep for children—sleep was "a small death" that requires sacrifice—while others volunteered their opinions about the difference between children's positive and negative aggression, proper discipline and the dangers of permissiveness, preschoolers' moral sense, and the role of television in the lives of youngsters. One exchange between fathers and mothers focused on the appropriateness of expressing strong emotions in the presence of offspring, another about the impact of parental squabbling in front of the children, and still a third about the proper timing of toilet training and weaning. Other men discussed whether preschoolers really wanted to please their parents, the value of nursery school versus staying home with mother, and the reasons for and ways of coping with sibling rivalry.[84]

Fathers of preteens and teenagers, of course, had different concerns. Although discussion ranged from the frequency of bathing to the proper size of allowances, parents paid particular attention to teenage sexuality. One man wanted to know if his twelve-year-old's lack of interest in girls was "normal," another worried about preteens' quest for popularity and the frequency of boy-girl parties among eleven-year-olds, and several others expressed concern about their children's incestuous impulses. The father of a twelve-year-old boy, for example, worried about his son's incestuous overtures—he "practically rapes his mother"—while another father found his daughter's request for a "Hollywood kiss" unnerving. Several fathers, noted the group leader, "showed a particularly keen awareness of the fact that their girls involved them in their fantasies of heterosexual relations," and another summed up the discussion about their children's sexuality by noting that "children's needs and readiness for heterosexual activities covered a wide range in this age group."[85]

These men were exceptional in taking the time to attend weekly discussion groups about child rearing. Most men did not. But in another sense they simply represented the epitome of the new postwar father, whose conception of his role extended well beyond breadwinning. Whether discussing their anxiety about the hospital delivery room or the teenage dance floor, these gatherings of fathers and mothers hinted at things to come. Their emphasis on the psychology of their children, their concern that small actions might have large repercussions, presaged later developments. These pioneering fathers of the 1950s would be followed later by literally hundreds of thousands of fathers in search of closer relationships with their children.

Sex-Role Sociology and Social Order

To post–World War II sociologists and psychologists, such paternal involvement boded well for the social and psychological development of children. Guided by the assumptions of functionalist sociology and convinced that proper gender identity was crucial to social order, these "experts" sought to discover the kind of child care, including paternal care, that produced children with appropriate sex-role characteristics. Their findings cheered those calling for a less dogmatic, more companionate mode of fathering. A 1956 analysis of 182 high school boys, for example, isolated 20 who tested high and 20 who tested low in masculine identification and then examined their relationship with their fathers. The findings were unequivocal: "[B]oys are more likely to identify with fathers whom they perceive as rewarding, gratifying, understanding, and warm than with fathers who are not perceived in these ways."[86] Or as David Mace noted in his praise of companionate fathers, "A boy who admires his dad and cherishes the happy hours they have spent together can accept his own masculine role smoothly and easily." Meanwhile his sister "will be forming, half-consciously, her ideal picture of what a man should be and of the kind of relationship she will one day have with her husband."[87]

None of the data confirmed the theory that "high masculine identification is a consequence of the father being threatening and punitive." Rather, families of highly masculine boys "appeared to be more persuasive, easygoing, more love-oriented, and less punitive in their disciplinary techniques"; moreover, they tended to come from homes where parents shared household tasks and fathers took an active role in child care.[88] Although some experts warned fathers not to become substitute mothers and "caricatures of women," most agreed that it was not important that the father himself be highly masculine or that he encourage his son in traditional masculine activities:

> In other words, it appears that, if a father is warm and nurturant in his relationship with his son, the latter is likely to become highly masculine, even if the father does not have this characteristic . . . and even if he does not encourage his son to participate in traditionally masculine activities. On the other hand, a ruggedly masculine, self-confident father who has poor relationships with his son is not likely to produce a highly masculine son, even if he actively attempts to stimulate his son's participation in typical male activities.[89]

Men's sense of their own responsibilities was in line with this analysis. Fathers saw themselves as role models for their offspring, but despite cultural fears that American boys risked emasculation, fathers put low emphasis on serving as explicitly "masculine" role models.[90] Only twelve of eighty-five fathers in one study conceptualized their obligations in these terms. The great majority highlighted fathers' role as guide and teacher, breadwinner, authority figure, companion, and even "contributor to the species."[91] Men took seriously their responsibility to bring their children to adulthood, but they did so by emphasizing their desire to become closer to their children and to inculcate in their off-spring desirable character traits and moral values. They might have ad-mired John Wayne or Fess Parker on the movie screen, but they felt no obligation to turn their sons into miniature versions of either at home.

Thus, the psychological studies of masculinity formation and the self-conceptions of fathers dovetailed. Fathers need not adopt a gruff, authoritative posture to prevent their sons from becoming sissies. Such an attitude, in fact, had precisely the opposite effect. Instead, sons and daughters profited from nurturing fathers who exemplified for both what modern masculinity should be. But they profited in other ways as well. If nurturant fathers produced masculine sons (and feminine daughters), they also produced tolerant, nonauthoritarian children. Al-though debate on what comprised appropriate levels of family democ-racy continued throughout the decade, all agreed that the authoritarian personality was a threat to democratic society.[92] With the memory of Nazism still fresh and Cold War rhetoric on the increase, inquiry into the roots of the authoritarian personality attracted the attention of so-cial scientists in the 1940s and 1950s, and part of their analysis centered on the relationship between paternal behavior and intolerance.

Again, research bore out the importance of family nurture and fa-therly love and affection. The highly prejudiced tended to see their fa-thers as stern and emotionally distant while those with low prejudice viewed their fathers as demonstrative, friendly, and affectionate: "In general, the fathers of the unprejudiced," wrote Else Frenkel-Brunswick, "seem to have spent a great deal of time playing and 'doing things' with their sons."[93] A nonthreatening, loving, emotionally involved father played a key role in establishing the psychological foundations of the unprejudiced man: "It makes it possible," Frenkel-Brunswick rea-soned, "for the son to include in his conception of masculinity some measure of passivity. Not feeling greatly threatened by their father, the unprejudiced man is apparently less afraid of losing his masculinity. He thus does not have to overcompensate for such fears by an overly rigid ego-ideal of aggressive toughness."[94]

By contrast, sons of dominating fathers often overcompensated by turning ego fragility into political intolerance. Although Frenkel-Brunswick was cautious about this finding—as she admitted, her sam-ple was very small—its significance, if true, was profound: "It would then be more understandable why the German family, with its long history of authoritarian, threatening father figures, could become susceptible to fascist ideology."[95] Threatened by their fathers, sons could never establish proper masculine identities. They were, therefore, attracted to political parties "where there is opportunity both for submission to the powerful and for retaliation upon the powerless."[96] The implications of this and other such studies were clear: authoritarian fathers produced authoritarian children, a finding that served well those pushing for more permissive fatherly behavior in the home.

Patriarchal, rigid, distant, overbearing fathers might produce proto-Nazis, but weak, uninvolved, ineffectual fathers had their own harmful impact on children and posed their own threat to social order. In extreme instances, such fathers literally drove their children crazy and rendered them incapable of functioning adequately. Specifically, psychologists and psychiatrists who worked with schizophrenics traced their patients' problems to aggressive, overanxious mothers and passive, subdued, indifferent fathers. All too often the schizophrenic's father was a retiring, ineffectual, withdrawn man married to a termagant who nagged and despised him; less often he was a domestic tyrant who hid basic inadequacies behind authoritarian bluster.[97] Common to both was a lack of genuine love for children and a disregard for children's emotional and intellectual growth, well-being, and autonomy. A study of 568 male schizophrenics conducted among U.S. Navy personnel, for example, found that schizophrenics had suffered disproportionately high losses of their fathers. For those not orphaned, many had been rejected by their fathers; in fact, "a rejecting father was the most frequently encountered pathological attitude."[98] This connection between weak fathers and schizophrenia was more obvious in a 1956 study conducted by psychiatrists from Yale University. Noting that the role of fathers was too often overlooked, the three authors argued that the fathers of schizophrenics often tended to be passive, immature, retiring, and inadequate. Of twelve carefully analyzed fathers, at least five assumed no responsibility for child care, and eight "were very distant and aloof."[99] In the same year, two psychologists reviewed the literature on male schizophrenia and concluded that the father's behavior "is generally reported to have been that of an emotional nonparticipant."[100]

But passive fathers and powerful mothers could do even worse. Experts also believed they played a critical role in the development of male homosexuality, a "fact" that aroused both pity and scorn in a society unremittingly opposed to same-sex relationships. Although authorities offered a host of complex psychological explanations to explain homosexuality, they agreed that the most common family dynamic was a powerful, overbearing mother and an uninvolved, detached father. Therapists concluded that homosexual men strongly favored their mothers over their fathers, in part because their fathers had shown them little or no love and affection.[101] Case reports by psychiatrists confirmed the frequency of this pattern. Mothers of homosexuals often had seductive relationships with their sons and sabotaged their sons' heterosexual desires. Fathers, for their part, were often absent and had little to do with their sons' development. One father, for example, "was obsessed with business and had little association with his wife and children. The patient thought of him as a stern man who failed to understand him, did not sympathize with his loneliness, and disparaged his ambitions."[102] A synthesis of American and British literature plus a study of British homosexuals came to the same basic conclusions. Fathers of homosexuals far more often than fathers of nonhomosexual neurotics tended to be absent, aloof, inept, or unassertive.[103]

Fathers not responsible for helping to create homosexual, schizophrenic, or authoritarian children might subvert the social order in another way by turning their children toward delinquency. The Jims, Judys, and Platos of the middle class and the ducktailed hoods and their girlfriends of the lower class came, researchers found, from broken homes and from homes lacking love, household routine, and refinement. In a study of almost five hundred delinquents and five hundred nondelinquent controls, the leading authorities on juvenile delinquency concluded that delinquents lacked warm relationships with either their fathers or their mothers: "only half as many fathers of the delinquents as of the nondelinquents (40.2%:80.7%) evidenced warmth, sympathy, and affection toward their boys."[104] Over 40 percent of delinquents' but only 16 percent of non-delinquents' fathers were indifferent to their children. (This difference, incidentally, was far greater than the corresponding comparison involving mothers.[105]) Likewise, the emotional ties of delinquent boys to their fathers were far weaker. If the fathers of delinquents had little interest in their sons, the sons felt the same about their fathers: three times as many delinquent sons evidenced indifference to their fathers; four times as many were hostile. Fifty-two percent of the nondelinquents found their fathers worthy of emulation; only 17 percent of the delinquents did so.[106] To Judge Samuel Leibowitz of Brooklyn's Kings County Court, the marginal position of fathers coupled with mothers who wield "absolute authority in a 'permissive household' lay at the root of the delinquent's rebellion, confusion, and unhappiness. The solution was simple: 'PUT FATHER BACK AT THE HEAD OF THE FAMILY.'"[107]

Fatherhood and Class Identity

The message to fathers in the decade of family togetherness and back-yard barbecues could hardly be clearer. Men's commitment to and involvement with their children had a decisive impact on personality development and on social order. But not all fathers, sociologists concluded, were so committed. It was middle-class men who most often treated their children in ways that promoted self-reliance, democracy, emotional stability, heterosexuality, and tolerance. If affluent blue-collar workers could drive their new cars to their new homes in Levittown, the parental dimensions of their lives lacked the expressive, affective, and egalitarian richness that allegedly characterized middle-class men's lives. Modes of fatherhood thus helped delineate class standing, strengthened female domesticity, and promoted an absorption in personal life.[108]

Social scientists who examined parental values and class standing ill-disguised their preferences behind a mask of functionalist objectivity. Writing in 1958, Urie Bronfenbrenner synthesized a generation of family studies by arguing that blue- and white-collar parents were, indeed, very different in their approaches to child rearing. Prior to World War II, the middle class had been more rigid in its early feeding, weaning, and toilet training practices, but since the war the middle class had become the more permissive. Influenced in part by child-rearing literature that lower-class parents did not read, middle-class fathers and mothers in the 1950s were more permissive than lower-class parents and more "'love-oriented' in discipline techniques." They had a "more acceptant, equalitarian relationship with their children" characterized by parental harmony, shared authority, paternal love, and fatherly involvement in the day-to-day affairs of the family. By contrast, lower-class parents were more demanding, strict, aggressive, and impulsive, and they had adopted as their own the once prominent middle-class emphasis on cleanliness, obedience, conformity, and control.[109]

Studies in the late fifties and early sixties supported and elaborated on Bronfenbrenner's synthesis. In a series of studies, the sociologist Melvin Kohn put Bronfenbrenner's assertions to the test by analyzing data from two hundred lower- and two hundred middle-class families in Washington, D.C. From interviews with mothers and fathers, Kohn concluded that although the two classes shared many child-rearing characteristics, they had fundamentally different parental values and objectives in discipline. Working-class family life centered around inculcating respectability and obedience in their children, middle-class around internalizing proper standards of conduct. For the middle class, the goal was a child who acted "according to the dictates of his own principles"; for the working class, the goal was to produce a child who obeyed parental demands.[110]

As to fatherly behavior per se, Kohn reported that middle-class sons turned more readily to their fathers for help or sympathy than did lower-class children, and that middle-class fathers—at least in the judgment of their wives—were more encouraging, involved, and willing to participate in leisure activities with their children; moreover, they assumed more of the burdens of day-to-day child care.[111] In light of these findings, it was no surprise that working-class mothers were more dissatisfied with their husbands' performance as fathers than were middle-class women. Working-class wives wanted husbands to be more affectionate and encouraging with the children and to play a more active role in setting limits. And though middle-class mothers wished husbands would assume more responsibility in rearing daughters, working-class mothers criticized their husbands for their uninvolvement with children of either sex: "Working-class fathers seem to play neither the directive role their wives would have them play, nor a highly supportive role. Rather, they seem to see child rearing as more completely their wives' responsibility."[112]

Describing these class differences was easier than accounting for them, but sociologists suggested the key lay in differing class needs. Blue-collar workers experienced standardization and direct supervision, their white-collar counterparts, self-direction and creative independence. "Working-class parents," wrote Kohn, "want their children to conform to external authority because the parents themselves are willing to accord respect to authority, in return for security and respectability." White-collar parents, in contrast, took for granted high income, stability, and respectability; their emphasis was on fostering self-direction, interpersonal relations, and "independence of action."[113] One set of goals led to an emphasis on obedience and constraint, the other to relative permissiveness and freedom; one mode led to sharply divided parental responsibilities, the other to a convergence of motherly and fatherly roles.

Underlying this evaluation of class and child rearing was a barely concealed attitude that middle-class values were the more desirable. With Nazism as a backdrop and the Cold War well under way, how could obedience, conformity, and dependence measure up against self-direction, freedom, and independence as desirable values to foster in children? That such values might play havoc with family unity and authority within families seems rarely to have entered into their analysis.

And yet, why should it? Functionalist theory masked the social scientists' own class bias, and their studies of masculine identification, the authoritarian personality, schizophrenia, homosexuality, and juvenile delinquency suggested that "normal" children were most likely to come from families imbued with middle-class patterns of child care.

Black Fathers and the "Tangle of Pathology"

Beyond the confines of academia, the comparison between white middle-class and white working-class modes of child rearing and fatherhood provoked little interest. Such was not the case when the comparison involved the far more volatile one of white and black families and white and black fathers. No domestic issue in the postwar period was more important than that of race relations, and thus, perhaps, it was not surprising that a 1965 report on the black family created a controversy that reverberates to this day. The report in question was officially titled *The Negro Family: The Case for National Action,* but most Americans came to know it by its author's name—"The Moynihan Report."[114]

The status of black fathers was at the center of Daniel P. Moynihan's analysis of the crisis facing black families. In the assistant secretary of labor's judgment, at the "heart of the deterioration of the fabric of Negro society is the deterioration of the Negro family."[115] What had initially caused this deterioration—now evidenced by high rates of marital dissolution, alarming increases in female-headed families, rising rates of illegitimacy, and burgeoning welfare roles—was slavery and the failure of Reconstruction. Denied equality and subject to racist oppression, black men had suffered particular hardships from slavery and Jim Crow. As Moynihan explained:

> When Jim Crow made its appearance towards the end of the 19th century, it may be speculated that it was the Negro male who was most humiliated thereby; the male was more likely to use public facilities, which rapidly became segregated once the process began, and just as important, segregation, and the submissiveness it exacts, is surely more destructive to the male than to the female personality. Keeping the Negro "in his place" can be translated as keeping the Negro male in his place: the female was not a threat to anyone.

Moynihan then explained how these forces undermined black fatherhood: "The very essence of the male animal, from the bantam rooster to the four-star general, is to strut." Black men, Moynihan bluntly reminded his readers, could not partake of such elemental masculine displays: "The 'sassy nigger' was lynched." Consequently, men could not take their rightful place as family head and the black family became increasingly matriarchal.

Slavery and the failure of Reconstruction had worked their destruction upon black men, but other factors had also destroyed black manhood and fatherhood. Drawing liberally from the work of E. Franklin Frazier, Moynihan argued that the urban migration of hundreds of thousands of blacks exacerbated the tendency to marginalize black fathers within their families. Plagued by under- or unemployment and thus unable to support their families, faced with the prospect of economic dependency on their working wives, black men in Northern cities became marginalized and powerless.[116] In Moynihan's memorable and controversial phrase, "a tangle of pathology" came to engulf the black family, one characterized by a matriarchal structure that, "because it is so out of line with the rest of the American society, seriously retards the progress of the group as a whole, and imposes a crushing burden on the Negro male and, in consequence, on a great many Negro women as well."[117] Given their residential proximity to the "pathology of the disturbed group," even middle-class black families could be caught in the matriarchal web. As Moynihan warned, "In a word, most Negro youth are in *danger* of being caught up in the tangle of pathology that affects their world, and probably a majority are so entrapped."[118]

This entrapment had dire consequences. Drawing on the works of other social scientists, Moynihan reported that black children with fathers present had higher IQ scores than those with fathers absent, that the alarming rates of juvenile delinquency among black youth could be attributed in part to the high rate of father absence, and that a much lower percentage of black than white male children discussed important life decisions with their fathers. At the root of all these problems lay the mother-dominated, fatherless black family that produced "most of the aberrant, inadequate, or antisocial behavior" afflicting black communities. The consequences for children, Moynihan bluntly asserted, were devastating: "Negro children without fathers flounder—and fail."[119]

The report ended with words that still provoke anger and controversy. In Moynihan's judgment, "the present tangle of pathology is capable of perpetuating itself without assistance from the white world." A national effort was needed "to strengthen the Negro family so as to enable it to raise and support its members as do other families." What this meant in practice followed from the substance of the report itself. Quoting again from E. Franklin Frazier, Moynihan called for a restoration of the black father to his rightful place at the head of the family: "Since the widespread family disorganization among Negroes has resulted from the failure of the father to play the role in family life required by American society, the mitigation of this problem must await those changes in the Negro and American society which will enable the Negro father to play the role required of him."

Originally written as an internal document for a small number of policymakers, the Moynihan Report became the subject of widespread controversy among government officials, media representatives, and civil rights workers.[120] At the heart of the controversy was a heated debate about the alleged pathology of the black family and black fatherhood. As the report's contents slowly leaked out over the summer of 1965, a number of critiques began to appear. Whereas some questioned the social science methodology of the document, others lambasted the report for implying that black family life—not poverty, discrimination, and unemployment—kept blacks in a second-class status. In two columns in the *Amsterdam News*, civil rights activist James Farmer minced no words in his sarcastic denunciation of the report:

> As if living in the sewer, learning in the streets and working in the pantry weren't enough of a burden for millions of American Negroes, I now learn that we've caught "matriarchy," and "the tangle of Negro pathology" . . . a social plague recently diagnosed by Daniel Moynihan in his celebrated report on "The Negro Family."[121]

Denouncing the report for "laying the primary blame for present-day inequalities on the pathological condition of the Negro family and community," Farmer chided Moynihan for implying "that Negroes in this nation will never secure a substantial measure of freedom until we learn to behave ourselves and stop buying Cadillacs instead of bread." Like other critics, Farmer believed that the report, by emphasizing the "pathology" of the black family, essentially blamed the victims for their problems: "It has been the fatal error of American society for 300 years to ultimately blame the roots of poverty and violence in the Negro community upon Negroes themselves." And to do so, Farmer cleverly and bitterly remarked, "is very much like curing Yellow Fever by painting the patient white and ignoring the mosquitoes."[122]

The harm of the Moynihan Report went even further. Farmer argued that the report's findings had already been seized upon by right-wing opponents of civil rights who used it to denounce "the Negro Revolution as the hysterical outburst of a mentally unbalanced subculture."[123] In addition, elected officials could use it "to divert practical anti-discrimination programs into an open season on 'pathological' Negroes." If the assumptions underlying the report became part of the white orthodoxy on racial questions, Farmer feared the worst: "In many ways, this report, when studied carefully, emerges in my mind as the most serious threat to the ultimate freedom of American Negroes to appear in print in recent memory."[124]

Although less harshly, other critics reiterated these charges and rebutted Moynihan's purported view of black males. The fault lay not with black men and black families but with racism, economic oppression, and discrimination. Impoverished black fathers left their families not because they were irresponsible or sick but because they, as was true of their fathers before them, could find no decent work. As Bayard Rustin explained, therapeutic efforts to bolster the esteem of black fathers were bound to fail without more fundamental change: "We could attempt to psychoanalyze poor negroes, to improve their self-image and self-esteem, but in the face of the economic realities, all our effort would be futile." Black families and black men did not need therapy but rather massive programs "to destroy the racial ghettos of America, house the black and white poor decently and create full and fair employment in the process." Only this kind of commitment would revitalize poor black family life and restore black fathers to the head of the household.[125]

As we shall see in the following chapter, the debate on black fatherhood and the structure of the black family sparked by the Moynihan Report is far from over. The report not only led to a reevaluation of the history of the black family—much of which undermined the historical assumptions of the report itself—but has continued to set the terms of the debate. Although Moynihan argued that he was misinterpreted by his critics, conservatives less attuned to nuance and qualification suggested at the time and have continued to argue that a "tangle of pathology" does, indeed, infect black families and that the solution for their ills must begin at home. Such ideas took on greater currency during the Reagan years as neoconservatives averred that Great Society programs since the mid-1960s only exacerbated the basic problems in black family stucture adumbrated by Moynihan in 1965.[126] Liberals, particularly academic liberals, responded more enigmatically. Historians tested Moynihan's history and found it wanting: their research has emphasized the strength and resilience of the black family in both slavery and freedom and the fact that urban poverty, not slavery and some ill-defined pathology, ultimately led to high rates of father-absenteeism in black families.[127] By contrast, social scientists reacted to Moynihan's call to arms by becoming "increasingly reluctant to research, write about, or publicly discuss inner-city social dislocations following the virulent attacks against Moynihan." The absent father, in other words, became a nonsubject.[128]

Toward the Future

The debate on the Moynihan Report reflected past assumptions about fatherhood and presaged today's conundrum about the issue. In the late 1940s and 1950s, social scientists, psychologists, and popular writers emphasized fathers' domestic responsibilities. Men, too, had an important part to play in the creation of well-adjusted children within a nurturant, child-centered home. Thus, fatherhood joined motherhood as a junior partner in the manufacture of the domestic mystique of the 1950s. The times, moreover, were propitious for middle-class fatherly absorption into private life: affluence, suburbanization, job security, and increased leisure gave millions of American men the time and money to focus on the private dimensions of their lives. Personal absorption coupled with relentless consumption became the hallmarks of middle-class life, nurturant fathering the mark of the middle-class man.

Nevertheless, this new consciousness of fatherly obligations did not challenge a gender-based division of labor. Social order and individual happiness depended on mothers who had chief responsibility for child rearing and fathers who supported their families and understood their emotional responsibilities. Families that did not fit this profile—female-headed black families for example—were described as pathological, a predictable assessment in a culture increasingly suffused with therapeutic values.

What is striking about the years from roughly 1920 to the 1960s are the continuities. Class and race differences existed and the Depression and World War II were interregnums of a sort, but the general outlines of the first phase of the new fatherhood were clear enough. Men supported families and played an important role in socializing their children. These two obligations could be in conflict as the demands of a rapidly growing consumer culture upped the breadwinning ante, but for fathers so inclined, a growing group of professionals were ready to offer advice on child rearing. Finally, throughout this period, social order and male breadwinning remained synonymous: threats to the latter—depression and war—undermined the former and prompted social policies meant to shore up the status of fathers.

This first phase of the new fatherhood is now over. While millions of American families still function within its terms, the reorganization of the household economy and the reemergence of feminism are in the process of destroying older assumptions about fatherhood. Wives and mothers working long hours for wages demand new behaviors of men or sullenly bear the burden of the "second shift." Feminists reject a gender-based division of labor and insist that fathers play a vital role not only in personality development but also in home maintenance and basic child care. These demands, in turn, have politicized fatherhood and left it culturally fragmented. Conservatives have answered the feminist challenge by hoping to restore lost paternal power while the therapeutically inclined have seen fatherhood as a way to break free of masculine chains or, conversely, as a way to get in touch with "the wildman" within men's souls. To understand these developments is to understand the politics of patriarchy and fatherhood, but before doing so we must explore the reorganization of men's lives during the last quarter-century.

10

Fatherhood and the Reorganization of Men's Lives, 1965–1993

S ETH STEIN, A SUCCESSFUL LAWYER, DESCRIBED THE UNDERLYING tension in his marriage: "Jessica has been very disappointed about my inability to do more in terms of the childrearing, and about my not sharing things fifty-fifty. She says I've left the childrearing to her." His wife, also a lawyer, insisted that she had sacrificed her career for his. As Stein put it, "She says she's cut twice as much time from her career as I've cut from mine." Nevertheless, he felt he could not live up to her standards: "She complains that I'm not like some imaginary other men, or men she knows, who take time with their children because they want to and know how important it is." His defense was his work, and her anger was an unavoidable byproduct of his commitments: "On the other hand, she understands the spot I'm in. So she holds it in until she gets good and pissed off, and then she lets me have it."[1]

Not all men joined Stein in resisting the demands of fatherhood. A college professor and father of three explained why he did 50 percent of the housework and child care: "My wife earns a third of what I earn. But as a public school teacher she's doing a job that's just as important as mine. She's an extraordinarily gifted teacher, and I happen to know she works just as hard at her teaching as I do at mine. So when we come home, she's as tired as I am. We share the housework and child-

care equally." Yet, even he admitted that his commitment was condi-
tional in some ways: "But if she were to take a job in insurance or real
estate, she'd just be doing another job. She wouldn't be making the
contribution she's making now. We haven't talked about it, but if that
were the case, I probably wouldn't break my back like this. She would
have to carry the load at home."[2]

The struggle of these two men to cope with their wives' outside employment represents one of the most significant developments in the
history of fatherhood during the last quarter-century. Nothing has
posed a greater challenge to the ideology of male breadwinning and
traditional male prerogatives than this transformation in the household
economy. Survey evidence suggests that American men have had a difficult time coping with the employment of their wives and tend to be
unhappier and have higher rates of mental distress than those whose
wives do not work outside the home. The reason, according to the experts, ultimately lay with men's sense of adequacy as providers: "According to the analysis based on the available measures," concluded a
recent investigation, "the most plausible explanation of the lower job
and life satisfaction of husbands of employed wives appears to lie in
their feelings of being less adequate as breadwinners for their
families."[3]

This strain on fathers' sense of identity and well-being has developed
with remarkable speed. In 1975, of the 84 percent of American children under eighteen who lived in two-parent families, 46 percent lived
in "traditional" families with breadwinning fathers and homemaking
mothers, but only 30 percent lived in families with both working mothers and fathers. Thirteen years later, approximately 78 percent of American children lived in two-parent families, but of that number, only 29
percent lived in families with nonwage-earning mothers, while 47 percent lived in dual-worker families.[4] Such a change has rendered traditional assumptions about fatherhood and breadwinning obsolete. It is
one thing to make a marginal commitment to home maintenance and
child care as sole breadwinner, but quite another when married to a
woman who holds down a full- or part-time job. Women's work, in
short, has destroyed the old assumptions about fatherhood and required new negotiations of gender relations. As a spate of books and
articles attest, these ongoing negotiations have become one of the
defining characteristics of the modern American home.

While thousands of fathers and mothers renegotiated gender boundaries, liberals, conservatives, and feminists tried to make sense of this
change in household economics. Never before had fatherhood become

so politicized; never before had so many new fathers proclaimed their commitment to child rearing. The politics of this debate are discussed in the next chapter, but while this debate was under way, a demographic revolution in the life experience of men was also taking place. Because of later marriage, declining fertility, and soaring divorce rates, the overall time men spent in family environments with children present dropped significantly. The irony did not escape researchers David Eggebeen and Peter Uhlenberg: "Thus, at the same time that increased attention is being given to the role of fathering, it seems likely that men, on average, are spending less time in living arrangements where there is an opportunity to occupy the role of father."[5]

Other trends suggest that "opportunity" may not be the right word. In some ways, men seem to be in full flight from the family. Thousands of divorced fathers fall behind in child-support payments or stop paying at all; thousands more make little effort to visit their children.[6] Others in large numbers refuse the claim of paternity altogether and abandon their children to their unwed mothers. Such realities make up part of a broader flight from traditional manly commitments that occurred in the post–World War II years. What ended in these years—or was at least severely eroded—was the equation of fatherhood and manhood. As Barbara Ehrenreich explained, by the end of the 1970s, "adult manhood was no longer burdened with the automatic expectation of marriage and breadwinning." Men had broken free. What was once quixotic had become acceptable, even respectable: "The man who postpones marriage even into middle age, who avoids women who are likely to become financial dependents, who is dedicated to his own pleasures is likely to be found not suspiciously deviant but 'healthy.'"[7]

All this suggests that the meaning of manhood and fatherhood can no longer be taken for granted. Fatherhood is talked about more, but understood less. It has lost cultural coherence. Breadwinning is still a critical part of fatherhood, but the fact remains that 25 million children under the age of eighteen live in dual-worker families.[8] Increased commitment to child care seems to define the new fatherhood, but how do we square men's sentiments with their well-documented resistance to carrying an equal load? Millions approvingly watch Dustin Hoffman's heartwarming transformation in *Kramer vs. Kramer*, but what about those "deadbeat dads" who make car payments but find it impossible to make child-support payments? Such questions have politicized fatherhood in the last two decades, but before analyzing the politics of fatherhood, we must understand the reorganization of men's lives over the last twenty years.

Women, Work, and the Transformation
of Male Breadwinning

For at least a century, fatherhood, breadwinning, and manhood were inextricably linked in American culture: men organized their lives and their identity around fatherly breadwinning. Much of this changed, however, in the last twenty-five years as millions of mothers entered the labor force. The movement of married women and mothers into the labor force has been well documented, but its consequences for men are sometimes overlooked. Today, millions of American fathers no longer have sole responsibility for family support. Just 23 percent of married women in 1950 with children under six worked for wages; in 1986, that figure had jumped to 54 percent. In 1950, 28 percent of women with children ages six to seventeen worked for wages, but by the mid-1980s the percentage had climbed to almost 70 percent. In the 1970s alone, the labor force participation rate for married women with preschool children rose nearly 15 percent, whereas the figure for married women with children in school went up over 12 percent. Today, two-job families compose almost 60 percent of all married couples with children.[9]

Many reasons account for the movement of mothers into the labor force, but researchers agree that the collapse of fathers' ability to support their families solely on their earnings is crucial to explaining the change.[10] Over the last twenty years, men's average weekly earnings (adjusted for inflation) have declined 14.3 percent. The rise in personal income, and hence the ability to support a family, that men took for granted in the post–World War II years no longer prevails. A thirty-year-old man in 1949 would see his real earnings increase by 63 percent by the time he turned forty, but the same man in 1973 would witness a 1 percent decline in his real average earnings over the same ten-year period.[11] This decline has put the squeeze on consumption. While young families in the 1950s might struggle for a few years, the father's expanding income would underwrite the cars, clothes, food, and home buying that became the mark of the modern middle class. With a stagnate income and rising costs, such optimism became a cruel generational joke. As late as 1976, 47 percent of homes were purchased on a single income, but as the 1980s came to a close, the figure had plummeted to only 21 percent. College tuition costs exhibited a similar trend: in 1970 tuition ate up 29 percent of family income; today the figure is 40 percent.[12]

Young men in their prime family-building years have been especially hard hit. As Jane Wilkie explained in her analysis of income trends over the last twenty-five years: "In the mid-1960s, 26% of all white men and 42% of all black men in this age group [20–34] had an income below the poverty level for a family of four. By 1987, these proportions had increased substantially. One-third (34%) of young white men and over one-half (56%) of all young black men had an income inadequate to support a family."[13] For these men, the alternatives were to postpone marriage, which many did—in 1965 nearly half of white and black men ages twenty to twenty-four were married but by 1988 that figure had fallen to less than one-fourth for white men and one-eighth for black men—or to establish dual-worker families.[14] Thus, for millions of American men, marriage and fatherhood were impossible without the earnings of a spouse, earnings that spelled the difference between outright poverty and marginal comfort or marginal comfort and reasonable security.

All is not bleak, but much has changed. Family income has continued to rise—median family income rose 13 percent between 1970 and 1990—but the good life increasingly comes with the help of two paychecks, not one.[15] In 1987, the median family income in traditional families (those with a sole male breadwinner) was $31,652; for dual-worker families, the same figure was $40,890.[16] Material comfort may still be within reach, but men and women have come to realize that the satisfaction of their families' ever-changing, ever-expanding needs requires two paychecks. Although men still earn the preponderance of family income, their wives contribute approximately one-third. As a consequence, power relationships within families have changed. Wives feel entitled to more support with home maintenance and child care. Some men concede the legitimacy of their wives' demands and either willingly or grudgingly increase their contributions; others resist in one way or another and condemn their wives to the "second shift." Regardless, mothers' participation in the labor force has challenged traditional paternal prerogatives regarding child care and housework.

The ultimate impact of this challenge will be far reaching. Women's work has indeed rendered the traditional attitudes and behaviors of fathers dysfunctional and obsolete, and as a wealth of evidence suggests, millions of men recognize this fact and want to play a more active part in child rearing. Before such hopes become a reality, however, the American corporate structure will have to change. Witnesses made these points repeatedly in testimony offered in June 1991 before the House Select Committee on Children, Youth, and Families. Cleverly called "Babies and Briefcases: Creating a Family-Friendly Workplace for Fathers," these hearings claimed that American fathers wanted to do more child care but often found their working and parenting lives in sharp conflict. James A. Levine, director of "The Fatherhood Project" in New York City, testified that "the number of men reporting a significant conflict between work and family life has increased sixfold, from 12 percent in 1977 to 72 percent in 1989."[17]

A variety of other surveys introduced as evidence supported Levine's findings. Forty-eight percent of fathers in metropolitan Washington, D.C., for example, claimed they reduced their working hours to spend more time with their children, and 23 percent reported they had passed up a promotion for the same reason.[18] In a 1990 poll by the *Los Angeles Times*, 39 percent of the fathers said they would quit their jobs if they could in order to spend more time with their children, and 28 percent felt their parental obligations hurt their careers. *Time* magazine reported that 48 percent of men between the ages of eighteen and twenty-four expressed an interest in staying home with their children. Another survey found that "74 percent of men said they would rather have a 'daddy track' job than a 'fast track' job," and a *Washington Post*/ABC News poll found that 43 percent of the fathers had actually cut back on their working hours to be with their children. *Fortune* magazine reported similar results, including the startling finding that more fathers than mothers thought companies should do more to help parents work out career and family responsibilities.[19] Perhaps Peter Lynch, one of the most successful mutual fund managers in the country, can speak for millions of American men in describing why he left his position to spend more time with his family: "Children are a great investment. They beat the hell out of stocks."[20]

Despite such desires, the hearings noted that most American corporations looked askance at paternal leave. A 1989 survey of medium and large private employers found that only 1 percent of employees had access to paid paternity leave and just 18 percent could take unpaid leave. Among Fortune 500 companies, only 37 percent provided for unpaid paternity leave, and of those companies, 90 percent "made no attempt to inform employees that such leave was available to new fathers." Worse, 63 percent of Fortune 500 executives felt "no leave" was reasonable and even employers that offered paternity leave felt "no length of [leave] time reasonable."[21] In testimony before Congress, Richard Salls, a successful pharmaceutical executive, described what such hostility meant in personal terms. Working for a corporation with no formal parental leave policy and a restrictive flextime program, Salls resigned his job to spend time with his two young sons, a decision that gave him the unsettling feeling "that I had committed a crime, a career suicide." Rebuffing his proposal to maintain some nontraditional working connection with the company, his superiors accepted the resignation of a man they had honored with an award only months before. Eighteen months later, Salls found the corporate world no more accommodating. He inquired about a job opening with his former company in March 1991. By late June, he still had heard no reply.[22]

Yet, not all the news was so grim. Chairwoman Patricia Schroeder, representative from Colorado, highlighted the efforts of several United States corporations to make work policies more flexible. Evidence garnered from a survey of 8,500 Du Pont employees, for example, found that 64 percent of the men expressed interest in a sick-child-leave policy and 35 percent responded favorably to paternity leave. Both of these percentages had risen sharply since a survey taken five years earlier. Du Pont responded to such concerns by expanding unpaid leave options and creating more flexible working arrangements. Similar actions were taken by Merck, a pharmaceutical company, and by the Los Angeles Department of Water and Power. The latter offered its 11,700 employees unpaid parental leave, child care, classes on fathering and stepfathering, peer support groups for fathers, electronic beepers for fathers whose partners were about to deliver (this program cut down on absenteeism as the birth day approached), breast-feeding coaching programs for fathers, and special events such as fathering fairs and father-child excursions to museums and sporting events.[23]

These pioneers represented what Representative Schroeder and others hoped would be the wave of the future. In their view, changes in the structure of the household economy were here to stay, and men clearly wanted to become more involved in their children's lives. For that to happen, the organization of work and the work culture would have to change: family leave, a variety of child-care options, and more flexible working hours were basic necessities. Managers and supervisors sensitive to family issues would be helpful as would counseling programs, stress reduction seminars, flexible vacation options, parenting seminars, and a host of financial support options to help fathers and mothers care for their offspring.[24] But why, James Levine asked, should American businesses undertake such far-reaching changes? "Because," he answered, "unless we put men back into the work family equation, we'll perpetuate the current pattern in which men are handicapped by feeling they can't risk more involvement in family life, and women are double handicapped, feeling they have to do it all, and being taken less seriously because of their family responsibilities."[25]

American men quite clearly are reconsidering their work and parenting responsibilities, and the American business community is slowly, sometimes grudgingly moving to recognize this change. Were the story to end here, all would be well, or at least better. But the story becomes less inspiring if we adopt a longer view. For much of this century, what is most striking is the continuity of many men's expectations and experiences and the historical resilience of the new fatherhood of the 1920s. In a follow-up to the Lynds' famous study, Theodore Caplow and four associates returned to Middletown in the late 1970s and found that "[s]ex differences in family roles in the United States do not seem to have changed much since the Lynds wrote about Middletown."[26] Fifty years after the first study, Middletown residents still believed that breadwinning and home repair fell largely to men, housekeeping and child care to women. And they acted on these beliefs: 77 percent of the husbands in the sample admitted that their wives did most of the child care, a high figure that was still less than the 89 percent of the wives reporting that they did virtually all the child care.[27] For their part, men earned bread: in over 80 percent of the families, men earned all or most of the family income.

Fathers' actual relationships with their children revealed a remarkable continuity as well. Despite some changes, fathers and children still disagreed over many of the same things in 1977 that they did in 1924— going out on school nights, grades, spending money, curfews. More important, children's identification with their fathers had changed very little over the years with over half claiming to be "quite close" or "extremely close" to their fathers. In fact, Caplow and his associates argued that their evidence "raises the possibility that the generation gap has been *narrowing*," especially among business-class families.[28] Nor had the paternal ideal changed much since the twenties. High school youths in 1924 and again in 1977 listed "spending time with his children" as the most desirable quality in a father and "respecting his children's opinions" as the second most. Caplow put the issue in terms congenial to the architects of the new fatherhood a half-century earlier: "What they [youth] wanted from their fathers then and now was their company."[29]

These Middletown fathers shared much with the new fathers of the 1920s. As their earlier counterparts had done, they had worked out a division of labor that made sense to them and their wives. Although wives and husbands disagreed over how much child care wives actually did, they both agreed that mothers had primary responsibility for child care, and each considered the other a capable parent. None of this is to say that the Middletown men of the 1970s were bad fathers, only that they were a good step or two behind the men fighting for flextime and paternal leave. Their traditionalism, however, should make us cautious in assessing the rate of overall change. Despite increases in mothers' wage work and the challenge posed by feminism, millions of fathers still hold to traditional views of fatherly responsibilities. That such is the case becomes even more evident when we examine the actual child-care performance of fathers.

The evidence suggests there is a sharp disjunction between what fathers think they should do at home and what they actually do. A 1978 national survey found that nearly 80 percent of men think that if husbands and wives both work, husbands should perform 50 percent of the housework and child care.[30] Such good intentions, however, are not borne out by actual behavior. Husbands of working women do, indeed, perform more child care and home maintenance, but the degree of change suggests more about men's ability to resist than to alter old patterns. Even in homes in which both partners work forty hours per week, men's total work week (paid and unpaid labor combined) is seventy hours, women's seventy-seven. This estimate is conservative because it does not include child care, something women do more of as well.[31] A 1983 study of white middle-class families in greater Boston found that working fathers married to working mothers spent only an extra forty-five minutes *each week* with their kindergarten-aged children than men married to full-time housewives. Summarizing their findings, the researchers concluded that "fathers spent significantly less time with children than did mothers regardless of whether the mothers were employed or at home."[32] After examining much of the research on men's housework and child care, Sylvia Hewlett concluded "that American men still do less than a quarter of all household tasks, and that married men's average time in family work has increased by only 6 percent in twenty years despite the massive shift of women into paid employment."[33]

None of these data should be surprising. Newspapers, magazines, and books like Arlie Hochschild's *The Second Shift* have kept the issue of women's double duty in the public eye for some time. The simple fact is that fathers resist because it is in their self-interest to do so. Child care, like housework, is often tedious, repetitious, and boring. Thus, even if men can be dragooned by their wives into doing it, they refuse to take responsibility for it. As Rosalind Barnett and Grace Baruch explain, fathers "might *perform* various tasks, but they were not responsible for 'remembering, planning, and scheduling' them." In their study of 160 middle-class fathers, 113 reported that they were not responsible for any child-care tasks; another 35 had responsibility for only one.[34] Michael Lamb has estimated that in two-worker families, fathers are engaged with their children about one-third as much as mothers, are accessible to their children about 65 percent as often, and take actual responsibility for child care only about 10 percent of the time.[35]

In short, fathers resist and mothers cope. In part this dynamic persists because men continue to exercise old options despite new realities and in part because fathers still do the major share of family breadwinning. As primary breadwinners, men confront a working world only now beginning to recognize their domestic responsibilities. Lack of flexibility and a work culture that denigrates men who take fathering seriously make it difficult for men to pull their weight at home. But the status of primary breadwinner also brings benefits. Thanks to a segmented labor force that consigns three-quarters of American working women to traditional "female jobs," employed wives (including those who work part-time) contribute only 26 percent of the family budget. Thus fathers and mothers logically put the man's work first. Maternity, not paternity, leave is the rule; mothers, not fathers, stay home to care for sick children; women, not men, visit the school principal, attend the daytime school program, or squeeze in an emergency shopping trip over their lunch hour. Thus, although many men no longer support their families on their wages alone, they continue at home to benefit from the wage gap. The prerogatives of male breadwinning live on, a remnant of a bygone era.

Reorganizing Men's Lives

Men's resistance to the demands of the new fatherhood goes well beyond figuring out ways to avoid changing diapers and cleaning house. One of the ironies of recent history is that amidst ubiquitous discussions about fatherly nurture and restructuring the workplace, a substantial number of men seem to be in flight from the family. The chief proponent of this view is social critic Barbara Ehrenreich who argues that men have been fleeing family commitments since World War II. In an ingenious analysis of a variety of postwar social trends, Ehrenreich suggests that men, not women, have led the "flight from commitment." Whether as "gray flannel dissidents," playboys, beatniks, counterculturists, or seekers of psychological "growth," American men have increasingly looked beyond marriage and fatherhood for meaning and personal gratification. Men who once assumed that only marriage and children could bring happiness and respectability now view alternative life choices with equanimity and even approval.

Ehrenreich's witty, irreverent analysis draws support from American social scientists who found that men and women in the 1970s emphasized marriage and parenthood less as a source of well-being than did their counterparts of the 1950s. In 1957 slightly over one-half the male and female respondents in one study believed the unwed were "either sick or immoral, too selfish or too neurotic to marry." Twenty years later the figure had fallen to 34 percent, prompting researchers Joseph Veroff, Elizabeth Douvan, and Richard A. Kulka to highlight "men and women's increased tolerance of people who reject marriage as a way of life."[36] More telling, the social scientists also found that over time people tended to take a dimmer view of marriage in general, a point of obvious importance to our story given the close connection between marriage and parenthood: in 1957, 44 percent of the sample emphasized the restrictiveness of marriage; that figure climbed to 59 percent by 1976. Nor were the differences especially striking between men and women when the responses were separated by sex. Overall, the evidence suggests a "remarkable similarity in men's and women's response to marriage in both years."[37]

As the stock of marriage declined, so, too, in some respects did that of parenthood. In the late 1950s, 63 percent of fathers had a "positive orientation" toward parenthood, a number that fell to 49 percent in 1976; likewise, whereas 27 percent of fathers perceived parenthood as generally "restrictive" in 1957, 43 percent did so in 1976. The attitude of mothers revealed similar trends, suggesting that men and women shared a common shift in values between 1957 and 1976. Even stronger was the change in attitude among childless men and women. Almost half the childless men in 1976, for example, perceived parenthood as largely restrictive.[38] This evidence does not mean that parenthood is unimportant in the lives of American men and women, but it does suggest, as Veroff and his colleagues conclude, "that parents are no longer *overly* invested in the role and more often think of it as a major but not all-encompassing aspect of their lives."[39]

These attitudinal changes have been mirrored by an actual demographic decline in men's investment in child rearing over the last thirty years. As the fertility rate fell, the age of marriage climbed, and divorce and out-of-wedlock birth rates soared after 1960, men increasingly "spend less time in living arrangements where there is an opportunity to occupy the role of father."[40] How much less time has been calculated by David Eggebeen and Peter Uhlenberg: "The most striking changes are a 43% reduction in the amount of time spent in family environments where young children are present (from an average of 12.34 years in 1960 to 7.0 years in 1980), and a complementary 49% increase in the amount of time spent outside of marriage (from 6.28 years in 1960 to 9.34 years in 1980)." By breaking the sample into age cohorts, the researchers found that most of the change could be accounted for by reorganization in the lives of younger men: for example, twenty- to twenty-nine-year-olds accounted for 58 percent of the increase in time spent outside of marriage, whereas men twenty-five to twenty-nine accounted for 34 percent of the total decrease in time spent in families with children under age six. "Taken together," write Eggebeen and Uhlenberg, "these findings indicate that men are spending less of their young adult years in environments where children are present."[41]

The irony is obvious: the emphasis on fatherly nurture of the 1970s, 1980s, and 1990s arose precisely when fatherhood for young men was becoming demographically less salient in American society. And although the welter of liberal, conservative, therapeutic, and feminist voices about fatherhood during the last couple of decades may have masked this change, the implications may be profound. If, as some researchers suggest, the experience of fatherhood promotes adult well-being and intrapersonal growth, stimulates nurturant and altruistic behavior, and challenges men to reassess the meaning of their lives, what, then, of men who do not have this experience?[42] Will they become selfish brutes, thereby fulfilling the grim predictions of some conservatives, or will they find other outlets for nurturance and other ways to clarify their basic values? What is clear is that increasing numbers of men will face this situation. As fatherhood becomes increasingly voluntary, the role of fatherhood and breadwinning in male identity will certainly decline. Men who would have once become fathers without question, who treated fatherhood as their fate, now face considerably less pressure to become such. A weighing of options is increasingly becoming the norm. Are children worth the time, effort, and money? Is the roller coaster of parenthood worth the ride? For some, it will surely be so, and in this new world of alternatives, these men, having considered the options, may become quintessential new fathers. Others may look for masculine identity in their work, a childless marriage, a series of relationships, or their leisure.[43] Regardless, what has occurred is nothing less than a sea change in the organization of men's lives whose full implications will not be evident until well into the next century.

The "Rebellion" of Fathers

Although these changes in men's lives stemmed in part from later marriages and smaller families, two other, far more explosive developments in American society over the last three decades—soaring rates of divorce and out-of-wedlock births—have shaken the very foundation of American life. Just how explosive can be gauged by the May 4, 1992, cover of *Newsweek* magazine, which sports a mug shot of a man on a wanted poster, above which is written the title of the issue's lead article, "Deadbeat Dads," and below the name of the pictured father and the amount he owes in child-support payments, some $22,000. Likewise, President George Bush's May 1992 commencement speech at Notre Dame on the disintegration of the two-parent family, the flap created by Vice President Dan Quayle in the same month when he criticized the television program "Murphy Brown" for allegedly "mocking the importance of fathers" and glamorizing out-of-wedlock births, and Bill Clinton's pledge at the Democratic National Convention to make delinquent fathers pay child support suggest that paternal neglect and malfeasance had entered election year politics.[44]

The roots of these two developments lie deep in history, but their impact has dramatically reshaped the lives of millions of Americans. Today some fifteen million American children grow up with little contact with their fathers. Of that number, ten million are the product of marital separation and divorce and five million the result of out-of-wedlock births. In the fifteen years following 1970, the number of American families rose by 20 percent but the number of female-headed families jumped by 51 percent. More significantly, the number of families headed by women with one or more children increased by 77 percent in these years. This demographic revolution had its greatest impact among black and Hispanic families, whose rates of female-headedness in the 1970s climbed by 108 and 164 percent, respectively. By the mid-1980s, 43 percent of all black families, 23 percent of Hispanic families, and 13 percent of white families were female-headed.[45]

Nothing has done more to separate fathers and children than the soaring divorce rate of the last three decades.[46] Its impact on American fatherhood has been both distressing and profound, largely because divorcing fathers have little contact with their children. Nor do they offer their children much in the way of financial assistance. In more than 90 percent of divorces, children remain with their mother and yet only about 60 percent of these women receive any child-support awards; moreover, the payment of these awards is erratic and unreliable. Recent government survey data found that just over half the mothers entitled to child support received the full amount, a quarter received partial payment, and over a fifth received nothing at all.[47] Fathers apparently chose to spend their money on other, allegedly more important priorities. A Denver study found that men's monthly car payments typically exceeded the amount requested of them for child support; sadly, these fathers were far more likely to be delinquent in supporting their own flesh and blood than on paying off their new Toyota.[48]

Even when men paid, most awards were not especially large. In the late 1980s, the average amount fathers paid was $2,700 per year, a figure that covers less than a quarter of the average cost of rearing a child and helps explain the financial difficulties of divorced women and their children. For the year 1989 alone, the child support payment "deficit" was approximately $5 billion and the overall deficit may run as high as $25 billion. This fact helps to explain why after divorce the standard of living of noncustodial fathers actually rises while that of mothers falls precipitously. One report from the mid-1980s found that women's standard of living dropped by about 30 percent in the first five years following divorce, while that of husbands rose 8 percent.[49] The unintended consequence of the divorce revolution, argues Lenore Weitzman, has been the relative or actual impoverishment of women and children. While the marriage lasted, these women and children occupied secure niches in the middle class; upon the breakup of the marriage, they were in economic freefall.

Many factors beside the dereliction of ex-husbands account for divorced women's economic difficulties—pay discrimination, child-care responsibilities, a segmented labor market, lack of marketable skills—but why do men fail to support their children? Why so many deadbeat dads? Theories abound, but one, put forth by the sociologist Frank Furstenberg, suggests that men tend to see marriage and fatherhood as a package, and that when the marriage ends, their sense of paternal responsibility wanes as well. This theory would help explain noncustodial fathers' dismal performance in paying child support and in even seeing their children. Tracking a representative sample of one thousand children from disrupted families between 1976 and 1987, Furstenberg and colleague Kathleen Mullan Harris found that 42 percent of the children had not seen their fathers at all during the previous year, 80 percent had not slept at their father's house in the previous month, and just slightly more than 15 percent saw their fathers once a week or more.[50] Some of these men were simply indifferent, but as Judith Wallerstein and Sandra Blakeslee rightfully point out, noncustodial fathers find it enormously difficult to maintain an active relationship with their children. Such fathers lack a clear definition of responsibility and authority. Their role is ambiguous, and many feel unneeded, even obtrusive when they see their children. Others avoid seeing their children to escape the pain, shame, and guilt they associate with their failed marriages.[51]

Thus, for many men the end of marriage brings with it a rapid deterioration in the father-child relationship: "As they watch their children grow up, seeing them every so often," write Wallerstein and Blakeslee, "men may feel a terrible guilt over having left them—and visits only seem to emphasize the discontinuity of the relationship. The father realizes, with each visit, that he is not part of the children's lives."[52] And if he is not part of their lives, his willingness to pay child support may evaporate as well. Men's explanations and excuses for not paying run the gamut. Some plead economic hardship; others believe their children do not need the money; some feel detached from their children and assume they are "getting by." Others withhold support, as one man put it in *Newsweek* magazine, to punish their ex-wives: it "was the only way I could hurt her."[53]

Regardless of their reasons or excuses, a large number of divorced fathers are financially irresponsible at best and incomprehensibly callous at worst. Despite recent efforts to force fathers to pay child support—for example, the Iowa attorney general plastered the state with ten thousand flyers listing the "10 Most Wanted Dads"; the state of Massachusetts has proposed a plan to revoke the trade and professional licenses of delinquent fathers; and President Clinton has pledged to make the issue a high priority policy in his administration—the fact remains that *"60 percent of divorced fathers contribute nothing at all to the financial support of their children."*[54] And yet the story becomes even bleaker. Fathers have more to give than just money, and their absence may have a devastating impact on children. This issue is politically loaded because it involves the viability and worthiness of families without fathers—a growing reality for millions of American women and children—and it is enormously complex owing to the inherit difficulty of assessing something so nebulous as "successful" family life and "healthy" psychological adjustment. Neither difficulty, however, has stopped researchers from trying to assess the problem, and when the methodological, evidenciary, and theoretical smoke is cleared, at least two relatively coherent positions can be seen, each with its own qualifications, limitations, and differences.

On one side, many studies argue that custodial mothers do a perfectly acceptable job of rearing children; on the other, many insist that the absence of the father causes serious problems for children. Typical of the first position is a cross-cultural study by Barbara Bilge and Gladis Kaufman of African, Eskimo, Indian, and American families. They argue that single-parent households occur in all societies, that such families are neither pathological nor inferior, and that marriage can be broken with no deleterious effects on children provided strong economic, social, and psychological support systems exist for the mother and her offspring.[55] Other analyses argue much the same. Researchers using personality inventory and other tests, for example, have argued that the measured self-esteem of children from divorced and intact families is similar, that the psychological profile of children of divorce differs little over the long term from that of children from intact homes, and that a stable home where parents are divorced is better for children than an intact home characterized by tension and bitterness. Other investigators report that children often see the divorce of their parents as unfortunate but a sensible thing under the circumstances, that children in divorced families considered themselves as accepted by their mothers and fathers as those from intact families, and that harmful impacts of divorce on children are caused less by father absence than by financial hardship.[56]

Many researchers who focus on father absence per se and not just on the children of divorce put forth similar positions. A study of some two hundred poor youth found no association between fatherlessness and psychopathology.[57] Another study of black children from lower-class backgrounds found no significant difference in the IQ, achievement, self-concept, and personality of those youngsters from father-present and father-absent homes. An investigation of black kindergarteners from homes with and without fathers revealed no difference in their academic preparedness, although those from homes with fathers present did somewhat better in terms of academic achievement.[58] Nor, another study found, did father absence significantly affect adult females' interpersonal relationships with men.[59] A review essay concluded that sex-role development and behavior is not impaired by the father's absence, that children in homes without fathers display good emotional development and self-esteem unless subject to undue stigmatization, and that intellectual development and rates of juvenile delinquency are shaped far more by social class than by father absence.[60]

Against this evidence, however, is a larger, ever-growing body of research stressing the harmful impact of father absence on the young. Certainly some of the most important work is the longitudinal study of sixty middle-class California families conducted by Judith S. Wallerstein and two associates.[61] Making contact with almost all the families five and then ten years after divorce, the researchers discovered that few fathers and children sustained a close and loving relationship. At the five-year mark, "The great majority of the father-child relationships had become emotionally limited over time . . . [and] offered little help to the child in dealing with the complex tasks of growing up." Some 70 percent were "emotionally insufficient to promote or even facilitate the growth and development of the child." In about 15 percent of the families, the father-child bond had become frozen in time and in another 30 percent the relationship had not kept pace with the child's maturation. Some relationships had become inappropriately eroticized and some quite clearly exploited the child to meet the needs of the father. In other families, the father-child bond had simply faded as fathers' interest in or ability to maintain the relationship declined. In these cases, children felt an acute sense of rejection and unworthiness.[62]

Not that the children wanted it this way. Even after ten years, many children tried to keep the relationship vital: "Yet we have also seen how poignantly the children hold on to an internal image, sometimes a fantasy image, of the absent or even the visiting father and how both fathers and children create phantom relationships with each other." Nor did the children's need for their father diminish over time. Wallerstein discovered quite the opposite: "We have seen that the children's need for their father continues and that it rises with new intensity at adolescence, especially when it is time for the children to leave home."[63] The story they tell, especially rich because it unfolds over ten and in some cases fifteen years, is one of loss, regret, abandonment, and sadness. It is a story of children who feel responsible for driving their fathers away, who try to make sense of their fathers' unfulfilled promises by creating fantasy relationships with their fathers. It is also a story of fathers who sometimes act with incomprehensible insensitivity and cruelty, or, more commonly, of men who simply drift away. Eighteen months after separating from his wife, one man admitted he seldom had contact with his children: "Look, I'll be honest. I've let myself grow away. Rosemary's [his ex-wife] new guy is their dad. He's doing a pretty good job. The kids don't seem to miss me that much." Five years after divorce, he had even less contact with his children and still assumed his absence meant little: "I'm ashamed to tell you, I haven't seen them, even though I live only a few blocks away. I haven't taken the time to see them. But I doubt that they miss me."[64]

He could not have been more wrong. In their follow-up interviews with this father's son and with other sons like him, Wallerstein found that fathers continued to maintain a critical role in the lives of their children: "When the father-son relationship is poor, the boy may suffer low self-esteem, poor grades, weak aspirations, and rejection. When the father-son relationship is good, where the father is regarded as moral and competent and the boy feels wanted and accepted by his father, then the boy's psychological health is likely to be good."[65] Likewise, the authors found that fathers maintained an enduring presence, for good or bad, in the lives of their daughters. Like their brothers, girls "have a powerful need to create a protective, loving father, one who would never intentionally let them down. . . . Without any sense of contradiction, they are able to maintain a benign image of the loving father side by side with a history of repeated rejections and failures."[66]

These children and their fathers passed like two ships in the night, the expectations and needs of the former unmet by the confusion, guilt, or simple neglect of the latter: "Most commonly, the father thinks he is doing his best while the child feels he or she is starving. The father thinks he is meeting his obligation, the child feels pushed to the periphery. The father thinks he is loving, the child feels rejected." These fathers, Wallerstein concluded, simply did not understand their own behavior and the needs of their children: "Most fathers in our study thought they had done reasonably well in fulfilling their obligations whereas three out of four of the children felt rejected by their fathers; they felt that their fathers were present in body but not in spirit."[67]

Although lacking the longitudinal and descriptive richness of Wallerstein's work, a host of researchers have come to similar conclusions. Everything from sleep disturbances to juvenile delinquency to teenage suicide has been attributed to divorce and consequent minimal contact with fathers. So, too, have drug use and psychological disorders. A whole series of studies contend that children from "broken homes" do more poorly in school. One study found that the math scores of children without fathers were especially prone to suffer, while another discovered that SAT scores differed dramatically among students from father-absent and father-present homes. After assessing these studies, Sylvia Hewlett suggested that "the decline in American educational performance over the past generation—which is most pronounced in science and mathematics—seems to be directly related to the rapid increase in the number of father-absent households. School failure may well have as much to do with the disintegration of families as with the quality of schools."[68]

Fathers have been disappearing from the lives of their children in another way as well. Perhaps the most shocking and one of the most publicized demographic changes in American family life in the last two decades has been the rise of out-of-wedlock births. Vice President Dan Quayle's 1992 election-year concern about television character Murphy Brown's "illegitimate" child only highlighted, in an unusual way, public concern about this problem. And the statistics, especially among the young, are alarming. In 1960 only 15 percent of teenagers who gave birth were unmarried; that figure climbed to 61 percent by the mid-1980s. Today approximately five hundred thousand unmarried teenage girls give birth each year. The problem is especially troubling among black families where one in three mothers is an unwed teenager.[69]

This issue has been much discussed, but behind the numbers are fathers who take little or no responsibility for their offspring. The question, of course, is why. The answers are complicated. Conservatives blame a misguided welfare state for the rise in out-of-wedlock births and female-headed families. In *Losing Ground*, Charles Murray argues that Great Society programs undercut male responsibility and thereby brought on the catastrophic rise in the number of female-headed families, out-of-wedlock births, welfare dependency, unemployment, crime, and poverty.[70] In his judgment, young fathers act irresponsibly because, ironically, they are acting rationally: the welfare state makes it economically illogical for young fathers to marry their pregnant girlfriends and to take menial jobs to support their families. It makes more economic sense for fathers and mothers to remain unmarried and dependent on welfare programs.[71]

Murray's ideas became influential in the Reagan administration's attack on the welfare state. Big, liberal, free-spending government inadvertently, perhaps with the best of intentions, destroyed homes and promoted paternal neglect. Moreover, although Murray was careful to point out the essential rationality of poor fathers' and mothers' decisions not to wed, his book fueled the argument that many poor men were sexually predatory and unwilling to shoulder the responsibilities of fatherhood. Such ideas were central to the assumptions of conservatives like George Gilder, but even some liberals could not dismiss them out of hand. The callousness of a young ghetto man who had fathered six children by four different women and supported none of them elicited disappointment and dismay from liberal Bill Moyers during his television special on the plight of the black family: "Well," the young man casually explained to Moyers, "the majority of the mothers are welfare. And welfare gives them the stipend for the month. So what I'm not doing, the Government does."[72]

Without question, some men are sexually predatory. Should their girlfriends of the moment become pregnant, many of these young fathers blithely assume the state will take care of breadwinning obligations. At one level, then, the conservative argument makes some sense, but a more comprehensive explanation of the rise of fatherless families, especially among the urban poor, requires more than criticism of the Great Society. Fortunately, William J. Wilson provides such an explanation in his influential book, *The Truly Disadvantaged*. Wilson argues that the soaring rates of female-headed families and out-of-wedlock births among the urban poor, especially blacks, cannot be understood without comprehending the interrelationships among historical, demographic, and economic changes. As millions of blacks migrated from the rural South to Southern and Northern cities throughout the twentieth century, they encountered persistent discrimination and limited economic opportunities. Furthermore, as Wilson explains, their transformation of the city's age structure promoted family instability. Minority migrants tended to be younger than white urban dwellers, and youth, as Wilson reminds us, is "associated with out-of-wedlock births, female-headed homes, and welfare dependency."[73]

As these young migrants streamed into the inner city, nonpoor urbanites moved out, thereby increasing the concentration of poverty and changing the class structure of America's urban minority neighborhoods.[74] This demographic shift, in Wilson's judgment, had far-reaching implications: "The net result in both the North and the South is that as the nation entered the last quarter of this century, its large cities continued to have a disproportionate concentration of low-income blacks who were especially vulnerable to recent structural changes in the economy."[75] The full impact of these structural changes is now evident. For the last three decades, the American economy has witnessed a far-reaching transformation as blue-collar jobs have declined and white-collar service jobs have expanded. As Wilson explained:

> Urban minorities have been particularly vulnerable to structural economic changes, such as the shift from goods-producing to service-producing industries, the increasing polarization of the labor market into low-wage and high-wage sectors, technological innovations, and the relocation of manufacturing industries out of the central cities.[76]

Many of these new service-related, suburban-based jobs have relatively high educational qualifications, which undermine the efforts of poor men, whites and nonwhites alike, to become breadwinners. New York City illustrates this transformation in terms of actual work opportunities. Between 1970 and 1984, New York City lost 492,000 jobs that required less than a high school education while gaining 239,000 jobs that required at least some higher education.[77] Many other cities showed similar if somewhat less dramatic trends, and the result has been devastating rates of unemployment for urban minority youth who suffer severe educational liabilities: "The fact that only 58 percent of all black young adult males, 34 percent of all black males aged eighteen to nineteen, and 16 percent of those aged sixteen to seventeen were employed in 1984 reveals a problem of joblessness for young black men that has reached catastrophic proportions."[78]

As middle- and working-class minorities have moved away from the central cities, those left behind face more than joblessness. For the young, in particular, "chances are overwhelming that [they] will seldom interact on a sustained basis with people who are employed or with families that have a steady breadwinner." What has been lost are the models that young men need if they are to see the connection between education and meaningful employment, hard work and economic success, two-parent families and financial stability.[79] Bereft of such models, young ghetto men become isolated from the social networks and institutions of mainstream society; thus, they are likely to adopt attitudes and behaviors not conducive to success in the larger society. Wilson explains the implications for would-be fathers and family breadwinners:

> Moreover, since the jobs that are available to the inner-city poor are the very ones that alienate even persons with long and stable work histories, the combination of unattractive jobs and lack of community norms to reinforce work increases the likelihood that individuals will turn to either underground illegal activity or idleness or both.[80]

Without jobs or even the prospect of jobs, young men are unlikely to take on the responsibilities of marriage, let alone the financial support of children. Wilson concludes that "the weight of existing evidence suggests that the problems of male joblessness could be the single most important factor underlying the rise in unwed mothers among poor black women."[81]

The Child-Fathers of Out-of-Wedlock Children

Without even the prospect of jobs, it is difficult for the young men discussed above to establish long-term relationships with either the mother of their children or the children themselves, but not for lack of trying. Behind the popular stereotype of the teenage father is often a troubled, naïve, and often confused young man who, against all odds, hopes to maintain a relationship with his children. That he so often fails stems not from a predisposition to hedonism and irresponsibility but from very real obstacles.[82]

Recent sociological literature has helped to dispel a variety of myths that developed in the 1940s and 1950s about teenage fathers. Such myths developed in the context of rising rates of out-of-wedlock births and Freudian speculations about young men's need to prove their masculinity.[83] Surveys, interviews, and casework studies, for example, have helped dispel the myth that teenage fathers are especially knowledgeable about sex. Evidence suggests that they share with other teenagers the low level of sex education characteristic of American youth. Nor does research confirm the vision of teenage fathers as sexual predators. Most couples have meaningful relationships, reject the idea that pregnancy is somehow the girl's fault, and overwhelmingly disagree that getting a girl pregnant is a sign of manhood.[84] In a study of ninety-five black teenage fathers in Tulsa, Chicago, and Columbus, for example, the young men expressed concern about the mother's and child's future and denied that "getting a girl pregnant proves that you are a man."[85] Finally, a good deal of evidence suggests that most teenage fathers have close emotional ties with their girlfriends, have known them from one to four years, and are anything but casual regarding their future as fathers. Most, in fact, want to participate actively in pregnancy, parenthood, and child rearing. Summarizing several studies, researcher Bryan Robinson writes:

> In one study, 91 percent of the adolescent males said they would provide financial support and 87 percent wanted to participate in child care. In another study, 96 percent of the unwed, expectant fathers said they planned to maintain close contact with the mother, to interact socially with the baby, and to help with the infant's physical care.[86]

Other investigators have found that teenage fathers want to know about pregnancy and birth and how to care for their infant after birth. Moreover, the great majority maintained regular contact with the mother during pregnancy and provided material support to her both before and after birth. Studies have also revealed that young fathers overwhelmingly want to interact with their baby and to participate in child care. A minister working with black teenage fathers found optimism despite the inability of the young men to provide much material support: "They no longer abandon their children. They are more responsible than that. . . . It is rare today to find a child of teenage parents who does not know his daddy. Part of this involvement is due to black men being aware of their role as nurturer and provider, rather than just procreator."[87]

The best intentions, however, cannot overcome the obstacles these young fathers face. Foremost, of course, is joblessness and the young men's inability to become breadwinners. This liability lies at the heart of so much of their economic misery, family discord, and parenting frustration.[88] These obvious economic limitations are compounded by the father's lack of education, unrealistic ideas about parenthood, and poor prospects for a stable relationship with the mother. Teenage fathers, for example, routinely receive less education than nonfathers. This setback puts them at a severe disadvantage compared with their classmates.[89] Nor are some young fathers realistic about the demands and responsibilities of parenthood. As one nineteen-year-old told Robinson:

My wife and I just don't get enough time together anymore. We can't do some of the things we'd like to do like just run out and see a movie. We always have to worry about a baby sitter—a sister sitter—or whatever you want to call her. . . . If we get in bed and try to talk, the baby will be crying in the next five minutes. They're just always there and you can't run from them.[90]

If, like this youth, the father and mother decide to marry—and some 90 percent do not—they stand a much higher chance of getting divorced than couples who have their first child after the age of twenty.[91]

Teenage parenting takes its toll on all parties, but that incurred by young fathers has only recently received much attention. Recent research, however, reveals that the problems of teenage fathers begin well before the birth of their offspring. Several studies document the anxiety, fear, shock, and depression young men feel during the mothers' pregnancy. In one study of twenty-six unwed expectant teenage fathers, three-fourths said they were not ready to assume the responsibilities of fatherhood.[92] The uncertainties of one young man could stand for those of thousands: "I've thought about it (fatherhood) a lot, and it scares me. Hell, I'll admit it—I'm not a grown man and I never try to pretend to be. I'm still, well, a child in a sense . . . I'll love it, but I'm not sure I'll know how to teach it and guide it."[93] Other studies of young fathers document feelings of emotional rejection, self-blame, guilt, and isolation, all of which may develop even before their child is born. Once the child arrives, teenage fathers often feel they have little control over critical decisions involving the baby, a situation that leaves them feeling confused and neglected. Nor do they have much confidence in their ability to support the child; in fact, one study of twenty teenage fathers who had married by the time of delivery found that all doubted their ability to become effective breadwinners. Other worries plagued them as well, including concern about the health of the mother and child, their ability to discipline and care for children, and their relationships with their partner, parents, and peers.[94]

When researchers actually interview young fathers and trace their lives, they find the youths differ markedly from the insensitive stereotypes that haunt the imagination of conservatives. Certainly some try to live out macho fantasies by impregnating women, but most do not. Most are naïve, scared young men whose adulthood is thrust on them at a time when they lack the means of handling its demands. More important, they live in a society that makes it impossible for them to do so. For hundreds of thousands of young American men, the historical link between fatherhood and breadwinning has been broken, and their inability to reforge that bond brings with it isolation, confusion, and sadness. It is a tragedy of profound dimensions.

The Kaleidoscope of Fatherhood

From the mid-nineteenth century until the post–World War II era, men had found identity in their role as family provider, but the economic and demographic foundations of this world came apart in the last quarter-century. Changes in the structure of the household economy coupled with rising rates of divorce, out-of-wedlock births, and female-headed families have called into question previous assumptions about fatherhood. The certainties of Ward Cleaver's domestic life have ebbed away, replaced by negotiations about housework and child care, discussions about "deadbeat dads" and single fathers, concerns about stepfathers and reconstituted families. More than ever before, diversity is the defining characteristic of American fatherhood.[95] The reorganization of men's lives has brought understandable concern. Few can take any solace in rising rates of out-of-wedlock births and female-headed families nor do "deadbeat dads" inspire much confidence. If men are truly in flight from the family, such a development marks a significant turn in American history. Until the last two decades, supporting a family was perhaps the definitive act of mature manhood, and if that is eroding, then men will be forced to find a new source of identity and self-respect. But perhaps the flight is more illusory than real. Perhaps the most significant change in the reorganization of men's lives is not their flight but their confusion. Men still find meaning as fathers as they struggle to discover new meanings for fatherhood. What has prompted these new meanings are changes in the structure of the household economy coupled with the rise of feminism. Together they have politicized fatherhood, the subject to which we now turn.

11

Patriarchy and the Politics of Fatherhood, 1970–1993

I N A ROOM FULL OF "SMOKE AND ANGER," SOME SIXTY MEN GATHERED in Portland in 1986 at the fifth annual meeting of the National Convention for Men. Denouncing "father bashing" and "female chauvinism," some went so far as to compare "the law's treatment of divorcing men to the Holocaust and Salem witchhunts." At issue were custody laws that allegedly favored mothers and discriminated against fathers. In the same year, the *New York Times Magazine* reported that millions of working fathers were now experiencing a conflict between family commitments and work obligations, a problem that Los Angeles lawyer and father John Kronstadt attributed to changing expectations of fatherhood: "Society hasn't lowered its level of job performance, but it has raised its expectations of our roles in our children's lives." Clearly, many men tried to fulfill these new expectations. A Pasadena father, for example, compared his experience with that of his own father: "My father has proudly stated that he never changed a diaper; I am similarly proud that I have changed hundreds."[1] Meanwhile, future fathers rushed to childbirth classes or signed up for classes in "baby massage." More sedentary sorts cheered Dustin Hoffman's Ted Kramer as he struggled with the pitfalls and triumphs of single fatherhood in the movie *Kramer vs. Kramer.* For Kramer, as for millions of other American men, fatherhood had become part of the therapeutic culture, a "growth experience" that enriched one's life, enlarged one's sense of self, and destroyed outmoded conceptions of masculinity.

Against these voices from the new fatherhood, critics complained of "deadbeat dads" who refused to provide child support, lazy fathers who condemned their wives to the "second shift," and dangerous fathers who treated incest as a patriarchal prerogative. Memoirs and psychological studies of grown children added to the dissent as "wounded children" bemoaned their fathers' absence from home and called them to task for their neglect, silence, and insensitivity. Criticism came from the other end of the political spectrum as well, as New Right thinkers and evangelical Christians joined in decrying the decline of paternal authority and in calling for a reinvigoration of traditional family values.

Dangerous or nurturing, ever-present or always absent, the patriarch of old or the pal of the new, fatherhood in recent decades has become a kaleidoscope of images and trends, a sure sign that it has lost cultural coherence. As a result, the identity that men once gained from fatherhood and breadwinning no longer prevails. Buffeted by powerful demographic, economic, and political changes, fatherhood in American culture is now fraught with ambiguity and confusion. Not surprisingly, so, too, are fathers themselves. Fred Farina can speak for a generation of men. As he and his wife contemplated divorce, he could not fathom being uninvolved in his children's upbringing: "I wanna be more than just the father image. I wanna be involved in the raising of those kids. I wanna see them, day after day, I wanna see them mature, I wanna see the cutting of their hair, the whole thing." Yet, his allegiance to traditional beliefs was not far below the surface: "I thought that as a man you couldn't raise children. It never came to my mind that children could be raised by their father and live with their father. I always thought it was a natural thing for kids to be raised by their mother."[2]

Farina's confusion is not difficult to understand. The "natural thing" for at least a century had been for mothers to rear children, fathers to support them. Fatherhood and manhood were inextricably linked in American culture: men organized their lives and their identity around fatherly breadwinning. Much of this changed, however, in the last twenty-five years under the influence of two profoundly important developments. As we have seen, the tremendous increase in the number of married women and mothers in the work force fundamentally challenged ideas about manhood, masculinity, and attendant breadwinning and fatherly responsibilities. Second, the effects of this change were augmented by the reemergence of feminism in the mid-1960s, which made all gender assumptions, including those about fatherhood, problematic. Together they prompted a far-reaching cultural debate about fatherhood never before known in American history.

Feminism and the Second Coming of the New Fatherhood

Family experts throughout the twentieth century have been calling for greater fatherly commitment to the home, but their cries took on new meaning with the reemergence of feminism, particularly its liberal strain, in the 1960s. Although concerns about personality development, sex-role socialization, and social order had been at the center of earlier calls for fatherly involvement, the feminist movement politicized this demand and with it fatherhood in general. What emerged after 1970 was a second, more political incarnation of the new fatherhood that had first emerged a half-century earlier. Prompted by feminism and women's rising work participation, this second version challenged men to share equally the nurture and daily care of their offspring. For this to happen, men had to become more than after-hour buddies and play-mates and take on the less appealing aspects of child care. As we have seen, men have not ignored this message—recall that in one sample of metropolitan Washington, D.C., fathers, 48 percent claim to have re-duced their working hours in order to spend more time with their chil-dren—but they have also demonstrated ingenious ways to resist the demands of parenthood. Others, even more clever as we shall see, have made fatherhood into a form of self-enhancing therapy. Regardless, although this second version of the new fatherhood bears superficial similarities to the first, its impact will ultimately be more profound be-cause its roots lie in basic changes in the household economy and in conceptions of gender. Having already discussed the first of these two transformations, let us turn to the second.

Both women and men have shaped the second coming of the new fa-therhood and provided its political meaning. Over the last twenty years, liberal women feminists have called repeatedly for reconceptualizing parental responsibilities and for restructuring the work environment to transform parenting. In a 1970 press release, the National Organization for Women (NOW) decried the assumption that child care was primar-ily a maternal responsibility: "[We believe] that the care and welfare of children is incumbent on society and parents. We reject the idea that mothers have a special child care role that is not to be shared equally by fathers."[3] In the same year NOW adopted a resolution stating that "marriage should be an equal partnership with shared economic and household responsibility and shared care of the children" and asked that institutions "acknowledge that parenthood is a necessary social service by granting maternal and paternal leaves of absence without prejudice and without loss of job security or seniority."

Although never key feminist demands, these assumptions and recommendations continued to be part of the liberal feminist agenda throughout the 1970s. At the end of the decade, for example, the White House Conference on Families called for increased child-care options, restructured jobs, flexible working hours, and the expansion of maternity and paternity leaves.[4] Moreover, liberal feminism began paying more attention to family matters and fatherhood. The National Organization for Women convened a conference in 1979 on the Future of the Family, and in a keynote address Betty Friedan applauded the "new fatherhood" and argued that "the family, instead of being enemy territory to feminists, is really the underground through which secretly they reach into every man's life." For Friedan, the family was "the new feminist frontier" and the "new man" one of its most important explorers.[5]

Such men, Friedan insisted, had already been blazing the trail. "A quiet movement" was under way among American males, who, despite feeling somewhat "awkward, isolated, confused," knew that manhood was in the midst of a historic change. Forced by the women's movement to change their lives yet enticed by the possibilities that such change offered, influenced by Vietnam protests and the sensibilities of the counterculture, alienated from increasingly meaningless work, men in the 1970s and 1980s began "disentangling themselves from definition by success in the work world and [shifted] toward a new defini-tion of themselves in the family and other new dimensions of self-fulfillment."[6] To make her case, Friedan cited a young Chicago executive who stepped off the fast track for the sake of fatherhood. Refusing to accept the extra assignments that could lead to a big promotion, the expectant father let his boss know the bad news: "We're having another child and I'm committed to sharing the responsibilities at home because my wife's going to law school at night." After assuring his employer that his decision would not affect his present performance, he then let the boss know that it was the extra work he rejected: "But I'm not taking on anything extra. My family is more important to me." The boss could only shake his head and lament, "That man isn't going to get far. Too bad. He was the pick of the litter."[7]

Male feminists elaborated these ideas, especially as they related to fatherhood. Inspired by feminist theory, critical of the increasing bureaucratization and routinization of work, and cognizant of changing gender relationships in general, men in the early 1970s began formulating a critique of traditional masculinity and made some of the earliest calls for a new, politically informed fatherhood. In the view of these men, the breadwinning role was anachronistic, dysfunctional, and a symbol of outmoded patriarchal prerogatives. Women's liberation, went their argument, encompassed male liberation from stereotypical assumptions about traditional male roles, including hoary notions of fatherly responsibilities. Fathers with working wives must assume 50 percent of the child care; otherwise, the promise of gender equality at the core of feminism would be unfulfilled. The feminist perspective on the "politics of housework" necessarily included the "politics of childcare," and for some men the "new fatherhood" of the 1970s, 1980s, and 1990s represented a genuine effort to fulfill the promises of the liberal feminist vision.

This liberal, ostensibly feminist perspective averred that traditional manhood and fatherhood were a kind of prison, a set of "roles" with unrealistic expectations that led men to do bad things and put them out of touch with their "real," more nurturing selves. Where this "true self" came from, as Tim Carrigan, Bob Connell, and John Lee pointed out in an important critique of men's studies, was not at all clear. But the theorists of the new manhood believed it was waiting to be unlocked by men intrepid enough to give up the old ways, bold enough to assume more nurturing relationships with their lovers, friends, and children. The problem lay, then, not in the structure of relationships but in the tyranny of roles and ultimately in the heads of men. The problem was one of character and misguided socialization, not power. Masculinity, and fatherhood with it, had to be modernized if men were to escape the oppression of sex-role confinement.[8]

Liberal Feminism, Fatherhood, and the Culture of Therapy

The new fatherhood thus became part of "male liberation," a movement defined not as struggling against the powerful but as breaking free of conventions.[9] As critics have pointed out, this perspective could lead to the mystification of patriarchal relations, to the view that men and women alike were victims of patriarchy, women for obvious reasons, men because patriarchal assumptions prevented them from "getting in touch with their feelings." Men could thus applaud feminists as fellow travelers on the road to human liberation and personal fulfillment, assumptions that ultimately eased into a therapeutic rather than a political perspective on fatherhood. While seemingly harmless, the implications of this development for feminism could be dire indeed. By deflecting attention from the political realm of social change to the private realm of the enhanced self, therapeutic visions of fatherhood could potentially hamper efforts to reconstruct gender relations.

And the vision was everywhere. In books, newspaper articles, newsletters, and radio and television programs, in classes for expectant fathers, new fathers, and fathers of children of every age, in university courses on fathering and in support groups of fathers in every conceivable situation, the message was more or less the same: the new, liberated father was a nurturing man.[10] Thus, men in Menlo Park, California, could learn infant massage to strengthen "parent-infant attachment" and promote "the physical and emotional well-being of babies." A class in Chicago offered new fathers the chance to "review recent research about the importance of father involvement during infancy" as well as practice "some basic baby-care skills (using dolls and real babies) such as holding, comforting, interacting with, diapering, feeding, and bathing." Men on the East Coast were not without similar resources. A course in Boston offered information about parenting and, perhaps more important, the reassurance that "pregnancy is a time of transition for the man *and* the woman and it is important for men to have the chance to be directly involved in this miracle." The course must have worked, because the director reported that men often exclaimed, "This is the first time anyone has asked me how I feel about the pregnancy."[11]

As the children grew, fathers had other sources on which to draw. In addition to a small library of books on fathering, men could take advantage of classes and workshops that helped them understand and nurture their preschoolers, grade schoolers, and teenagers. Everything from standard child development instruction, to "Saturday with Daddy" outings, to songfests, field trips, and father-child potlucks, to a "Warm Line" telephone service were available to men hoping to amplify and solidify the child-father bond. Even men behind bars could get help. Inmates at the Hennepin County, Minnesota, Adult Corrections Facility could take a series of programs meant to enhance father-child relations. One novel program allowed inmate fathers to read children's stories into cassette tapes that were then sent, along with the book itself and a Polaroid picture of the father, to their child.[12]

All of this was not only good for the child but beneficial to the psychological well-being of fathers. Whereas the new fatherhood of the 1920s to mid-1960s emphasized the benefits children would receive from such attention, the therapeutic impact of such a perspective on fathers went more or less unexplored. Not so in the 1970s and 1980s.

Now the new fatherhood would not only help children; it would also enhance men's lives, heighten their self-awareness, and reorient masculine attitudes. Such happy results were especially likely if men availed themselves of the readings, workshops, and seminars that proliferated in the years after 1970. Men in San Francisco, for example, could visit the "Parents Place" and talk with other men about "child development, their own roles as fathers, and the 'worries, joys, and values' which the men share as parents of young children." In the eyes of their group leader, "Fathers share their feelings quite openly and serve as a valuable source of support and information for each other." At the "For Dads Only" program in Baton Rouge, men had the opportunity to discuss feelings of paternal inadequacy and their sadness about "being 'neglected' while their wives are getting so much attention." A fathers' support group in Cambridge, Massachusetts, helped men overcome "the limits that male socialization can place on their involvement in childrearing and nurturing," while fathers in Arlington, Massachusetts, came away from a support group "more positive about their ability to have mutually satisfying relationships with their children." The same happy result befell fathers who attended a Brooklyn discussion group. Participants had the chance "to share honestly and openly their insights, fears, and experiences with like-minded peers." Such mutual support worked its magic. The men left with "'a growing confidence and self-esteem' and a re-affirmation of the excitement, challenge, and commitment with which a number of men are approaching the 'experience of nurturing.'"[13]

Such a transformation must have been heady indeed for men who had entered the class full of self-doubt and anxiety. Nor were they alone. The countless newspaper and magazine articles, hundreds of programs and workshops, and scores of books on the new fatherhood speak to changes in the behavior and expectations of American men. Evidence presented to Congress in June 1991 documented fathers' willingness to get out of the "rat race" and on to the "daddy track." Witnesses described their commitment to being real care givers and the differences it had made in their lives.[14] Quite clearly, many American men want to be more than breadwinners and some have quite willingly taken on the onerous tasks of child rearing, but beyond a vague desire to "spend more time with their families," it is not exactly clear what most American fathers expect from the new fatherhood. As we have already seen, most do not want the drudgery of daily child care—diapering, feeding, dressing, cleaning up after, chauffeuring, and the like, that keeps families running. What men apparently want is companionship and the chance to nurture. To liberal feminists, such desires translate into the hope that such men will ultimately become better humans. Best-selling author Letty Pogrebin, for example, finds that "children are discovering their 'other parent' and men are discovering their 'other selves.' Fathers are ripping off the stiff patriarchal collars of *their* fathers; men are writing about the old kind of father who couldn't tell his children his love or his fears, who 'kept still and died in silence.'"[15] She applauds the men who attend baby showers, push carriages, and demand paternity leave and takes comfort in changes in advertising images of fathers, the proliferation of child-care courses for boys, and the erosion of "the absurd linkage of Father with Breadwinner."[16]

Likewise, Friedan's feminism contains a therapeutic perspective that reveals how easily the political can slide into the psychological. As men turn away from machismo and begin to explore their "messy" personal feelings, as they start becoming real fathers to their offspring, they become better, more self-fulfilled people. One man who quit his advertising job to write a novel described to Friedan the new freedom he felt: "I go over to the dock with the kids and their bikes after they get home from day camp. I look forward to putting them to bed every night; they like to talk then." His new life as a father and writer left him positively exhilarated at the end of the day: "I go to bed tingling all over."[17] Friedan's optimism about such men is standard fare among liberal feminists from both the men's and the women's movement. It accords with the assumption that men can shuck off outmoded roles with the help of education classes, flextime, paternity leaves, and less sexist television advertising. But the vaguely feminist politics underlying this view have little depth and ultimately give way to the therapeutic assumption that fatherhood—while perplexing and anxiety-producing—is also good therapy. If all goes well, it can be a growth experience, an enriching odyssey that can help men understand the truer, more sensitive self entombed within the hard shell of masculinity.[18]

Fatherhood and the Psychologists

Liberal feminists drew support from the psychological community. Spurred on by changes in family structure, feminism, the reality of the new fatherhood, and changing assumptions about parent-child relations in general, scholars began researching the father-child bond from every conceivable angle. What followed was a geometric increase in the number of articles about fatherhood that reflected a host of different major perspectives and signaled a shift of important dimensions. Parenthood was no longer synonymous with motherhood. Although debates of every kind raged within this literature, one clear result was to legitimate fatherhood as a field of study and to recognize its growing cultural importance. How fathers interacted with their infants, what degree of bonding developed between fathers and children, and the affiliative behavior (smiling, vocalization) of infants toward fathers all came under scrutiny. So, too, did fathers' role in socialization, including analyses of father-child play, maternal versus paternal styles of interaction, and comparisons between the interactions of mothers and fathers with daughters and sons. Summarizing scores of such studies, Michael Lamb concluded that "[f]athers and mothers both appear to be psychologically salient to their children from the time the children are infants" and thereafter adopt different roles as mothers become more responsible for nurturing and physical care and fathers for play and allegiance to cultural norms.[19]

Much the same could be said for research on fathers' role in sex-role development. The literature is inconclusive, at times even contradictory, but its cumulative weight is to legitimate the psychological significance of fatherhood. Some researchers argue that fathers more consistently desire sons than do mothers, that boys in turn develop a preference for their fathers, and that this preference ultimately leads to healthy sex-role identification. Others approach the question of sex-role socialization from the perspective of modeling and argue that "warm, nurturant, and involved" fathers have the most masculine sons, whereas others suggest that fathers "who are seen as heads of their household have more masculine sons and [that] the masculinity of sons is lower when the father plays a feminine role at home."[20] The results of this research, in short, are ambiguous, but they, too, underscore the importance of fathers to children's lives.

Other research has followed a similar course. Important debates continue about fathers' role in moral development and intellectual achievement. One study concluded, for example, that "fathers who felt positively about childrearing had sons who identified with them and displayed an internalized morality," and another "reported significant mother-child similarity in moral judgment but little father-child similarity."[21] Research on fathers' ability to promote or retard social competence and psychological adjustment has also prompted considerable interest and sparked an ongoing debate. As Michael Lamb surveyed this vast outpouring of psychological literature, he expressed dismay about its shortcomings, but the studies did confirm two key findings of importance to the new fatherhood: "[T]he masculinity of sons and femininity of daughters is greatest when fathers are nurturant and participate extensively in childrearing. . . . The most influential fathers appear to be those who take their role seriously and interact extensively with their children."[22]

Evidence seemed to suggest that children simply needed the presence of a father. Research on children reared in homes without fathers reported that boys tended to be less masculine or, ironically, hypermasculine compared with boys reared in homes with fathers. Father absence promoted poorer moral development, more juvenile delinquency, and a deterioration in boys' school performance, whereas paternal presence was associated with ease in establishing solid peer friendships and, later, successful heterosexual relationships.[23] After an exhaustive survey of the research literature on sex-role development, Henry Biller affirmed the importance of fatherly nurture to children's lives: "The optimal situation for the child is to have both an involved mother and involved father. The child is then exposed to a wider degree of adaptive characteristics."[24] Summarizing twenty years of her research on father-child relationships, Norma Radin told Congress that nurturing fathers promoted more favorable attitudes toward women's work, higher levels of intellectual functioning among sons (the evidence for daughters was more ambiguous), better social functioning and peer relationships, and a greater ability to empathize with others.[25]

Psychologists and child development specialists have thus added their support for the new fatherhood in the context of an approving culture. The flood of articles about fatherhood and the "daddy track," the birth classes and workshops on fathering, and the interest in reorganizing the workplace all suggest that the new fatherhood has gained an important measure of cultural legitimacy. It is good politics and good therapy. It is also good psychology. In a nation perplexed about family values, it is comforting to learn that nurturant, involved fathers will produce happier, smarter, better-adjusted children.

The New Fatherhood and Class Identity

The new fatherhood has also gained cultural legitimacy because it has become an important marker of class.[26] In a world in which even middle-class men cannot adequately support their families without their wives' wages, older styles of fatherhood no longer make sense. Men can neither claim the solitary status of breadwinning nor the prerogatives that come with that status. This being the case, fathers have made a virtue of necessity. They embrace an expanded role for themselves that is publicly commended and yet largely free of the onerous aspects of child rearing that still fall to women. Leading this call have been middle-class men, veritable symbols of the new fatherhood. In advertisements, movies, television shows, magazine testimonials, and newspaper features, more often than not the new father is a middle-class man trying to balance a busy career with the demands of basic child care and paternal nurture. Never mind that such men may actually create more work than they contribute.[27] What counts is their intentions and their sensibilities. Fathers who attend "expectant parent" classes, do an occasional load of laundry, spend "quality time" in creative play with their children, approvingly watch Ted Kramer's change from soulless advertising man to liberated father, or sympathize with the struggles of Steve Martin in *Parenthood* can feel not only good about the person they are becoming but superior to those in social classes below them. Life may be hectic in the middle class and the husband's paycheck insufficient to cover family expenses, but at least these men can take solace in leading private lives of a better sort than blue-collar working stiffs. From this perspective, the perambulator-pushing, diaper-changing, Little League-coaching suburban father is marking out class boundaries.

The new fatherhood as a marker of social class becomes clearer in light of the general experience of the middle class in the 1970s and 1980s. Beset by anxieties ranging from the youth revolt of the late 1960s to the stagflation of the 1970s, the economically hard-pressed middle class suffered what Barbara Ehrenreich has called a "fear of falling." Faced with soaring housing costs, rising tuition, and insufficient male paychecks, the middle class looked for ways to set itself off from the working class. This effort took a variety of forms, most notably the creation of a blue-collar stereotype perhaps best symbolized by television character Archie Bunker. In sociology texts, Hollywood productions, television shows, and magazine articles, blue-collar workers (inevitably male) appeared as ethnocentric, authoritarian, intolerant, and bigoted buffoons or as menaces to society.[28] By implication, of course, the middle-class male was all those things the working-class male was not, including more nurturing, tolerant, flexible, and knowledgeable in his approach to fatherhood. Thus, although social class is actually a poor predictor of fathers' involvement in child care, it is not surprising that the popular image of the new father was, and is, relentlessly middle class.[29] After all, these are the men most receptive to liberal feminism and its hope for a restructuring of traditional gender relationships. So, too, these are the men who staff the agencies of the therapeutic culture and trust in its agents, the ones most likely to take advantage of a "Fathers' Day Out" program or a workshop on good parenting, the men who staff the corporate bureaucracies experimenting with flextime and paternity leaves.

The new fatherhood, then, can become a badge of class, a sign that one has the knowledge, time, and inclination to embrace more progressive visions of parenting. On one side of the abyss, Archie Bunker screams nonsense at his son-in-law; on the other, yuppie Ted Kramer learns the exquisite joys of rearing children. The new fatherhood thus becomes part of a middle-class strategy of survival in which men accommodate to the realities of their wives' careers and the decline of their breadwinning capabilities. For these men, pushing a pram becomes less the sign of a wimp than a public symbol of their commitment to a more refined, progressive set of values than those held by working-class men still imprisoned by outdated ideas of masculinity.

Dangerous Fathers

Pram-pushing fathers may be staking out class boundaries, enhancing their own sense of good feeling, or actually doing a stint on the "second shift." Regardless of how we interpret their motivations, we generally applaud their behavior. But feminists have alerted us to a darker side of fatherhood as well. While most fathers do not harbor violent or incestuous intent toward their children, some do, and one of the achievements of feminism has been the rediscovery of family violence, particularly the role of husbands and fathers in perpetrating such violence. For a variety of reasons, researchers ignored child abuse throughout much of the twentieth century and rediscovered it only in the postwar period, thanks to a variety of historical changes, especially the reemergence of feminism.[30] Feminism demystifies family relationships and recognizes the centrality of gender to social analysis, a point made by Wini Breines and Linda Gordon in their analysis of family violence: "[W]e see the family and family violence, like all other historical phenomena, as produced within a gendered society in which male power predominates."[31] From the feminist perspective, the victimization of women and children by husbands and fathers is rooted in patriarchy and will not disappear until male supremacy ends.

This central assumption has helped researchers ask new questions about child abuse. For example, although evidence suggests that fathers and mothers each commit about one-half the child abuse in the United States (excluding incest, which is overwhelmingly committed by males), feminists have pointed out an obvious but overlooked point:

fathers do far less child care than mothers and spend demonstrably fewer hours with their offspring but nevertheless still abuse their children at rates equal to those of their wives; moreover, perhaps the fact that mothers abuse their children at all stems from their own subordination within a sexist society that leaves many mothers—particularly the impoverished and the single—feeling isolated, trapped, and angry.

Nor do feminists shrink from recognizing the complexity of the matter. Family violence, they insist, must be understood within its historical and cultural context and with an appreciation of class, race, ethnic, and generational variation. Furthermore, as Breines and Gordon explain, each act of violence is fraught with psychological as well as cultural meaning: "[N]o act of violence is merely the expression of a social problem (or a culture) such as poverty or unemployment or male dominance; each is also the personal act of a unique individual."[32] The ongoing task for feminists has been to explain the interrelationship of these factors, an effort already made by those who have studied the crime of incest, a special form of child abuse.[33] In fact, over 90 percent of incest assailants are males, and a similarly high percentage of their victims are female. And although brother-sister incest is far more common than father-daughter, experts estimate that the latter occurs in over 1 percent of families, a figure that translates into hundreds of thousands of victims.[34] Recent evidence suggests that the figure may be considerably higher. In a study of 930 women in San Francisco, 4.5 percent had been sexually abused by their fathers before the age of eighteen. If this figure holds for the population at large, 45,000 out of every one million women are victimized by their fathers before their eighteenth birthday.[35]

These victims were largely ignored until feminists brought attention to the sexual crimes of fathers. Part of this willful ignorance can be traced to Freud, who initially accepted then dismissed as fantasy his female patients' descriptions of father-daughter incest.[36] Part, too, can be traced to a tradition of blaming "collusive mothers" for the incestuous acts of fathers. From this perspective, incompetent, unbalanced, cold, and above all sexually frigid wives acted as catalysts for their husbands' illicit sexual behavior with their daughters. If blame could not be placed on mothers, still another part of the prefeminist tradition insisted that seductive daughters themselves were to blame for their fathers' actions.[37] Alfred Kinsey and his colleagues likewise consistently downplayed both the reality and the harmfulness of cross-generational incest.[38] Above all, incest remained hidden from view because it was simply a particularly brutal expression of unequal power relations within families. In other words, it was embedded within patriarchy.

As feminists began to decode family relationships, the tradition of blaming the victims of incest for the crimes of fathers came under withering attack. In both scholarly works and more popular offerings, writers insisted that father-daughter incest represented patriarchy at its rawest. Louise Armstrong, who describes her own incestuous victimization in *Kiss Daddy Goodnight,* draws a tight connection between incest and patriarchy: "Our understanding of incest as a longstanding male prerogative, a routine behavior traditionally permitted to men, was based on history, based on theory, and, of course utterly corroborated by women's testimony. For centuries, men have molested their children because it has been their privilege to do so."[39] Sarah Begus and Pamela Armstrong argue much the same: "The sexual assault on female children is part of the pervasive sexual abuse of women in patriarchy. Incest is a process wherein a father teaches his daughter the social relations of heterosexual sex: male aggression and power."[40] They could hardly be more blunt in asserting the implications of this relationship: "Moreover, it seems clear that as long as patriarchal power relations exist in any society, every child is a potential incest victim, and every father a potential rapist."[41]

Clinical evidence and first-person testimonials expose the complexity and the tragedy of father-daughter incest. Reading victims' accounts is an excursion into a world of denial, pain, confusion, and loss. It is a world of daughters who may feel enraged and yet stubbornly maintain affection for their abusive fathers, of young girls consumed by guilt and fear, of mothers paralyzed by shame and powerlessness, and, worst of all, of fathers who feel no remorse. That father-daughter incest is especially tragic is born out by evidence compiled by Diana Russell in her study of 930 San Francisco women. Russell found that victims of father-daughter incest reported considerably more trauma than victims of other kinds of incest, in part because fathers more likely imposed vaginal intercourse, abused their daughters more frequently, and were more likely to use physical force than other incest perpetrators.[42] Looking back, one young woman recalled the long-term damage she suffered because of her father's repeated abuse: "I was very emotionally upset as a teenager and a young adult. I was angry. I don't know what else to say. I was an unstable person. I flunked out of three colleges." Another woman obliquely commented on the anxiety and guilt she still felt because of her stepfather's predations: "It inhibited me for a long time. There has to be a certain kind of trust for me to have sex with a male. Every time anyone makes a sexual comment or yells at me on the street, I ask myself, 'What kind of image am I projecting? Is it the way I walk, or dress, or look?'"[43]

Against the sadness of such daughters falls the callousness of the fathers. Incestuous fathers seldom seek treatment or stop their assaults. In a study of forty incestuous families, Judith Herman found that not one father voluntarily stopped the abuse. Once charged with incest, many fathers use all the power at their disposal, including efforts to turn other family members against the victim, to fight the charges. And they are often successful. Evidence suggests that incest offenders are notoriously difficult to prosecute.[44] Rather than remorse, many of these men display an appalling insensitivity and a tendency to blame everyone but themselves for the breakdown in sexual order. And why should they not? If incest is an extreme expression of patriarchy, then one would expect its perpetrators to defend themselves in its terms.

Fatherhood and the Defense of Patriarchy

For feminists, father-daughter incest is a manifestation of patriarchy at its worst and will cease only when male supremacy gives way to egalitarian relations. To that end, feminists and advocates for the men's movement hope that the new fatherhood will be a progressive step in redefining American manhood, a step in line with building more equality between husbands and wives and more nurturing, meaningful relationships between fathers and children. To critics from the right, however, such changes merely signify the erosion of traditional relationships on which the good of society depends. What society desperately needs, they argue, is not the new fatherhood but the reassertion of traditional paternal authority: "The family is an organization," writes conservative psychiatrist Harold Voth, "and it is consistent with all known patterns of animal behavior, including that of man, that the male should be the head of the family." Although fathers should be "loving, compassionate, understanding, capable of gentleness and the like . . . all should know he is the protector, the one who is ultimately responsible for the integrity and survival of the family." Such knowledge, Voth assured his readers, is a prerequisite of success: "It is known that the most successful families are those where all members, including the wife, look up to the father-husband."[45]

Worried that American families were in deep trouble, convinced that the welfare system sapped the strength of fathers, galvanized by the battle against feminism and the Equal Rights Amendment (ERA), conservatives like Voth fought back in the 1970s and 1980s, hoping to forestall the corrosive effects of social and political change by reasserting paternal authority within families and reemphasizing men's obligation to support their dependents. Families needed clear lines of authority that only a father could provide: "There must be no role confusion between the mother and father," asserts Voth, "and though . . . distributions of responsibility and authority exist, everyone in the family must also know, appreciate and respect the fact that the father has the overall responsibility for the family; he is its chief executive, but like all good executives he should listen to all within his organization."[46] With this authority came responsibility. Men had the time-honored obligation to support their wives and children, an obligation firmly established by law but now under siege by misguided proponents of feminism. In the view of conservatives, traditional laws insured "the right of a woman to be a full-time wife and mother, and to have this right recognized by laws that obligate her husband to provide the primary financial support and a home for her and their children, both during their marriage and when she is a widow."[47] These laws originated in biology and religion: "Since God ordained that women have babies," writes antifeminist leader Phyllis Schlafly, "our laws properly and realistically establish that men must provide financial support for their wives and children."[48]

But feminism put all this at risk. What was at stake for conservative women in the battle for the ERA, for example, was the legitimacy of women's and children's claims on men's income. The stakes were high: "The Equal Rights Amendment," warned Schlafly, "would invalidate all the state laws that require the husband to support his wife and family and provide them with a home, because the Constitution would then prohibit any law that imposes an obligation on one sex that it does not impose equally on the other."[49] Such a turn of events would leave women doubly burdened: "ERA would impose a constitutionally mandated legal equality in all matters, including family support. This would be grossly unfair to a woman because it would impose on her the double burden of financial obligation plus motherhood and homemaking." Schlafly was certainly right on the last point. As she put it, "The law cannot address itself to who has the baby, changes the diapers, or washes the dishes."[50]

And men were more than willing to let women assume the burden of the "double shift." Underlying much of the conservative defense of patriarchy, as Barbara Ehrenreich has pointed out, was the deep suspicion that men, free of traditional obligations, would simply refuse to support their families. The fear persisted that men supported dependents only so long as it was convenient, a situation that would only become worse by passage of the ERA, which would destroy the legal foundations of male obligation.[51] Schlafly spoke for millions of anti-ERA homemakers in denouncing the proposed amendment: "The moral, social, and legal evil of ERA is that it proclaims as a constitutional mandate that the husband no longer has the primary duty to support his wife and children."[52] Hence the deep hostility to feminism on the part of Phyllis Schlafly and her supporters: it was a force that meant to help women but in reality helped legitimate male irresponsibility. In a culture eviscerated by the collapse of traditional family values, men acted responsibly only if their wives (and the obligations they felt toward their children) compelled it: "Man's role as family provider," Schlafly writes, "gives him the incentive to curb his primitive nature. Everyone needs to be needed. The male satisfies his sense of need through his role as provider for the family." If this need were subverted by feminist impulses, warned Schlafly, a man "tends to drop out of the family and revert to the primitive masculine role of hunter and fighter."[53]

This grim view was most fully developed by best-selling author George Gilder, who, in *Sexual Suicide* and *Wealth and Poverty*, argued that men were fundamentally brutes who became good citizens and productive workers only because women made them so. Sex—irresponsible, insatiable, and unrelenting—drove men, and this primal, destructive, and uncivilizing force could be checked only by women and children: "A married man . . . is spurred by the claims of family to channel his otherwise disruptive male aggressions into his performance as a provider for a wife and children." By extending men's horizons beyond the fulfillment of their sexual impulses, fatherhood gives men a vision of the future: "The woman gives him access to his children, otherwise forever denied him; and he gives her the product of his labor, otherwise dissipated on temporary pleasures. The woman gives him a unique link to the future and a vision of it; he gives her faithfulness and a commitment to a lifetime of hard work."[54]

Traditional breadwinning cooled male ardor and deflected it into worthwhile channels, but woe to the society that allowed women to intrude into this male domain: "A society of relatively wealthy and independent women will be a society of sexually and economically predatory males. . . . If they cannot be providers, they have to resort to muscle and phallus."[55] And muscle and phallus do not for good social order make; what does is men and women bound "to identities as fathers and mothers within the 'traditional' family." Children encourage respectability, the work ethic, and economic productivity among fathers, commitments that restrain men's sexuality and counteract antisocial behavior. In the view of the New Right, writes the sociologist Allen Hunter, "anarchic male energy is disciplined not by civic virtue in the society at large but by sexual responsibility toward one woman and economic responsibility to her and their offspring."[56] In short, fatherhood disciplines men to accept their responsibilities and obligations in the face of a variety of forces—feminism, humanism, godlessness, the welfare state—working to destroy conservatives' visions of social order.

In the view of the New Right, the contemporary liberal state has relentlessly encroached on parental authority and responsibilities and has sapped the initiative of breadwinners. To conservatives, as Allen Hunter has explained, "judicial activism and liberal, humanist social legislation have threatened the traditional family by penetrating it with instrumental, individualistic values, and by creating a paternalistic state which takes over child-rearing from parents and subverts the market." The image is one of the family under siege by the so-called "new class," the welfare bureaucrats and social planners so despised by New Right thinkers.[57] These architects of liberalism subvert male authority by eroding female dependence on male breadwinning. Worse, they create unemployment and poverty by causing family breakdown. Dusting off the assumptions put forth in the Moynihan Report, conservatives argue that it is family breakdown that causes poverty, not poverty that causes family breakdown. And family breakdown, as George Gilder explains in his inimitable fashion, came when the welfare state usurped paternal responsibilities to wives and children: "The man has the gradually sinking feeling that his role as provider, the definitive male activity from the primal days of the hunt through the industrial revolution and on into modern life, has been largely seized from him; he has been cuckolded by the compassionate state." With male breadwinning made optional, a father "feels dispensable, his wife knows he is dispensable, his children sense it." Men respond by leaving their wives and children and reverting to a less civilized state, exhibiting "that very combination of resignation and rage, escapism and violence, short horizons and promiscuous sexuality that characterizes everywhere the life of the poor."[58]

Fathers' Rights

Gilder's apocalyptic vision of fathers stems from a peculiar mix of Victorian biology and political conservatism, but his position has received support from other quarters as well. Into this camp fall "fathers' rights" activists and, more enigmatically, followers of the poet Robert Bly. By using the language of equality and appealing to the assumptions of the new fatherhood, the former turn feminist assumptions on their head and complain of the oppression of males in custody awards. By worrying about the absense of fathers and invoking the spirit of the "wildman" to overcome "softness," the latter hope to remasculinize American society by rediscovering the power of fathers.

The fathers' rights movement began as part of "men's liberation" in the 1970s. This larger movement initially reflected the desire of men on the left to align with feminism and to stake out and legitimate new modes of masculinity. The goal, in essence, was to reconstruct masculinity in order to free men's softer, more sensitive selves from the prison of machismo. One way to do so was to emphasize men's ability to nurture, and thus men's movement writers embraced the new fatherhood as a way to transcend the flinty reserve allegedly characteristic of an earlier generation of breadwinning drones. As we have already seen, this vision of manhood had within it as much therapy as politics, and by the mid to late 1970s the liberal feminism of some of these men ironically legitimated efforts to rectify the iniquities of child custody awards in divorce suits.[59] For how could divorced men remain loving, committed new fathers and how could they gain the deep personal satisfactions that came with parenthood if courts routinely marginalized them in divorce settlements?

What these men shared was a feeling of intense, palpable anger at a system they deemed stacked against them.[60] In meetings all over America, aggrieved fathers gathered to voice their frustration and hostility toward the courts, social workers, and most of all their ex-wives for cutting them off from their children. Part therapy group, part reform movement, the fathers' rights organizations combined feminism's language of equal rights with the vocabulary of male nurturance to fight for change. Their goal was to overcome the decades-old assumption that mothers were the more capable parent and to insist that fathers be assured continued involvement in the lives of their children. By the mid-1980s, over two hundred fathers' rights organizations with names such as Fathers for Justice (Mobile, Alabama), Fathers United for Equal Justice (Eliot, Maine), and Fathers Are Capable Too (Lubbock, Texas) had sprung up in virtually every state and were lobbying successfully for the reform of custody laws.[61] In fact, by the end of the 1980s men's groups had played key roles in passing joint custody bills in more than thirty states.

One cannot read these fathers' accounts without sympathizing with their loss, frustration, and anger. Their stories reverberate with tales of vindictive ex-wives, uncooperative, obstructionist social workers, and inattentive, insensitive judges. They tell, too, of children turned against them by maniacal former spouses, of specious sexual abuse allegations that destroyed peace of mind, of their dawning sense that they would be forever alienated from their children. At a meeting of the Equal Rights for Fathers organization in New York City, one father's anger could stand for that of thousands of others:

> I see my kid every weekend but it's become a nightmare. Lately, my six-year-old son acts terrified. My ex-wife has accused me, in front of him, of physically abusing him when I'm alone with him. Last time he threw up as soon as he got into the car. I know my wife is angry with me, but does she have a right to destroy my relationship with my child in order to revenge herself?

Deeply moved by this man's testimony, another participant said simply, "Fathers love their children," and then repeated the statement as if to underscore the point and reaffirm his own pain.[62]

The most frequent complaint is that ex-wives make visitation impossible and that courts do little or nothing to enforce fathers' visitation rights. (Fathers' rights activists, it deserves note, reject the term *visitation* and argue that it should be called *parenting time*. Said one activist, "Fathers are not cousins once removed or casual friends of the family; they don't *visit* their own children."[63]) Their concerns are not without foundation. One study found that 40 percent of custodial wives admitted they had refused, at least once and for punitive reasons, to allow their ex-husbands to see their children in the first two years after divorce. Another investigation found that 20 percent of divorced wives saw no benefit to fathers' continued involvement with their children and worked actively to sabotage their efforts to do so.[64]

Clearly these fathers' grievances must be taken seriously and their frustrations deserve sympathy. One cannot read accounts of men denied access to their children for months on end without feeling their sadness and loss, nor can one read of men falsely accused of sexually abusing their children without sharing their bitterness. But another dimension to this debate deserves attention. In the judgment of critics, the fathers' rights movement has taken the language of shared parenting and the new fatherhood and used it to increase men's control over women. As part of a wider backlash against women's gains, the fathers' rights movement increases men's legal control over their children outside marriage while effective day-to-day care of children remains where it always has been—with mothers.

Thus, critics argue that joint custody, the principal demand of the fathers' rights movement, empowers men but has nothing positive to offer women. Mandatory joint custody legislation misses the point that mothers almost always provide primary care both before and after divorce. Despite this imbalance, fathers in joint custody arrangements gain equal legal control over their children's lives without, in essence, having to assume equal responsibility for their care: "Joint legal custody," writes Carol Smart, "would not involve men in the daily care of children, but it would enhance their access rights and would mean that they had to be consulted over major issues concerning the child." Moreover, as Smart notes, because joint custody presupposes equality in decision making about the children, when conflicts arise the custodial parent (in most cases, women) would be open to increased surveillance by the courts.[65] Thus, under joint custody arrangements women remain as the primary care givers but are subject to the enhanced power of their ex-husbands backed by the power of the state. How, they ask, can such a development benefit them?

Critics also worry that the fathers' rights movement poses even greater dangers. Although most fathers do not request custody, when they do they increasingly gain it. In a California study from the late 1970s, 63 percent of fathers who requested custody received it, up from 35 percent in 1968 and 37 percent in 1972. Of contested cases settled by trial, fully one-third of the awards went to fathers. Other studies reveal success rates of fathers in contested cases ranging from 40 to 50 percent, evidence that belies the claim of fathers' rights activists that men suffer terrible discrimination in divorce court. That women receive custody in about 90 percent of divorce cases obscures the fact that most men do not request custody. When they do, they have a good chance of receiving it even though in most instances women have been the primary care givers.[66]

In many, perhaps most instances, the good intentions of these men should not be questioned. Single fathers are a rapidly growing segment of the population—in 1991 almost 15 percent of single parents were fathers, up from 10 percent in 1980—and their triumphs and struggles have begun to attract both popular and scholarly attention. In an article "It's Not Like Mr. Mom," *Newsweek* offered profiles of several such men and chronicled how single fatherhood had changed their lives, changes that were novel, it is worth noting, only because they happened to men, not women. Their stories were heartwarming, even inspiring, but they should not obscure an important point made by feminist critics of the politics of custody. Although fathers' rights activists use the rhetoric of equality to their advantage, critics point out that caretaking is not an equal proposition in most American homes.[67] The choice in custody suits is not between two parents who provide care equally but between one parent who does most of the care giving and another who does far less. That courts and legislatures have increasingly couched the matter in abstract terms of equality devalues care giving and conceals women's real work in rearing children. Worse, by seeking to avoid an automatic preference for mothers and holding instead to a sex-neutral standard in settling custody disputes, courts weigh equally fathers' financial support against mothers' nurturance. A feminist critic of the fathers' rights movement, Nancy Polikoff, rejects the logic of this equation:

> But the only appropriate purpose of a sex-neutral standard is to require evaluation of who is providing primary nurturance without automatically assuming it to be the mother; its purpose should not be to eliminate the importance of nurturance from the custody determination and equate the provision of financial support with the provision of psychological and physical needs.[68]

The obvious point is to extend equality to nurturing fathers, not to equate paternal financial support with maternal nurture.

Feminists have pointed out other difficulties women encounter in courts attracted to the assumptions of the fathers' rights movement. Mothers who do less than everything may draw the negative attention of judges, whereas fathers who do a bit more than nothing attract positive comment. Other judges tend to see mothers who work outside the home in the same light as fathers who do so, ignoring that working mothers also tend to do most of the child care during the "second shift." Thus, a Missouri appellate court could state that "if the mother goes and returns as a wage earner like the father, she has no more part in the responsibility [of child care] than he."[69] Courts have gone even further and criticized working mothers' ability to care for their children, a prejudice working fathers seldom encounter. So, too, divorcing mothers new to the labor market who must take time out for training and education appear less settled and stable to judges than ex-husbands who have a long employment history. Finally, if courts use financial support as a criterion for custody—and they have—mothers clearly find themselves in a difficult spot: "At a time when the myth that men are unfairly denied custody has pervaded public consciousness," writes Polikoff, "judges can latch on to the father's economic superiority as a reason to support paternal custody."[70]

Feminists argue not that the principle of equality should be ignored, not that a sex-neutral standard in custody awards is wrong, but that in practice judges have devalued mothers' work and have hopelessly confused the real nature of family life and child care by adhering to abstractions that work against women's interests. Polikoff puts the feminist case forcefully: "The concern lies with mothers who lose custody although they have performed the primary nurturing role throughout the marriage. A system that produces such a result is one that penalizes women and children, denigrates the mothering role, and shifts yet another form of social control to men."[71] The fathers' rights movement, the emergence of joint custody statutes, and the evolution of case law custody decisions over the last decade are, in the judgment of feminists, perfect examples of patriarchy at work. Only a system that gives custody preference to the primary caretaker—in most cases mothers, but in some fathers—is truly fair and congruent with the reality of child care in America.

Fathers and Wildmen

Fathers' rights organizations are not alone in lamenting the sundering of ties between fathers and children. Other men have sought more unconventional ways to bind male generations together. Around campfires and in sweat lodges, thousands of American men have gathered to recapture their lost manhood, find their missing fathers, and learn the ancient lessons that they can one day pass on to their sons. At the center of this movement stands poet Robert Bly, who, in workshops and a best-selling book, has inspired thousands of men to try to get in touch with their "deep masculinity." Bly's basic message is neither complicated nor historically novel. Sharing the anxiety of Boy Scout leaders at the turn of the century and Philip Wylie in the 1940s, Bly worries about the effeminacy of American culture and fears that the authority of fathers, and elder men in general, has declined. Such men, he argues, no longer lead the rituals that help young boys discover the true nature of manhood. Instead, fathers have become increasingly remote and irrelevant in the lives of young boys. Bly traces this development to changes in economic structure, especially the separation of male work from the home. As he puts it in *Iron John*, "When the office work and the 'information revolution' begin to dominate, the father-son bond disintegrates. If the father inhabits the house only for an hour or two in the evenings, then women's values, marvelous as they are, will be the only values in the house." And the process begins for boys when they are hardly beyond the womb: "One could say that the father now loses his son five minutes after birth."[72] As the boy becomes increasingly estranged from his father, he becomes distrustful of him and of other older men as well. The generational continuity between males is broken and young men, as Bly writes, become uneasy with their own masculinity:

If the son learns feeling primarily from the mother, then he will probably see his own masculinity from the feminine point of view as well. He may be fascinated with it, but he will be afraid of it. He may pity it and want to reform it, or he may be suspicious of it and want to kill it. He may admire it, but he will never feel at home with it.

Through the telling of old tales and myths and the enactment of rituals, Bly hopes to help men end this estrangement and to salve the wounds caused by remote, absent, and judgmental fathers.

To do so, Bly holds workshops, gives lectures, and tries to create "ritual spaces" where men may rediscover "the wildman" at the bottom of their psyches. Some of his efforts and those of his followers make easy targets for ridicule, especially the wildmen gatherings that have attracted thousands of participants. There is, indeed, something silly about tax lawyers and accountants lolling in the mud, groping about on all fours, and howling fiercely at the night. Surely most of us would feel uncomfortable snake-dancing to the beat of drums or climbing into a makeshift sweat lodge with other male seekers. But there is something real about these men's sense of loss and their alienation from their fathers. Trip Gabriel, who attended a wildmen gathering in Texas, found some of it awkward and some of it hokey, but he was also struck by the participants' anguish about their fathers. As the group leader, for example, began to chant the words "Dad," "Father," and "Daddy," men began to cry, first hesitantly and then "their anguish burst forth in heaving sobs that rolled through the grove. Beside me, Jim cried freely. A couple of places to my right, a man gasped, 'Hug me!' and he was embraced by the man next to him."[73]

If the fifty thousand or so men who have attended such gatherings had experiences anything like those described by Gabriel, there are probably many thousands more who feel a similar sense of loss.[74] Bly has clearly touched a sensitive nerve in American males, who may indeed feel out of touch with their masculinity and estranged from their fathers. But behind the bonfires, drumming, dancing, and anguish lies a politics that feminists find troubling. Bly, they assert, is opposed to feminism and wants to reestablish the power of men. Bly rejects such a characterization, expresses sympathy for the women's movement, and argues that the men's movement runs on a parallel track with that of feminism.[75] Feminists remain unconvinced.

Although critic Jill Johnston was "beguiled and moved" by Bly when she saw him on a 1990 Bill Moyers television special, she later concluded that "his program for men, as defined in *Iron John,* depends strictly on women playing their traditional roles at home."[76] More pointedly, she, along with Susan Faludi, author of the best-selling *Back-*

lash: The Undeclared War against American Women, see no coincidence in Bly's concerns about masculinity and the power of fathers and the rise of a more general animosity toward feminism. "Bly became a champion of men," writes Johnston, "at a time when many males were enduring a crisis of masculine identity in the wake of feminism. He and others . . . began seeing what they euphemistically called 'soft males'— limp men with low self-esteem and a heightened vulnerability to women, men suffering a remoteness from their fathers and a feminization of sorts because of the women's movement."[77] To Johnston, the drumming and chanting in the "ritual space" of meetings that exclude women are simply efforts by men to recapture lost power. Such men like to see themselves as victims—"wounded," as Bly puts it—but in fact "white men are not an oppressed group." Warming to her subject, Johnston has little time for Bly's male-segregated gatherings: "These meetings smack of the paranoid and racist overreactions of the David Dukes of this world, who feel that white (male) societies are threatened by black advances, however minuscule these advances actually are."[78]

Johnston is too harsh here, but her general point is on the mark. Despite Bly's protestations, his movement is not on a parallel track with feminism nor does it understand feminism's central insight. Gender is historically and socially constructed. Thus, Bly's ahistorical, unchanging, natural poles of "masculine" and "feminine" to which people allegedly gravitate are little more than mythopoetic tropes that shore up rather than tear down male dominance. Finding lost fathers may only multiply the number of men who control women.

The Fragmentation of Fatherhood

Lamaze coaches and deadbeat dads, daddy trackers and child deserters, wildmen and wimps, new fathers and old patriarchs, they are all part of American culture and the politics of gender. For each of these groups, fatherhood means something different. For one, the emphasis is on infant bonding, for another on starting a new family after the failure of the old. One group of men hopes to restructure work to facilitate father-child contact, another searches for lost fathers in a sweat lodge in north Texas, still a third hopes to restore men to their breadwinning preeminence. Despite these differences, fatherhood remains an important source of male identity. A survey of fathers in the mid-1970s found that 84 percent would rather be known as good fathers than good workers.[79] Yet, the meaning of "good" has become ever more elusive and political. Feminists and conservatives continue to argue over the politics of fatherhood, the former seeing new, liberating possibilities for men in dual-worker families, the latter only dangerous threats to social order.

The history of fatherhood in the twentieth century helps us understand the roots of this cultural confusion. For over a hundred years, male breadwinning undergirded patriarchal authority, helped define male identity, and even provided some commonalities for fathers across the chasms of race and class. But its hold was always tenuous. Fathers who could not support their families—breadlosers—suffered terribly. Some grew depressed and grimly hung on; others simply left. But the problems were cultural as well as economic. The authority of immigrant fathers was eroded by the power of American culture, but so, too, was that of middle-class fathers. The former found their children pulled away by the lure of American life, the latter by the rise of a youth peer culture and a consumer society. Although experts praised the emotional ties of fathers and children, their bonds were in many ways becoming increasingly economic. What fathers could buy for their offspring became a critical marker of successful family life.

Nor should the impact of the state on fatherhood be ignored. Some actions have shored up the power of breadwinners—the WPA or the GI Bill—while others have reduced it. Over the course of the century, for example, the state has given some attention to mothers and children seeking protection from cruel or irresponsible fathers. The therapeutic culture of the twentieth century likewise played an important role in the relocation of paternal power. Good fathers earned bread, but they also interacted with their children in ways delineated by self-styled experts interested in staking out new professional terrain. As fathering became part of the therapeutic milieu, rearing children became less the exercise of authority and more the search for personal "growth." Helping men in this search were therapists of one stripe or another who ran the workshops, taught the classes, and wrote the articles that kept the enterprise of the new fatherhood alive and well. Their converts were legion, a phenomenon that led Barbara Ehrenreich to wonder mischievously "why every man who changed a diaper has felt impelled, in recent years, to write a book about it."[80]

These changes worked at the edges of the breadwinner ideal, their impact limited by the sheer weight of a gendered division of labor. For most of the twentieth century, the new fatherhood asked that men support their families, function as role models, and provide what time they could for their children's emotional and intellectual development. For their part, fathers tried to meet these obligations, constrained as they were by the obligations of work and a consumer and youth culture that tugged at their children's affections and interests. But the relative continuity of social expectations and men's experiences gave way in the years after 1970. The reorganization of the household economy and the rise of feminism transformed male breadwinning and female domesticity from the cultural norm to one alternative out of many. Out of these changes came the second incarnation of the "new" fatherhood with its profound potential to alter family relationships and men's lives. While for some it simply became another way to feel better—one more form of therapy in a culture of therapies—for others the new fatherhood might well bring about a reordering of one's life.

These changes have left fatherhood fragmented and fathers uncertain. Some men hold on to past assumptions, others embrace new possibilities; some resist doing child care, others offer workshops on how to do it better. "Daddy trackers" think they have an answer, but so, too, does Pat Robertson. Meanwhile, most American fathers go off to work in the morning and renegotiate the boundaries of parenthood in the evening, all in a culture that lacks any coherent and unified vision of what fathers and fatherhood should be. None of this should be taken as a lament for the lost power of fathers. Throughout this century, fatherhood has been an integral part of patriarchy. Breadwinning has not been without burdens, but it has bestowed great privilege as well. So long as fatherhood, breadwinning, family stability, and social order remained linked, women's claims to economic justice could be dismissed and men's commitment to child care could remain marginal.

Recent developments have challenged these assumptions. Fatherhood has become politicized; its terms are unclear, its very meaning contested. It will remain as such for some time. There will be those who pine for old verities, and those who resist the onerous tasks of child care; those who avoid child-support payments, and those who abuse their children. Such realities cannot be denied. But there is room for optimism as well. Millions of fathers are becoming more involved with their children, and millions more express the desire to become so. Recent survey evidence suggests that active "fathering" is now a strong male life-goal and that public opinion takes a more favorable view toward men who do housework.[81] While mothers still do most of the routine child care, fathers are slowly assuming more of the burden. This trend will continue. The task now is to restructure the working world and our assumptions about American family life in ways that recognize its remarkable diversity. Clearly many fathers want to become genuine care givers; clearly many mothers want to be part of the work force. Surely in the years ahead social policies can be developed that will allow men and women to do both.

NOTES

Chapter 1. Introduction: From Breadwinner to "Daddy Tracker"

1. Marion Elderton, ed., *Case Studies of Unemployment Compiled by the Unemployment Committee of the National Federation of Settlements* (Philadelphia: University of Pennsylvania Press, 1931): 194–201; Aimee Lee Ball, "The Daddy Track," *New York* (October 23, 1989): 57.
2. Robert S. Weiss, *Staying the Course: The Emotional and Social Lives of Men Who Do Well at Work* (New York: Free Press, 1990): 193–94.
3. Quoted in Jacquelyn Dowd Hall, James Leloudis, Robert Korstad, Mary Murphy, Lu Ann Jones, and Christopher Daly, *Like a Family: The Making of a Southern Cotton Mill World* (Chapel Hill: University of North Carolina Press, 1987): 163–64.
4. Lillian Breslow Rubin, *Worlds of Pain: Life in the Working-Class Family* (New York: Basic Books, 1976): 36.
5. Robert S. Lynd and Helen Merrell Lynd, *Middletown: A Study in American Culture* (New York: Harcourt, Brace and World, 1956; first published 1929): 149.
6. Weiss, *Staying the Course,* 96.
7. Samuel Osherson, *Finding Our Fathers: How a Man's Life Is Shaped by His Relationship with His Father* (New York: Fawcett Columbine, 1986): 6. Osherson focuses on father-son relationships, but the general point holds for father-daughter bonds as well.
8. Lynd and Lynd, *Middletown,* 149.
9. These figures come from John Modell, *Into One's Own: From Youth to*

Adulthood in the United States, 1920–1975 (Berkeley: University of California Press, 1989): 221, and Steven Mintz, "New Rules: Postwar Families (1955–Present)," in Joseph M. Hawes and Elizabeth I. Nybakken, eds., *American Families: A Research Guide and Historical Handbook* (New York: Greenwood Press, 1991): 197.

10. Clifford E. Clark, Jr., "Ranch-House Suburbia: Ideals and Realities," in Lary May, ed., *Recasting America: Culture and Politics in the Age of Cold War* (Chicago: University of Chicago Press, 1989): 171–91.

11. Elaine Tyler May develops this theme at length in *Homeward Bound: American Families in the Cold War Era* (New York: Basic Books, 1988).

Chapter 2. Breadwinning and American Manhood, 1800–1920

1. Robinson quoted in Philip Greven, *The Protestant Temperament: Patterns of Child-Rearing, Religious Experience, and the Self in Early America* (New York: New American Library, 1977): 37; Lincoln Steffens, "Becoming a Father at 60 Is a Liberal Education," *American Magazine* 106 (August 1928): 48. What follows is based on the extensive secondary literature on the American family. For those interested in further reading, Steven Mintz and Susan Kellogg provide an excellent overview and extensive citations in their book, *Domestic Revolutions: A Social History of American Family Life* (New York: Free Press, 1988).

2. Mintz and Kellogg analyze the transformation of family life from the eighteenth to the nineteenth century in *Domestic Revolutions*, chapter 3. Three essays chart the general changes in American fatherhood since the seventeenth century: John Demos, "The Changing Faces of Fatherhood: A New Exploration in Family History," in Stanley Cath, Alan Gurwitt, and John M. Ross, eds., *Father and Child: Developmental and Clinical Perspectives* (Boston: Little, Brown, 1982): 425–50; Joseph Pleck, "American Fathering in Historical Perspective," in Michael Kimmel, ed., *Changing Men: New Directions in Research on Men and Masculinity* (Newbury Park, Calif.: Sage, 1987): 83–97; and E. Anthony Rotundo, "American Fatherhood: A Historical Perspective," *American Behavioral Scientist* 29 (September/October 1985): 7–25.

3. Mintz and Kellogg, *Domestic Revolutions*, 21–22; Carole Shammas, "The Domestic Environment in Early Modern England and America," *Journal of Social History* 14 (Fall 1980): 3–24.

4. Mintz and Kellogg, *Domestic Revolutions*, 20.

5. Greven, *Protestant Temperament*, 152, 160, 164, 170–71, 178–79, 184, 198, 227–33.

6. Mary Beth Norton, *Liberty's Daughters: The Revolutionary Experience of American Women, 1750–1800* (Boston: Little, Brown, 1980); Linda Kerber, *Women of the Republic: Intellect and Ideology in Revolutionary America* (Chapel Hill: University of North Carolina Press, 1980). For a view of the

Revolution that emphasizes the continuities in women's experiences before and after the war, see Joan H. Wilson, "The Illusion of Change: Women and the American Revolution," in Alfred Young, ed., *The American Revolution: Explorations in the History of American Radicalism* (DeKalb: Northern Illinois University Press, 1976).

7. Ruth Bloch, "American Feminine Ideals in Transition: The Rise of the Moral Mother, 1785–1815," *Feminist Studies* 4 (June 1978): 101–26.

8. E. Anthony Rotundo, "Manhood in America: The Northern Middle Class, 1770–1920," Ph.D. diss., Brandeis University, 1982, 344–45.

9. Alexis de Tocqueville, *Democracy in America*, vol. 2 (New York: Vintage, 1945): 205.

10. Hal S. Barron, *Those Who Stayed Behind: Rural Society in Nineteenth-Century New England* (Cambridge: Cambridge University Press, 1984): 72, 80–111.

11. Ibid., 71–72.

12. On the rise of the middle class, see Stuart M. Blumin, *The Emergence of the Middle Class: Social Experience in the American City, 1760–1900* (Cambridge: Cambridge University Press, 1989); on early suburbanization, see Sam Bass Warner, Jr., *Streetcar Suburbs: The Process of Growth in Boston, 1870–1900* (Cambridge, Mass.: Harvard University Press, 1962).

13. John Modell, Frank Furstenberg, Jr., and Theodore Hershberg, "Social Change and Transitions to Adulthood in Historical Perspective," *Journal of Family History* (Autumn 1976): 7–32.

14. Mary Ryan, *Cradle of the Middle Class: The Family in Oneida County, New York, 1790–1865* (Cambridge: Cambridge University Press, 1981): 167–68.

15. Ryan, *Cradle of the Middle Class*, 168. Most immigrant laborers and unskilled workers established their own households in their twenties, well before their middle-class counterparts.

16. Ibid., 172.

17. Ibid., 167.

18. Carroll Smith-Rosenberg, "The Female World of Love and Ritual: Relations between Women in Nineteenth-Century America," *Signs* 1 (Autumn 1975): 1.

19. Both planters are quoted in Jane Turner Censer, *North Carolina Planters and Their Children: 1800–1860* (Baton Rouge: Louisiana State University Press, 1984): 29–30.

20. Daniel Blake Smith, *Inside the Great House: Planter Family Life in Eighteenth-Century Chesapeake Society* (Ithaca: Cornell University Press, 1980): 40–46, 49; also see Censer, *North Carolina Planters and Their Children*, 31. Censer's evidence suggests that planter fathers were openly affectionate toward their children and hoped to be their confidants. See 59–61.

21. Censer, *North Carolina Planters and Their Children*, 38–64. Steven M. Stowe discusses the relationship among planter parents, their adolescent children, and the educational experience of these children in "The Rhetoric of Authority: The Making of Social Values in Planter Family Correspondence," *Journal of American History* 73 (March 1987): 916–33.

22. Quoted in Censer, *North Carolina Planters and Their Children*, 49, 53.

23. Ibid., especially chap. 5.

24. Bertram Wyatt-Brown, *Southern Honor: Ethics and Behavior in the Old South* (Oxford: Oxford University Press, 1982): 118.

25. Wyatt-Brown, *Southern Honor*, 122. Wyatt-Brown makes the point that these practices were not isolated among the upper class. As late as 1940, over 70 percent of men in one rural Kentucky sample carried their fathers' names. Jane Censer downplays the link between patriarchy and child-naming practices and suggests that naming practices tied the newborn to both sides of his or her family. See *North Carolina Planters and Their Children*, 32–33.

26. Wyatt-Brown, *Southern Honor*, 167. Wyatt-Brown discusses the relationship among fathers, sons, and honor at length; see 149–74.

27. Quoted in Herbert Gutman, "Persistent Myths about the Afro-American Family," *Journal of Interdisciplinary History* 6 (Autumn 1975): 204–5.

28. These generalizations come from Herbert Gutman's *The Black Family in Slavery and Freedom, 1750–1925* (New York: Vintage, 1977; first published by Pantheon, 1976). Carl Degler provides a useful survey of the black family in *At Odds: Women and the Family in America from the Revolution to the Present* (New York: Oxford University Press, 1980): 111–32.

29. The phrase "tangle of pathology" is from Daniel P. Moynihan's famous and controversial 1965 report on the black family. Herbert Gutman discusses this report in light of his research on the history of the black family in *The Black Family in Slavery and Freedom*, 461–69.

30. Gutman, *The Black Family in Slavery and Freedom*, 191.

31. Quoted in Eugene Genovese, *Roll, Jordan, Roll: The World the Slaves Made* (New York: Vintage, 1976; first published 1972): 492.

32. Quoted in Genovese, *Roll, Jordan, Roll*, 486. Genovese also notes that archaeological excavations of old slave quarters reveal that fish and game supplemented the slaves' protein-deficient diets. More than likely, fathers supplied the great majority of this food. See 487.

33. Quoted in Gutman, *The Black Family in Slavery and Freedom*, 36.

34. Genovese, *Roll, Jordan, Roll*, 486.

35. Mintz and Kellogg, *Domestic Revolutions*, 70.

36. Quoted in Mintz and Kellogg, *Domestic Revolutions*, 70. Degler provides a useful summary of the statistical evidence on slave family disruption by sale in *At Odds*, 119–20.

37. Degler, *At Odds*, 128. See, too, Gutman, "Persistent Myths about the Afro-American Family," 195–96, and Frank F. Furstenberg, Jr., Theodore Hershberg, and John Modell, "The Origins of the Female-Headed Black Family: The Impact of the Urban Experience," *Journal of Interdisciplinary History* 6 (Autumn 1975): 211–33.

38. Paul J. Lammermeier, "The Urban Black Family of the Nineteenth Century: A Study of Black Family Structure in the Ohio Valley, 1850–1880," *Journal of Marriage and the Family* 35 (August 1973): 44–56.

39. This trend became more intense in the half-century after 1940. Herbert

Gutman has described the process as a "modern enclosure" movement; see *The Black Family in Slavery and Freedom,* 466–69.

40. Gutman, "Persistent Myths about the Afro-American Family," 207.

41. Gutman, "Persistent Myths about the Afro-American Family," 205–10; Furstenberg, Hershberg, and Modell, "The Origins of the Female-Headed Black Family," 211–33.

42. Pitirim Sorokin and Carle C. Zimmerman, *Principles of Rural-Urban Sociology* (New York: Henry Holt, 1929): 340.

43. Ibid., 341, 345.

44. Ibid., 347–49.

45. Ibid., 350–51, 365–66.

46. In his analysis of family sociology in the 1920s and 1930s, Christopher Lasch analyzes Zimmerman's critique of the sociological infatuation with the "companionate" family; see Lasch, *Haven in a Heartless World: The Family Besieged* (New York: Basic Books, 1977): 44–49.

47. Ernest W. Burgess, *The Adolescent in the Family: A Study of Personality Development in the Home Environment* (New York: Appleton-Century, 1934): 339–44.

48. Ibid., 340, 343.

49. Ibid., 166–68, 171; see, too, Paul Landis, *Rural Life in Process* (New York: McGraw-Hill, 1940): 152.

50. Laura Amos, "As a Student Sees Farm Life," in *Farm Youth: Proceedings of the Ninth National Country Life Conference* (Chicago: University of Chicago Press, 1927): 21.

51. The Genesee County study was by W. A. Anderson in Cornell University Agricultural Experiment Station Bulletin, no. 607 (1934), summarized by Dwight Sanderson, "The Rural Family," *Journal of Home Economics* 29 (April 1937): 224. Wallace is quoted in Landis, *Rural Life in Process,* 217. This evidence did not mean that the venerable practice of fathers granting lands to sons was dead. For example, a study of rural Wisconsin in the early twentieth century found that 30 percent of transfers in land titles were from father to son. The study by C. J. Galpin appeared in a research bulletin published by the University of Wisconsin Agricultural Experiment Station in 1919 and was cited in J. H. Kolb and Edmund deS. Brunner, *A Study of Rural Society: Its Organization and Changes* (Boston: Houghton Mifflin, 1935): 42.

52. Landis, *Rural Life in Process,* 105, 435–36. On farmers' suspicions of schools, see Bird T. Baldwin, Eva A. Fillmore, and Lora Hadley, *Farm Children: An Investigation of Rural Child Life in Selected Areas of Iowa* (New York: Appleton, 1930): 45–48, 100–104. Rural school reformers criticized the backwardness of the one-room schoolhouse and proposed consolidation, professionalization, and curricular changes as antidotes. These efforts, especially the latter, presupposed that farmers could no longer even teach their children how to farm anymore. On rural school reform, see Barron, *Those Who Stayed Behind,* 46–47.

53. Landis, *Rural Life in Process,* 211.

54. Sanderson, "The Rural Family," 224.

55. Edward N. Clopper, *Rural Child Welfare: An Inquiry by the National Child Labor Committee* (New York: Macmillan, 1922): 85. Emphasis in original.

56. Proceedings of the Ninth National Country Life Conference, *Farm Youth* (Chicago: University of Chicago Press, 1927): 68.

57. Landis, *Rural Life in Process,* 214–15.

58. The studies by Mather and Thurow are both cited in Landis, *Rural Life in Process,* 153, and Sanderson, "The Rural Family," 225.

59. Burgess, *The Adolescent in the Family,* 133, 345.

60. Landis, *Rural Life in Process,* 152–53, 347, 453.

61. The data on movie attendance are from Burgess, *The Adolescent in the Family,* 170. In one survey from the 1930s, rural youth were far more critical of where they lived than were urban youth: over 70 percent of the youth living in towns under 2,500 and over 40 percent of those living in open-country farms expressed dissatisfaction with where they lived; by contrast, only 18 percent of boys and 10 percent of girls from suburbs and cities did so; see Howard M. Bell, *Youth Tell Their Story: A Study of the Conditions and Attitudes of Young People in Maryland between the Ages of 16 and 24* (Washington, D.C.: American Council on Education, 1938): 38–40.

62. E. L. Morgan and M. W. Sneed, "The Activities of Rural Young People in Missouri," *Missouri Agricultural Experiment Station Bulletin,* no. 269 (Columbia, Missouri, 1937).

63. A new study of the memoirs of men and women who grew up on the Midwestern frontier argues that beneath ritualistic praise for rural life ran a deep subcurrent of hostility to the constant work, grim isolation, harsh weather, and parental demands characteristic of life in this region; see Liahna Babener, "Bitter Nostalgia: Recollections of Childhood on the Midwestern Frontier," in Elliott West and Paula Petrik, eds., *Small Worlds: Children and Adolescents in America, 1850–1950* (Lawrence: University Press of Kansas, 1992): 301–20.

64. Michael Grossberg, "Who Gets the Child? Custody, Guardianship, and the Rise of a Judicial Patriarchy in Nineteenth-Century America," *Feminist Studies* 9 (Summer 1983): 235–60; Robert L. Griswold, *Family and Divorce in California, 1850–1890: Victorian Illusions and Everyday Realities* (Albany: State University of New York Press, 1982), 154; Lee E. Teitelbaum, "Family History and Family Law," *Legal History Program Working Papers,* Working Paper #1, Institute for Legal Studies, University of Wisconsin, 26–27.

65. *Reports of Cases Determined in the Supreme Court of the State of California, 1860,* XIV, 2d ed. (San Francisco: Bancroft and Whitney, 1887), 513–19.

66. Quoted in Teitelbaum, "Family History and Family Law," 28.

67. On the law and custody, see Grossberg, "Who Gets the Child?" 235–60.

68. David Rothman, *The Discovery of the Asylum: Social Order and Disorder in the New Republic* (Boston: Little, Brown, 1971), 235–36.

69. Quoted in Teitelbaum, "Family History and Family Law," 69.

70. Quoted in ibid., 22.

71. Eileen Boris and Peter Bardaglio, "The Transformation of Patriarchy: The Historic Role of the State," in Irene Diamond, ed., *Families, Politics, and Public Policy: A Feminist Dialogue on Women and the State* (New York: Longman, 1983): 70–93. On the shifting fortunes of children in the late nineteenth and early twentieth centuries, see Viviana A. Zelizer, *Pricing the Priceless Child: The Changing Social Value of Children* (New York: Basic Books, 1985); also see Robert McGlone, "Suffer the Children: The Emergence of Modern Middle-Class Family Life, 1820–1870," Ph.D. diss., University of California, Los Angeles, 1971, 104–6, 121–22, 131–32ff, 147, 149–50, 158–59, 266–69, 271, 276; Daniel T. Rodgers, "Socializing Middle-Class Children: Institutions, Fables, and Work Values in Nineteenth-Century America," *Journal of Social History* 13 (1980): 354–67; Bernard Mergen, "The Discovery of Children's Play," *American Quarterly* 27 (1975): 399–420. Susan Strasser discusses the home economics movement in *Never Done: A History of American Housework* (New York: Pantheon, 1982): 202–23. Also see Glenna Matthews, *Just a Housewife: The Rise and Fall of American Domesticity* (New York: Oxford University Press, 1987).

72. Susan Strasser discusses early twentieth-century child experts in *Never Done*, 224–41.

Chapter 3. Breadwinning on the Margin: Working-Class Fatherhood, 1880–1930

1. Marion Elderton, ed., *Case Studies of Unemployment Compiled by the Unemployment Committee of the National Federation of Settlements* (Philadelphia: University of Pennsylvania Press, 1931): 32–36.

2. John Bodnar, *The Transplanted: A History of Immigrants in Urban America* (Bloomington: Indiana University Press, 1985): 76.

3. Ibid., 72. Here Bodnar notes that the family economy was very much a part of European life. In some respects, a transplantation of family strategies from Europe to America occurred.

4. Claudia Goldin, "Family Strategies and the Family Economy in the Late Nineteenth Century: The Role of Secondary Workers," in Theodore Hershberg, ed., *Philadelphia: Work, Space, Family, and Group Experience in the Nineteenth Century* (Oxford: Oxford University Press, 1981): 277–310.

5. Jacquelyn Dowd Hall et al., *Like a Family: The Making of a Southern Cotton Mill World* (Chapel Hill: University of North Carolina Press, 1987): 61.

6. Tamara Hareven, *Family Time and Industrial Time: The Relationship between the Family and Work in a New England Industrial Community* (Cambridge: Cambridge University Press, 1982): 73–75.

7. Quoted in John Bodnar, Roger Simon, and Michael P. Weber, *Lives of Their Own: Blacks, Italians, and Poles in Pittsburgh, 1900–1960* (Urbana: University of Illinois Press, 1982): 244. Although fathers also found work for daughters, doing so was not nearly as important as finding work for sons;

whereas young men could look forward to a life of breadwinning, young women were expected to leave the work force once they married and became pregnant.

8. Hareven, *Family Time and Industrial Time,* 99. On kin clustering in the Amoskeag mills, see 85–101.

9. Ibid., 167; John Modell, Frank Furstenburg, Jr., and Theodore Hershberg, "Social Change and Transitions to Adulthood in Historical Perspective," *Journal of Family History* 1 (Autumn 1976): 7–32.

10. U.S. Congress, Senate. *Woman and Child Wage-Earners,* I: 436–37.

11. Hall et al., *Like a Family,* 162.

12. Hareven, *Family Time and Industrial Time,* 190.

13. Ibid., 193. Leonore Kosloff, a Lithuanian Jew who came to America in 1901, dutifully helped her family when her asthmatic father could no longer work: "I accepted my responsibility to help support my family even though this meant I wouldn't go to high school. I wanted to go to school, but I knew this was not possible. I was willing to help my mother because I had a sense of togetherness." Quoted in Elizabeth Ewen, *Immigrant Women in the Land of Dollars: Life and Culture on the Lower East Side, 1890–1925* (New York: Monthly Review Press, 1985): 100. Ewen provides other examples of young people readily helping to support their families on 101, 104–5.

14. John Bodnar, *Workers' World: Kinship, Community, and Protest in an Industrial Society, 1900–1940* (Baltimore: Johns Hopkins University Press, 1982): 28.

15. Bodnar, et al., *Lives of Their Own,* 148, 154. Daniel D. Luria offers a Marxist interpretation of the meaning of home ownership in "Wealth, Capital, and Power: The Social Meaning of Home Ownership," *Journal of Interdisciplinary History* 7 (Autumn 1976): 261–82.

16. Bodnar et al., *Lives of Their Own,* 153.

17. Ibid., 159. In 1930, 52.2 percent of foreign-born whites owned their own homes but only 38.1 percent of native-born whites did.

18. Olivier Zunz, *The Changing Face of Inequality: Urbanization, Industrial Development, and Immigrants in Detroit, 1880–1920* (Chicago: University of Chicago Press, 1982): 152. At the Amoskeag, parents sent their children to the mills to help buy a home, a decision that curtailed the completion of their children's educations. Hareven also noted that during the 1922 strike, some workers crossed the picket line rather than give up their homes. Hareven, *Family Time and Industrial Time,* 360.

19. Howard Chudacoff offers a useful overview and interpretation of mobility studies in "Success and Security: The Meaning of Social Mobility in America," in Stanley Kutler and Stanley Katz, eds., *The Promise of American History: Progress and Prospects* (Baltimore: Johns Hopkins University Press, 1982): 101–12. James A. Henretta offers a pointed critique of the mobility literature in "The Study of Social Mobility: Ideological Assumptions and Conceptual Bias," *Labor History* 18 (Spring 1977): 164–78.

20. Stephan Thernstrom, *The Other Bostonians: Poverty and Progress in the*

American Metropolis, 1880–1970 (Cambridge, Mass.: Harvard University Press, 1973): 232–33.

21. Hareven, *Family Time and Industrial Time,* 361.
22. Ibid., 362.
23. Ibid.
24. Bodnar, *The Transplanted,* 65.
25. Thernstrom, *The Other Bostonians,* 243–47.
26. W. O. Saunders, "Getting Acquainted with Father: A Confession," *American Magazine* 95 (February 1923): 39, 174, 177. It is unclear whether Saunders's father was an immigrant, but the text suggests as much.
27. Ewen, *Immigrant Women in the Land of Dollars,* 109. Irving Howe also notes the shifting fortunes of fathers and mothers in the Jewish community: "It was from her place in the kitchen that the Jewish housewife became the looming figure who would inspire, haunt, and devastate generations of sons. She realized intuitively that insofar as the outer world tyrannized and wore down her men, reducing them to postures of docility, she alone could create an oasis of order." *World of Our Fathers* (New York: Harcourt, Brace, Jovanovich, 1976): 174, 254.
28. White House Conference on Child Health and Protection, *The Young Child in the Home: A Survey of Three Thousand American Families,* John Anderson, Chairman (New York: Appleton-Century, 1936): 77–84. Whereas about one-half to two-thirds of fathers in the highest two classes read both magazine and newspaper articles about child care, only 12 to 13 percent did so in the lowest two classes. Among fathers in the "slightly skilled trades," 24 percent had at least one foreign-born parent; the same figure for day laborers was 38 percent (352).
29. Ibid., 108.
30. Ibid., 237.
31. Ibid., 211, 213.
32. Thomas Bell, *Out of This Furnace: A Novel of Immigrant Labor in America* (Pittsburgh: University of Pittsburgh Press, 1976; first published in 1941 by Little, Brown): 168.
33. Neil M. Cowan and Ruth Schwartz Cowan, *Our Parents' Lives: The Americanization of Eastern European Jews* (New York: Basic Books, 1989): 196.
34. Kathy Peiss, *Cheap Amusements: Working Women and Leisure in Turn-of-the-Century New York* (Philadelphia: Temple University Press, 1986): 15–16. Investigator quoted in Peiss, 16.
35. Quoted in ibid., 17. On working-class saloons, see Roy Rosenzweig, *Eight Hours for What We Will: Workers and Leisure in an Industrial City, 1870–1920* (Cambridge: Cambridge University Press, 1983): 35–64, and Jon M. Kingsdale, "The 'Poor Man's Club': Social Functions of the Urban Working-Class Saloon," *American Quarterly* 25 (October 1975): 472–89.
36. Elderton, *Case Studies of Unemployment,* 17–18.
37. *Twelfth U.S. Census, Occupations,* lxxxix–xciii, 219.

38. Alexander Keyssar, *Out of Work: The First Century of Unemployment in Massachusetts* (Cambridge: Cambridge University Press, 1986): 50.

39. Ibid., 320–26.

40. Although workers under 20 were the most likely to leave, 25 percent of male blue-collar workers in their twenties and almost 17 percent of such men in their thirties left the town of Brockton, Massachusetts, in a single year, 1900–1901. See ibid., 126.

41. Ibid., 143–76. These strategies for survival were also noted by the social workers in their case reports in Elderton, *Case Studies of Unemployment.*

42. Quoted in Keyssar, *Out of Work,* 165.

43. Elderton, *Case Studies of Unemployment,* 129.

44. Ibid., 136.

45. Ibid., 155.

46. Ibid., 291. For other cases in which men expressed a reluctance to accept charity, see Elderton, 241, 288, 295, 300, 303, 316, 343.

47. Ibid., 39–41.

48. Ibid., 85.

49. Ibid., 236. For other examples of men suffering severe depression owing to their unemployment, see 6, 43–44, 87, 118, 133, 208, 221, 255, 268, 270, 283, 369.

50. Ibid., 126.

51. Ibid., 14–15.

52. Ibid., 62.

53. Ibid., 63–64.

54. Ibid., 74.

55. Ibid., 216–17.

56. Ibid., 351.

57. Ibid., 334.

58. Ibid., 390.

59. Ibid., 71. Other men also withdrew their attention from their children because of unemployment; see 94, 134, 341.

60. Ibid., 28–29. For other case reports of men who suffered shame because of their economic situation, see 81, 101, 114–15, 164, 221, 340.

61. Ibid., 44.

62. Ibid., 104. For other examples of cases in which children lost respect for their father and/or fathers became irritable or abusive toward their children because of unemployment, see 69, 99, 104, 133, 175, 179, 258, 272, 363.

63. On the history of juvenile delinquency, see Anthony M. Platt, *The Child Savers: The Invention of Delinquency,* 2d ed. (Chicago: University of Chicago Press, 1977; first published 1969), and Joseph Kett, *Rites of Passage: Adolescence in America, 1790 to the Present* (New York: Basic Books, 1977): 254–58.

64. Elderton, *Case Studies of Unemployment,* 69.

65. Ibid., 158.

66. Ibid., 116–17.

67. Ibid., 208–9.
68. Neil R. McMillen, *Dark Journey: Black Mississippians in the Age of Jim Crow* (Urbana: University of Illinois Press, 1989): 113, 118–21, 141–43.
69. Ibid., 118–21, 126.
70. Ibid., 129.
71. Ibid., 125.
72. Ibid., 160–61.
73. Elizabeth Pleck offers a useful summary of the data on black household structure in *Black Migration and Poverty: Boston, 1865–1900* (New York: Academic, 1979): 183–84.
74. Bodnar et al., *Lives of Their Own*, 31–32.
75. Pleck, *Black Migration and Poverty*, 166, 183–84.
76. Herbert G. Gutman, "Persistent Myths about the Afro-American Family," *Journal of Interdisciplinary History* 6 (Autumn 1975): 181–210.
77. A variety of theories have sought to explain higher rates of female-headed families among blacks. Some scholars, notably E. Franklin Frazier and Daniel Moynihan, have suggested that the legacy of slavery was the decisive factor; others have suggested that imbalanced urban sex ratios, specifically a surplus of women, were key; a third line of argument focuses on high rates of black male mortality. After careful consideration of this evidence, historian Elizabeth Pleck found them wanting and poses the alternative discussed here; see Pleck, *Black Migration and Poverty*, 167–87.
78. Pleck, *Black Migration and Poverty*, 173–75. Pleck did find that the presence of children retarded black men's rate of desertion. Among couples who could be traced from one manuscript census to the next between 1870 and 1900, the rate of separation or desertion in late nineteenth-century Boston was 14 percent for childless black husbands and only 9 percent for black fathers. These figures come from longitudinal data of married couples traced from the 1870 to the 1880 census and from the 1880 to the 1900 manuscript census schedules.
79. To recognize the pain of this loss is not, of course, to belittle the hardship of black women because of men's absence. Bereft of male support, black mothers who headed families found it extraordinarily difficult to provide for their children in an economy that foreclosed virtually all economic opportunities for black women. Surely many of these women were depressed or outraged when it became clear their husbands were gone for good. Surely many such mothers found it all but impossible both to rear their children and to be the principal breadwinner for the family. On black women's participation in the labor force, see Claudia Goldin, "Female Labor Force Participation: The Origin of Black and White Differences, 1870 and 1880," *Journal of Economic History* 37 (March 1977): 87–112.
80. Bodnar et al., *Lives of Their Own*, 91.
81. Ibid., 92.
82. Ibid., 36.
83. On declining craft work for blacks, see Gutman, *The Black Family in Slavery and Freedom*, 27–28.

84. Bodnar et al., *Lives of Their Own*, 36–37.
85. Eileen Boris and Peter Bardaglio, "The Transformation of Patriarchy: The Historic Role of the State," in Irene Diamond, ed., *Families, Politics, and Public Policy: A Feminist Dialogue on Women and the State* (New York: Longman, 1983): 70–93. Also see Stanley Katz, "Legal History and Family History: The Child, the Family, and the State," *Boston College Law Review* 21 (July 1980): 1025–36, and Carol Brown, "Mothers, Fathers, and Children: From Private to Public Patriarchy," in Lydia Sargent, ed., *Women and Revolution: A Discussion of the Unhappy Marriage of Marxism and Feminism* (Boston: South End Press, 1981): 239–68.
86. Boris and Bardaglio, "The Transformation of Patriarchy, 70.
87. Eli Zaretsky, "The Place of the Family in the Origins of the Welfare State," in Barrie Thorne, ed., *Rethinking the Family: Some Feminist Questions* (New York: Longman, 1982): 195.
88. Viviana A. Zelizer, *Pricing the Priceless Child: The Changing Social Value of Children* (New York: Basic Books, 1985): 56–59.
89. Ibid., 64.
90. Quoted in ibid., 69.
91. *Report on Condition of Woman and Child Wage-Earners,* I: 353.
92. Quoted in ibid., 69–70.
93. The long story of child labor legislation is well told in Zelizer's *Pricing the Priceless Child,* 64–112. By the turn of the century, twenty-eight states had some kind of child labor legislation, most of which was vague, unenforceable, and full of loopholes. In 1916 Congress passed the first federal law banning the products of child labor from interstate and foreign trade, but after being challenged by opponents, the law was declared unconstitutional in 1918. A similar law, passed in 1919, met the same fate in 1922. In the 1920s Congress passed a constitutional amendment to allow Congress to regulate child labor, but it met a dismal fate in the states with only a handful ratifying it. The same thing happened in the early 1930s. Effective national regulation of child labor came only with the reforms of the New Deal, first in the short-lived National Industrial Recovery Act, then in the landmark 1938 Fair Labor Standards Act.
94. Quoted in Zelizer, *Pricing the Priceless Child,* 71.
95. Mrs. A. O. Granger, "The Work of the General Federation of Women's Clubs against Child Labor," *AAAPSS* 24 (May 1905): 104.
96. David J. Rothman, *Conscience and Convenience: The Asylum and Its Alternatives in Progressive America* (Boston: Little, Brown, 1980): 253.
97. Ibid., 205–35.
98. Ibid., 216–17, 232.
99. Ibid., 212.
100. Quoted in ibid., 221, from Victor Arnold, "What Constitutes Sufficient Grounds for the Removal of a Child from His Home, *Proceedings of the Child Conference,* 1910: 345.
101. Quoted in Rothman, *Conscience and Convenience,* 223. Emphasis in the original.
102. Ibid., 234.

103. On seventeenth-century laws regarding abuse of children, see Elizabeth Pleck, *Domestic Tyranny: The Making of Social Policy against Family Violence from Colonial Times to the Present* (New York: Oxford University Press, 1987): 17–33. The account that follows draws heavily from Pleck and from Linda Gordon, *Heroes of Their Own Lives: The Politics and History of Family Violence* (New York: Penguin, 1988).

104. Gordon, *Heroes of Their Own Lives,* 46–47.

105. Ibid., 48–55.

106. Ibid., 50–51.

107. Ibid., 55–57.

108. Ibid., 60–69.

109. Ibid., 72–73.

110. Martha May, "The 'Problem of Duty'" Family Desertion in the Progressive Era," *Social Service Review* (March 1988): 40–60. Savage quote, 43.

111. Ibid., 47. Charity officials did note that women could contribute to male abandonment if they kept house poorly or acted irritably and insensitively toward their husbands.

112. Ibid., 44. Reformers' lack of sympathy toward the deserter overlooked the fact that nearly one-fourth of the male deserters suffered from unemployment.

113. Ibid., 49–50.

114. Ibid., 52–54.

115. Gordon, *Heroes of Their Own Lives,* 73.

116. Ibid., 100.

117. Ibid.

118. Ibid., 103–5. Despite considerable opposition from social workers, states established mothers' pensions for single women because they were needed and women demanded them.

119. Pleck, *Domestic Tyranny,* 127–29; Gordon, *Heroes of Their Own Lives,* 289–99.

Chapter 4. Fatherhood, Immigration, and American Culture, 1880–1930

1. Leonard Covello, *The Heart Is the Teacher* (New York: McGraw-Hill, 1958): 29–31.

2. Robert Anthony Orsi, *The Madonna of 115th Street: Faith and Community in Italian Harlem, 1880–1950* (New Haven: Yale University Press, 1985): 120–21. These displays most often occurred in the *domus,* a term that refers to the family but, more broadly, to "the foundation of their understanding of the good and the basis of their moral judgment" (xix). Orsi argues that the domus was something of a Freudian hothouse, that "oedipal rivalries raged right on the surface of the life of the domus" (119–20).

3. Ibid., 120–21. Orsi contends that Italian mothers actually dominated the domus. Fathers maintained a ceremonial power as patriarch, but real power

resided with mothers, who administered discipline, controlled the family finances, regulated their children's courtships, and functioned as peacemaker. Orsi rightfully recognizes the limits of this power and sees it as a kind of "cage" (133–35, 145–46). Sydney Weinberg suggests that many Jewish families exhibited the same pattern: Men were the "ceremonial leaders" of the household but women often exercised day-to-day power in less obtrusive, more private ways. Weinberg, *The World of Our Mothers: The Lives of Jewish Immigrant Women* (Chapel Hill: University of North Carolina Press, 1988): 132–33.

4. Weinberg, *The World of Our Mothers,* 133–34.

5. Cited in Orsi, *The Madonna of 115th Street,* 129.

6. Ibid., 120.

7. Covello cited in ibid., 120–21.

8. Leah Morton (pseudonymn for Elisabeth Stern), *I Am a Woman—and a Jew* (New York: J. H. Sears, 1926): 1.

9. Anzia Yezierska, *Bread Givers* (New York: Persea Books, 1975; first published by Doubleday in 1925): 9–10.

10. On the mothers' role as buffer, see Weinberg, *The World of Our Mothers,* 123, 130.

11. Anzia Yezierska, *Red Ribbon on a White Horse* (New York: Persea Books, 1950): 72.

12. Yezierska, *Bread Givers,* 65, 296–97. A similar theme appeared in the popular and path-breaking movie *The Jazz Singer,* starring Al Jolson, adapted from the play by Samson Raphaelson.

13. Hutchins Hapgood, *The Spirit of the Ghetto* (Cambridge, Mass.: Belknap Press of Harvard University Press, 1967; first published in 1902): 23.

14. Ibid., 27.

15. Ibid., 26.

16. Ibid., 26–27.

17. Lincoln Steffens, *The Autobiography of Lincoln Steffens* (New York: Literary Guild, 1931): 244–45.

18. Ibid., 245. Perhaps the cause was, indeed, lost. In his recent book *The Jews in America,* Arthur Hertzberg argues that the "evidence of the destruction of the role of the father is overwhelming." Unable to support their families on their wages, bewildered by a culture they could scarcely understand, Jewish fathers receded into the background or even deserted, their place taken by a new cultural figure—the Jewish mother: Hertzberg, *The Jews in America: Four Centuries of an Uneasy Encounter: A History* (New York: Simon and Schuster, 1989): 196–98. Hertzberg notes that Jewish charities united in 1911 to establish the National Desertion Bureau, whose sole purpose was to find wayward husbands so that they might contribute to the support of their families. The bureau dealt with over 100,000 cases.

19. Julius Drachsler quoted in Elizabeth Ewen, *Immigrant Women in the Land of Dollars: Life and Culture on the Lower East Side, 1890–1925* (New York: Monthly Review Press, 1985): 187.

20. Rose Cohen, *Out of the Shadow* cited in Irving Howe and Kenneth Libo, eds., *How We Lived: A Documentary History of Immigrant Jews in America, 1880–1930* (New York: Richard Marek Publishers, 1979): 130.

21. Howe and Libo, eds., *How We Lived,* 51–52.

22. Covello, *The Heart Is the Teacher,* 24–25.

23. Yezierska, *Bread Givers,* 135.

24. Quoted in Ewen, *Immigrant Women in the Land of Dollars,* 73.

25. Weinberg, *The World of Our Mothers,* 112.

26. Hapgood, *The Spirit of the Ghetto,* 28; also see Hertzberg, *The Jews in America,* 201.

27. Weinberg, *The World of Our Mothers,* 112.

28. Mary Antin, *The Promised Land* (Boston: Houghton Mifflin, 1911): 271.

29. Ibid., 272.

30. Budd Schulberg, *What Makes Sammy Run?* (New York: Random House, 1941): 237.

31. Weinberg, *The World of Our Mothers,* 115–16.

32. Yezierska, *Red Ribbon on a White Horse,* 33. Although this book is often referred to as Yezierska's autobiography, it is actually a mixture of fact and fiction. See Carol B. Schoen, *Anzia Yezierska* (Boston: Twayne, 1982): 104.

33. Quoted in Ewen, *Immigrant Women in the Land of Dollars,* 189–90.

34. Hapgood, *The Spirit of the Ghetto,* 23.

35. In Detroit in 1900, for example, 43 percent of Irish boys and girls ages twelve to twenty attended school compared with 26 percent of Polish boys and girls. See Zunz, *The Changing Face of Inequality,* 234, table 9.7.

36. Reed Ueda, *Avenues to Adulthood: The Origins of the High School and Social Mobility in an American Suburb* (Cambridge: Cambridge University Press, 1987): 132, 147.

37. Ibid., 136.

38. Ibid., 151–52.

39. On the work culture of department stores, see Susan Porter Benson, *Counter Cultures: Saleswomen, Managers, and Customers in American Department Stores, 1890–1940* (Urbana: University of Illinois Press, 1981). Peiss describes the changing work structure for women in turn-of-the-century New York in *Cheap Amusements: Working Women and Leisure in Turn-of-the-Century New York* (Philadelphia: Temple University Press, 1986): 38–45.

40. Peiss, *Cheap Amusements,* 45–49; see also Leslie Woodcock Tentler, *Wage-Earning Women: Industrial Work and Family Life in the United States, 1900–1930* (New York: Oxford University Press, 1979): 58–80.

41. Cited in Peiss, *Cheap Amusements,* 64.

42. Stuart Ewen and Elizabeth Ewen, *Channels of Desire: Mass Images and the Shaping of American Consciousness* (New York: McGraw-Hill, 1982): 81–108.

43. Peiss, *Cheap Amusements,* 50.

44. Ibid.

45. Ibid., 101–3.

46. Ibid., 99.

47. Ibid., 98.

48. Ibid., 70.

49. Yezierska, *Bread Givers,* 2–6.

50. Quoted in Ewen, *Immigrant Women in the Land of Dollars,* 106.

51. Cited in Orsi, *The Madonna of 115th Street,* 112; also see 109–49 for a general discussion of parent-child conflict among Italian immigrants and their children. Conflicts between fathers and children were, as a rule, sharper than those between mothers and children because mothers often played the role of buffer between Old World fathers and children immersed in the nascent culture of the young.

52. Milton Meltzer, *Starting from Home: A Writer's Beginnings* (New York: Puffin, 1988): 85–87.

53. Alfred Kazin, *A Walker in the City* (New York: Harcourt, Brace and World, 1951): 21–22.

54. Ewen, *Immigrant Women in the Land of Dollars,* 192–93.

55. Selma Berrol, "Immigrant Children at School, 1880–1940," in Elliott West and Paula Petrik, eds., *Small Worlds: Children and Adolescents in America, 1850–1950* (Lawrence: University Press of Kansas, 1992): 42–60; David Tyack, *The One Best System: A History of American Urban Education* (Cambridge, Mass.: Harvard University Press, 1974): 230. "Americanization" efforts were not limited to schoolchildren. The Ford Motor Company announced a profit-sharing plan in 1914 that required participating workers to learn English and to demonstrate evidence of "manhood and thrift." Other industrialists joined with Ford in promoting night schools for the Americanization of immigrant workers. See Zunz, *The Changing Face of Inequality,* 311–18; also John J. Bukowczyk, *And My Children Did Not Know Me: A History of the Polish Americans* (Bloomington: Indiana University Press, 1987): 67–69.

56. Cited in Berrol, "Immigrant Children at School," 57.

57. Tyack, *One Best System,* 242. Tyack notes that attitudes toward schooling varied among ethnic groups. Eastern European Jews, for example, were well known for their emphasis on formal education whereas Italians, by contrast, placed considerably less importance on extended formal schooling. See Tyack, 248–54.

58. William H. Maxwell, "Education of the Immigrant Child," in *Education of the Immigrant,* abstracts of papers read at a public conference under the auspices of the New York–New Jersey Committee of the North American Civic League for Immigrants, held at New York City, May 16 and 17, 1913 (Washington, D.C.: U.S. Bureau of Education, Bulletin, No. 51, 1913): 18.

59. Quoted in Tyack, *One Best System,* 237.

60. Ibid., 237. Tyack notes that some educators began to realize that such prejudices were counterproductive. By 1913 the U.S. Commissioner of Education called on schools to respect the integrity of immigrant cultures while slowly transforming immigrant children into model American citizens (238–39).

61. Maxwell, "Education of the Immigrant Child," 19.
62. Stephan F. Brumberg, *Going to America, Going to School: The Jewish Immigrant Public School Encounter in Turn-of-the-Century New York City* (New York: Praeger, 1986): 75–78.
63. Ibid., 126–33.
64. Ibid., 82.
65. Leonard Covello, *The Teacher in the Urban Community* (Totawa, N.J.: Littlefield, Adams, 1970): 41, 43. On Italians and American education see Salvatore J. LaGumina, "American Education and the Italian Immigrant Response," in Bernard J. Weiss, ed., *American Education and the European Immigrant: 1840–1940* (Urbana: University of Illinois Press, 1982): 61–77.
66. Charles Bernheimer, assistant head of University Settlement House on the Lower East Side, quoted in Ewen, *Immigrant Women in the Land of Dollars,* 88.
67. Tyack, *One Best System,* 183–84. By 1900 thirty-one states had passed compulsory school attendance laws, most requiring attendance from eight to fourteen years of age.
68. John Bodnar, "Schooling and the Slavic-American Family, 1900–1940," in Weiss, *American Education and the European Immigrant,* 78–95.
69. Jerre Mangione, *Mount Allegro* (Boston: Houghton Mifflin, 1942): 225.
70. Quoted in Ewen, *Immigrant Women in the Land of Dollars,* 194.
71. Both quotes from ibid., 195.
72. Ronald H. Bayor, *Neighbors in Conflict: The Irish, Germans, Jews, and Italians of New York City, 1929–1941* (Baltimore: Johns Hopkins University Press, 1978): 16.
73. Elderton, ed., *Case Studies of Unemployment,* 194–201.
74. Attitudes about schooling differed greatly from one ethnic group to another. For a sophisticated analysis of such differences, see Joel Perlmann, *Ethnic Differences: Schooling and Social Structure among the Irish, Italians, Jews, and Blacks in an American City, 1880–1935* (Cambridge: Cambridge University Press, 1988).
75. Quoted in Tyack, *One Best System,* 241–42.
76. Walter E. Weyl, "Jan, the Polish Miner," *The Outlook* 94 (March 26, 1910): 716.
77. Bukowczyk, *And My Children Did Not Know Me,* 71.

Chapter 5. The Invention of the New Fatherhood, 1920–1940

1. James J. Corbett, "If I Had a Son," *Saturday Evening Post* 197 (May 2, 1925): 8–9.
2. The term *masculine domesticity* has been borrowed from Margaret Marsh; see her two essays, "Suburban Men and Masculine Domesticity, 1870–1915," *American Quarterly* 40 (June 1988): 165–86, and "From Separation to Togetherness: The Social Construction of Domestic Space in American

Suburbs, 1840–1915," *Journal of American History* 76 (September 1989): 506–27.

3. Stuart M. Blumin, "The Hypothesis of Middle-Class Formation in Nineteenth-Century America: A Critique and Some Proposals," *American Historical Review* 90 (April 1985): 312.

4. T. J. Jackson Lears, "From Salvation to Self-Realization: Advertising and the Therapeutic Roots of the Consumer Culture, 1880–1930," in T. J. Jackson Lears and Richard W. Fox, eds., *The Culture of Consumption: Critical Essays in American History, 1880–1980* (New York: Pantheon, 1983): 3–37.

5. Blumin, "The Hypothesis of Middle-Class Formation," 332. Blumin's citations are a useful bibliography on the history of the formation of the middle class in the nineteenth century.

6. Steven Mintz and Susan Kellogg, *Domestic Revolutions: A Social History of American Family Life* (New York: The Free Press, 1988): 108.

7. On fraternal rituals, see Mark C. Carnes, "Middle-Class Men and the Solace of Fraternal Ritual," in Mark C. Carnes and Clyde Griffen, eds., *Meanings for Manhood: Constructions of Masculinity in Victorian America* (Chicago: University of Chicago Press, 1990): 37–52, and his book, *Secret Ritual and Manhood in Victorian America* (New Haven: Yale University Press, 1989).

8. Mintz and Kellogg offer a fine overview of the emergence of the companionate family in *Domestic Revolutions,* 107–31.

9. What follows draws heavily from Lears, "From Salvation to Self-Realization," and from his book *No Place of Grace: Antimodernism and the Transformation of American Culture, 1880–1920* (New York: Pantheon, 1981).

10. Michael S. Kimmel, "The Contemporary 'Crisis' of Masculinity in Historical Perspective," in Harry Brod, ed., *The Making of Masculinities: The New Men's Studies* (Boston: Allen and Unwin, 1987), 138. Before the Civil War, almost 90 percent of American men were farmers or self-employed businessmen, a figure that fell to less than one-third by 1910. On the importance of personality in twentieth-century culture, see Warren Sussman's essay, "'Personality' and the Making of Twentieth-Century Culture" in his collection of essays, *Culture as History: The Transformation of American Society in the Twentieth Century* (New York: Pantheon, 1984): 271–85.

11. Lears, *No Place of Grace,* 22–23. Bruce Barton's popular book, *The Man Nobody Knows: A Discovery of Jesus* (Indianapolis: Bobbs-Merrill, 1925), depicted Christ as a go-getting businessman and abundant-life therapist. Lears's essay, "From Salvation to Self-Realization," includes a perceptive analysis of Bruce Barton, 30–37. On Barton also see Warren Sussman, "Culture Heroes: Ford, Barton, Ruth," in his collection, *Culture as History,* 122–49.

12. On changes in nineteenth-century conceptions of masculinity, see my essay, "Divorce and the Legal Redefinition of Victorian Manhood," in Carnes and Griffen, eds., *Meanings for Manhood,* 96–110. Some men embraced feminist visions of masculinity. Leading educators at women's colleges were especially prominent in this regard and saw in women's education not a threat to femi-

ninity but the salvation of the female sex. Animated by similar sentiments, other men boldly proclaimed their support for women's suffrage, backed women's claims to autonomy within marriage, and agitated for easier divorce laws to free women from oppressive husbands. For such men, calls for expanded female career opportunities, even for wives and mothers, followed naturally from their principles, as did support for sexual reform and birth control. See Kimmel, "The Contemporary 'Crisis' in Masculinity," 150, and Ellen K. Trimberger, "Feminism, Men, and Modern Love: Greenwich Village, 1900–1925," in Ann Snitow, Christine Stansell, and Sharon Thompson, eds., *Powers of Desire: The Politics of Sexuality* (New York: Monthly Review Press, 1983): 131–52. The responses to this seeming crisis in masculinity were diverse. Some men turned virulently antifemale and constructed new biological explanations to explain women's alleged innate inferiority; others called for a resuscitation of manliness through rugged living, the Boy Scouts, or military endeavors; still a third group sought to escape into the manly world of saloons, political parties, or fraternal organizations. The variant that resonated powerfully within the middle class, however, called for fathers to spend more time with their children, especially their sons. The popular literature of the early twentieth century contains story after story of fathers who passed on valuable, manly lessons to their sons while fishing, building models, or playing ball. Now more than ever, sons needed fathers who could devote time to their sons' welfare. Those who failed to do so encountered steady criticism. See Peter Filene, *Him/Her/Self: Sex Roles in Modern America*, 2d ed. (Baltimore: Johns Hopkins University Press, 1986; first published 1974), 78. As Filene put it, "More important, changing attitudes toward the family made the absence of men not merely a situation, but an accusation. The minor contribution of fathers was interpreted as a masculine failure."

13. Lears, "From Salvation to Self-Realization," 11; Lears, *No Place of Grace*, chap. 1; and Sussman, "'Personality' and Twentieth-Century Culture," 271–85.

14. Lears, "From Salvation to Self-Realization," 13–14; also, Sussman, "'Personality' and Twentieth-Century Culture," 277.

15. Christopher Lasch, *Haven in a Heartless World: The Family Besieged* (New York: Basic Books, 1977): chaps. 2, 4.

16. Ernest R. Groves, *The Drifting Home* (Boston: Houghton Mifflin, 1926): 39–41; Ernest Groves, "Social Influences Affecting Home Life," *American Journal of Sociology* 31 (September 1925): 231–32; William Ogburn, "The Family as an Institution in Modern Society," in Edward Reuter and Jessie Runner, eds., *The Family: Source Materials for the Study of Family and Personality* (New York: McGraw-Hill, 1931): 155–56; Paula Fass, *The Damned and the Beautiful: American Youth in the 1920s* (New York: Oxford University Press, 1977): 96–97.

17. Groves, *Drifting Home*, 5–9, 28–33; Ernest Mowrer, *Family Disorganization: An Introduction to a Sociological Analysis* (Chicago: University of Chicago Press, 1927): 4–7, 21–22.

18. Groves, *Drifting Home,* 32; Groves, "Social Influences," 235.

19. Ernest R. Groves and Gladys H. Groves, *Parents and Children* (Philadelphia: Lippincott, 1928), 150.

20. Ibid., 29–30; also see Grace Fletcher, "Bringing Up Fathers," *Ladies Home Journal* 44 (September 1927): 35.

21. Groves, "Social Influences," 232.

22. Groves, *Drifting Home,* 3–4. Lincoln Steffens discussed the advantage of being a first-time father at the age of sixty. Unlike young fathers who were "busy and vain" and spend little time with their children, a father of Steffens's age had time to dote on his son: "What young husband would let his foolish young wife go forth to make a name for herself, while he stayed home to mind the baby? What self-respecting young father would encourage the mother of his child to avoid the menial tasks of the cradle, in order to perform them himself?" But in doing such tasks, Steffens found remarkable rewards: "Only a shameless grandfather would do what I have done for Pete, and yet, by doing it, I have discovered that for ages women have been elbowing us men out of one of the greatest happinesses of life." Steffens, "Becoming a Father at 60 Is a Liberal Education," *American Magazine* 106 (August 1928): 48.

23. Ernest Burgess, "The Family as a Unity of Interacting Personalities," *Family* 7 (March 1926): 3–9; Fass, *The Damned and the Beautiful,* 109–11.

24. Fass, *The Damned and the Beautiful,* 112, 115. Ronald L. Howard also analyzes American family sociology in the 1920s in *A Social History of American Family Sociology, 1865–1940* (Westport, Conn.: Greenwood Press, 1981): 63–94, as does Christopher Lasch, more critically, in *Haven in a Heartless World: The Family Besieged* (New York: Basic Books, 1979).

25. See Marsh, "Suburban Men" and "From Separation to Togetherness."

26. Groves and Groves, *Parents and Children,* 127–28.

27. Lorine Pruette, *The Parent and the Happy Child* (New York: Henry Holt, 1932): 53.

28. Fletcher, "Bringing Up Fathers," 199. Also see Pruette, *The Parent and the Happy Child,* 53.

29. Groves and Groves, *Parents and Children,* 128. The Groveses feared the impact of too much mothering, a situation that could warp the child's personality and lead to maternal fixation, a barrier to the child's "growth," independence, and self-reliance (119–23). Such concerns received some credibility in Meyer Nimkoff's 1928 study of 1,300 young men and the same number of young women. His data revealed that both sons and daughters were more obedient to their mothers and that children, regardless of sex, confided more often in their mothers than fathers. Most surprising of all, both sons and daughters spent more recreation time with their mothers: "Parent-Child Intimacy: An Introductory Study," *Social Forces* 7 (December 1928): 244–49.

30. Lasch, *Haven in a Heartless World,* 24–25, 31–35.

31. In *Haven in a Heartless World,* Lasch argues that sociologists in the 1930s paid little attention to parent-child relationships and emphasized instead the importance of husband-wife intimacy: "In sociological theory, parenthood and

child rearing, when they were dealt with at all, dwindled to by-products of marriage" (40). Although the focus may have been on husband-wife relations and marital adjustment studies, there were sociologists and popular family writers deeply concerned about fatherhood and sex-role socialization.

32. Robert Foster, "Editorial," *Child Study* 16 (March 1939): 134. See, too, the *New York Times,* July 8, 1938, 10; the *New York Times,* February 26, 1939, II, 5; and James L. Hymes, Jr., "School: A Woman's World," *Child Study* 16 (March 1939): 138. Hymes worried that not only boys suffered because of inadequate exposure to men: "Where does Mary in school find the man with whom she can work out her position as a girl, and her future position as a woman? Where can she find a man who can help her, simply through a relationship, to build up her conceptions of men—their behavior, their possibilities, their attitudes?"

33. Hymes, Jr., "School: A Woman's World," 137.

34. Dorothy Blake, "Fathers Should Be Seen and Heard," *American Home* 14 (August 1935): 199, 225; Mary E. Overholt, "For Fathers Only," *Parents' Magazine* 7 (July 1932): 39.

35. Everett Duvall, "Child-Parent Social Distance," *Sociology and Social Research* 21 (May–June 1937): 462. Duvall's study included comparisons by social class; he concluded from his study of over 450 Los Angeles twelve- to seventeen-year-old boys and girls that "the tendency for children to be closer to their mothers than to their fathers was greater among underprivileged children than among average children and was also greater among the girls of both groups than for boys of both groups." He also found that children whose fathers were poor were less likely to see their fathers as models than were those from average economic circumstances. Duvall discovered that as the children aged, their "social distance" from fathers increased more rapidly than from mothers (460–62). Also see H. Meltzer, "Children's Attitudes to Parents," *American Journal of Orthopsychiatry* 5 (July 1935): 244–65.

36. Joseph Pleck, "The Theory of Male Sex Role Identity: Its Rise and Fall, 1936 to the Present," in Miriam Lewin, ed., *In the Shadow of the Past: Psychology Views the Sexes* (New York: Columbia University Press, 1983): 206.

37. Ibid., 207–8.

38. Ibid., 208–10.

39. This quote is from a speech by Caroline B. Zachary, research director of the Progressive Education Association, before a conference of elementary educators at Teachers College, *New York Times,* July 8, 1938, 10.

40. Estelle Barnes Clapp, "Growing Up with Father," *Child Study* 16 (March 1939): 139; also, Hiram Motherwell, "For Fathers Only," *Parents' Magazine* 10 (April 1935): 20–21. James Warbasse disagreed with the need for fatherly heroism: "[Children] just as honestly respect the real superiority of their fathers. They evaluate this knowledge and experience. We parents do not need to place ourselves on a pedestal. Children know our real worth." Warbasse, "Fathers as Pals," *Parents' Magazine* 11 (August 1936): 74.

41. Helen Witmer, "Influence of Parental Attitudes on the Social Adjustment of the Individual," *American Sociological Review* 2 (October 1937): 762.

42. *New York Times,* February 21, 1937, 19. Caroline Zachary warned that a dominant mother and an absent father could create an overly docile son: "He loves his mother, identifies himself with her and accepts her domination happily." *New York Times,* February 26, 1939, II, 5.

43. Lawrence K. Frank, "The Father's Role in Child Nurture," *Child Study* 16 (March 1939): 136.

44. Clapp, "Growing Up with Father," 139.

45. Henry C. Fulcher, "My Son and I Go Fishing," *Parents' Magazine* 5 (May 1930): 32; H. J. Hobbs, "For Fathers Only," *Parents' Magazine* 10 (February 1935): 32; W. J. Weir, "For Fathers Only," *Parents' Magazine* 12 (October 1937): 14.

46. *New York Times,* April 3, 1938. Lewis Leary argued that the future of daughters lay in the hands of fathers: "But, if you want her to be happy, take time to be a friend of hers. If you want her to be intelligent, talk with her. If you want her to be dependable, trust her. If you want her to understand men, let her understand you. If you want her to be good, be good yourself." Leary, "A Girl Needs Her Father," *Parents' Magazine* 11 (April 1936): 61. Daughters who became close companions of their fathers gained an appreciation of their fathers' wisdom and experience. See William H. Spence, "Fathers and Daughters," *Parents' Magazine* 12 (September 1937): 80.

47. Leary, "A Girl Needs Her Father," 30.

48. Ibid.

49. *New York Times,* July 8, 1938, 10.

50. Ibid., February 26, 1939, II, 5. Zachary noted that children who saw little of their fathers encountered problems when they reached adolescence: "Girls frequently find it difficult to adjust to masculine relationships and boys show submissive attitudes due to the domination of mothers and women teachers." *New York Times,* July 8, 1938, 10.

51. Phyllis Jackson, "Good Fathers Get Together," *Parents' Magazine* 11 (February 1936): 47.

52. Clifford Parcher, "A Get-Acquainted Program for Commuting Fathers," *American Home* 22 (October 1939): 25. On the same point, E. H. Felix, "Share Your Boy's Hobby," *Parents' Magazine* 6 (March 1931): 78; Mary Overhold, "For Fathers Only," *Parents' Magazine* 7 (July 1932): 4; Harold Page, "For Fathers Only," *Parents' Magazine* 10 (December 1935): 85.

53. Page, "For Fathers Only," 85.

54. Many articles appear on the need for such planning; see, for example, Page, "For Fathers Only," 85; Henry B. Lent, "I Am a Week-end Father," *Parents' Magazine* 6 (September 1931): 17; Parcher, "A Get-Acquainted Program for Commuting Fathers," 25, 110; Robert Miller, "For Fathers Only," *Parents' Magazine* 11 (December 1936): 40; Clapp, "Growing Up with Father," 139–40.

55. Phyllis Jackson, "Good Fathers Get Together," *Parents' Magazine* 11 (February 1936): 47, 62. A study of fifty University of Wisconsin freshmen found that male students with "stable" personalities were those who "have progressed to the stage of father-identification, at least to the point of enjoy-

ing his companionship, idealizing him and accepting commands and punishments from him rather than from the mother." See Ross Stagner, "The Role of Parents in the Development of Emotional Instability," *American Journal of Orthopsychiatry* 8 (January 1938): 128.

Testimonials in the 1930s about the joy and worth of father-child companionship abound; see, for example, Miller, "For Fathers Only," 40; Fulcher, "My Son and I Go Fishing," 32–33, 77; Felix, "Share Your Boy's Hobby," 26, 78–79; H. B. Lent, "I Am a Weekend Father," 17; John H. McMurtie, "For Fathers Only," *Parents' Magazine* 7 (August 1932): 9; Raymond F. Yates, "For Fathers Only," *Parents' Magazine* 7 (October 1932): 8; and Donald MacMillan, "A Boy Must Believe in Himself," *Parents' Magazine* 11 (February 1936): 44. Apparently these calls for companionship were well placed; a survey of two thousand children ages ten to twenty reported that companionship with fathers was a frequently stated desire: "To go fishing with dad was revealed as the unfilled desire of many boys" (*New York Times*, April 28, 1937, 25). Another survey of one thousand children reported frequent complaints about a lack of companionship with their parents, especially the father who often "says he is too busy." See Lindwood Chase, "What 1,000 Children Think of Parents," *Parents' Magazine* 12 (February 1937): 9.

56. Clapp, "Growing Up with Father," 139–40. Fathers occasionally complained that companionate relations with their children took too much time: "But I swear that I will not give them my all. I am going to hold something back for myself." That "something" was leisure. Another complained that his first child monopolized his time, but with the arrival of a second child and a move to a new neighborhood full of children, he now enjoyed being a part-time father and "no longer an unwilling, full-time slave to my son." See Anonymous, "For Fathers Only," *Parents' Magazine* 12 (November 1937): 12, and Benjamin Carroll, "For Fathers Only," *Parents' Magazine* 12 (December 1937): 116.

57. Cecile Pilpel and Anna W. M. Wolf, "Parents' Questions: Study Group Department," *Child Study* 16 (March 1939): 145.

58. Frank, "The Father's Role in Child Nurture," 135.

59. Howard Stephenson, "For Fathers Only," *Parents' Magazine* 10 (November 1935): 14.

60. Anonymous, "Mistakes I've Made with My Boy," *Parents' Magazine* 11 (July 1936): 51.

61. Mildred Thurow, "Succeeding as a Family," *Parents' Magazine* 10 (June 1935): 24, 60–61. A symposium on "How Parents Handle the Smoking Problem" in *Parents' Magazine* revealed five fathers' allegiance to these values. Each took a somewhat different approach, but none an autocratic one. See "How Parents Handle the Smoking Problem," *Parents' Magazine* 10 (April 1935): 17–18. Also see Page, "For Fathers Only," 27, 85; Anonymous, "How We Nearly Lost Our Son and Daughter," *Parents' Magazine* 11 (January 1936): 16–17, 52–55; Frederick Hall, "For Fathers Only," *Parents' Magazine* 11 (September 1936): 92; and John Scotford, "For Fathers Only," *Parents' Magazine* 12 (July 1937): 82. Estelle Barnes Clapp

warned of the dangers to the child's sense of security when all disciplinary problems were left to the father in "Growing Up with Father," 140, 156.

62. Frank Richardson, "How Good a Father Are You?" *Parents' Magazine* 10 (June 1935): 36, 77–79.

63. Thurow, "Succeeding as a Family," 61. The article concluded that a lack of paternal dominance was one of several key factors that made for successful family life. Thurow had earlier listed "little dominance of father in home" as one of thirteen key factors that promoted successful family life; see *New York Times,* April 8, 1934, II, 2.

64. *New York Times,* January 27, 1936, 7.

65. As Lasch put it in *Haven in a Heartless World:* "Relations within the family took on the same character as relations elsewhere; individualism and the pursuit of self-interest reigned even in the most intimate of institutions. Parental authority came to rest purely on the provision of material services, at the same time that industrialization of production and bureaucratization of welfare undermined the family's capacity to manipulate economic rewards. Parents without property to pass on to their offspring could exact obedience only by appealing to a sense of duty, deference, or filiopiety, in other words to hierarchical principles having little place in a society based on rational self-interest" (35–36). Lasch added that the sociologists who uncovered this insight backed off from its implications: "Instead of showing how the modern child increasingly judged his parents according to their ability to provide goods and services, and how the parents in turn attempted to justify their authority in a way that merely strengthened appeals to enlightened self-interest, the Chicago sociologists forgot self-interest and concentrated their entire attention on the family's 'affectional' function" (36).

66. On Zimmerman, see Lasch, *Haven in a Heartless World,* 44–49.

67. Frank, "The Father's Role in Child Nurture," 136. Ernest Osborne expressed similar sentiments and warned that "the domination of an unreasonable, brow-beating father influences the child's attitudes toward authority most decidedly." Such a child became abjectly obedient to all authority (and hence vulnerable to fascist ideology) or unreasonably disobedient. Osborne, "The Family's Contribution to Democracy," *Parents' Magazine* 12 (November 1937): 84. Michael Frobish's useful survey of family ideology reveals these trends in more detail in "The Family and Ideology: Cultural Constraints on Women, 1940–1960," Ph.D. diss., University of North Carolina at Chapel Hill, 1983.

68. Joseph Pleck argues that the sex-role paradigm was not fully articulated until the mid-1930s; see his essay, "The Theory of Male Sex-Role Identity," 21–38.

69. Groves and Groves, *Parents and Children,* 135.

70. Grace Fletcher argued that autocratic fathers were becoming increasingly uncommon and that they were unwelcome in American homes. Fathers who tried to lay down the law would, at best, confront unattentive children and, at worst, face children threatening to leave home. See "Bringing Up Fathers," 35, 199.

71. Groves and Groves, *Parents and Children,* 36.

72. Steffens, "Becoming a Father at 60 Is a Liberal Education," *American Magazine* 106 (August 1928): 48.

73. Clarence B. Kelland, "It's Fun Being a Father," *American Magazine* 103 (January 1927): 146. Emphasis in the original. Chester T. Crowell used somewhat more florid prose to describe the same thing: "Once children are accepted as associates rather than duties, living with them becomes a lot of fun—much more fun than grown people can supply. . . . They are eager to go not only half but nine-tenths of the way toward a companionship so beautiful that it comes close to perfection." Crowell, "Notes of an Amateur Father," *American Mercury* 3 (October 1924): 142.

74. Anonymous, "What I Owe My Father," *American Magazine* 95 (March 1923): 170. Family life, in the words of Judge Florence Allen, was "a partnership in which the father has not fulfilled his obligations when he has simply paid the rent or lifted the mortgage or settled the grocery bill. That isn't the way human character grows. Human character doesn't grow by just having a physical soil in which to plant itself. Human character needs the sunshine of affection and comradeship." Florence Allen, "Significant Factors in Home Life as Revealed through the Courts," *Journal of Home Economics* 20 (December 1928): 856. The Groveses make the same point in *Parents and Children*, 131, as does Pruett, *The Parent and the Happy Child*, 56. Some fathers lamented that becoming a friend to their children was difficult, if not impossible. With sadness and resignation, Frederic Van de Water admitted, "I am by no possible stretch of the imagination my son's pal at present. There are few things for which I have tried harder to be, or at which I have been less successful. . . . We have played together, my son and I; he politely and puzzledly; I grimly and determinedly. By and by we have given it up, both of us immensely bored and relieved." See "Confessions of a Dub Father," *Ladies Home Journal* 42 (May 1925): 25, 97–98.

75. Kelland, "It's Fun Being a Father," 144.

76. Pruette, *The Parent and the Happy Child*, 67.

77. Groves and Groves, *Parents and Children*, 142. Similar sentiments were expressed by a writer in the *Ladies Home Journal* who advised men to put less emphasis on economic success in order to spend more time with their children, thereby gaining "a rich trove of memories of hours spent in playing and learning together." Fletcher, "Bringing Up Fathers," 199.

78. E. W. Bok, "What Else Did Father Do?" *Scribner's Magazine* 72 (December 1922): 660–64.

79. Ibid.; also see Chester T. Crowell, "It's a Wise Father Who Can Answer His Own Child," *American Magazine* 100 (October 1925): 18–19, 72, 74.

80. See W. O. Saunders, "A Father Who Took No Pleasure in His Children: A True Story," *American Magazine* 100 (November 1925): 49, 107, 110. Father-child closeness had other benefits as well. Family experts in the 1920s and 1930s worried about crime, divorce, delinquency, and other sources of disorder and traced such problems to psychological pathologies caused by family disunity; therefore, if family disunity could be reduced, social disorder would

decline. To make this turn of events a reality, families had to become more tolerant, open, flexible, and, above all, affectionate. In the modern world, only this type of family would produce strong, secure, well-adjusted children who would become socially responsible adults. As a child, "the individual must learn to love and be loved, to give and receive tenderness and affection. . . . Failure to learn this will handicap the individual as a personality in all his or her activities." See Lawrence Frank, "Some Aspects of Education for Home and Family Life," in *Papers on Parent Education Presented at the Biennial Conference of the National Council of Parent Education,* November 1930 (New York, 1931), 47, quoted in Fass, *Damned and the Beautiful,* 100.

81. White House Conference on Child Health and Protection (henceforth, WHC), *The Young Child in the Home: A Survey of Three Thousand American Families,* John Anderson, Chairman (New York: Appleton-Century, 1936): 73–78.

82. Although few fathers in any class listened to radio shows regularly, fathers in the upper and middle classes spent more time listening to such programs than fathers on the bottom rungs of the occupational ladder. Likewise, middle-class fathers were more likely than their working-class counterparts to attend child study groups and parent-teacher association meetings. Whereas 6 percent of professional men attended child study groups and 15.5 percent went to PTA meetings, the figures for day laboring fathers was 2.1 percent and 4.2 percent, respectively. WHC, *The Young Child in the Home,* 79–81. Grace Nies Fletcher suggested that fathers made up almost 50 percent of the members of parent-teacher and child study groups, but she offered no firm evidence to support her claim. She also alluded to several Pennsylvania cities where fathers had established their own child study groups. Fletcher strongly supported education for fatherhood because it "cannot help but cement the bond of common interest between husbands and wives, a bond too often sorely strained by present marriage conditions." See "Bringing Up Fathers," 199. Perhaps the height of middle-class fatherly involvement in parent education were the husbands who participated in the Vassar summer euthenics program. Joining their wives on weekends, these men studied a variety of topics about family life, including lectures designed to improve fathers' child-rearing abilities. Reporter Dorothy Woolf wrote that though a woman may believe in the information and tips she learns during the week, "she cannot carry them out at home unless her husband is in sympathy with them. For this reason most of the women are anxious for their husbands to join them for the week-end lectures." Woolf, "Euthenics Taught in Vacation Study," *New York Times,* August 3, 1930, III, 7. On euthenics at Vassar, also see "Class for Homemaking Husbands," *New York Times,* March 12, 1927, 14, and "Husbands Invited to Euthenics School," *New York Times,* March 10, 1927, 13.

83. WHC, *The Young Child in the Home,* 237.

84. Ibid., 236–37.

85. Ibid., 210–13.

86. Approximately 60 percent of parents in the upper two social classes spanked

their one- to five-year-olds; by contrast, almost 80 percent of parents in the lower two classes used corporal punishment. Similarly, over 70 percent of mid- to upper-class parents (fathers included) used reasoning—at least at times—to discipline their youngsters ages one to five, a technique that only 40 to 50 percent of fathers and mothers in the lower classes employed. As the children aged, this disparity increased. While poorer parents relied on scolding with their six- to twelve-year-olds, more affluent fathers and mothers used appeals to reason: almost 90 percent of professional-class parents relied, at least in part, on reasoning, a technique used by barely 30 percent of the laborers; see WHC, *The Young Child in the Home*, 213–20.

87. WHC, *The Young Child in the Home*, 221. Experts emphasized that mothers and fathers must present a united front when disciplining children. As one adviser put it, "The father should never take the part of the child who is resisting the attempt of the mother to exact obedience." In the best homes, "Neither parent ever sided with a child against the other. When the father said, 'Mother and I have decided,' the children knew that it was really a joint decision, and concurred. . . . Above all, he must avoid argument with her in their presence, and unhesitatingly give his support to all her efforts in maintaining authority." See William R. P. Emerson, "The Hundred Per Cent Father," *Woman's Home Companion* 49 (October 1922): 20.

88. Kelland, "It's Fun Being a Father," 54–55; 144–46.

89. White House Conference on Child Health and Protection (henceforth, WHC), *The Adolescent in the Family: A Study of Personality Development in the Home Environment*, Ernest W. Burgess, Chairman (New York: Appleton-Century, 1934): 7.

90. Ibid., 6–7. Although the Burgess report minimized the relationship between social class and personality development, it did emphasize that "the average level of family relations and of personality adjustment of the children is somewhat higher for urban than for rural children." In so doing, Burgess and his colleagues repudiated those who praised the alleged stability, harmony, and wholesomeness of rural life. In their judgment, the hurly-burly urban environment produced better-adjusted children than did more bucolic settings.

91. Ibid., 143, 287–98. In light of Burgess's general theory, family unity emerged as a key variable in assessing personality development. Unified families, according to the theory, should engender strong personality development; fractious families, by contrast, would give rise to children with weak personality development. Again, the data seemed to confirm Burgess's theory: among boys and girls, those who had no criticisms of their parents had better personality development than those who did. For boys, 52 percent of those with no criticisms of their parents—Burgess's indicator of family unity or its absence—had good personality development while only 30 percent of those who criticized their fathers, 29 percent of those who found fault with their mothers, and 16 percent of those who registered complaints about both had good personality adjustment. For girls, the same basic relationship held. Children from "unified" homes also tended to be "more compliant socially" and more exemplary in their classroom behavior, evidence leading Burgess to

conclude that "while lack of intimacy between parents and children does not necessarily produce emotional and social maladjustment in the child, there is a definite tendency for more children from poorly organized homes than from homes with a high degree of harmony and intimacy to be maladjusted." See WHC, *The Adolescent in the Family*, 135–36.

92. Ibid., 145.

93. Ibid., 147. This respondent added that the closeness she had with her father and mother was not shared by many of her college classmates: "Very few of my friends confide in their parents. They say that they (the parents) would not understand. I am certainly happy that I have always wanted to confide in mother and father" (147). Chester T. Crowell, whose oldest of five children was twelve and whose youngest was three, would have won the plaudits of this respondent: "Above all, I accept the children as equals and grown persons, so that they feel no embarrassment in telling me their own thoughts." Crowell, "Notes of an Amateur Father," *American Mercury* 3 (October 1924): 137–42.

94. WHC, *The Adolescent in the Family*, 151.

95. Ibid., 153.

96. Ibid., 154.

97. Ibid., 195–96. A similar relationship existed for girls. Among girls who confided in their mothers "very much," 87 percent received sex education from parents; among those who confided "very little," 53 percent received sex education in the home.

98. Ibid., 201.

99. Ibid., 209–10.

100. Ibid., 197.

101. Ibid., 202.

102. Ibid., 205.

103. Ibid., 195–96, 231.

104. Ibid., 157. Chase Going Woodhouse's analysis of "250 successful families" likewise documented the importance of fatherly involvement in the family. In these families, both parents kept abreast of advances in child development and psychology and encouraged their children's independence: "A Study of 250 Successful Families," *Social Forces* 8 (June 1930): 511–32. Also see H. Meltzer, "Children's Attitudes to Parents," *American Journal of Orthopsychiatry* 5 (July 1935): 244–65, and Meltzer, "Economic Security and Children's Attitudes to Parents," ibid. 6 (October 1936): 590–608; Percival Symonds, "A Study of Parental Acceptance and Rejection," ibid. 8 (October 1938): 679–88. Three University of California psychologists compared parent-child relationships in two generations (those born circa 1900 and those born in 1927–28) and concluded that fathers' involvement with and affection for both sons and daughters was higher in the second generation than in the first. See Wanda Bronson, Edith Katten, and Norman Livson, "Patterns of Authority and Affection in Two Generations," *The Journal of Abnormal and Social Psychology* 58 (March 1959): 143–52.

105. These letters are all from the Angelo Patri Papers in the Library of Congress.

Filed by date, the letters are either typed or handwritten and include Patri's typed reply. To protect the confidentiality of these men and their children, all names have been omitted from the citations. Ralph LaRossa, a sociologist at Georgia State University, is making an exhaustive analysis of the Patri letters as part of his work on the history of American fatherhood during the interwar years.

106. Kimball Young noted the anxiety of middle-class parents regarding their children's education: "Anxiously ambitious mothers and fathers of the bourgeois classes, in particular, upon discovering through mental tests high abilities in their children are often given over to intense concern with the educative process." See Young, "Parent-Child Relationships: Projection of Ambition," *Family* 8 (May 1927): 69.

107. Letter to Angelo Patri, October 25, 1926, Box 4, Angelo Patri Papers, Library of Congress (APP-LC).

108. Letters to Angelo Patri, February 22, 1926, Box 4, and June 2, 1926, APP-LC. Problems with children's lying and stealing appear with some frequency in the letters to Patri.

109. Letters to Angelo Patri, January 19, 1925, Box 2, and October 25, 1926, Box 4, APP-LC.

110. Letter to Angelo Patri, April 18, 1925, Box 3, APP-LC.

111. Letter to Angelo Patri, February 2, 1925 (misdated as 1924), Box 2, APP-LC.

112. Letter to Angelo Patri, June 11, 1925, Box 3, APP-LC.

113. Letter to Angelo Patri, August 17, 1925, Box 3, APP-LC.

114. See, for example, letters to Angelo Patri, April 19, 1934, Box 28, and May 2, 1934, Box 28, APP-LC.

115. Letters to Angelo Patri, September 29, 1932, Box 20, and September 29, 1936, Box 32, APP-LC; also see letters to Angelo Patri, February 25, 1929, Box 8; July 6, 1932, Box 18; December 1, 1932, Box 22; and November 14, 1933, Box 24, APP-LC.

116. Letters to Angelo Patri, September 15, 1932, Box 20, and November 15, 1926, Box 4, APP-LC; also see letter to Angelo Patri, April 21, 1937, Box 27, APP-LC.

117. Letters to Angelo Patri, June 21, 1932, Box 18; October 26, 1926, Box 4; and November 1929, Box 12, APP-LC.

118. Letter to Angelo Patri, undated (Patri's reply is July 7, 1928), APP-LC.

119. Letter to Angelo Patri, November 9, 1925, Box 3, APP-LC.

120. Letter to Angelo Patri, July 1932, Box 18, APP-LC.

121. Letter to Angelo Patri, October 9, 1924, Box 2, APP-LC.

122. Letter to Angelo Patri, November 17, 1929, Box 12, APP-LC.

123. Letter to Angelo Patri, June 30, 1925, Box 3, APP-LC.

124. Letter to Angelo Patri, February 12, 1925, Box 2, APP-LC.

125. Letter to Angelo Patri, February 6, 1934, Box 26, APP-LC.

126. Letter to Angelo Patri, September 1924, Box 2, APP-LC; in the same box, also see a letter of October 4, 1924.

127. Letter to Angelo Patri, January 2, 1925, Box 2, and January 30, 1929, Box 8,

APP-LC. Similar worries about a young child's academic failures appeared in the letter of a Chicago bank executive. See the letter of March 25, 1925, Box 3.

128. Letter to Angelo Patri, December 12, 1925, Box 3, APP-LC.

129. Letter to Angelo Patri, January 16, 1926, Box 3, APP-LC; also see letters of November 17, 1926, Box 4; April 26, 1933, Box 24; and November 3, 1933, Box 24, APP-LC.

130. Letter to Angelo Patri, January 30, 1936, Box 30, APP-LC.

131. Letter to Angelo Patri, August 16, 1932, APP-LC.

132. Letter to Angelo Patri, February 24, 1931, Box 14, APP-LC.

133. Letter to Angelo Patri, January 15, 1926, Box 3, APP-LC.

134. Letter to Angelo Patri, February 17, 1929, Box 8, APP-LC.

135. Letter to Angelo Patri, October 25, 1924, Box 2, APP-LC. Kimball Young described at length the frustration and misguided anxiety of a father who could not admit to himself that his son was simply not college material: "Parent-Child Relationships: Projection of Ambition," 69–70.

136. Letter to Angelo Patri, December 5, 1925, Box 3, APP-LC.

137. Letter to Angelo Patri, November 17, 1926, Box 4, APP-LC; also see a letter of October 11, 1932, Box 20.

138. Charlotte Perkins Gilman, *The Home: Its Work and Influence* (New York: Charlton, 1910), and Gilman, *Women and Economics: The Economic Factor between Men and Women as a Factor in Social Evolution* (New York: Harper and Row, 1966; first published in 1898).

139. Lisa Duggan, "The Social Enforcement of Heterosexuality and Lesbian Resistance in the 1920s," in Amy Swerdlow and Hanna Lessinger, eds., *Class, Race, and Sex: The Dynamics of Control* (Boston: Hall, 1983): 85–87.

140. Carroll Smith-Rosenberg, *Disorderly Conduct: Visions of Gender in Victorian America* (New York: Knopf, 1985): 265, 275–78, 281; Duggan, "The Social Enforcement of Heterosexuality," 85–87.

141. Popular magazine articles about fathers focused almost exclusively on men's involvement with their children in activities, visits, trips, hobbies, sports, and the like. The other popular image of father was as a wise counselor, especially to sons. Few had much to say about men's assuming domestic chores. One article even celebrated that mothers did the work of child rearing while fathers had all the fun with the children: Anonymous, "The Greatest American Invention," *Outlook* 122 (July 23, 1919): 463–64.

142. Lincoln Steffens implied as much in "Becoming a Father at 60 Is a Liberal Education," *American Magazine* 106 (August 1928): 48. Steffens suggested that "busy and vain" young fathers avoided the menial tasks associated with child rearing.

143. Ella Winter, "The Advantages of Marrying an Older Man," *American Magazine* 106 (September 1928): 29.

144. Ruth Cowan, *More Work for Mother: The Ironies of Household Technology from the Open Hearth to the Microwave* (New York: Basic Books, 1983); see too Glenna Matthews, *Just a Housewife: The Rise and Fall of Domesticity in*

America (New York: Oxford University Press, 1987); and Susan Strasser, *Never Done: A History of American Housework* (New York: Pantheon, 1982).

145. Carol Brown, "Mothers, Fathers, and Children: From Private to Public Patriarchy," in Lydia Sargent, ed., *Women and Revolution: A Discussion of the Unhappy Marriage of Marxism and Feminism* (Boston: South End Press, 1981).

Chapter 6. The Cultural Contradictions of the New Fatherhood, 1920–1940

1. Letter to Angelo Patri and his reply, October 6, 1924, Box 2, Angelo Patri Papers, Library of Congress (APP-LC).
2. These examples come from the following letters to Patri: February 14, 1931, Box 14; March 1931, Box 14; June 21, 1932, Box 18; December 29, 1925, Box 3; June 23, 1925, Box 3; April 18, 1925, Box 3; June 1928, Box 6; February 26, 1931, Box 14; March 12, 1931, Box 14; and April 5, 1934, Box 28, APP-LC.
3. Steven Mintz and Susan Kellogg provide a useful survey of these developments in *Domestic Revolutions: A Social History of American Family Life* (New York: Free Press, 1988): 120–23.
4. Letter to Angelo Patri, April 8, 1934, Box 28, and Patri's reply April 24, 1934, Box 28, APP-LC. Although both the father and mother signed the letter to Patri, from the text of the letter, it is clear that the father wrote it.
5. Reply of Angelo Patri, February 10, 1925, Box 2, APP-LC.
6. Letter to Angelo Patri, January 14, 1925, Box 2, and Patri's reply, January 17, 1925, Box 2, APP-LC.
7. Reply of Angelo Patri, December 4, 1924, Box 2, APP-LC.
8. Reply of Angelo Patri, November 16, 1925, Box 3, APP-LC. Patri gives similar advice to a father troubled by the recalcitrance of his adolescent son. See reply of Patri, July 7, 1928, Box 6, APP-LC.
9. Reply of Angelo Patri, January 20, 1925, Box 2, APP-LC; also see reply of Patri, January 7, 1925, Box 2, APP-LC.
10. Reply of Angelo Patri, October 10, 1924, Box 2, APP-LC. Other self-styled experts chided fathers who refused to follow the advice of specialists. One doctor devised a 100-point scale for evaluating fathers and explained how disregard of expert advice affected one's score: "But because the matter of health is so fundamental to every department of family life it is necessary to call attention to the fact that the father's responsibility is not ended when he calls a doctor and pays the bills. If he fails to do his part in following out the physician's instructions; if his own habits give a bad example by letting a good time take precedence over health; if he fails to interest himself in the school life and daily activities of his children; if he leaves all their training to the mother because he is preoccupied with his work, then he is not entitled to the full twenty-five points which we have allowed for Ideals and Character." William R. P. Emerson, "The Hundred Per Cent Father," *Woman's Home Companion* 49 (October 1922): 20.

11. Letters to Angelo Patri, July 7, 1932, and August 31, 1932, APP-LC.

12. Letter to Angelo Patri, February 23, 1932, APP-LC. Other fathers chastised themselves for being too strict. Worried about his son's irritability and effeminacy, a father assured Patri that the boy was not indulged: *"He is not spoiled.... Possibly we deny or restrain him too much for it seems to me that every time he makes a request we say NO."* (Emphasis in original.) Letter to Angelo Patri, October 9, 1924, Box 2, APP-LC.

13. Letter to Angelo Patri, November 2, 1932, APP-LC.

14. Letter to Angelo Patri, February 6, 1936, Box 30, APP-LC.

15. Letter to Angelo Patri, December 6, 1933, and Patri's reply, December 19, 1933, APP-LC.

16. Letter to Angelo Patri, May 23, 1934, APP-LC.

17. Frank Ward O'Malley, "A Plea for Young Male Parents," *Saturday Evening Post* 192 (January 1920): 150.

18. Ralph P. Bridgman, "Ten Years' Progress in Parent Education," *AAAPSS* 151 (September 1930): 34–37; also see Ernest Groves, "Parent Education," *AAAPSS* 160 (March 1932): 216–22; Helen Merrell Lynd, "Parent Education and the Colleges," *AAAPSS* 160 (March 1932): 197–204.

19. Barbara Ehrenreich and Deidra English, *For Her Own Good: 150 Years of Experts' Advice to Women* (Garden City, N.Y.: Anchor Press, 1978): 186–88; Bridgman, "Ten Years' Progress in Parent Education," 36–37; William I. Thomas and Dorothy Swaine Thomas, *The Child in America: Behavior Problems and Programs* (New York: Knopf, 1928): 295–329. The most thorough treatment of parent education appears in the volume published by the White House Conference on Child Health and Protection (hereafter, WHC), *Parent Education: Types, Content, Method,* Sidonie M. Gruenberg, Chairman (New York: Century, 1932).

20. Bridgman, "Ten Years' Progress in Parent Education," 37.

21. Ibid., 38.

22. Ibid. All the parent education groups received a constant stream of expert advice and research data from the child development research centers that reached national prominence during the 1920s. The Universities of Iowa, Minnesota, and California, Teachers College at Columbia, and the Merrill-Palmer School in Detroit all established child development research centers that played critical roles in developing parent education. In 1924, for example, the Iowa Station established a parent education division to disseminate information to parents and "to induce parents to look at their children objectively as well as subjectively." The station organized child study groups, coordinated the efforts of various state organizations interested in parent education, and conducted conferences and held seminars on child rearing. The other centers pursued similar kinds of projects. On the research stations, see ibid., 39. In the 1920s two basic approaches to child rearing vied for attention. One minority stream, culminating in the work of the behaviorist John B. Watson, distrusted affection, emphasized regimentation, and extolled the virtues of positive and negative reinforcements in shaping children's charac-

ter. The other, more dominant stream stressed affection, love, tenderness, and understanding within the family. Both streams, as Paula Fass has suggested, emphasized personality development; both wanted to make parenthood into a profession. The two approaches radically disagreed, however, on how best to shape the ever-elusive "well-adjusted personality." For an insightful analysis of Watson and this debate in general, see Paula Fass, *The Damned and the Beautiful: American Youth in the 1920's* (New York: Oxford University Press, 1977): 100–107.

23. White House Conference on Child Health and Protection (hereafter, WHC), *The Young Child in the Home: A Survey of Three Thousand American Families,* John E. Anderson, Chairman (New York: Appleton-Century, 1936): 78. Whereas from 80.7 to 90.6 percent of mothers in the top three social classes read newspapers or magazine articles on child care, the same figure for fathers ranged from 41.7 to 65.0 percent. This relationship held true for fathers and mothers in the lower four classes as well: 34.5 to 75.4 percent of mothers but only 12.1 to 35.1 percent of fathers in the lower four classes read newspaper or magazine articles on child care.

24. Ibid., 79–81. Overall, slightly more than 50 percent of 2,531 mothers but only 25 percent of 2,471 fathers tuned in such radio offerings. So, too, almost 20 percent of all mothers but fewer than 3 percent of all fathers attended a child study group. Fathers attended parent-teacher associations at slightly better than half the rate of mothers (9.6 percent to 17.8 percent). While fewer than 1 percent of fathers attended both a child study group and a parent-teacher association, 9.2 percent of all mothers did so.

25. John Anderson, "The Clientele of a Parental Education Program," *School and Society* 26 (August 6, 1927): 178–79, 181.

26. Barbara Ehrenreich and Deidre English describe child-rearing experts as "a new source of patriarchal authority." See *For Her Own Good,* 189. For women, the parent education movement was fraught with irony. Mothers shaped, consumed, and disseminated the knowledge of child experts and in so doing increased their leverage over less informed fathers. On the other hand, some middle-class mothers may have become dependent on experts for guidance; moreover, their intensive involvement with parent education simultaneously heightened the identification of womanhood with motherhood. To be a woman was to be a mother; to be a good mother was to be an informed mother. Such an identification obviously worked against the interests of women who wished to expand female involvement to the world beyond the home.

27. One well-known expert charged that many fathers were either indifferent to or overtly opposed to mothers' efforts to use new child-rearing knowledge; see Lawrence Frank, "The Father's Role in Child Nurture," 135. Frederic Van de Water argued that fathers needed advice about rearing children more than mothers because the latter could rely on instinct. Unfortunately, most of the available child-rearing information was directed at mothers, a fact with dire consequences for fatherhood: "The average male parent, unless he is one

of the rare inspired, is a self-taught blunderer, a well-meaning dub." He went on to write that he wished he "knew how to be a fair, enlightened, and scientific parent." See Van de Water, "Confessions of a Dub Father," *Ladies Home Journal* 42 (May 1925): 25, 97–98. Chester T. Crowell expressed similar sentiments in "Notes of an Amateur Father," *American Mercury* 3 (October 1924): 137–42.

28. Lucia Clow, "Motherless Families," *The Family* 9 (March 1928): 11–14.

29. Frank Ward O'Malley, "A Plea for Young Male Parents," *Saturday Evening Post* 192 (January 1920): 18–19, 149–50, 153.

30. Margarete Simpson, *Parent Preferences of Young Children* (New York: Teachers College, Columbia University, 1935): 25, 31–33. For a fuller treatment of parental preference studies in the 1920s and 1930s, also see my essay, "Ties that Bind and Bonds that Break: Children's Attitudes toward Fathers, 1900–1930," in Paula Petrik and Elliot West, eds., *Small Worlds: Children and Adolescents in America* (Lawrence: University Press of Kansas): 255–74.

31. WHC, *The Young Child in the Home*, 228–29.

32. Ibid., 228–33.

33. WHC, *Adolescent in the Family*, 133. Meyer Nimkoff's study of almost 3,000 young adults (1,336 males and 1,336 females) found a similar pattern. Only about one-half the sons and only one-fifth as many daughters confided as completely in their fathers as in their mothers; see Nimkoff, "Parent-Child Intimacy," *Social Forces* 7 (December 1928): 244–49.

34. WHC, *Adolescent in the Family*, 134–35, 370.

35. Nimkoff, "Parent-Child Intimacy," 244–47, 249. Younger children apparently looked at fathers somewhat differently. When a St. Louis psychologist asked 150 children (average age twelve) to say the first ten things that came to mind when they heard the words "father" and "mother," the children described their father as playmates more frequently than their mothers. For example, "plays with me" was included 121 times in regard to fathers, only 49 times in association with mothers. The children associated fathers with "outdoor games" 38 times, mothers zero. However, 69 expressions of "love," "like," and "loyalty" went to mothers, only 27 to fathers. In general, children more often mentioned their fathers as companions than their mothers. Without making too much of this evidence, it does suggest that younger children tended to see their fathers as pals, even playmates, a point of no small significance both to the issue of "masculine domesticity" and to the household division of labor. See H. Meltzer, "Children's Attitudes to Parents," *American Journal of Orthopsychiatry* 5 (July 1935): 244–65.

36. WHC, *Adolescent in the Family*, 134–35, 370. Fifty-two percent of boys and 65 percent of girls who "almost always" confided in their fathers had good personality adjustment compared with only 33 percent of boys and the same percentage of girls who "almost never" told their fathers their "joys and troubles." A later study of 1,500 high school youth also found them much more willing to confide in their mothers than in their fathers. Seventy-one percent

talked over their problems with their mothers; only 31 percent did so with their fathers. See Melvin J. Williams, "Personal and Familial Problems of High School Youths and Their Bearing Upon Family Education Needs," *Social Forces* 27 (March 1949): 279–85.

37. For an analysis of the contrast between the old and the new middle class, see C. Wright Mills, *White Collar: The American Middle Classes* (New York: Oxford University Press, 1956). On the rise of the middle class, see Stuart Blumin, *The Emergence of the Middle Class: Social Experience in the American City, 1760–1900* (Cambridge: Cambridge University Press, 1989).

38. T. J. Jackson Lears, "From Salvation to Self-Realization: Advertising and the Therapeutic Roots of the Consumer Culture, 1880–1930," in Lears and Richard W. Fox, eds., *The Culture of Consumption: Critical Essays in American History, 1880–1980* (New York: Pantheon, 1983): 3–37.

39. Stuart A. Rice, "Undergraduate Attitudes toward Marriage and Children," *Mental Hygiene* 13 (October 1929): 788–93.

40. Robert S. Lynd, "The People as Consumers," in *Recent Social Trends in the United States: Reports of the President's Research Committee on Social Trends,* vol. 2 (New York: McGraw-Hill, 1933): 867.

41. Ibid., 866–67. The key link between the producer and the consumer was advertising, a medium that came of age in the 1920s. In 1929 alone, businesses spent almost 1.8 billion dollars—2 percent of the national income, fifteen dollars per capita—to advertise their products (Lynd, "The People as Consumers," 872). Daniel Horowitz explores the cultural debate about consumption in the early twentieth century by contrasting the restraint advocated by Ellen Richards with the relative license advocated by Martha Bruere in Daniel Horowitz, "Frugality or Comfort: Middle Class Styles of Life in the Early Twentieth Century," *American Quarterly* 37 (June 1985): 239–59.

42. Lynd, "The People as Consumers," 857. Rising wages and expansion in available credit heightened people's ability to consume. By the 1920s installment sales made up almost 15 percent of all retail sales, including 75 percent of radios, 60 percent of furniture and automobiles, and 50 percent of electrical household goods. See Lynd, "The People as Consumers," 862.

43. Such desires became more elaborate as one's income improved. Not surprisingly, poorer Americans spent a relatively high percentage of their income on food and rent, whereas those with more comfortable incomes could afford to buy more discretionary items. Affluent families with annual incomes over $6,500 spent 50 percent or more of their money on a vast array of consumer items, including approximately $100 per year each on gifts, entertainment of guests, family vacations, automobiles, and music lessons. See Lynd, "The People as Consumers," 893–95. The Lynds found persistent rumors in Middletown that some families purchased a car solely to increase the social prestige of their high school offspring. See Robert S. Lynd and Helen M. Lynd, *Middletown: A Study in Modern American Culture* (New York: Harcourt, Brace World, 1956; first published 1929): 137.

44. Letter to Angelo Patri, August 21, 1925, Box 3, AAP-LC.

45. Letter to Angelo Patri, December 29, 1925, and January 7, 1926, Box 3, APP-LC.

46. Letter to Angelo Patri, May 29, 1934, APP-LC.

47. Lynd and Lynd, *Middletown,* 80–81.

48. Ibid., 87.

49. Anonymous, "These Modern Husbands," *Nation* 124 (January 12, 1927): 39.

50. Lynd, "The People as Consumers," 866.

51. Feminist analyses of housework rightfully point out that consumption by women to maintain the household is socially necessary and often unrecognized labor that benefits the entire family but often does little or nothing for women personally.

52. Stuart Ewen, *Captains of Consciousness: Advertising and the Social Roots of the Consumer Culture* (New York: McGraw-Hill, 1976): 131, 136; also see Stuart Ewen and Elizabeth Ewen, *Channels of Desire: Mass Images and the Shaping of American Consciousness* (New York: McGraw-Hill, 1982).

53. WHC, *The Adolescent in the Family,* 163–65.

54. Ibid., 166.

55. George A. Lundberg, Mirra Komarovsky, and Mary A. McInerny, *Leisure: A Suburban Study* (New York: Columbia University Press, 1934): 183–84. Commuter families did, however, tend to spend their evenings within the home at a higher rate than noncommuter families; so, too, suburban children spent many evenings at home. The authors do note, however, that although suburban families spent time in the home together, they often pursued their own interests there.

56. Groves and Groves, *Parents and Children,* 150; also, Groves, *The Drifting Home,* 28–29.

57. Letter to Angelo Patri, April 30, 1933, APP-LC.

58. Lynd and Lynd, *Middletown,* 137, 257–58, 522. Earl H. Bell found the same conflict between parents and children over the use of the car in small-town Iowa. He also found frequent clashes between the generations over spending money: "Age Group Conflict and Our Changing Culture," *Social Forces* 12 (December 1933): 237–43. Likewise, Florence Kelly worried about the impact on family unity of the automobile and new amusements in "Future of the Family," *Century* 112 (September 1926): 623.

59. This evidence comes from a letter in the Patri files that is not to Patri but to a physician; see the letter of June 22, 1928, Box 6, APP-LC. The man wrote Patri for advice the next day and included a copy of the letter he sent to the doctor with the one he sent to Patri.

60. Lynd and Lynd, *Middletown,* 265–67. Only 21 percent of 337 high school boys and 33 percent of 423 high school girls attended movies more often with their parents than without them. Burgess's figures confirmed the findings of the Lynds: adolescents attended the movies with boyfriends about 27 percent of the time, with girlfriends about 26 percent of the time, and with parents about 12 percent of the time. See WHC, *The Adolescent in the Family,* 170.

61. Ibid., 267–68.

62. Ellen Rothman provides an excellent analysis of middle-class courtship in *Hands and Hearts: A History of Courtship in America* (New York: Basic Books, 1984).

63. For a complete description of nineteenth-century courtship, see Rothman, *Hands and Hearts*; for twentieth-century developments, see Beth Bailey, *From Front Porch to Back Seat: Courtship in Twentieth-Century America* (Baltimore: Johns Hopkins University Press, 1988): 13–24.

64. Bailey, *From Front Porch to Back Seat*, 17.

65. Ibid., 26–27. Bailey notes that the rise of dating and the resulting break from parental supervision was often attributed to the advent of the automobile. Although it is true that cars offered youth mobility and privacy, the automobile simply accelerated trends in dating that were already under way. See Bailey, *From Front Porch to Back Seat*, 18. Bailey notes not only that dating undercut the power of parents—she focuses on mothers—but that it shifted the balance of power from young women to young men.

66. Lynd and Lynd, *Middletown*, 138.

67. Ibid., 139.

68. Ibid., 141.

69. Ibid., 142, 522.

70. Paula Fass provides an astute analysis of college youth culture in the 1920s in her book, *The Damned and the Beautiful*; Reed Ueda does the same for high school youth in *Avenues to Adulthood: The Origins of the High School and Social Mobility in an American Suburb* (Cambridge: Cambridge University Press, 1987).

71. Lynd and Lynd, *Middletown*, 135, 522. From the Middletown evidence, it is impossible to say whether both mothers and fathers objected to their children's evening activities. The examples of parental complaints come from mothers, but whether or not fathers shared their wives' attitudes, many fathers saw little of their teenage children in the after-school hours. Focusing on a slightly younger group of children—eighth-, ninth-, and tenth-graders—Burgess found that urban boys and girls spent far less time at home in the evenings than their rural counterparts: 54 percent of the boys and 62 percent of the girls spent three evenings per week or fewer at home; by contrast, the figure for rural boys was 23 percent and for rural girls, 27 percent. WHC, *The Adolescent in the Family*, 167.

72. On suburban leisure in the late twenties and early thirties, see Lundberg, Komarovsky, and McInerny, *Leisure: A Surburban Study*, 112, 176–82.

73. Samuel Osherson, *Finding Our Fathers: How a Man's Life Is Shaped by His Relationship with His Father* (New York: Fawcett Columbine, 1986): 6.

Chapter 7. Fathers in Crisis: The 1930s

1. Robert S. McElvaine, *Down and Out in the Great Depression: Letters from the "Forgotten Man"* (Chapel Hill: University of North Carolina Press, 1983): 72.

2. Quoted in Steven Mintz and Susan Kellogg, *Domestic Revolutions: A Social History of American Family Life* (New York: Free Press, 1988): 138.

3. In an effort to study the impact of the Depression on families, Winona Morgan in 1933 reinvestigated over 300 families first studied by Ruth Lindquist in 1927. The fathers in Lindquist's original study were overwhelmingly middle class—either professionals or businessmen along with smaller numbers of retailers, highly skilled workmen, and farmers—and far exceeded the national average in education. Morgan found that over 80 percent of these men occupied the same class position as before and that only 2 percent were unemployed as of 1933. Morgan, *The Family Meets the Depression: A Study of a Group of Highly Selected Families* (Minneapolis: University of Minnesota Press, 1939): 11–12, 15–16.

4. Cecile Pilpel and Anna W. M. Wolf, "Parents' Questions: Study Group Department," *Child Study* 16 (March 1939): 144. Predictably, the experts opined that with proper planning a father could spend his Sundays with his children and still make time for a round of golf.

5. Letters to Angelo Patri, June 20, 1932, Box 18; December 28, 1932, Box 22; and July 1932, Box 18, Angelo Patri Papers, Library of Congress (APP-LC).

6. Jessie Bernard, "The Good Provider Role: Its Rise and Fall," *American Psychologist* 36 (January 1981): 3–5. Mirra Komarovsky described at some length the relationship between breadwinning and male identity in *The Unemployed Man and His Family* (New York: Dryden, 1940): 74–83. When reporters asked Glen Craig of Muncie, Indiana—head of the most "typical" family from the most "typical" town in America—what he desired in life, he explained "that he had no particular ambitions except to provide for his family." *New York Times,* October 18, 1938, 27. The Lynds found the same sentiments expressed by other Muncie residents when they revisited the town in the thirties: Robert S. Lynd and Helen M. Lynd, *Middletown in Transition: A Study in Cultural Conflicts* (New York: Harcourt, Brace and World, 1937): 176. An unemployed crane operator paid allegiance to the breadwinning role in a conversation with a welfare worker: "He said that he could not allow himself to become discouraged because, after all, it was up to him to get a job so that he could support his family." See Elizabeth Dixon and Grace Browning, *Social Case Records: Family Welfare* (Chicago: University of Chicago Press, 1938): 9.

7. Robert S. McElvaine, *The Great Depression: America, 1929–1941* (New York: Times Books, 1984): 75.

8. *New York Times,* November 10, 1933, 30. These figures came from a survey of 2,566 families by the Milbank Memorial Fund and the United States Public Health Service.

9. *New York Times,* II, January 24, 1932, 1. Writers who emphasized the salutary impact of the Depression tended to focus on its impact upon family loyalty and mutual help and support. See, for example, Robert Cooley Angell, *The Family Encounters the Depression* (Gloucester, Mass.: Peter Smith, 1965): 58, 60, 84–85. Some believed the family spent more time together

because of the crisis, others that wastefulness and indulgence had declined. One woman described how the hard times had forced her family to learn "self-reliance, thrift, and industry" and had increased the time her husband and sons spent together. See *New York Times,* July 14, 1932, 18; *New York Times,* April 25, 1933, 7; *New York Times,* XIII, December 20, 1936, 3; Morgan, *The Family Meets the Depression,* 61–62, 63, 68; and Komarovsky, *The Unemployed Man and His Family,* 49–55.

10. A similar point is made by John F. Bauman and Thomas H. Coode, *In the Eye of the Great Depression: New Deal Reporters and the Agony of the American People* (DeKalb: Northern Illinois University Press, 1988).

11. Angell, *The Family Encounters the Depression,* 91.

12. Ibid., 143.

13. Ibid., 212; for other examples, see 219, 237, 252–53; see also E. Wight Bakke, *Citizens without Work: A Study of the Effects of Unemployment upon the Workers' Social Relations and Practices* (New Haven: Yale University Press, 1940): 110ff. There are always those who want to make a silk purse out of a sow's ear: "For those who will," wrote personnel director R. O. Beckman, "the depression, instead of acting as a force or repression and destruction, becomes a challenge, an exceptional opportunity for the rediscovery of personality as a jewel of priceless worth." Beckman, "Mental Perils of Unemployment," *Occupations* 12 (December 1933): 35.

14. Komarovsky, *The Unemployed Man and His Family,* 50–55.

15. Ibid., 105–7.

16. Ibid., 107–8. Komarovsky suggested that lenient, affectionate, and nonassertive fathers retained their authority despite losing their jobs as did traditional patriarchs whose power the children accepted as legitimate.

17. The two major studies that emphasized family unity in coping with the Depression were Ruth Cavan and Katherine Ranck, *The Family and the Depression: A Study of One Hundred Chicago Families* (Chicago: University of Chicago Press, 1938), and Angell, *The Family Encounters the Depression.*

18. McElvaine, *Down and Out in the Great Depression,* 59.

19. Ibid., 72.

20. Ibid., 76.

21. Ibid., 130.

22. Ibid., 160. Harry Emerson Fosdick, pastor of Riverside Church in New York City, empathized with the plight of such men in a speech before representatives of 242 family welfare agencies: "I think I would want to blow the lid off if my children had to go hungry. Some of my friends marvel at the spread of radicalism. I wonder why there is so little of it." *New York Times,* November 21, 1934, 21.

23. Komarovsky, *The Unemployed Man and His Family,* 80–81.

24. Douglas Thom, "Mental Hygiene and the Depression," *Mental Hygiene* 16 (October 1933): 569. An unemployed carpenter told an investigator that all he wanted was "just a moderately decent living, maybe a home of his own, a chance for his children to get a proper education," see Komarovsky, *The Unemployed Man and His Family,* 8.

25. Komarovsky, *The Unemployed Man and His Family,* 74.

26. James M. Reinhardt and George R. Boardman, "Insecurity and Personality Disintegration," *Social Forces* 14 (October 1935–May 1936): 240–49.

27. Cavan and Ranck, *The Family and the Depression,* 59–60. For other examples, see Angell, *The Family Encounters the Depression,* 80, 165–66, 255, and McElvaine, *Down and Out in the Great Depression,* 55, 158.

28. Cavan and Ranck, *The Family and the Depression,* 127.

29. McElvaine, *Down and Out in the Great Depression,* 159. Investigators periodically mentioned fathers who threatened or actually committed suicide under the stress of unemployment; see, for example, Morgan, *The Family Meets the Depression,* 92, and Cavan and Ranck, *The Family and the Depression,* 61–63, 104–6. Investigators noted that some fathers became abusive because of unemployment: William Haber, "The Effects of Insecurity on Family Life," *AAAPSS* 196 (March 1938): 37; Melvin Vincent, "Relief and Resultant Attitudes," *Sociology and Social Research* 20 (September–October 1935): 28; and Komarovsky, *The Unemployed Man and His Family,* 95.

30. McElvaine, *Down and Out in the Great Depression,* 117.

31. Bessie A. McClenahan, "The Child of the Relief Agency," *Social Forces* 13 (May 1935): 561.

32. James M. Williams, *Human Aspects of Unemployment and Relief: With Special Reference to the Effects of the Depression on Children* (Chapel Hill: University of North Carolina Press, 1933): 69, 71, 73.

33. McClenahan, "The Child of the Relief Agency," 561; also see Komarovsky, *The Unemployed Man and His Family,* 92. Glen Elder found that middle-class men suffered greater psychological setbacks than their working-class counterparts when unemployment struck. Glen H. Elder, *Children of the Great Depression: Social Change in the Life Experience* (Chicago: University of Chicago Press, 1974).

34. Komarovsky, *The Unemployed Man and His Family,* 35; also see Marion Elderton, "Unemployment Consequences on the Home," *AAAPSS* 154 (March 1931): 62.

35. Komarovsky, *The Unemployed Man and His Family,* 39. Komarovsky quotes another father along the same lines: "Now that I am at home all day I get irritated with the children, and they feel that I have become a nag. When I used to work I would ask my wife in the evening, 'Were Johnny and Willie good boys today?' and then I would either punish them or reward them. And that's how it should be" (85).

36. Haber, "The Effects of Insecurity on Family Life," 39–40.

37. Komarovsky, *The Unemployed Man and His Family,* 14, 46, 76. Robert Angell notes similar examples in *The Family Encounters the Depression,* 220, as does E. Wight Bakke in *Citizens without Work,* 120. Samuel Stouffer and Paul Lazarsfeld speculate on the loss of paternal authority due to unemployment in *Research Memorandum on the Family in the Depression* (New York: Social Science Research Council, 1937): 113–14.

38. Komarovsky, *The Unemployed Man and His Family,* 41.

39. Henry C. Shumacher, "The Depression and Its Effect on the Mental Health

of the Child," *Mental Hygiene* 18 (April 1934): 287. Also see Komarovsky, *The Unemployed Man and His Family,* 97–98.

40. Komarovsky, *The Unemployed Man and His Family,* 93, 99–101. Robert Angell describes a case in which an employed daughter of a jobless father likewise became "the mainstay of the family in the outside world." See Angell, *The Family Encounters the Depression,* 48–49. Some investigators found that the Depression caused adolescent males to rethink their obligations to their families. Speaking of a young Ohio boy, a New Deal reporter remarked that "he like others his age were growing up determined to live their own lives without assuming the overwhelming responsibility that support of their families now on relief would bring." See John F. Bauman and Thomas H. Coode, *In the Eye of the Great Depression,* 84.

41. Komarovsky, *The Unemployed Man and His Family,* 100.

42. See, for example, Angell, *The Family Encounters the Depression,* 48–49, 98, 155, 157, 166, 170; Bakke, *Citizens without Work,* 133–38; Komarovsky, *The Unemployed Man and His Family,* 27; and Cavan and Ranck, *The Family and the Depression,* 61, 83, 94–95.

43. Beckman, "Mental Perils of Unemployment," 30.

44. Pauline Young, "The New Poor," *Sociology and Social Research* 17 (January–February 1933): 242.

45. *New York Times,* October 16, 1932, 24; see also Dorothy O'Rourke, "Fifty Family Deserters: An Inquiry into the Reasons for Their Desertion," *Smith College Studies in Social Work* 1 (June 1931): 395. Quoting one expert, O'Rourke noted that "many men may confidently be relied upon to desert on each occasion of their wives' confinement, unable or willing to face the problem of financing the additional expense."

46. Young, "The New Poor," 241. A relief worker made much the same point: "In a home stricken by unemployment there is constant talk of lack of food, the menace of the landlord, the cost of fuel and the need for new clothes. There is little wonder that a male member of the family is likely to say to himself: 'If I leave home now there will be one less to provide for, and it will be easier for the women folks to get help from charity.' And this thought comes to the thinking men and boys; not the morons." *New York Times,* October 16, 1932, 24.

47. Towne Nylander, "Wandering Youth," *Sociology and Social Research* 17 (July–August 1933): 560–61.

48. Williams, *Human Aspects of Unemployment and Relief,* 111.

49. Ibid.

50. Ibid. William Mathews, director of the Emergency Work and Relief Bureau in New York City, noted the relationship among unemployment, family abandonment by fathers, and juvenile crime, see *New York Times,* October 16, 1932, 24.

51. *New York Times,* October 16, 1932, 24; also *New York Times,* July 18, 1932, 11.

52. Williams, *Human Aspects of Unemployment and Relief,* 102.

53. Ibid., 104–5.

54. Ibid., 107.

55. On the New Deal and work relief see, for example, William W. Bremer, "Along the 'American Way': The New Deal's Work Relief Programs for the Unemployed," *Journal of American History* 62 (December 1975): 636–52; William R. Brock, *Welfare, Democracy, and the New Deal* (Cambridge: Cambridge University Press, 1988): 270–79, 329–30, 353–54; James T. Patterson, *America's Struggle against Poverty, 1900–1980* (Cambridge, Mass.: Harvard University Press, 1981): 63–67; William E. Leuchtenburg, *Franklin D. Roosevelt and the New Deal, 1932–40* (New York: Harper and Row, 1963): chap. 6; Bauman and Coode, *In the Eye of the Great Depression*, 90, 110; Michael Katz, *In the Shadow of the Poorhouse: A Social History of Welfare in America* (New York: Basic Books, 1986): 213–47.

56. Lois Scharf, *To Work and To Wed: Female Employment, Feminism, and the Great Depression* (Westport, Conn.: Greenwood, 1980): 123.

57. Alice Kessler-Harris, *Out To Work: A History of Wage Earning Women in the United States* (New York: Oxford University Press, 1982): 262–64. Despite such discrimination, Kessler-Harris does note the very real benefits female workers received under New Deal legislation. On discrimination against women in New Deal projects, also see Scharf, *To Work and To Wed*, 122–25.

58. *New York Times,* IV, March 10, 1935, 7.

59. *New York Times,* VII, June 2, 1935, 2. "Give a man a dole and you save his body and destroy his spirit," Hopkins once told an audience; "give him a job and pay him an assured wage, and you save both the body and the spirit." Hopkins quoted in Bremer, "Along the 'American Way,'" 637.

60. Folks quoted in Bremer, "Along the 'American Way,'" 637–38.

61. *New York Times,* IV, March 10, 1935, 7.

62. *New York Times,* VII, June 2, 1935, 2.

63. *New York Times,* IV, February 17, 1935, 11.

64. Harry L. Hopkins, *Spending to Save: The Complete Story of Relief* (New York: Norton, 1936): 172.

65. For an excellent analysis of the guiding assumptions of the WPA and the problems that beset it, see Bremer, "Along the 'American Way,'" 643–52, and Katz, *In the Shadow of the Poorhouse*, 228–33.

66. Kessler-Harris, *Out To Work,* 251.

67. Quoted in ibid., 256.

68. Ibid., 255, 256.

69. Quoted in Scharf, *To Work and To Wed,* 45.

70. Scharf, *To Work and To Wed,* 46–50; Kessler-Harris, *Out To Work,* 257.

71. George Gallup, *The Gallup Poll: Public Opinion, 1935–1971,* Vol.1, 1935–1948 (New York: Random House, 1972): 39, 131. In the 1938 survey, 19 percent of men but 25 percent of women approved "of a married woman earning money in business or industry if she has a husband capable of supporting her," but 75 percent of the women and 81 percent of the men opposed the employment of such women. In 1938, Massachusetts voters in thirty cities and towns approved two to one a referendum granting the legisla-

ture the right to enact restrictions against the employment of wives. See
Scharf, *To Work and To Wed*, 55.

72. Scharf, *To Work and To Wed*, 53–55 and chap. 4; Kessler-Harris, *Out To Work*, 257.

73. Quoted in Scharf, *To Work and To Wed*, 61.

74. U.S. Congress, House, *Hearings before the Committee on the Civil Service on H.R. 5051*, *"To Amend Married Persons' Clause,"* 74th Cong., 1st sess., 1935, 72.

75. Kessler-Harris, *Out To Work*, 259.

Chapter 8. Fatherhood, Foxholes, and Fascism, 1940–1950

1. This war bond advertisement, funded by Felt and Tarrant Manufacturing Company of Chicago, appeared in *Time*, June 12, 1944, 63.

2. Psychiatrist David Levy reported that work had the power to transform men's psyches, including their sexual abilities. One man who had been rendered sexually impotent by unemployment "became adequate sexually as well as otherwise" once he went back to work. The agency reporting this case stated many other men had exactly the same experience, see Levy, "The War and Family Life: Report for the War Emergency Committee," *American Journal of Orthopsychiatry* 15 (January 1945): 144; see also 141, 143–46.

3. On the relationship between the war and the family, see Dennis Lee Frobish, "The Family and Ideology: Cultural Constraints on Women, 1940–1960," Ph.D. diss., University of North Carolina at Chapel Hill, 1983, and Elaine Tyler May, *Homeward Bound: American Families in the Cold War Era* (New York: Basic Books, 1988): 57–78.

4. Frobish, "The Family and Ideology," 30–31, 34–35.

5. Ibid., 37–38.

6. Ibid., 56.

7. Ernest Burgess, "The Effect of War on the American Family," *American Journal of Sociology* 48 (November 1942): 352; for similar sentiments, see Ernest Mowrer, "War and Family Solidarity and Stability," *AAAPSS* 229 (September 1943): 100–101; Lawrence Frank, "The Family in the National Emergency," in Sidonie M. Gruenberg, ed., *The Family in a World at War* (New York: Harper and Brothers, 1942): 67.

8. Quoted in Frobish, "The Family and Ideology," 62.

9. On these points, see Susan Hartmann, *The Home Front and Beyond: American Women in the 1940s* (Boston: Twayne, 1982); May, *Homeward Bound*, 58–91; and Frobish, "The Family and Ideology."

10. Robert Westbrook, "'I Want a Girl, Just Like the Girl That Married Harry James': American Women and the Problem of Political Obligation in World War II," *American Quarterly* 42 (December 1990): 588. Emphasis in original.

11. Robert Westbrook offers an astute analysis of Rockwell's "Four Freedoms" in "Fighting for the American Family: Private Interests and Political Obligations

in World War II," in Richard Wightman Fox and T. J. Jackson Lears, eds., *The Power of Culture: Critical Essays in American History* (Chicago: University of Chicago Press, 1993): 195–201. On soldiers' motivations, see Samuel Stouffer, et al., *The American Soldier: Combat and Its Aftermath*, vol. 2 (Princeton, N.J.: Princeton University Press, 1949): 105–91.

12. Ibid., 201. One father expressed this sense of private obligation rather well. Fearing that a bill in Congress might forbid the drafting of fathers, he pleaded with his draft board to draft him: "Give me a break," he wrote the chairman of the Polk County, Iowa, draft board, "as I've so much more to fight for than some of the younger boys who, after all, are just beginning to live. My family will be in good hands while I'm in there pitching." *New York Times*, September 19, 1943, 4.

13. *Time*, May 15, 1945, 45.

14. *Newsweek*, March 12, 1945, 113.

15. *Time*, June 26, 1944, 7. Many advertisements pictured children either at home without their fathers or in scenes of reunion with them. One war bond ad sponsored by Commercial Solvents Corporation portrayed a little boy, apparently a newspaper seller, buying a war bond with his earnings. The caption read, "Return Ticket for Dad" (*Time*, June 12, 1944, 95).

16. *Life*, January 8, 1945, 15. Westbrook notes that posters and ads pictured the enemy as a threat to the family, particularly its weaker members. See "American Women and the Problem of Political Obligation in World War II," 592–95. The essentially private nature of most soldiers' conception of war aims came through in the remark of a GI who displayed considerable disquiet once his aims had been attained: "It's funny the way things work out. When I was in Normandy my morale was kept up by the knowledge that I was fighting for home, family and normalcy. Now that I have all three again I lack the morale necessary to go on and face the little problems which make up my day to day existence," see John Cuber, "Family Readjustment of Veterans," *Marriage and Family Living* 7 (Spring 1945): 28–29. Roy Grinker and John Spiegel likewise noted the private motivations of most GIs and offered as one source of disillusionment the tendency of GIs to idealize their homes and to view their return "as a rebirth after the personal psychological death symbolized by repetitive combat missions." Grinker and Spiegel, *Men under Stress* (Philadelphia: Blakiston, 1945): 181, 185. George Pratt examines the same process in *Soldier to Civilian: Problems of Readjustment* (New York: McGraw-Hill, 1944): 123.

17. *Newsweek*, February 19, 1945 (inside of front cover).

18. *Life*, January 8, 1945, 45.

19. *Newsweek*, December 20, 1943, 44. Emphasis in original.

20. *Time*, June 12, 1944, 98.

21. John Slawson, "The Adolescent in a World at War," *Mental Hygiene* 27 (October 1943): 531–35; Slawson called for expansion of social service agencies to help meet the crisis of venereal disease, especially for the establishment of special clinics to deal with infected young girls. He also argued that

juvenile delinquency could be curbed, in part, if young boys had father substitutes once their own fathers went off to war. Also see George Gardner,
"Child Behavior in Nation at War," *Mental Hygiene* 27 (July 1943): 353–69.
Gardner emphasized the importance of women staying at home to supervise
their children and the importance of Sunday schools, boys clubs, YMCAs, and
the like, in preventing juvenile delinquency. See, too, Gardner's article, "Sex
Behavior of Adolescents in Wartime," *AAAPSS* 236 (November 1944): 60–66,
and Ernest Groves and Gladys Groves, "The Social Background of Wartime
Adolescents," *AAAPSS* 236 (November 1944): 26–32. For secondary sources
on juvenile delinquency, James Gilbert's *A Cycle of Outrage: America's
Reaction to the Juvenile Delinquent in the 1950s* (New York: Oxford
University Press, 1986) is very useful, especially 24–41. The Senate held hear-
ings on wartime juvenile delinquency in late 1943 and early 1944; see U.S.
Congress, Senate, Subcommittee of the Committee on Education and Labor,
Hearings on Wartime Health and Education: Juvenile Delinquency, Parts 1,
4, 78th Congress, 1944 (hereafter cited as *Hearings: Juvenile Delinquency*).

22. Journals and popular periodicals were filled with discussions of wartime insta-
    bility; for a sampling, see H. J. Locke, "Family Behavior in Wartime,"
    Sociology and Social Research 27 (March-April 1943): 277–84; Esther E.
    Twente, "The Impact of War upon the Husband-Wife Relationship in the
    Rural Family," *Family* 24 (October 1943): 226–31; James H. S. Bossard,
    "Family Backgrounds of Wartime Adolescents," *AAAPSS* 236 (November
    1944): 33–42; Eleanor Clifton, "Some Psychological Effects of the War as
    Seen by the Social Worker," *Family* 24 (June 1943): 123–28; Henry L.
    Zucker, "Working Parents and Latchkey Children," *AAAPSS* 236 (November
    1944): 43–50; Ernest Burgess, "The Effect of War on the American Family,"
    American Journal of Sociology 48 (November 1942): 343–52; and Ernest
    Mowrer, "War and Family Solidarity and Stability," *AAAPSS* 229 (September
    1943): 100–106.

23. Gardner, "Child Behavior in Nation at War," 361.

24. Gilbert, *Cycle of Outrage*, 29; also see J. Edgar Hoover, "There Will Be a
    Post-War Crime Wave Unless—," *Rotarian* 66 (April 1945): 12–14; J. Edgar
    Hoover, "Wild Children," *American Magazine* 136 (July 1943): 40–41, 103–5;
    "Who's to Blame for Juvenile Delinquency?" *Rotarian* 68 (April 1946): 20–24;
    Gardner, "Child Behavior in a Nation at War," 353–69; Slawson, "The
    Adolescent in a World at War," 531–48; Gardner, "Sex Behavior of
    Adolescents in Wartime," 60–66.

25. *Hearings: Juvenile Delinquency*, Part 1, 70.

26. Ibid., 104; see also 153. William Healy, director of the Judge Baker
    Guidance Center in Boston, testified, "Where there is a father or even an
    older brother in the service, a boy is apt, we find, to feel that he can do
    pretty much as he pleases" (6). Healy likely derived this assertion from a
    study of youth in Massachusetts conducted by the staff of the Judge Baker
    Clinic. The findings were reported in Gardner, "Child Behavior in a Nation
    at War," 353–69.

27. *Hearings: Juvenile Delinquency,* Part 1, 263.

28. See the testimony, for example, of Eliot Ness, director of the Social Protection Division in the Office of Community War Services, in *Hearings: Juvenile Delinquency,* Part 1, 85–86; Arnold Gesell, director of the Clinic of Child Development, Yale University, ibid., 166–67, 222, 224; Victor Scafati, truant officer, New Haven, Connecticut, ibid., 171–72; Franklin Adams, ibid., 172–73; Joseph Anderson, executive secretary of the American Association of Social Workers, ibid., 257. Also see Gardner, "Sex Behavior of Adolescents in Wartime," 66.

29. See, for example, the testimony of Eliot Ness: *Hearings: Juvenile Delinquency,* Part 1, 95, and juvenile court Judge Michael J. Scott, ibid., 261–63; also see comments by the chairman of the committee, Senator Claude Pepper, ibid., 267. Experts worried about sons who earned more than their fathers. Discussing this problem, Eleanor Clifton asked rhetorically, "'How,' a father asks himself, 'can I control or guide this cocksure young person who can get for himself more than I have ever been able to give him?'" See Clifton, "Some Psychological Effects of the War as Seen by the Social Worker," 126; on this point, also see Groves and Groves, "The Social Background of Wartime Adolescents," 28.

30. Daniel Boone, "No Substitute for Father," *Rotarian* 65 (August 1944): 32. John Slawson, executive director of the Jewish Board of Guardians in New York City, worried about the absence of male role models among social workers who worked with boy delinquents: "We should also face the problem of the absence of the male as an ego ideal in our treatment programs. Devising methods of treatment by female case-workers and substitutions in the home for male ego ideals becomes a challenging responsibility for the mature professional women workers of to-day." Slawson, "The Adolescent in a World at War," 546.

31. U.S. Congress, Senate, Subcommittee on Military Affairs, *Hearings on Married Men Exemption: Drafting of Fathers,* 78 Cong. 1st sess., 1943, revised consolidated print, 2 (hereafter cited as *Hearings: Drafting of Fathers*). For the military's perspective, also see the testimony of Colonel Francis Keesling, Jr., chief liaison and legislative officer of the Selective Service System, 12; General Joseph E. McNarney, U.S. Army, 20–25, 31; Robert P. Patterson, under secretary of war, 51–52; Brig. General Ray E. Porter of the War Department General Staff, 98; Rear Admiral Randall Jacobs, chief of naval personnel, U.S. Navy, 105ff; and General George C. Marshall, chief of staff, 246ff.

32. *Hearings: Drafting of Fathers,* 32. For other examples of the armed services' viewpoint, see 52–53, 86. One letter to the *New York Times* argued that giving fathers special protection "runs counter to every American ideal." *New York Times,* September 20, 1943, 20.

33. *New York Times,* September 15, 1943, 16.

34. *Hearings: Drafting of Fathers,* 4–5.

35. Ibid., 5, 7.

36. Ibid., 170. Also see 272. Wheeler argued (225) that fathers would make poorer soldiers than unmarried men: "You cannot tell me that the right kind of father is going into the Army and leave his children and not know whether his wife has to go to work in order to support them. You cannot tell me that he is going to be as good a soldier as he would if he did not have any children." On this issue also see 45, 76, 259, 265, 302. Military officials directly challenged Wheeler on this point (45, 224–25, 302), as did, by implication, the testimonials of fathers actually in the service. As one put it, "We're just soldiers like everybody else around here, and most of us are damned good ones too." See "Fathers in the Army," *New York Times Magazine,* October 10, 1943, 36.

37. *Hearings: Drafting of Fathers,* 56–58.

38. Ibid., 58; also 206, 219.

39. Ibid., 379.

40. Ibid., 206.

41. Ibid., 310.

42. Ibid., 191.

43. Ibid., 346.

44. *New York Times,* September 15, 1943, 17. Wheeler mentions this poll in the *Hearings: Drafting of Fathers,* 128.

45. *Hearings: Drafting of Fathers,* 390.

46. Ibid., 129, 190.

47. Ibid., 391.

48. Ibid., 218.

49. Ibid., 388–89; for other letters, see 272–73, 279, 386–87, 389–93, 400–401, 403–4.

50. *New York Times,* September 17, 1943, 23; also from the *New York Times,* see September 7, 1943, 25; September 12, 1943, 9; October 11, 1943, 11, and from the *Hearings: Drafting of Fathers,* 391–92, 403. Three draft board members resigned in Whitehall, New York, stating they could "no longer conscientiously classify pre–Pearl Harbor fathers, and some of them fathers of four and five children, in Class 1-A when childless men were still being deferred for reasons we consider insufficient and local boards being apparently nothing more or less than a 'rubber stamp'" (*New York Times,* October 11, 1943, 11).

51. *Hearings: Drafting of Fathers,* 347–48.

52. Ibid., 350. Other academics, Charlotte Towle among them, expressed similar concerns: "That the pregnant woman and the mother of children needs the support, psychological as well as economic, of her husband during wartime is also well recognized. The absence of the father has a different import for children at different ages, but at all times he is needed." See Towle, "The Effect of the War upon Children," *Social Service Review* 17 (June 1943): 154.

53. Key military officials repeatedly testified that labor power needs required the drafting of fathers. In response to one question about the necessity of drafting fathers, General Marshall testified: "We have to have the 446,000 men. We

have to have them, if we are to go about this war in a businesslike manner."
See *Hearings: Drafting of Fathers,* 250. Wheeler faced opposition not only
from the military but from leading newspapers as well. The *New York Times*
lampooned his military knowledge, reminding its readers that Wheeler had
opposed the Selective Service Act of 1940, voted to uphold the arms
embargo, and opposed Lend-Lease. As a *Times* editorial sarcastically put it,
"Mr. Wheeler has written his own record as an expert on national defense."
See *New York Times,* September 17, 1943, 20. Bernard Baruch was one of
many who deferred to the needs of the military: "No cheese-paring. No trad-
ing down. Give him [General Marshall] what he needs." See *New York Times,*
September 23, 1943, 1.

54. Joseph Pleck, "The Theory of Male Sex Role Identity: Its Rise and Fall, 1936
to the Present," in Miriam Lewin, ed., *In the Shadow of the Past: Psychology
Views the Sexes* (New York: Columbia University Press, 1983): 205–25.

55. Roy Helton, "The Inner Threat: Our Own Softness," *Harper's Magazine* 181
(September 1940): 337–43.

56. Philip Wylie, *Generation of Vipers* (New York: Holt, Rinehart, and Winston,
1955; first published 1942): 198–99, 200, 208.

57. David Levy, *Maternal Overprotection* (New York: Columbia University Press,
1943): 150–55; Amram Scheinfeld, "Are American Moms a Menace?" *Ladies
Home Journal* 62 (November 1945): 138, 140. Also see Nancy Staver, "The
Use of a Child Guidance Clinic by Mother-Dominant Families," *Smith
College Studies in Social Work* 14 (March 1943): 367–88.

58. Edward Strecker, *Their Mothers' Sons: The Psychiatrist Examines an
American Problem* (Philadelphia: Lippincott, 1946): 18. On Strecker, also see
New York Times, April 28, 1945, 11.

59. Strecker, *Their Mothers' Sons,* 75–90.

60. Ibid., 71, 167, 172–73.

61. Ibid., 211–13, 219.

62. Juliet Danziger, "Life without Father," *New York Times Magazine,* May 7,
1944, 16; Robert Havighurst, et al., *The American Veteran Back Home: A
Study of Veteran Readjustment* (New York: Longmans, Green and Co., 1951):
46.

63. Janet Landes, "Daddy Comes First," *Parents' Magazine* 19 (November 1944):
154; for other examples, also see Barbara Bosanquet, "Far-Away Father,"
Woman's Home Companion 70 (June 1943): 6; *New York Times,* May 26,
1945, 12; Danziger, "Life without Father," 16, 47; Catherine Mackenzie,
"Absent Fathers," *New York Times Magazine,* April 9, 1944, 29; Reuben Hill,
"The Returning Father and His Family," *Marriage and Family Living* 7 (May
1945): 31–33; John Waldman, "Attention New Fathers," *Parents' Magazine*
21 (May 1946): 37, 48; Juliet Danziger, "Daddy Comes Home on Leave,"
Parents' Magazine 19 (October 1944): 29ff; Gladys Denny Shultz, "Life without Father," *Better Homes and Gardens* 22 (June 1944): 12, 77.

64. John Waldman, "Attention New Fathers," *Parents' Magazine* 21 (May 1946):
48. Some experts offered advice to families when the father did not go to war,

especially the importance of informing children of their fathers' contributions to the war effort despite his absence from the military. See Ruth H. Freund, "When Father Stays Home from War," *Parents' Magazine* 20 (April 1945). On January 8, 1945, *Parents' Magazine* announced it had produced a supplement for overseas fathers. In it, fathers would learn "what children are like, what they need from their parents, what fun children are, how to write them letters and how to participate in the life of the family, even though absent." *New York Times,* January 9, 1945, 22.

65. Laura C. Reynolds, "Calling All Fathers: Stretch Your Fathering to Include Neighbor Children with Dads in the Service," *Parents' Magazine* 20 (March 1945): 33, 102; Hope Bennett, "Living without Father," *Parents' Magazine* 18 (July 1943): 20–21, 57; Milton Rosenbaum, "Emotional Aspects of Wartime Separations," *The Family* 24 (January 1944): 340.

66. Mackenzie, "Absent Fathers," 29. In the same article, Milton Levine of the New York City Bureau of Child Hygiene argued that a father substitute was especially important for the emotional health of boys aged five to fifteen, because their masculine development was at stake.

67. Ada Hart Arlitt, "How Separation Affects the Family," *Marriage and Family Living* 5 (February 1943): 21.

68. David Levy, "War and Family Life," *American Journal of Orthopsychiatry* 15 (January 1945): 147–49. For a sampling of psychological case studies involving father absence, see Pratt, *Soldier to Civilian,* 178–79; Rosenbaum, "Emotional Aspects of Wartime Separations," 339–40; Shultz, "Life without Father," 77; Ray E. Baber, "Marriage and the Family after the War," *AAAPSS* 229 (September 1943): 170–71; Clifton, "Some Psychological Effects of the War," 125; Sterling Johnson, "Effect of Selective Service," *The Family* 23 (July 1942): 173–75; Edward McDonagh and Louise McDonagh, "War Anxieties of Soldiers and Their Wives," *Social Forces* 24 (December 1945): 195–200; Reuben Hill, "The Returning Father and His Family," *Marriage and Family Living* 7 (May 1945): 32–33; George E. Gardner and Harvey Spencer, "Reactions of Children with Fathers and Brothers in the Armed Forces," *American Journal of Orthopsychiatry* 14 (January 1944): 36–43.

69. Reuben Hill, *Families under Stress: Adjustment to the Crises of War Separation and Reunion* (New York: Harper and Brothers, 1949): 64. Hill's classic study of 135 Iowa families does argue that most of the 289 children in the study coped well with their father's departures but that in twenty-one families (15 percent), there were children who remained maladjusted for their father's entire absence.

70. Clifton, "Some Psychological Effects of the War," 125.

71. Hill, *Families under Stress,* 62.

72. Amelia Igel, "War Separation and Father-Child Relations," *The Family* 26 (March 1945): 4, 6–7, 8–9; also see Pratt, *Soldier to Civilian,* 175–77, and Hill, *Families under Stress,* 57–58, 61.

73. Virginia Moore, "When Father Comes Marching Home," *Parents' Magazine*

20 (January 1945): 16–17, 112; Whitman M. Reynolds, "When Father Comes Home Again," *Parents' Magazine* 20 (October 1945): 28, 71, 74–76; also see Madeleine Dixon, "Father Takes a Hand," *Parents' Magazine* 21 (April 1946): 146–47, and Mackenzie, "When Father Comes Home," 27. In September 1945, the Child Study Association of America published a pamphlet, "Father Comes Home," to help fathers and families readjust to reunion; see *New York Times,* September 19, 1945, 28. The child expert Ada Arlitt warned mothers "particularly against making the father the person who is going to do the punishing which the mother has not had time to take care of." In her judgment, "Discipline should be transferred to the father very slowly." The *New York Times,* May 26, 1945, 12. Also see Coleman Griffith, "The Psychological Adjustments of the Returned Servicemen and Their Families," *Journal of Home Economics* 36 (September 1944): 385–89, and Cynthia Nathan, "Servicemen Face Discharge with Hope and Fear," *The Family* 26 (March 1945): 91–97. Some believed mere advice to parents would not be enough. The Salvation Army opened a psychiatric clinic to deal with "war jitters," including problems associated with children's and fathers' adjustment to each other. The Jewish Social Service Association established a committee to help veterans and their families readjust after the war; see *New York Times,* October 24, 1944, 17, and February 11, 1945, 34.

74. Hill, *Families under Stress, passim.*
75. The key research on the question of father absence and child development was conducted in a series of postwar investigations at Stanford University. The findings were published in Lois Meek Stolz, ed., *Father Relations of War-Born Children: The Effect of Postwar Adjustment of Fathers on the Behavior and Personality of First Children Born While the Fathers Were at War* (Stanford: Stanford University Press, 1954). Included in the collection were several chapters by Stolz titled "The Father-Interview Study" as well as the following by other psychologists: Erika Chance, "Father's Perception of Self and First-Born Child"; Edith M. Dowley and William L. Faust, "Characteristics of War-Born Children as Revealed by Mothers"; Alberta Engvall, "Comparison of Mother and Father Attitudes Toward War-Separated Children"; Nancy Guy Stevenson, Leonard Ullmann, and Lois Meek Stolz, "Behavior of War-Separated Children in Group Situations"; Margaret S. Faust, "Children as Revealed in Projective-Play Situations" and "Father-Child Relations in Story Completions"; Joyce M. Ryder, "Aggression with Balloons, Blocking, and Doll Play"; Laverne C. Johnson, D. Bob Gowin, and Lois Meek Stolz, "Father-Child Relations as Revealed by Dramatic-Play Completions." A chapter ends the collection with a case study as an example and a useful general summary and interpretation. Several of the contributors had written unpublished master's theses on the subject of fathers separated from their children by the war. Other psychologists who studied this issue include George R. Bach, "Father-Fantasies and Father-Typing in Father-Separated Children," *Child Development* 17 (March–June 1946): 63–80; and Robert Sears, M. H. Pintler, and Pauline Sears, "Effect of Father Separation

on Pre-School Children's Doll Play Aggression," *Child Development* 17 (December 1946): 219–43.

76. Stolz, *Father Relations of War-Born Children*, 39.

77. Ibid.

78. Reuben Hill, "The Returning Father and His Family," *Marriage and Family Living* 7 (September 1945): 31; see also Hill, *Families under Stress*, 85.

79. Stolz, *Father Relations of War-Born Children*, 33. Reuben Hill found that slightly fewer than 10 percent of his sample of 135 fathers considered family responsibilities onerous; Hill, *Families under Stress*, 85; on this point, also see Pratt, *Soldier to Civilian*, 187, and the remarks of Luther Woodward, a staff member of the National Committee for Mental Hygiene, in *New York Times*, January 24, 1945, 18.

80. Stolz, *Father Relations of War-Born Children*, 36.

81. Ibid.

82. Ibid., 40, 48, 69–70. Other investigators confirmed this evidence. Reuben Hill found that in almost 15 percent of his sample of 135 families, "the children had grown so close to the mother or another relative in the father's absence that they resented the return of the father, or accepted him as a companion but refused to accept him as a disciplinarian—so there was conflict between father and children." See Hill, *Families under Stress*, 85. Hill along with John Cuber also reported that many veterans simply felt irrelevant to their children: Hill, "The Returning Father and His Family," 31–32, and Cuber, "Family Readjustment of Veterans, *Marriage and Family Living* 7 (September 1945): 29. Testimony from fathers who did not go off to war reflected entirely different sentiments. One nonseparated father described his return from work: "Every time I came home Harry would run out and want a surprise or want to go on a drive or something . . . He has always been closer to me than to my wife." Stolz, *Father Relations of War-Born Children*, 49.

83. Stolz, *Father Relations of War-Born Children*, 42–43; also Havighurst et al., *The American Veteran Back Home*, 83–84.

84. Ibid., 34–35.

85. Paul Byers, "My Son Teaches Me to Be a Father," *Parents' Magazine* 20 (July 1945): 92.

86. Stolz, *Father Relations of War-Born Children*, 172.

87. Ibid., 171.

88. Ibid., 37.

89. Ibid., 37, 43.

90. Ibid., 45. Stolz reported that fathers' harsh discipline sparked "extreme disagreements" with mothers.

91. Ibid., 44–45, 141–42.

92. Ibid., 62–63, 165–66. Stolz discusses this issue from a more theoretical perspective in "The Effect of Mobilization and War on Children," in E. A. Richards, ed., *Proceedings of the Midcentury White House Conference on Children and Youth* (Raleigh, N.C.: Health Publications Institute, 1951): 111–22. In "The Returning Father and His Family," Reuben Hill notes

fathers' importance as appropriate sex-role models for their sons and daughters. See Hill, "The Returning Father and His Family," 31.

93. Stolz, *Father Relations of War-Born Children*, 64.

94. Ibid., 57, 65.

95. Ibid., 70.

96. Ibid.

97. Ibid., 70–72, 94, 140, 142–43, 319–20. War-separated fathers did more actual child care with their second child than their first, a pattern exactly the opposite of fathers who were not separated from their firstborn (121).

98. Ibid., 146–47, 321–22.

99. Ibid., 322.

100. Paul Fussell suggests that for soldiers and writers alike, World War II occurred in an "ideological vacuum." The romance, idealism, and moral purpose associated with World War I seemed to disappear in the general carnage and anonymity of World War II. What appeared in their place was silence. See *Wartime: Understanding and Behavior in the Second World War* (New York: Oxford University Press, 1989): 129–43.

101. Hill, "The Returning Father and His Family," 31.

102. John Hersey, *Into the Valley: A Skirmish of the Marines* (New York: Knopf, 1965; first published 1943), quoted in Fussell, *Wartime*, 141.

103. Hill, "The Returning Father and His Family," 32.

Chapter 9. Fatherhood and the Great American Barbecue, 1945–1965

1. The most extensive analysis of family ideology in the 1950s is Michael Frobish, "The Family and Ideology: Cultural Constraints on Women," Ph.D. diss., University of North Carolina, 1983. On consumption, family life, and the Cold War, see Elaine Tyler May, *Homeward Bound: American Families in the Cold War Era* (New York: Basic Books, 1988): 162–82.

2. Cynthia Rice Nathan, "Servicemen Face Discharge with Hope and Fear," *The Family* 26 (March 1945): 91–93; John Cuber, "Family Readjustment of Veterans," *Marriage and Family Living* 7 (September 1945): 28–29; Reuben Hill, "The Returning Father and His Family," *Marriage and Family Living* 7 (September 1945): 32.

3. On postwar discrimination against working women, see William Chafe, *The American Woman: Her Changing Social, Economic, and Political Role, 1920–1970* (New York: Oxford University Press, 1972): 174–95, and Ruth Milkman, *Gender at Work: The Dynamics of Job Segregation by Sex during World War II* (Urbana: University of Illinois Press, 1987): 99–127.

4. Waller quoted in Chafe, *The American Woman*, 176.

5. "Fortune Survey," *Fortune* 34 (August 1946): 8, 10, 14.

6. Chafe, *The American Woman*, 180.

7. As Chafe points out in his analysis of the *Fortune* magazine survey, people tolerated female employment so long as it did not conflict with women's

familial obligations. Wage-working mothers of small children faced far more opposition than women whose children were over sixteen. See Chafe, *The American Woman*, 189. These same assumptions help explain why working women received markedly lower wages than men and why the labor force remained gender-segregated: because men worked to support a family while women worked for "pin money" or to supplement their husband's income, men needed higher wages. Thus, men's financial obligation to their wives and children—their breadwinning role—legitimated gender segregation and discriminatory wages in the work force. In the job market, men benefited from the obligations of fatherhood while women, by contrast, were handicapped by those of motherhood.

8. See the analyses offered in William Graebner, *The Age of Doubt: American Thought and Culture in the 1940s* (Boston: Twayne, 1991), and May, *Homeward Bound*.

9. Barbara Ehrenreich, *The Hearts of Men: American Dreams and the Flight from Commitment* (New York: Anchor, 1984): 14–17.

10. Arthur Miller, *Death of a Salesman*, in Harold Clurman, ed., *The Portable Arthur Miller* (New York: Penguin, 1971): 16, 57.

11. Ehrenreich, *The Hearts of Men*, 18.

12. Ibid., 23.

13. Ovesey quoted in ibid., 25.

14. The "reproductive consensus" is analyzed in detail in May, *Homeward Bound*, chap. 6. In his insightful analysis of the baby boom's impact on American culture, Landon Jones uses the term *procreation ethic* to describe much the same assumptions. See Jones, *Great Expectations: America and the Baby Boom Generation* (New York: Ballantine, 1981), chap. 2.

15. Jones, *Great Expectations*, 31.

16. Joseph Veroff, Elizabeth Douvan, and Richard A. Kulka, *The Inner American: A Self-Portrait from 1957 to 1976* (New York: Basic Books, 1981): 215, 217.

17. A companion survey in 1976 to the 1957 study found that 84 percent of fathers would rather be known as good fathers than good workers. See Veroff, Douvan, and Kulka, *The Inner American*, 216. On fatherhood and identity, see, too, Ruth Tasch, "Interpersonal Perceptions of Fathers and Mothers," *Journal of Genetic Psychology* 87 (September 1955): 59–65.

18. Harold Justin, "It's a Man's Job Too!" *Parents' Magazine* 26 (September 1951): 165; Warren R. Ross, "Father Reports: My Baby's Done a Lot for Me," *Parents' Magazine* 32 (November 1957): 127.

19. Ruth Tasch, "The Role of the Father in the Family," *Journal of Experimental Education* 20 (June 1952): 339–46.

20. May, *Homeward Bound*, 146. One writer sharply criticized television's portrayal of fathers: "All in all, Dad is pictured as a helpless, hopeless, overgrown boy who, left to his own devices, couldn't possibly last the year out." Bill Gale, "TV Makes a Fool out of Dad: Domestic Comedy," *American Mercury* 84 (February 1957): 37. Bruno Bettelheim made a similar point in "Fathers

Shouldn't Try to Be Mothers," *Parents' Magazine* 31 (October 1956): 40.

21. May, *Homeward Bound,* 146. On television in the 1950s, see Ella Taylor, *Prime Time Families: Television Culture in Postwar America* (Berkeley: University of California Press, 1989): 17–41.

22. Sears interview, F-11, 2; F-14, 2. The evidence from the Sears interviews formed the basis of Robert R. Sears, Lucy Rau, and Richard Alpert, *Identification and Child Rearing* (Stanford: Stanford University Press, 1965). The typed transcripts, from which this and other quotations in this chapter were drawn, are available at the Henry A. Murray Center, Radcliffe College, 2 boxes. The author would like to thank Robert Sears for allowing photocopying of the interview transcripts for my use on this research project. Henceforth, all references to the transcripts will contain Sears's name, the code number of the interview, and the page number. The punctuation of the typed transcripts was idiosyncratic at times. Therefore, on occasion I have made a few minor changes for the sake of clarity or because nothing was served by reproducing the original punctuation. (For example, I have used only two hyphens for the typist's occasional five or six to make a dash.)

23. Sears interview, F-16, 2; F-34, 2.

24. Sears interview, F-28, 2.

25. Sears interview, F-7, 2. Many other fathers expressed their belief that mothers should spend their time at home rather than in the work force. See, for example, F-17, 1; F-25, 2; F-30, 2; F-35, 2; F-44, 3. A few men, however, approved of mothers working for wages; see, for example, F-12, 2; F-23, 2; F-40, 2.

26. Sears interview, F-42, 2.

27. Sears interview, F-44, 2.

28. Sears interview, F-3, 1. (Because of a typographical error on the interview transcript, this page is actually the second page, but it is numbered "1.")

29. Sears interview, F-7, 1.

30. Sears interview, F-14, 1–2.

31. Sears interview, F-8, 2.

32. Sears interview, F-20, 2.

33. Sears interview, F-32, 2.

34. Sears interview, F-41, 3. Almost all the other fathers interviewed by Sears and his associates displayed a similar insouciance about the responsibilities of fatherhood. See, for example, F-10, 2; F-11, 1; F-19, 1; F-21, 2; F-22, 1; F-24, 1; F-26, 2; F-30, 3. There were a couple of exceptions, notably one man who responded about becoming a father: "It scared the hell out of me. Yeah, it still does" (see F-23, 1).

35. O. Spurgeon English and Constance Foster, "How Good a Family Man Is Your Husband," *Parents' Magazine* 27 (September 1952): 36. Irene Josselyn recognized that some men recoiled from infant care but assured fathers it was not "emasculating to give an infant a bottle unless it is done in the emotional framework of being a substitute mother." See Josselyn, "Cultural Forces, Motherliness and Fatherliness," *American Journal of Orthopsychiatry* 26

(April 1956): 268. Unlike most experts, M. Robert Gomberg, the executive director of Jewish Family Service, worried that fathers were being asked to devote too much time to daily chores and child rearing. See Gomberg, "The Father as a Family Man," *New York Times Magazine,* September 6, 1953, 34.

36. See three articles by Theodore B. Johannis, all in *The Coordinator:* "Participation by Fathers, Mothers and Teenage Sons and Daughters in Selected Household Tasks" 6 (June 1958): 61–62; "Participation by Fathers, Mothers and Teenage Sons and Daughters in Selected Family Economic Activity" 6 (September 1957): 15–16; and "Participation by Fathers, Mothers and Teenage Sons and Daughters in Selected Child Care and Control Activity" 6 (December 1957): 31–32; also see Marvin E. Olsen, "Distribution of Family Responsibilities and Social Stratification," *Marriage and Family Living* 22 (February 1960): 60–65; William Dyer and Dick Urban, "The Institutionalization of Equalitarian Family Norms," *Marriage and Family Living* 20 (February 1958): 53–58; Ruth Tasch, "The Role of the Father in the Family," *Journal of Experimental Education* 20 (June 1952): 319–61; and Nathan Ackerman, "The Principle of Shared Responsibility of Child Rearing," *International Journal of Social Psychiatry* 2 (Spring 1957): 280–91.

37. Tasch, "The Role of the Father in the Family," 341. Nearly two-and-one-half times as many fathers reported that daily care of children caused "problems" rather than promoted "satisfactions."

38. Rachel Elder, "Traditional and Developmental Conceptions of Fatherhood," *Marriage and Family Living* 11 (Summer 1949): 98–100ff.

39. Dorothy Koehring, "Needed: Full-Time Fathers," *National Parent Teacher* 49 (February 1955): 8.

40. Sears interview, F-2, 2.

41. Sears interview, F-42, 3.

42. Sears interview, F-5, 2.

43. Sears interview, F-44, 3. A host of fathers noted that they did little day-to-day care. See, for example, F-3, 2; F-8, 4; F-9, 2; F-10, 2; F-11, 3; F-25, 3; F-34, 2–3; F-36, 2. Some fathers, however, did report doing considerable daily care, but in almost all these cases, they saw themselves as "helpers" or "playmates." See, for example, F-12, 3; F-20, 2–3; F-27, 2; F-32, 2; F-38, 3.

44. Jones, *Great Expectations,* 42. On consumption in post–World War II suburbia, see William H. Whyte, Jr., *The Organization Man* (New York: Simon and Schuster, 1956): chap. 24.

45. Tasch, "The Role of the Father in the Family," 348–49.

46. T. Jackson Lears, "From Salvation to Self-Realization," 3–17.

47. Tasch, "The Role of the Father in the Family," 349.

48. Jones, *Great Expectations,* 51.

49. Bettelheim, "Fathers Shouldn't Try to Be Mothers," 125. In this article, Bettelheim dissents from the many voices calling for fathers to participate more actively in the daily care of their young children: "Unfortunately, this is somewhat empty advice," wrote Bettleheim, "because the male physiology and that part of his psychology based on it are not geared to infant care"

(125). He went on to argue that such involvement could even be emasculating and that while women fulfilled themselves through motherhood, men fulfilled themselves through engagement in the world (126).

50. On teenage spending in the 1950s and 1960s, see Jones, *Great Expectations,* 73–74, 84–86.

51. May, *Homeward Bound,* 164 and all of chap. 7.

52. Ibid., 164. As May points out, Americans spent their money on their homes, not on personal or luxury items. In the four years immediately after World War II, Americans bought over 20 million cars and refrigerators, 5.5 million stoves, and 11.6 million television sets (166).

53. Most of the growing number of wives and mothers who worked for wages did so to enhance the buying power of their families. On this point, see May, *Homeward Bound,* 167, and Winifred Wandersee, *Women's Work and Family Values, 1920–1940* (Cambridge, Mass.: Harvard University Press, 1981).

54. These last several quotes are drawn from May's detailed analysis of the Kelly survey; see *Homeward Bound,* 176–80.

55. David Mace, "Fathers Are Parents Too," *Women's Home Companion* 80 (June 1953): 9, 11.

56. Vidal is quoted in Ehrenreich, *The Hearts of Men,* 28.

57. The term *other-directed* comes from David Riesman's famous book of 1950, *The Lonely Crowd: A Study of the Changing American Character* (New Haven: Yale University Press, 1950).

58. Miller, "Death of a Salesman," 27, 58.

59. Miller, "Death of a Salesman," 132.

60. Quoted in Ehrenreich, *The Hearts of Men,* 30.

61. "The New American Domesticated Male," *Life* (January 4, 1954): 43.

62. Quoted in Ehrenreich, *The Hearts of Men,* 32.

63. Ehrenreich, *The Hearts of Men,* 32.

64. David Riesman (in collaboration with Reuel Denney and Nathan Glazer), *The Lonely Crowd,* 3–35.

65. Whyte, Jr., *The Organization Man,* part VII.

66. O. Spurgeon English and Constance J. Foster, *Fathers Are Parents Too* (New York: Belmont, 1962; first published by Putnam, 1951): 17. Also see their article, "How Good a Family Man Is Your Husband?" 36–37ff, in which they warn wives not to undermine their husbands' efforts to become good fathers.

67. Russell Smart, "What Is Father's Part in Discipline?" *Parents' Magazine* 27 (November 1952): 85; see also Dorothy Koehring, "Needed: Full-Time Fathers," *National Parent-Teacher* 49 (February 1955); 8; Andrew Takas, "What Children Need from Dad," *Parents' Magazine* 28 (May 1953): 44ff; C. B. Palmer, "Life with Father (1955 Model)," *New York Times Magazine* (January 23, 1955), 15; and Nancy Cleaver, "Are You a Dud as a Dad?" *American Home* 44 (August 1950): 21.

68. Josselyn, "Cultural Forces, Motherliness and Fatherliness," 268.

69. Ibid., 270.

70. David Mace, "Fathers Are Parents Too," *Women's Home Companion* 80 (June 1953): 9; Gunnar Dybwad and Helen Puner likewise wrote that "it's not the *quantity* of time he spends with his children that's important, but the quality." Dybwad and Puner, "Be Fair to Father," *Parents' Magazine* 33 (June 1958): 96. Mace argued that work often kept men and their children apart but also criticized wives for monopolizing child rearing. Such interference could have dire consequences: "Many a modern husband would have had neither the time nor the inclination to run after someone else's wife if his own had set herself to forge, between him and his children, those deep bonds of tenderness which are a true father's joy and pride."

71. Dybwad and Puner, "Be Fair to Father," 39, 94. Dybwad was the director of the National Association for Retarded Children; Puner was an associate editor of *Parents' Magazine*. See, too, Nathan Ackerman, "The Principle of Shared Responsibility of Child Rearing," *International Journal of Social Psychiatry* 2 (Spring 1957): 280–91; Miriam Selchen, "What Are Fathers For?" *Parents' Magazine* 32 (June 1957): 72.

72. Dybwad and Puner, "Be Fair to Father," 94–96; also see Dorothy Barclay, "The Men in Children's Lives," *New York Times Magazine*, June 19, 1955, 38; Gale, "TV Makes a Fool out of Dad," 35–39. There were writers who were cautious about the worth of men's involvement in the home; see M. Robert Gomberg, "Father as a Family Man," *New York Times Magazine*, (September 6, 1953), 34, and especially Bettelheim, "Fathers Shouldn't Try to Be Mothers," 40–41ff. Bettelheim argued that male physiology and "that part of his psychology based on it are not geared to infant care" (125). Unlike women who fulfill themselves through motherhood, men find no such ultimate satisfaction in fatherhood. Rather, a man gains meaning by making a contribution to society as a whole, and by conveying to his children "what a man should be like in meeting life, in mastering it and its responsibilities" (127). In his book *Paradoxes of Everyday Life,* Milton Sapirstein argued that men may resent their loss of paternal authority when they accede to their wives' desires to establish democratic families. Sapirstein added that such men often withdraw from their families because their wives, in collusion with child experts, make these fathers seem inadequate. Dorothy Barclay discusses Sapirstein's work in "Rights of Man Around the House," *New York Times Magazine*, October 2, 1955, 48.

73. Almost all the fathers in the Sears study recognized a sharp division of labor between men and women; one of the best was offered by subject F-40, 32–33. Also see Ruth Jacobson Tasch's detailed survey of eighty-five fathers, "The Role of the Father in the Family," *Journal of Experimental Education* 20 (June 1952): 319–61.

74. Tasch, "The Role of the Father in the Family," 349.

75. Ibid., 350–51.

76. Ibid., 350, 352.

77. This evidence is from the Sears interviews. The two examples of fatherly affection and participation included in the text came from interviews with

Father #3, 32, and Father #9, 21. Many other fathers (all somehow associated with Stanford University) expressed similar sentiments. See, for example, F-2, 31; F-3, 32; F-4, 38; F-7, 32, 34; F-8, 45; F-11, 26.

78. Sears interview, F-26, 35.

79. Sears interview, F-2, 31.

80. Sears interview, F-12, 35. The fathers in the Sears study were not unique. Tasch found that father-child companionship was the greatest source of paternal satisfaction among her eighty-five subjects. The meaning of such companionship became clearer as Tasch explored father-child interaction; for example, 87 percent of the men spent time with their children on intellectual pursuits, including trips to libraries or museums, reading and telling stories, playing intellectual games, helping with homework, and the like. The same percentage also reported engaging in activities to improve their children's physical abilities, from rough-and-tumble play, to games, to outdoor pastimes and organized sports, to backyard construction projects. Over 90 percent of the fathers also noted that they took their children on short trips to visit relatives or on excursions to ballparks, theaters, playgrounds, beaches, or amusement parks. See Tasch, "The Role of the Father in the Family," 320–21.

81. Tasch, "The Role of the Father in the Family," 342–43.

82. Ibid., 322–24.

83. Records of the Child Study Association of America, Social Welfare History Archives, University of Minnesota, "Expectant Couples Group," Box 28, Folder 287, 1949–1954; "Preparation for Parenthood," Group II, Box 28, Folder 288, 1955; "Preparation for Parenthood Group," Box 28, Folder 288, 1957; "Preparation for Parenthood," Box 28, Folder 288, 1958.

84. Records of the Child Study Association of America, Social Welfare History Archives, University of Minnesota, "Record of Discussion Group for Parents of Pre-School Children, Box 28, Folder 290, 1957.

85. Records of the Child Study Association of America, Social Welfare History Archives, University of Minnesota, "Record of Parent Discussion Group," Box 28, Folder 290, 1957.

86. Donald Payne and Paul Mussen, "Parent-Child Relationships and Father Identification among Adolescent Boys," *Journal of Abnormal and Social Psychology* 52 (May 1956): 360; similar conclusions appear in Paul Mussen and Luther Distler, "Masculinity, Identification, and Father-Son Relationships," *Journal of Abnormal and Social Psychology* 59 (November 1959): 353. Also see Dorothy Koehring, "Needed: Full-Time Fathers," *National Parent Teacher* 49 (February 1955): 8–9. Although the social scientists did not cite the works of Edward Strecker or Philip Wylie on the harmful impact of "momism" on American manhood, clearly such a concern helped to animate such research. See Strecker, *Their Mother's Sons: The Psychiatrist Examines an American Problem* (Philadelphia: Lippincott, 1946), and Wylie, *Generation of Vipers* (New York: Farrar and Rinehart, 1942).

87. Mace, "Fathers Are Parents Too," 11.

88. Paul Mussen and Luther Distler, "Child-Rearing Antecedents of Masculine

Identification in Kindergarten Boys," *Child Development* 31 (1960): 93–95. In the judgment of Andre Fontaine, sustained fatherly involvement helped sons avoid becoming sissies. Fontaine, "Are We Staking Our Future on a Crop of Sissies? *Better Homes and Gardens* 29 (December 1950): 154–56, 159–60.

89. Paul Mussen and Eldred Rutherford, "Parent-Child Relations and Parental Personality in Relation to Young Children's Sex Role Preferences," *Child Development* 34 (September 1963): 596. Mussen and Rutherford found that highly feminine daughters were apt to have highly masculine fathers (601). On concerns about fathers becoming caricatures of mothers, see Dorothy Barclay, "Men in Children's Lives," *New York Times Magazine*, June 19, 1955, 38.

90. Fears of homosexuality abounded in the 1950s; on this point see May, *Homeward Bound*, 94–96.

91. Tasch, "The Role of the Father in the Family," 347, 354.

92. Michael Frobish charts the changing fortunes of the democratic family in the 1950s in "Family and Ideology," chaps. 5–7; also see Sonya Michel, "American Women and the Discourse of the Democratic Family," in Margaret Randolph Higonnett et al., eds., *Behind the Lines: Gender and the Two World Wars* (New Haven: Yale University Press, 1987): 154–67.

93. Else Frenkel-Brunswick, "Parents and Childhood as Seen through the Interviews," in T. W. Adorno et al., eds., *The Authoritarian Personality*, part I (New York: Wiley, 1964; originally published 1950): 361.

94. Ibid., 364–65.

95. Ibid., 370.

96. Ibid. See, too, Jack Block, "Personality Characteristics Associated with Fathers' Attitudes toward Child Rearing," *Child Development* 26 (March 1955): 44, and Solis Kates and Lutfy Diab, "Authoritarian Ideology and Attitudes on Parent-Child Relationships," *Journal of Abnormal and Social Psychology* 51 (July 1955): 14.

97. Suzanne Reichard and Carl Tillman, "Patterns of Parent-Child Relationships in Schizophrenia," *Psychiatry* 13 (May 1950): 250–51, 253. In 76 percent of the cases analyzed by Reichard and Tillman (60/79), the mother was the dominant parent, the father passive and uninvolved.

98. C. W. Wahl, "Some Antecedent Factors in the Family Histories of 568 Male Schizophrenics of the United States Navy," *American Journal of Psychiatry* 113 (September 1956): 206, 209.

99. Theodore Lidz, Beulah Parker, and Alice Cornelison, "The Role of the Father in the Family Environment of the Schizophrenic Patient," *American Journal of Psychiatry* 113 (August 1956): 127, 131; also see Ruth Lidz and Theodore Lidz, "The Family Environment of Schizophrenic Patients," *American Journal of Psychiatry* 106 (November 1949): 332–45.

100. Melvin Kohn and John Clausen, "Parental Authority Behavior and Schizophrenia," *American Journal of Orthopsychiatry* 26 (April 1956): 298. The authors found that 43 percent of schizophrenic men reported a combination of

strong maternal and weak paternal authority; none of the normal men reported this pattern. Forty percent of schizophrenic women reported this pattern, but so did 20 percent of the normal women. Weak fathers apparently had a more decisive impact on sons than daughters. On schizophrenia and fatherhood, also see James McKeown and Conrad Chyatte, "The Behavior of Fathers as Reported by Normals, Neurotics, and Schizophrenics," *American Catholic Sociological Review* 15 (December 1954): 332–40. In their study of 157 male and female schizophrenics, 85 neurotics, and 292 normal men and women, McKeown and Chyatte found that fathers of normals were "encouraging," those of neurotics "antagonistic," and those of schizophrenics "superficial" in their relationships with their children. The authors pointed out that they were analyzing associations, not causation: "[T]here is no way of determining . . . if a schizophrenic got that way because his father was Superficial, or whether he perceives his father as Superficial because he is schizophrenic" (337).

101. D. J. West, "Parental Figures in the Genesis of Male Homosexuality," *International Journal of Social Psychiatry* 5 (Autumn 1959): 85–86.

102. Lawrence Kolb and Adelaide Johnson, "Etiology and Therapy of Overt Homosexuality," *Psychoanalytic Quarterly* 24 (October 1955): 508, 511; also Daniel Brown, "The Development of Sex-Role Inversion and Homosexuality," *Journal of Pediatrics* 50 (May 1957): 616.

103. West, "Parental Figures in the Genesis of Male Homosexuality," 92; also see Harry Gershman, "Psychopathology of Compulsive Homosexuality," *American Journal of Psychoanalysis* 17 (1957): 58–72, and Charles Berg, "The Problem of Homosexuality (I)," *American Journal of Psychotherapy* 10 (October 1956): 696–708, and "The Problem of Homosexuality (II)," ibid. 11 (January 1957): 65–79.

104. Sheldon Glueck and Eleanor Glueck, *Unraveling Juvenile Delinquency* (New York: Commonwealth Fund, 1950): 125.

105. Ibid.

106. Ibid., 127.

107. Anonymous, "Put Father Back," *America* 98 (March 15, 1958): 682.

108. Richard Sennett, *The Fall of Public Man* (New York: Vintage, 1976); Christopher Lasch, *Haven in a Heartless World: The Family Besieged* (New York: Basic Books, 1977), and Lasch, *The Culture of Narcissism: American Life in an Age of Diminishing Expectations* (New York: Norton, 1978).

109. Urie Bronfenbrenner, "Socialization and Social Class through Time and Space," in Eleanor Maccoby, Theodore Newcomb, and Eugene Hartley, eds., *Readings in Social Psychology,* 3d ed. (New York: Holt, Rinehart, and Winston, 1958): 409–21, 423. Bronfenbrenner did suggest that working-class attitudes and practices were beginning to converge with those of the middle class.

110. Melvin Kohn and Eleanor Carroll, "Social Class and the Allocation of Parental Responsibilities," *Sociometry* 23 (December 1960): 372–73; Melvin Kohn, "Social Class and the Exercise of Parental Authority," *American Sociological Review* 24 (June 1959): 353, 364–65; Melvin Kohn, "Social Class

and Parental Values," *American Journal of Sociology* 64 (January 1959): 341.

111. Kohn and Carroll, "Social Class and the Allocation of Parental Responsibilities," 382, 385. Kohn's data came from interviews with both mothers and fathers.

112. Ibid., 391–92. On class and fatherhood, see, too, Martin Hoffman, "Power Assertion by the Parent and Its Impact on the Child," *Child Development* 31 (1960): 129–43; William H. Sewell, "Social Class and Childhood Personality," *Sociometry* 24 (December 1961): 340–56; L. Pearlin and Melvin Kohn, "Social Class, Occupation, and Parental Values: A Cross-National Study," *American Sociological Review* 31 (August 1966): 466–79; Bernard Rosen, "Social Class and the Child's Perception of the Parent," *Child Development* 35 (December 1964): 1151; Mirra Komarovsky, *Blue-Collar Marriage* (New Haven: Yale University Press, 1962): 73–81. In the postwar period, sociologists continued the tradition of equating parenthood with motherhood; for example, Evelyn Millis Duvall's interesting article, "Conceptions of Parenthood," had nothing to say about fatherhood but instead offered a provocative analysis of mothers' attitudes toward parenthood among Jewish, non-Jewish, white, and black women from a variety of class backgrounds: Duvall, "Conceptions of Parenthood," *American Journal of Sociology,* 52 (November 1946): 193–203.

113. Melvin Kohn, "Social Class and Parent-Child Relationships: An Interpretation," *American Journal of Sociology* 68 (January 1963): 475–76, 477; also see David Aberle and Caspar Naegele, "Middle-Class Fathers' Occupational Role and Attitudes toward Children," *American Journal of Orthopsychiatry* 22 (April 1952): 366–78. The parental focus on fostering creativity, initiative, and self-reliance to insure their children's (read sons') future success in the middle class is curious in light of the persistent concern that middle-class occupations promoted relentless conformism among their white-collar denizens. See Ehrenreich, *The Hearts of Men,* 30–41; also Michael Zuckerman, "Dr. Spock: The Confidence Man," in Charles Rosenberg, ed., *The Family in History* (Philadelphia: University of Pennsylvania Press, 1975): 179–207.

114. *The Negro Family: The Case for National Action* (Washington, D.C.: United States Government Printing Office, 1965; reprinted by Greenwood Press, Westport, Conn., 1981). Lee Rainwater and William L. Yancey examine the report and the controversy surrounding it in *The Moynihan Report and the Politics of Controversy* (Cambridge, Mass.: M.I.T. Press, 1967). On the report's impact on future research on the black family and black fatherhood, see William J. Wilson, *The Truly Disadvantaged: The Inner City, the Underclass, and Public Policy* (Chicago: University of Chicago Press, 1987): 6, 8, 15.

115. *The Negro Family: The Case for National Action,* 5.

116. Ibid., chap. 3.

117. Ibid., 29.

118. Ibid., 29–30. Emphasis in original.

119. Ibid., 35–45.

120. For an exhaustive analysis of the controversy surrounding the Moynihan Report, see Rainwater and Yancey, *The Moynihan Report and the Politics of Controversy*. Included in Rainwater and Yancey's book is a reprint of the report as well as a host of responses to it.

121. Rainwater and Yancey, *The Moynihan Report and the Politics of Controversy*, 410.

122. Farmer's columns are reprinted in Rainwater and Yancey, *The Moynihan Report and the Politics of Controversy*, 409–13.

123. Rainwater and Yancy, *The Moynihan Report and the Politics of Controversy*, 409–13. Farmer's fears were not without foundation. Writing a month before Farmer's two columns appeared, conservative columnists Rowland Evans and Robert Novak reported that President Johnson's White House Conference on Civil Rights failed to give the Moynihan Report a fair hearing. In their judgment, the conference had been scuttled by black leaders—among them Bayard Rustin, "who has never disguised his doctrinaire Socialist view that the root of the Negro's misery is the American economic system"—unwilling to face up to the implications of the Moynihan Report: "To examine critically the generations-old habits of the Northern Negro and seek self-improvement would be for them a return to the discredited 'Uncle Tom' preachments of Booker T. Washington." Instead, black leaders "insisted that the Federal Government and the Federal Government alone could relieve the torment of the urban Negro." As part of their indictment of the civil rights leadership, the two reporters accused it of "Negro racism" and of knowing "only how to put its hand out to Uncle Sam." The Evans and Novak column is reprinted in Rainwater and Yancey, *The Moynihan Report and the Politics of Controversy*, 380–82. The sociologist Herbert Gans shared Farmer's concerns and worried that "the findings on family instability and illegitimacy can be used by right-wing and racist groups to support their claim that Negroes are inherently immoral and therefore unworthy of equality." Gans's criticisms of the Moynihan Report appeared in *Commonwealth* and, in a slightly longer version, in Rainwater and Yancey, *The Moynihan Report and the Politics of Controversy*, 445–57. Conservative Southern newspapers made use of the report, sometimes reprinting large sections of it in an effort to show just how "ill" black families were. On this point, see Rainwater and Yancey, 399.

124. Farmer's column of December 18, 1965, is reprinted in Rainwater and Yancey, *The Moynihan Report and the Politics of Controversy*, 411.

125. Rustin's article, "Why Don't Negroes . . ." originally appeared in *America*, June 4, 1966, and is reprinted in Rainwater and Yancey, *The Moynihan Report and the Politics of Controversy*, 417–26. Gans also worried that the report "could lead to a clamor for pseudo-psychiatric programs that attempt to change the Negro family through counseling and other therapeutic methods." See Rainwater and Yancey, 450. Critics of the report drew upon the work of Ralph Dreger and Kent Miller, who had argued in a 1960 article that differences in black and white psychological functioning stemmed more from

class than racial differences. See Dreger and Miller, "Comparative Psychological Studies of Negroes and Whites in the United States," *Psychological
Bulletin* 57 (1960): 361–402.

126. Charles Murray, *Losing Ground: American Social Policy, 1950–1980* (New
York: Basic Books, 1984).

127. Frank Furstenberg, Theodore Hershberg, and John Modell, "The Origins of
the Female-Headed Black Family: The Impact of the Urban Experience,"
Journal of Interdisciplinary History 6 (August 1975): 211–33; Elizabeth H.
Pleck, "The Two-Parent Household: Black Family Structure in Late
Nineteenth-Century Boston," *Journal of Social History* 6 (Fall 1972): 3–31;
Herbert Gutman, *The Black Family in Slavery and Freedom, 1750–1925*
(New York: Pantheon, 1976); A. H. Walker, "Racial Differences in Patterns of
Marriage and Family Maintenance, 1890–1980," in S. M. Dornbusch and
M. H. Strober, eds., *Feminism, Children, and New Families* (New York:
Guilford, 1985).

128. Wilson, *The Truly Disadvantaged*, 15.

Chapter 10. Fatherhood and the Reorganization of Men's Lives, 1965–1993

1. Arlie Hochschild, *The Second Shift* (New York: Avon, 1989): 116.

2. Ibid., 224–25.

3. Graham Staines, Kathleen J. Pottick, and Deborah A. Fudge, "Wives'
Employment and Husbands' Attitudes toward Work and Life," *Journal of
Applied Psychology* 71 (February 1986): 118–28; also see Ronald C. Kessler
and James A. McRae, Jr., "The Effects of Wives' Employment on the Mental
Health of Married Men and Women," *American Sociological Review* 47
(April 1982): 216–27.

4. Howard Hayghe, "Children in 2-Worker Families and Real Family Income,"
Monthly Labor Review 112 (December 1989): 48–49.

5. David Eggebeen and Peter Uhlenberg, "Changes in the Organization of
Men's Lives: 1960–1980," *Family Relations* 34 (April 1985): 251–57.
Eggebeen and Uhlenberg estimate that the average number of years men
ages twenty to forty-nine spend in families where children live declined 40
percent between 1960 and 1980. In 1960 the average was slightly over twelve
years; by 1980 it was seven years.

6. Sylvia Ann Hewlett, *When the Bough Breaks: The Cost of Neglecting Our
Children* (New York: Basic Books, 1991): 88–94. Hewlett reports that over 40
percent of divorce settlements have no child support provisions. Of mothers
entitled to child support, only 51 percent receive the full amount, another 25
percent receive only partial payment, and 23 percent receive no support
whatsoever. Nor are fathers much better about visitation. In a sample of one
thousand children of divorce tracked between 1976 and 1987, 42 percent had
not seen their fathers once during the previous year and only 16 percent saw
their fathers once a week or more.

7. Barbara Ehrenreich, *The Hearts of Men: American Dreams and the Flight from Commitment* (New York: Anchor, 1984): 12.

8. Hayghe, "Children in 2-Worker Families and Real Family Income," 48.

9. Hoschschild, *The Second Shift,* 2; Robert L. Daniel, *American Women in the 20th Century: The Festival of Life* (San Diego: Harcourt, Brace, Jovanovich, 1987): 379.

10. For a general discussion of the factors that propelled married women into the labor force, see Kingsley Davis, "Wives and Work: A Theory of the Sex-Role Revolution and Its Consequences," in Sanford M. Dornbusch and Myra H. Strober, eds., *Feminism, Children, and the New Families* (New York: Guilford, 1988): 67–86.

11. Steven Greenhouse, "The Average Guy Takes It on the Chin," *New York Times,* III, July 13, 1986, 1, 10.

12. Hewlett, *When the Bough Breaks,* 74; also see Kevin Phillips, "The Collapse of the Middle Class," *New Perspectives Quarterly* 7 (Fall 1990): 41–44.

13. Jane Riblette Wilkie, "The Decline in Men's Labor Force Participation and Income and the Changing Structure of Family Economic Support," *Journal of Marriage and the Family* 53 (February 1991): 117.

14. Wilkie, "The Decline in Men's Labor Force Participation," 118.

15. Robert J. Samuelson, "How Our American Dream Unraveled," *Newsweek,* March 2, 1992, 35.

16. Hayghe, "Children in 2-Worker Families and Real Family Income," 50.

17. Prepared statement of James A. Levine, "Babies and Briefcases: Creating a Family-Friendly Workplace for Fathers," *Hearings before the Select Committee on Children, Youth, and Families,* 102nd Cong., 1st sess., June 11, 1991, p. 33.

18. Ibid., p. 4

19. Ibid., 4–5, 38, 69–71, 142.

20. Ibid., 142.

21. Ibid., 6.

22. Ibid., 134–38.

23. Ibid., 2–3, 16–21, 26.

24. A list of "family-oriented" options for employers appears in "Babies and Briefcases," 6–9; also see Ellen Galinsky, "Trends in Corporate Family-Supportive Policies," *Marriage and Family Review* 15 (1990): 75–94.

25. "Babies and Briefcases," 30.

26. Theodore Caplow, Howard M. Bahr, Bruce A. Chadwick, Reuben Hill, and Margaret Holmes Williamson, *Middletown Families: Fifty Years of Continuity and Change* (Minneapolis: University of Minnesota Press, 1982): 66

27. Ibid., 68–71.

28. Ibid., 146; also 144–47. Emphasis in original.

29. Ibid., 149–50.

30. Joan Huber and Glenna Spitze, *Sex Stratification: Children, Housework, and Jobs* (New York: Academic 1983).

31. Beth Anne Shelton, *Women, Men and Time: Gender Differences in Paid*

Work, Housework and Leisure (New York: Greenwood, 1992): 147.

32. Rosalind C. Barnett and Grace K. Baruch, "Correlates of Fathers' Participation in Family Work," in Phyllis Bronstein and Carolyn Pape Cowan, eds., *Fatherhood Today: Men's Changing Role in the Family* (New York: Wiley, 1988): 72. The Barnett and Baruch article contains a useful bibliography on fathers' participation in child care and housework. Also useful are Shelton, *Women, Men and Time;* Joseph H. Pleck, *Working Wives, Working Husbands* (Beverly Hills: Sage, 1985); Alexander Szalai, ed., *The Use of Time: Daily Activities of Urban and Suburban Populations in Twelve Countries* (The Hague: Mouton, 1972); and Hochschild, *The Second Shift,* 277–79. Scores of articles on this subject appear in social science journals.

33. Sylvia Ann Hewlett, *A Lesser Life: The Myth of Women's Liberation in America* (New York: Warner, 1986): 88–89. The division of household labor remains relentlessly gender-segregated. Mothers cook, wash dishes, vacuum, and diaper; fathers do household repairs, yard work, lawn mowing, and snow shoveling. This division tends to hold firm even within homes in which men do many hours of housework. On this point, see Sampson Lee Blair and Daniel T. Lichter, "Measuring the Division of Household Labor: Gender Segregation of Housework among American Couples," *Journal of Family Issues* 12 (March 1991): 91–113.

34. Barnett and Baruch, "Correlates of Fathers' Participation in Family Work," 72.

35. Lamb suggests that the analysis of parental involvement with children must differentiate among engagement, accessibility, and responsibility. For example, a father may have regular engagement with a child (feeding, bathing, and so on) and be relatively accessible to meet the child's needs and yet take little responsibility for keeping track of the child's clothes, school supplies, medical appointments, and the like. See Lamb, "Introduction: The Emergent American Father," in Michael E. Lamb, ed., *The Father's Role: Cross-Cultural Perspectives* (Hillsdale, N.J.: Lawrence Erlbaum, 1987): 3–25. Ralph LaRossa discusses these and other points in "Fatherhood and Social Change," *Family Relations* 37 (October 1988): 451–57.

36. Joseph Veroff, Elizabeth Douvan, and Richard A. Kulka, *The Inner American: A Self-Portrait from 1957 to 1976* (New York: Basic Books, 1981): 191.

37. Ibid., 173.

38. Ibid., 214–15.

39. Ibid., 203. Emphasis in original.

40. Eggebeen and Uhlenberg, "Changes in the Organization of Men's Lives: 1960–1980," 252. The total fertility rate declined from 3.8 in 1960 to 1.8 in 1980, while the median age of first marriage for men rose from 22.8 in 1960 to 23.4 in 1979. The divorce rate increased 150 percent in the same twenty years.

41. Ibid., 253.

42. These psychological implications for fathers are raised by Eggebeen and

Uhlenberg based on the research of Michael Lamb, "Influence on the Child on Mental Quality and Family Interaction during the Prenatal, Perinatal, and Infancy Periods," in R. M. Lerner and G. B. Spanier, eds., *Child Influences on Marital and Family Interaction: A Life Span Perspective* (New York: Academic, 1978): 132–61; R. A. Fein, "Research on Fathering: Social Policy and an Emergent Perspective," *Journal of Social Issues* 34 (Winter 1978): 122–35; and Ross Parke, *Fathers* (Cambridge, Mass.: Harvard University Press, 1981). See Eggebeen and Uhlenberg, "Changes in the Organization of Men's Lives: 1960–1980," 256.

43. These implications are discussed in Eggebeen and Uhlenberg, "Changes in the Organization of Men's Lives: 1960–1980," 256–57. The authors also speculate that the reduction in men's involvement with young children may result in less political attention and less monies directed at programs and facilities for children. Will childless men, for example, support taxation for schools, recreation programs, child nutrition programs, and the like?

44. *New York Times,* May 21, 1992, A1, A12. The article also noted that President Bush's advisers would try to make the decline of the American two-parent family a major campaign issue. On Clinton's comments, see *Washington Post Weekly* 10 (January 11–17, 1993): 32.

45. U.S. Bureau of the Census, *Current Population Reports,* Series P-23, no. 107, "Families Maintained by Female Householders, 1970–1979" (Washington, D.C.: Government Printing Office, 1980); also see Wilson, *The Truly Disadvantaged,* 26–29.

46. Hewlett, *When the Bough Breaks,* 41.

47. *Child Support and Alimony, 1987,* U.S. Bureau of the Census, *Current Population Reports,* Series P-23, no. 167, June 1990, 3, table B. This evidence is cited in Hewlett, *When the Bough Breaks,* 89. A host of studies confirms the delinquency of fathers in paying child support; see, for example, Walter Johnson, *Policy Implications of Divorce Reform: The Illinois Example* (Springfield, Illinois: Sangamon State University Press, 1979): 123–30; Richard Peterson, *Women, Work, and Divorce* (Albany: State University of New York Press, 1989): 93; Joyce A. Arditti, "Child Support Noncompliance and Divorced Fathers: Rethinking the Role of Paternal Involvement," in Sandra S. Volgy, ed., *Women and Divorce/Men and Divorce: Gender Differences in Separation, Divorce and Remarriage* (New York: Haworth, 1991): 107–19; also in the Volgy volume, see James R. Dudley, "Exploring Ways to Get Divorced Fathers to Comply Willingly with Child Support Agreements," 121–35; see, too, Thomas J. Espenshade, "The Economic Consequences of Divorce," *Journal of Marriage and the Family* 41 (August 1979): 615–25.

48. Cited in Hewlett, *When the Bough Breaks,* 89, from Lucy Marsh Yee's "What Really Happens in Child Support Cases: An Empirical Study of the Establishment and Enforcement of Child Support Orders in the Denver District Court," *Law Journal of Denver* 57 (1980): 21–36. Articles on fathers' failure to pay child custody appeared in popular periodicals with some regu-

larity in the 1980s; see, for example, P. Wingert, "And What of Deadbeat Dads," *Newsweek* 112 (December 19, 1988): 66; P. Simpson, "Making Sure Dad Pays Up," *Ms.* 16 (May 1988): 65ff; C. Berman, "Why Fathers Don't Pay," *McCalls* 115 (May 1988): 51–54; M. Takas, "Collecting Child Support: Why Uncle Sam Won't Help," *Vogue* 177 (November 1987): 58.

49. On the child support "deficit," see Edward Walsh, "Going After Fathers Who Turn Their Backs," *Washington Post Weekly* 10 (January 11–17, 1993): 32. On the economic impact of divorce, see Greg J. Duncan and Saul D. Hoffman, "A Reconsideration of the Economic Consequences of Marital Dissolution," *Demography* 22 (November 1985): 485–97; Robert S. Weiss, "The Impact of Marital Dissolution on Income and Consumption in Single-Parent Households," *Journal of Marriage and the Family* 46 (February 1984): 115–27. Lenore Weitzman's often quoted though hotly debated statistic was even more alarming. In California, women's standard of living allegedly declined by 73 percent after divorce while men's went up by 42 percent. See Lenore J. Weitzman, *The Divorce Revolution* (New York: Free Press, 1985): 323. In *Backlash: The Undeclared War against American Women* (New York: Crown, 1991), Susan Faludi suggests that Weitzman's statistic is probably grossly inflated (21–23).

50. The Furstenberg and Harris study is cited in Hewlett, *When the Bough Breaks,* 90–91; also see Frank Furstenberg and Christine Winquist Nord, "Parenting Apart: Patterns of Childrearing after Marital Disruption," *Journal of Marriage and the Family* 47 (November 1985): 874. A study of forty middle-class children ages twelve to eighteen found that most had contact with the noncustodial parent less than once a month. See Benjamin Schlesinger, "Children's Viewpoints of Living in a One-Parent Family," *Journal of Divorce* 5 (Summer 1982): 1–23. By contrast, a study of white, middle-income, non-custodial fathers who had been divorced an average of only eight months found that 70 percent saw their children at least twice a month; see Mary Ann Koch and Carol Lowery, "Visitation and the Noncustodial Father," *Journal of Divorce* 8 (Winter 1984): 47–65. All evidence suggests that over time, non-custodial fathers' contact with their children steadily falls.

51. Judith S. Wallerstein and Sandra Blakeslee, *Second Chances: Men, Women, and Children a Decade after Divorce* (New York: Ticknor and Fields, 1989): 235.

52. Ibid.

53. Steven Waldman, "Deadbeat Dads," *Newsweek* 119 (May 4, 1992): 48.

54. Hewlett, *A Lesser Life,* 62; emphasis in original. On recent efforts to tighten up child support collection, see Walsh, "Going After Fathers Who Turn Their Backs."

55. Barbara Bilge and Gladis Kaufman, "Children of Divorce and One-Parent Families: Cross-Cultural Perspectives," *Family Relations* 32 (January 1983): 59–71.

56. Berthold Berg and Robert Kelly, "The Measured Self-Esteem of Children from Broken, Rejected and Accepted Families," *Journal of Divorce* 2

(Summer 1979): 363–69; Richard Kulka and Helen Weingarten, "The Long-Term Effects of Parental Divorce in Childhood on Adult Adjustment," *Journal of Social Issues* 35 (Fall 1979): 50–78; Barbara H. Long, "Parental Discord vs. Family Structure: Effects of Divorce on the Self-Esteem of Daughters," *Journal of Youth and Adolescence* 15 (February 1986): 19–27; David W. Reinhard, "The Reaction of Adolescent Boys and Girls to the Divorce of Their Parents," *Journal of Clinical Psychology* 6 (Summer 1977): 21–23; Jane Teleki et al., "Parental Child-Rearing Behavior Perceived by Parents and School-Age Children in Divorced and Married Families, *Home Economics Research Journal* 13 (September 1984): 41–51; Nancy Donahue Colletta, "The Impact of Divorce: Father Absence or Poverty?" *Journal of Divorce* 3 (Fall 1979): 27–35.

57. Paul Adams and Jeffrey H. Horovitz, "Psychopathology and Fatherlessness in Boys," *Child Psychiatry and Human Development* 10 (Spring 1980): 135–42.

58. Linda Collier et al., "The Effect of the Father-Absent Home on 'Lower Class' Black Adolescents," *Educational Quest* 17 (1973): 11–14; Patrick C. Fowler and Herbert C. Richards, "Father Absence, Educational Preparedness and Academic Achievement: A Test of the Confluence Model," *Journal of Educational Psychology* 70 (August 1978): 595–601.

59. Jill A. Bannon and Mara L. Southern, "Father-Absent Women: Self-Concept and Modes of Relating to Men," *Sex Roles: A Journal of Research* 6 (February 1980): 75–84.

60. Barbara G. Cashion, "Female-Headed Families: Effects on Children and Clinical Implications," *Journal of Marital and Family Therapy* 8 (April 1982): 77–85. On the inconsistencies of the literature on father absence, see, for example, Elizabeth Herzog and Cecelia E. Sudia, "Children in Fatherless Families," in *Review of Child Development Research,* Vol. 3, Child Development and Social Policy (Chicago: University of Chicago Press, 1973): 141–231, and Lamb, "Fathers and Child Development," 27–30.

61. The five-year follow-up is by Judith Wallerstein and Joan Berlin Kelly, *Surviving the Breakup: How Children and Parents Cope with Divorce* (New York: Basic Books, 1980): 235–63; the ten-year follow-up is by Wallerstein and Sandra Blakeslee, *Second Chances: Men, Women, and Children a Decade after Divorce* (New York: Ticknor and Fields, 1989).

62. Wallerstein and Kelly, *Surviving the Breakup,* 238–63; quotes from 238.

63. Wallerstein and Blakeslee, *Second Chances,* 302; also see Wallerstein and Kelly, *Surviving the Breakup,* 235–63.

64. Wallerstein and Blakeslee, *Second Chances,* 219–20.

65. Ibid., 238.

66. Ibid., 243. One of the authors' more troubling findings was what they called the "sleeper effect." Although girls seemed to fare better psychologically than boys immediately after divorce, the daughters as they grew older experienced a profound suspicion that their own romantic relationships would ultimately fail and that they would somehow be betrayed by the men in their lives: "Doubtless the basic father-daughter relationship serves as a template for the relationships these women anticipate with other men." See 56–67.

67. Wallerstein and Blakeslee, *Second Chances,* 238.

68. Hewlett, *When the Bough Breaks,* 94. Hewlett analyzed studies emphasizing the harmful impact of divorce and father absence upon children, 88–94. Representative examples of such studies are Paul D. Allison and Frank F. Furstenberg, "How Marital Dissolution Affects Children: Variations by Age and Sex," *Developmental Psychology* 25 (July 1989): 540–49; Mark A. Fine et al., "Long Term Effects of Divorce on Parent-Child Relationships," *Developmental Psychology* 19 (September 1983): 703–13; Sheila Fitzgerald Krein and Andrea H. Beller, "Educational Attainment of Children from Single-Parent Families: Differences by Exposure, Gender and Race," *Demography* 25 (May 1988): 221–33; Norma Radin, "The Role of the Father in Cognitive, Academic, and Intellectual Development," in *The Role of the Father in Child Development,* ed. Michael E. Lamb (New York: Wiley, 1981): 410–11; Lyn Carlsmith, "Effect of Early Father Absence on Scholastic Aptitude," *Harvard Educational Review* 34 (1964): 3–21; John Guidubaldi and Joseph D. Perry, "Divorce, Socioeconomic Status, and Children's Cognitive-Social Competence at School Entry, *American Journal of Orthopsychiatry* 54 (July 1984): 459–68; and John Guidubaldi et al., "The Impact of Parental Divorce on Children: Report of the Nationwide NASP Study," *School Psychology Review* 12 (Fall 1983): 300–323.

69. Hewlett, *When the Bough Breaks,* 41.

70. Charles Murray, *Losing Ground,* passim.

71. Ibid., 156–62.

72. The CBS documentary "The Vanishing Family: Crisis in Black America," aired on January 25, 1986; for a review, see *New York Times,* January 25, 1986, 3.

73. Wilson, *The Truly Disadvantaged,* 37.

74. Ibid., 49–55.

75. Ibid., 34–35. Wilson noted that the migration trend has now been reversed for blacks and that the 1970s, for example, witnessed an actual outmigration of blacks from the central cities. For the first time in the twentieth century, the population of inner-city blacks is no longer being replenished by migrants.

76. Ibid., 39.

77. Ibid., 39–41.

78. Ibid., 43. The problem of joblessness among the urban poor has been exacerbated by the general weakness of the national economy in recent years coupled with increased labor force competition from women (44–45).

79. Ibid., 56.

80. Ibid., 60–61.

81. Ibid., 73.

82. For an overview and extensive review of the literature on young fathers, see Bryan E. Robinson, *Teenage Fathers* (Lexington, Mass.: Lexington Books, 1988).

83. N. Reider, "The Unmarried Father," *American Journal of Orthopsychiatry* 18 (April 1948): 230–37; S. Futterman and J. B. Livermore, "Putative Fathers," *Journal of Social Casework* 28 (May 1947): 174–78.

84. Shirley Brown, "The Commitment and Concerns of Black Adolescent Parents," *Social Work Research and Abstracts* 19 (Winter 1983): 27–34.

85. Leo Hendricks, "Unmarried Black Adolescent Fathers' Attitudes toward Abortion, Contraception, and Sexuality: A Preliminary Report," *Journal of Adolescent Health Care* 2 (1982): 199–203.

86. Robinson summarizes these data in *Teenage Fathers,* 31–32; for examples of relevant studies, see M. A. Redmond, "Attitudes of Adolescent Males toward Adolescent Pregnancy and Fatherhood," *Family Relations* 34 (July 1985): 337–42; Ouida E. Westney, O. Jackon Cole, and Theodosia L. Munford, "Adolescent Unwed Prospective Fathers: Readiness for Fatherhood and Behaviors toward the Mother and the Expected Infant," *Adolescence* 21 (Winter 1986): 901–11; and Arthur B. Elster and Susan Panzarine, "Teenage Fathers: Stresses during Gestation and Early Parenthood," *Clinical Pediatrics* 22 (October 1983): 700–703.

87. Robinson, *Teenage Fathers,* 32. Robinson is quoting Reverend Richard Banks, curate of Christ the King Center in Charlotte, North Carolina.

88. Robinson reviews the social science literature on the problems faced by teenage fathers in *Teenage Fathers,* 39–69.

89. Josefina Card and Lauress Wise, "Teenage Mothers and Teenage Fathers: The Impact of Early Childrearing on the Parents' Personal and Professional Lives," *Family Planning Perspectives* 10 (July-August 1978): 199–205.

90. Robinson, *Teenage Parents,* 42–43.

91. Ibid., 42.

92. Westney, Cole, and Munford, "Adolescent Unwed Prospective Fathers," 901–11.

93. Quoted in Robinson, *Teenage Fathers,* 57, from a 1983 study by Susan Panzarine and Arthur B. Elster, "Coping in a Group of Expectant Adolescent Fathers: An Exploratory Study," *Journal of Adolescent Health Care* 4 (1983): 117–20.

94. Elster and Panzarine, "Teenage Fathers," 700–703. Robinson surveys the literature on the problems of young fathers in *Teenage Fathers,* 57–60.

95. For a recent overview of the literature on social class and fatherhood, see Rebecca J. Erickson and Viktor Gecas, "Social Class and Fatherhood," in Frederick W. Bozett and Shirley M. H. Hanson, eds., *Fatherhood and Families in Cultural Context* (New York: Springer, 1991): 114–37. For a review essay comparing fatherhood among blacks, Hispanics, Asians, and Native Americans, see Alfredo Mirande, "Ethnicity and Fatherhood," in Bozett and Hanson, 53–82.

Chapter 11. Patriarchy and the Politics of Fatherhood, 1970–1993

1. John Leo, "Men Have Rights Too," *Time* 128 (November 24, 1986): 87; Gail Gregg, "Putting Kids First," *New York Times Magazine,* April 13, 1986, 47; Leah Yarrow, "Fathers Speak Out," *Parents' Magazine* 60 (September 1985): 168.

2. Anthony Astrachan, *How Men Feel: Their Response to Women's Demands for Equality and Power* (New York: Anchor, 1986): 244–45.

3. Judith Hole and Ellen Levine, *Rebirth of Feminism* (New York: Quadrangle, 1971): 305.

4. Betty Friedan, *The Second Stage* (New York: Summit, 1981): 108.

5. Ibid., 102–3.

6. Ibid., 125–33.

7. Ibid., 137. Some variation of Friedan's story appeared in countless magazine and newspaper articles. See, for example, Aimee Lee Ball, "The Daddy Track," *New York* 22 (October 23, 1989): 52–60. Hollywood added its voice with the enormously popular *Kramer vs. Kramer,* whose hero, played by Dustin Hoffman, discovers the true meaning of fatherhood when his wife leaves to find herself. Hollywood also explored the lives of fathers unwilling or unable to make the journey taken by Hoffman; see, for example, *The Great Santini* or, slightly earlier, *I Never Sang for My Father.* For a sharp critique of the politics behind Hollywood's infatuation with fatherhood, see Molly Haskell, "Lights . . . Camera . . . Daddy!" *Nation* 236 (May 28, 1983): 673–75.

8. Tim Carrigan, Bob Connell, and John Lee, "Toward a New Sociology of Masculinity," *Theory and Society* 14 (September 1985): 551–603. On the "new manhood" in general, see Warren Farrell's *The Liberated Man: Beyond Masculinity* (New York: Random House, 1974), Mark Fasteau's *The Male Machine* (New York: McGraw-Hill, 1974), and Herb Goldberg's *The Hazards of Being Male: Surviving the Myth of Masculine Privilege* (Plainview, N.Y.: Nash, 1976); on fatherhood specifically, see Arthur and Libby Colman's *Earth Father/Sky Father: The Changing Concept of Fathering* (Englewood Cliffs, N.J.: Prentice-Hall, 1981), James Levine's *Who Will Raise the Children? New Options for Fathers (and Mothers)* (Philadelphia: Lippincott, 1976), or Ross Parke's *Fathers* (Cambridge, Mass.: Harvard University Press, 1981).

9. Carrigan, Connell, and Lee, "Toward a New Sociology of Masculinity," 568–69.

10. The Fatherhood Project at Bank Street College of Education compiled an exhaustive list of classes, services, and programs available to fathers. See Debra G. Klinman and Rhiana Kohl, *Fatherhood U.S.A.* (New York: Garland, 1984). Hundreds of such programs and services were ultimately identified.

11. These examples are from Klinman and Kohl, *Fatherhood U.S.A.,* 6, 11–12.

12. Ibid., 62–63, 134–35.

13. Ibid., 92–94, 96, 98–99.

14. "Babies and Briefcases: Creating a Family-Friendly Workplace for Fathers," *Hearing before the Select Committee on Children, Youth, and Families,* House of Representatives, 102nd Cong., 1st sess., June 11, 1992. See the statements by Gordon Rothman and Richard J. Salls, 10–15, 134–37.

15. Letty C. Pogrebin, *Family Politics: Love and Power on an Intimate Frontier* (New York: McGraw-Hill, 1983). Pogrebin is the author of the very popular *Growing Up Free: Raising Your Child in the 80s* (New York: McGraw-Hill, 1980).

16. Pogrebin, *Family Politics,* 205–11.

17. Friedan, *The Second Stage,* 153.

18. Thousands of fathers, of course, do perform the less glamorous tasks of child rearing *and* still find it rewarding. Testifying before Congress, Richard J. Salls described how he gave up a high-paying corporate job to be home with his two young sons. He found the trade-off tremendously satisfying: "It's been almost eighteen months now, and I don't hesitate to note that it has been the most rewarding period of my life. . . . I simply cannot put into words the importance and value that I feel this time together with them has meant to each of us." My point is not to ignore men like Salls but to recognize that they are exceptional. For his testimony, see "Babies and Briefcases," 137.

19. Michael Lamb offers a lengthy and indispensable review of the vast literature on fathers and child development in "Fathers and Child Development: An Integrative Overview," in Michael Lamb, ed., *The Role of the Father in Child Development* (New York: Wiley, 1981): 1–70. Lamb's bibliography has over seven hundred entries. In the same collection, Henry Biller offers a useful literature review and a comprehensive bibliography in his article, "The Father and Sex Role Development," 319–58.

20. Lamb, "Fathers and Child Development," 17–20.

21. Ibid., 20.

22. Ibid., 24.

23. Ibid., 27–29.

24. Biller, "The Father and Sex Role Development," 349–50.

25. "Babies and Briefcases," 76–85. Radin is a researcher on child development at the University of Michigan School of Social Work.

26. Joseph Veroff, Elizabeth Douvan, and Richard A. Kulka, *The Inner American: A Self-Portrait from 1957 to 1976* (New York: Basic Books, 1981): 216.

27. Heidi I. Hartmann, "The Family as the Locus of Gender, Class and Political Struggle," *Signs* 6 (Spring 1981): 366–94.

28. Barbara Ehrenreich, *Fear of Falling: The Inner Life of the Middle Class* (New York: Pantheon, 1989): 107–20.

29. Rosalind Barnett and Grace K. Baruch, "Correlates of Fathers' Participation in Family Work," in Phyllis Bronstein and Carolyn Pape Cowan, eds., *Fatherhood Today: Men's Changing Role in the Family* (New York: Wiley, 1988): 75.

30. These changes, beginning in the mid-1950s, include a general sense that the family was in crisis, of which family violence was seen as a symptom; an emphasis on child-centered families and permissiveness, which rendered child abuse increasingly unacceptable; a culture of self-exposure that legitimated speaking and writing about what had once been unmentionable; a focus on environmentalist social thought that could turn even abusers into victims of a sort and thus encourage their exposure; and, most significantly, the reemergence of feminism, which prompted a thoroughgoing analysis of

family power relations, including relations of abuse. See Wini Breines and Linda Gordon, "The New Scholarship on Family Violence," *Signs* 8 (Spring 1983): 491.

31. Breines and Gordon, "The New Scholarship on Family Violence," 493.

32. Ibid., 530.

33. For a thoughtful analysis of incest in twentieth-century America, see Linda Gordon, *Heroes of Their Own Lives: The Politics and History of Family Violence, Boston, 1880–1960* (New York: Penguin, 1988): chap. 7; also see Sarah Begus and Pamela Armstrong, "Daddy's Right: Incestuous Assault," in Irene Diamond, ed., *Families, Politics, and Public Policy: A Feminist Dialogue on Women and the State* (New York: Longman, 1983): 236–49.

34. David Finkelhor, *Sexually Victimized Children* (New York: Free Press, 1979): 88. Kinsey reported that 1.5 percent of the women surveyed in his study had been sexually molested by their fathers, whereas Judith Herman and Lisa Hirschman estimated that between 2 and 3 percent of their psychotherapy clients had been so. Despite the difficulty of gathering reliable statistics on father-daughter incest, the rough congruence of these estimates bodes well for their credibility. See Judith Herman and Lisa Hirschman, "Father-Daughter Incest," *Signs* 2 (Summer 1977): 735–56, and Diana E. H. Russell, *The Secret Trauma: Incest in the Lives of Girls and Women* (New York: Basic Books, 1986): 59–91.

35. Russell, *The Secret Trauma*, 10. In these statistics, Russell did not differentiate between biological fathers and stepfathers. When she did so, she found that "women who were raised by a stepfather were over seven times more likely to be sexually abused by him than women who were raised by a biological father" (234).

36. Jeffrey Moussaieff Masson, *The Assault on Truth: Freud's Suppression of the Seduction Theory* (New York: Farrar, Straus and Giroux, 1984); Russell, *The Secret Trauma*, 5–9. The impact of the Freudian interpretation, as Russell points out, has been far-reaching: "The Freudian legacy, then, is to discount the reality of incestuous abuse and, where discounting is impossible, to blame the child for being the one who wanted the sexual contact in the first place."

37. For examples, see Ruth S. Kempe and C. Henry Kempe, *Child Abuse* (Cambridge, Mass.: Harvard University Press, 1978), and Susan Forward and Craig Buck, *Betrayal of Innocence: Incest and Its Devastation* (New York: Penguin, 1978).

38. Russell, *The Secret Trauma*, 6–9.

39. Louise Armstrong, "Making an Issue of Incest," in Dorchen Leidhold and Janie G. Raymond, eds., *The Sexual Liberals and the Attack on Feminism* (New York: Pergamon, 1990): 49.

40. Begus and Armstrong, "Daddy's Right," 236. Judith Herman, one of the foremost authorities on father-daughter incest, argues that the incest taboo works less strongly between fathers and daughters than mothers and sons for the simple reason that the latter is an affront to the power of fathers and thus

cannot be tolerated in a patriarchally structured society. By contrast, no such threat is posed by the former, and though most fathers respect the incest taboo, some do not. It is a measure of the strength and reach of patriarchy that it has taken the organized power of women to bring the transgressions of this small minority to light; see Herman and Hirschman, "Father-Daughter Incest," 735–56, and Herman (with Lisa Hirschman), *Father-Daughter Incest* (Cambridge, Mass.: Harvard University Press, 1981).

41. Begus and Armstrong, "Daddy's Right," 239.
42. Russell, *The Secret Trauma,* 231–32. Again, Russell found significant differences between stepfathers and biological fathers. The former abused their daughters over longer periods and were more likely to use verbal threats than biological fathers; however, the actual use of force showed no statistical difference (236).
43. Ibid., 238–39, 247.
44. Begus and Armstrong, "Daddy's Right," 243.
45. Harold M. Voth, *The Castrated Family* (Kansas City: Sheed, Andrews, and McMeel, 1977): 2, 4.
46. Ibid., 4.
47. Ehrenreich, *The Hearts of Men,* 146.
48. Phyllis Schlafly, *The Power of the Christian Woman* (Cincinnati: Standard Publishing, 1981): 78.
49. Ibid., 79.
50. Ibid., 80.
51. Ehrenreich, *The Hearts of Men,* 144–49.
52. Schlafly, *The Power of the Christian Woman,* 83.
53. Ibid., 103.
54. George Gilder, *Wealth and Poverty* (New York: Basic Books, 1981): 69–70.
55. George Gilder, *Sexual Suicide* (New York: Quadrangle, 1973): 97.
56. Allen Hunter, "Children in the Service of Conservatism: Parent-Child Relations in the New Right's Pro-Family Rhetoric," unpublished manuscript read at the Legal History of the Family Symposium, Madison, Wisconsin (Summer 1985): 1, 10; also see Hunter, "Virtue with a Vengeance: The Pro-Family Politics of the New Right," Ph.D. diss., Brandeis University, 1985.
57. On the "new class," see Ehrenreich, *Fear of Falling,* 144–95. Almost any issue of the Moral Majority's *Liberty Report* or any publication from Gary Bauer's group, "Focus on the Family," contains an attack on the "new class" and a call for the reestablishment of traditional families.
58. Gilder, *Wealth and Poverty,* 115, 122; for similar sentiments, see Charles Colson, *Against the Night: Living in the New Dark Ages* (Ann Arbor: Servant, 1989): 75.
59. On the history of the men's movement, see Carrigan, Connell, and Lee, "Toward a New Sociology of Masculinity," 564–78.
60. For examples of fathers' grievances, see Jane Young, "The Fathers Also Rise: Battling to Stay in Their Children's Lives," *New York* 18 (November 18, 1985): 50ff; John Leo, "Men Have Rights Too," *Time* 128 (November 24,

1986): 87–88; *New York* 21 (January 11, 1988): 42–49; *New York Times Magazine,* January 26, 1986, 31; *Ms.* 14 (February 1986): 67–68.

61. A complete list of fathers' rights organizations as of 1984 appears in Klinman and Kohl, *Fatherhood U.S.A.,* 155–77.

62. Young, "The Fathers Also Rise," 53.

63. Ibid. Emphasis in original.

64. Ibid., 55.

65. Carol Smart, "Power and the Politics of Child Custody," in Carol Smart and Selma Sevenhuijsen, eds., *Child Custody and the Politics of Gender* (London: Routledge, 1989): 19–21; also see Nancy D. Polikoff, "Gender and Child-Custody Determinations: Exploding the Myths," in Irene Diamond, ed., *Families, Politics, and Public Policy: A Feminist Dialogue on Women and the State* (New York: Longman, 1983): 192, 196.

66. Polikoff, "Gender and Child-Custody Determinations," 184–85.

67. "It's Not Like Mr. Mom," *Newsweek* 120 (December 14, 1992): 70–71, 73; Polikoff, "Gender and Child-Custody Determinations," 187; see also Martha Fineman, "The Politics of Custody and Gender: Child Advocacy and the Transformation of Custody Decision Making in the U.S.A.," in Smart and Sevenhuijsen, eds., *Child Custody and the Politics of Gender,* 27–50.

68. Polikoff, "Gender and Child-Custody Determinations," 188.

69. Ibid.

70. Ibid., 190.

71. Ibid., 193.

72. Robert Bly, *Iron John: A Book about Men* (Reading, Mass.: Addison-Wesley, 1990): 20–21.

73. Trip Gabriel, "Call of the Wildmen," *New York Times Magazine,* October 14, 1990, 39.

74. The figure of fifty thousand comes from Gabriel, "Call of the Wildmen," 38. On the dilemma of contemporary fatherhood, see Samuel Osherson, *Finding Our Fathers: How a Man's Life Is Shaped by His Relationship with His Father* (New York: Fawcett Columbine, 1986).

75. Gabriel, "Call of the Wildmen," 39.

76. Jill Johnston, "Why Iron John Is No Gift to Women," *New York Times Book Review,* February 23, 1992, 28.

77. Johnston, "Why Iron John Is No Gift to Women," 29. To Johnston, the story of *Iron John* is really the story of Bly's life and his alienation from his father. Without recounting all the parallels she sees between Bly's life and the story of male initiation he tells in *Iron John,* suffice it to say his belated rapprochement with his father occurred about the time he turned against the world of mothers and *his* mother and began helping men find the "positive father substance." Susan Faludi analyzes Bly in *Backlash: The Undeclared War against American Women* (New York: Crown, 1991): 304–12.

78. Johnston, "Why Iron John Is No Gift to Women," 31.

79. Veroff, Douvan, and Kulka, *The Inner American,* 216.

80. Barbara Ehrenreich, *The Worst Years of Our Lives: Irreverent Notes from a Decade of Greed* (New York: Harper Perennial, 1991): 140.

81. Shirley Sloan Fader, "Are Men Changing? Nine Reasons Why Men Feel More Pressure to Please Their Wives and Put Their Families First," *Working Mother* (February 1993): 48–51.

INDEX

Abandonment of family, 151–52, 310*n*45, 310*n*46

Adolescence: father's importance during, 96–97; parent preferences during, 133–34, 303*n*33; sex education and, 106–7; unemployment of father and, 149, 150, 151

Advertising: consumption and, 138, 196, 304*n*41; military themes in, 161, 164–65, 166, 313*n*15; new fatherhood in, 250, 253

African-Americans. *See* Black families; Black fathers

Alienation: father-child relationship and, 3, 134; fathers and, 141–42, 200–201

American Association of University Women, 128

Amoskeag Mills, 38, 39, 41, 277*n*18

Anderson, John, 42

Antin, Mary, 75

Arlitt, Ada Hart, 175

Armstrong, Louis, 256

Armstrong, Pamela, 256

Authority of father: compulsory attendance laws and, 31, 32, 81, 82, 84, 119, 286*n*67; consumerism and, 138; defense of patriarchy and, 257–58; disciplining children and, 100, 104, 296*n*87; immigrant fathers and, 60, 61, 69, 81, 84; individualism and, 100–102, 293*n*65, 293*n*67, 293*n*70; new

fatherhood and, 100, 104, 296*n*87; 1950s fathers and, 203, 204–5; nineteenth-century attitudes on, 11, 30; rural life and, 27; state involvement in family life and, 31–32, 65–66; unemployment and children's rebellion against, 150–51, 152–53, 309*n*37, 310*n*50; unemployment survival related to degree of, 50–51, 145–46, 279*n*63, 308*n*16; wages earned by children and, 38–39; working-class fathers and, 50–51, 56, 65–66, 279*n*63; work relief programs and, 156; youth culture and, 140

Automobiles: advertising for, 164, 165, 166; leisure time and, 139, 140, 305*n*55

Barnett, Rosalind, 227

Baruch, Grace, 227

Baseball, 73–74

Beckman, R. O., 151

Begus, Sarah, 256

Bell, Thomas, 42

Bettelheim, Bruno, 196

Bilge, Barbara, 233

Biller, Henry, 252

Bisno, Abraham, 80

Black families: absence of fathers in, 53–54, 214–15, 280*n*78; breadwinning and, 4; current state of, 237–38; dependence on children's wages in, 52; effects of divorce on, 234; female-headed, 22, 53–55, 217,

231, 280*n*77, 280*n*79; income trends for, 223; slavery and, 20–22, 54

Black fathers: breadwinning and, 4; economic independence of children and, 55; forces undermining, 213–14; Moynihan Report on, 213–17, 331*n*123; need for supplemental income by, 52–54; out-of-wedlock births and, 240; schooling attitudes of, 55–56; slavery and role of, 20, 22–23; working-class experiences of, 52–56. *See also* Black fathers

Blakeslee, Sandra, 232

Bly, Robert, 260, 265–67

Bodnar, John, 55

Bok, Edward, 102

Boys. *See* Sons

Brandt, Lilian, 63

Breadwinning, 8; adult children's residence and, 15–16; alienation and despair with failure in, 199–201; baby boom in 1950s and, 187–95; black fathers and, 20–23; changes in meaning of, 4–5, 92, 93; child-care responsibilities and, 12–13, 18, 19, 130–32; child-labor laws and, 58–59; consumption and, 135–37, 197–99, 304*n*43; courts on, 64–65; economic conditions and, 7, 13–14; family life reformers and, 62–63, 64–65; farming and, 23–29; father-daughter relationships and, 16–17; fathers' control over their own futures and, 14–15; feminism and, 7, 258–59; Great Depression and, 143–44, 159; income trends and, 222–23; industrialization and, 13–17; legal changes affecting, 29–31; male dominance of, 3–4, 186–87; male identity connected with, 2, 144, 221, 307*n*6; new fatherhood concepts and, 6–7, 90–91, 130–32, 244, 259–60, 287*n*12; 1950s fatherhood and, 186, 194; nineteenth-century focus on, 10–33; occupational ties between fathers and sons and, 14–15, 16, 21–22, 23, 134–35; parent education movement and, 129; psychic costs of, 137; reorganization of men's lives and, 222–28; roots of change for, 11–13; slavery and, 20–22, 54; Southern economic conditions and, 17–19; state involvement in family life and, 31–32; therapeutic culture affecting, 32–33; unemployment and, 45–46; working-class fathers and, 35–39, 66–67; working women and, 4, 156–57, 222–23; work relief programs and, 154–55

Breines, Wini, 254, 255

Bronfenbrenner, Urie, 211

Burgess, Ernest, 92–93, 94, 99, 104, 105, 106, 108, 134, 138, 163

Bush, George, 231

Businesses: Americanization of immigrant workers in, 285*n*55; effects of drafted men on, 169–70; family leave and, 224–25, 246; father-son relationships and, 134–35; postwar employment of women in, 188

Capitalism, 13, 36, 44, 134

Caplow, Theodore, 226

Carrigan, Tim, 247

Child abuse, 61–65, 254–57, 282*n*103

Child-care and child-rearing practices: absent fathers during wartime and, 179–80; child study movement on, 32, 103, 129, 295*n*82, 302*n*24; child-support payments and, 221, 231–32, 332*n*6, 335*n*48; class differences in, 211–13; conflicts between working lives and, 223–24, 243; continuity of traditional views of, 227–28, 334*n*33, 334*n*35; custody decisions and, 233–34, 262–65; expert advice on, 12–13, 121–23, 128–29, 131–32, 302*n*24, 302*n*26; family leave policies and, 224–25, 246; government agencies and, 157; grandparents and, 179–80; as mother's primary role, 3, 101, 130–32, 187, 226; new fatherhood concepts and, 7, 88, 101, 116–17, 130–32, 246–47; 1950s fathers and, 187, 193–95, 203, 212, 323*n*35, 326*n*72; nineteenth-century approaches to, 12–13, 32–33; parent preferences of children and, 132–34, 142; public opinion on, 224, 227; reorganization of men's lives and, 219–20, 221; scientific mothering concept in, 32–33; Southern white plantation economy and, 18, 19; working-class fathers and, 42

Child labor: attitudes of parents toward, 58; black families and, 55; economic independence resulting from, 55, 79, 141, 315*n*29; family's dependence on, 36, 38–39, 47–48, 85–86, 150–51, 277*n*13; immigrant families and, 76, 85–86; laws governing, 57–59, 281*n*93; schooling and, 81–82; unemployment of father and, 150–51, 310*n*40; working-class families and, 57–58

Children: central cities and conditions for, 238–39; consumption and, 137–38, 196–97; current redefinitions of fatherhood and, 248–49; effects of divorce on, 233–36, 338n68; men's identity connected with, 2; nineteenth-century and religious reevaluation of, 11–12; wartime advertisements using, 165, 313n16. *See also* Daughters; Father-child relationships; Father-daughter relationships; Father-son relationships; Mother-child relationships; Mother-daughter relationships; Mother-son relationships; Sons

Children's Bureau, 32, 163, 167

Child Study Association of America, 127–28

Child study movement, 32, 103, 129, 295n82, 302n24

Child-support payments, 221, 231–32, 244, 332n6, 335n48

Civilian Works Administration, 154

Civil rights movement, 215, 331n123

Class: child rearing and, 211–13; new fatherhood and identity in, 89–90, 252–54; 1950s fatherhood and, 187; reading time related to, 103–4; unemployment effects and, 309n33. *See also* Middle-class *and* Working-class *headings*

Clinton, Bill, 231, 233

Cold War, 8, 208, 212

Commission on Children in Wartime, 163

Commuting, 139, 305n55

Connell, Bob, 247

Consumption: advertising and, 138, 304n41; breadwinning and, 135–37, 197–99, 304n43; children and, 137–38, 196–97; family life changes and, 135, 142; leisure activities and, 79; middle class and, 89, 186; 1950s fatherhood and, 186, 187, 195–96, 325n52; success equated with, 197, 198; television and, 196; unemployment and, 149; wartime advertisements and, 165–66; working women and, 222, 325n53

Corbett, Jim, 88

Corporations: family leave policies in, 224–25, 246; working women in, 188

Courts: fathers' rights movement and divorce in, 264–65; male desertion and, 63–64; nineteenth-century right to child custody in, 30. *See also* Juvenile court system

Courtship, 140

Cousins, Norman, 157

Covello, Leonard, 68–69, 70, 74, 80, 84, 85

Craft work, 13, 15, 23, 35–36, 41, 56, 280n83

Crime: family violence and, 254–57; fathers as soldiers and, 167; unemployment and, 152

Culture: Americanization of immigrant children within, 72–74, 75–77, 82–83, 86, 87, 285n60; emphasis on personal life in, 91–92; immigrant fathers and dilemmas of, 71, 74, 87; new fatherhood concept and, 6, 244–45; rural life and, 25; working women and, 157. *See also* Therapeutic culture

Custody of children: child-support payments and, 221, 231–32, 332n6, 335n48; fathers' rights movement and, 260, 261–63; joint, 262–63; mothers and, 233–34, 243; nineteenth-century right to, 30

Daniels, John, 86

Dating behavior, 140–41, 306n65

Daughters: fathers as role models for, 93–94, 95, 97; industrialization and domestic focus of, 16, 17; leisure activities of, 78–79; parent preferences of, 132–33; sexual behavior of, 79–80. *See also* Father-child relationships; Father-daughter relationships; Mother-daughter relationships

Death of a Salesman (Miller), 189, 199–200

Democracy, home as classroom for, 162, 163

Depression: absent fathers during wartime and, 1; unemployment and, 46–47, 66

Desertion of family, 151–52, 310n45, 310n46

Discipline of children, 100, 104, 180, 211, 296n87

Division of labor: continuity of views of, 227–28, 334n33, 334n35; fathers' rights movement and, 261–64; feminism and, 5; men's monopoly of desirable jobs in, 3–4; 1950s fathers on, 194; unemployment and, 151; working women and, 4, 163–64

Divorce, 92, 287n12; children and, 231, 233–36, 338n68; child-support payments after, 221, 231–32, 332n6, 335n48; economic difficulties after, 232, 336n49; father-child relationship after, 232–33, 244, 336n50; fathers' rights movement and, 261–64; nineteenth-century changes in, 30; postwar changes in, 229–30

Doctors, advice sought from, 124–25, 131–32

Domesticity: continuity of views of, 227–28; "masculine domesticity" concept and, 89,

116–17, 286n2; new fatherhood concepts of, 6, 115–18; working women and, 188, 227

Douvan, Elizabeth, 229

Draft boards, 171, 316n50

Dybwad, Gunnar, 203

Economic factors: changes in fatherhood and, 7–8; dating and, 140–41; redefinitions of breadwinning and, 13–14; reorganization of men's lives and, 220–21

Education: Americanization of immigrants and, 285n55; black fathers and, 55–56; child labor and, 81–82; compulsory attendance laws and, 31, 32, 81, 82, 84, 119, 286n67; effects of divorce on, 234; expert advice sought on, 119–20; immigrant fathers' attitudes toward, 74, 82, 84–85, 285n57, 286n74; impact of teachers in, 83–84; new fatherhood and, 109, 112–14, 298n106; out-of-wedlock births and, 240; rural life and, 27–28, 274n52; slavery and black families and, 21; Southern white plantation economy and, 18; sports and, 73–74, 77–78; unemployment of father related to performance in, 153; working-class fathers and, 55–56. *See also* Parent education

Eggebeen, David, 221, 229–30

Ehrenreich, Barbara, 189, 190, 200–201, 221, 228, 253, 258, 268

Elliot, John, 145

English, O. Spurgeon, 201–2

English language, 72, 74–75, 83, 285n55

Entertainment. *See* Leisure time

Equal Rights Amendment, 257, 258, 259

Equal Rights for Fathers, 262

Experts: absent fathers during wartime, views of on, 167, 175–77; advice from, 32, 108–15, 121–25, 129, 131–32, 301n22, 302n23, 302n24, 302n26; discussion groups and, 205–6; fatherhood redefinitions and, 8, 98–99, 124–25, 245, 291n55, 292n56; new fatherhood and, 6, 98–102, 103, 120–26, 295n82; 1950s fathers and, 186, 201–4, 217; nineteenth-century practices and, 12–13, 32–33

Factory work, 13–15, 23, 35–36

Faludi, Susan, 266–67

Family: changes in meaning of breadwinning within, 3–5; class identity and, 89–90; as classroom for democracy, 162, 163; consumption and changes in, 135, 142; dependence on child's wages, 36, 38–39, 47–48, 85–86, 150–51, 156, 277n13; female-headed, 22, 53–55, 217, 231, 280n77, 280n79; feminism and redefinitions of concepts of, 5–6; interacting personalities theory of, 93, 94, 99, 104, 146; men's identity connected with, 2; middle-class conceptions of ideal model of, 66; nineteenth-century attitudes on, 11–12; social interaction time in, 138–39; state government's involvement in, 7, 92; unemployment and relationships within, 48–50, 151–54; wartime drafting of fathers and, 172, 316n52. *See also* Black families; Immigrant families; Middle-class families; Working-class families

Family leave policies, 224–25, 246

Farm economy, 23–29, 90; authority of father in, 28–29; children's views of fathers in, 29, 275n61, 275n63; conflicts in, 29; industrialization and, 12, 13; intergenerational unity and, 23–25; land ownership and, 27, 274n51; migration to cities and, 27, 29; occupational ties between fathers and sons and, 14–15, 28–29

Farmer, James, 215–16, 331n123

Father-child relationships: affection and companionship of 1950s fathers in, 204–5, 207, 327n80; alienation in, 3, 134, 141–42; child-support payments and, 221, 231–32, 332n6, 335n48; continuity of traditional experiences in, 226–27; custody of children and, 261–62; dependence on child's wages and, 36, 38–39, 47–48, 150–51, 156, 277n13; divorce and, 232–33, 336n50; economic activity of child in, 15–16, 55, 79, 141; education and schooling decisions and, 18, 21; generational conflict in, 72–74, 80–81; importance of fatherly involvement in, 297n104; leisure activities and, 42–43; new fatherhood concepts and, 6–7, 88, 101–2, 105–6, 142, 297n93; nineteenth-century attitudes on, 11–12; psychological perspectives on, 250–52; rural life and, 24–25, 26, 29; slavery and, 20–22; social interaction time for, 138–39; Southern white plantation economy and, 17–19; time spent with children in, 6, 202–3, 229–30; unemployment and, 49–50, 148–50, 151–52, 155, 279n62, 310n45, 310n46; wartime absence of fathers in, 175–76, 178–82, 320n82;

Father-child relationships (cont.)
working-class families and, 42–43, 48–50;
work time of father and, 2–3, 224, 245.
See also Father-daughter relationships;
Father-son relationships
Father-daughter relationships: divorce and
effects on, 235, 337*n*66; economic independence of daughters in, 79; immigrant
families and, 69–70; incest and, 255–57;
industrialization and, 16–17; 1950s
fathers and, 191, 195, 205; schooling
issues in, 84–85; unemployment and,
153, 155. *See also* Father-child relationships
Fatherhood: breadwinning concepts of, 3–5;
complexities of understanding, 1–2; current welter of voices on, 8–9, 247–50;
defense of patriarchy and, 257–60; economic conditions, 7–8; experts affecting
meaning of, 8; fathers' rights movement
and, 260–65; feminism and redefinitions
of, 5–6, 9, 90, 245–47, 287*n*12; manhood
equated with, 221; new fatherhood definitions of, 88–89, 90, 287*n*12; 1950s
fathers on, 190–94, 322*n*17, 323*n*34. *See
also* New fatherhood
Fathers: children's preferences for, 132–34,
142, 303*n*33, 303*n*34; family leave for,
224–25, 246; nineteenth-century status
of, 30–31; out-of-wedlock births and,
236–37, 239–42; as role models, 93–94;
support of families by, 258–59. *See also*
Black fathers; Immigrant fathers;
Middle-class fathers; New fatherhood;
Working-class fathers
Father-son relationships: dating behavior
and, 140–41; divorce's effects on, 235;
domineering fathers in, 208–9; earnings
of son and, 315*n*29; family business and,
134–35; homosexuality in son and role of,
209–10; industrialization and, 14–16;
juvenile delinquency and, 210; masculine
identification in, 207, 208; 1950s fathers
and, 206–10; occupational ties in, 14–15,
16, 21–22, 23, 37–38, 135, 276*n*7; recov-
ering bonds in, 265–67; rural life and,
27–29; schizophrenia in son and, 209,
328*n*97, 328*n*100; schooling issues in,
85–86; Southern white plantation economy and, 18–19; wartime absence of
father and, 176, 177, 318*n*73. *See also*
Father-child relationships
Fathers' rights movement, 261–63
Federal Economy Act of 1932, 157, 158, 159
Federal government: Great Depression and,

146, 148; position of working women
within, 157–58; work relief programs of,
154–56
Feminism: backlash against, 5–6; breadwin-
ning and, 7; family violence and, 255;
fatherhood redefinitions and, 5–6, 9, 269;
male liberation movement and, 247–48;
men's critiques of fatherhood influenced
by, 246–47; new fatherhood and, 90, 115,
186, 217, 244–47, 253, 287*n*12
Foster, Constance J., 201–2
Foster, Robert, 94–95
Frank, Lawrence, 99, 100–101
Frazier, E. Franklin, 214
Frenkel-Brunswick, Else, 208
Freud, Sigmund, 255
Friedan, Betty, 246, 250
Furstenberg, Frank, 232

Gabriel, Trip, 266
Gallup polls, 170, 311*n*71
Gender roles: absent fathers during wartime
and, 180–81; division of labor and, 3–4,
156, 226; feminism and, 5, 244–45, 246,
253; Great Depression and, 145; indus-
trialization changes and, 16
Genovese, Eugene, 21
Gilder, George, 237, 259, 260
Girls. *See* Daughters
Goldwyn, Samuel, 71
Gordon, Linda, 64, 254, 255
Government. *See* Federal government; State
government
Great Depression, 143–44; changes in
fatherhood concepts and, 7–8, 143–44,
159–60; children's responses to, 148–50;
magnitude of, 144–45; sense of failure
during, 143, 146–47
Great Society programs, 216, 237
Greene, Thomas G., 171
Groves, Ernest, 91, 92, 101, 139
Groves, Gladys, 92, 101, 139
Gutman, Herbert, 20, 23, 56

Hall, G. Stanley, 32
Hapgood, Hutchins, 71–72, 75, 77
Hareven, Tamara, 38
Harris, Kathleen Mullan, 232
Herman, Judith, 257
Hertzberg, Arthur, 283*n*18
Hewlett, Sylvia, 227, 236
High schools, 77–78, 114
Hill, Reuben, 176
Hispanic families, 231
Hochschild, Arlie, 227

Holt, Luther Emmett, 32
Homosexuality, 8, 173; ignoring marriage and fatherhood and slide toward, 189–90; role of parents in development of, 209–10
Hoover, J. Edgar, 167, 169
Hopkins, Harry, 155, 156, 311n59
Housing, 40, 56, 196, 222, 277n15
Howells, William Dean, 45
Hunter, Allen, 260
Hymes, James, Jr., 95

Identity of men: breadwinning central to, 2, 144, 159, 307n6; children and, 2; new fatherhood and, 252–54; reorganization of men's lives and, 220; wages earned by children and, 151
Igel, Amelia, 176
Immigrant families: breadwinning and, 4; children's financial obligations to, 85–86; economic independence of children in, 55; mothers in, 69
Immigrant fathers, 68–87; ambiguous position of, 71–72, 87; Americanization of children of, 72–74, 75–77, 82–83, 86, 87, 285n60; attitudes toward education of, 82, 84–85, 285n57, 286n74; authority of, 60, 61, 69, 81, 84; breadwinning and, 4; businesses and, 285n55; compulsory school laws and, 82, 286n67; daughters and, 69–70; family life reformers and, 62; generational conflict and, 72–74, 80–81; Jewish families and, 70–71, 72–74; language problems and, 72, 74–75; leisure activities and, 73–74, 79–80; meaning of success to, 76–77; occupational mobility of children and, 41; reliance on children by, 74–75; religious issues and, 72–73; schooling and, 81–86; unemployment and, 46; youth culture and, 77–81
Incest, 255–56
Individualism: effects of unemployment on, 154; new fatherhood and, 100–2, 293n65, 293n67, 293n70; rural life and, 24
Industrialization: breadwinning concepts and, 13–17; children's financial dependence on fathers and, 15–16; household economic changes and, 13–14; mother-daughter relationships and, 16–17; occupational ties between fathers and sons and, 14–15, 16; Southern farm economy and, 17, 19
Industrial Revolution, 8, 260

Infant Care (Children's Bureau), 32
International Ladies' Garment Workers' Union, 80
Italian families, 1, 2, 4, 68–69, 70, 74, 80, 84–85, 282n3

Jenkins, Henry E., 84
Jewish families, 70–71, 72–74, 75, 76, 278n27, 283n3, 283n18
Johnston, Jill, 266–67
Joint custody, 262–63
Jones, Landon, 190
Juvenile court system, 7, 32, 140; therapeutic culture and, 60; working-class families and, 59–61
Juvenile delinquency, 8, 252; absent fathers during wartime and, 167, 168, 169, 313n21, 315n30; divorce and, 236; 1950s fathers and, 210; unemployment of fathers and, 50–51, 152–53, 279n63, 310n50

Kaufman, Gladis, 233
Kazin, Alfred, 81
Kelly, E. Lowell, 198
Kendall, Frank, 14
Kessler-Harris, Alice, 156–57
Khrushchev, Nikita, 8, 197
Kinsey, Alfred, 255
Koehring, Dorothy, 194
Kohn, Melvin, 211–12
Komarovsky, Mirra, 146, 147
Kramer vs. Kramer (movie), 221, 243, 253, 254
Kronstadt, John, 243
Kulka, Richard A., 229

Labor force. *See* Work force
Lamb, Michael, 227, 251
Landis, Paul, 27
Land ownership, 27, 274n51
Language, 72, 74–75, 83, 84, 285n55
Laws and legislation: changes in fatherhood concepts and, 7; child labor, 57–59, 281n93; compulsory attendance, 31, 32, 81, 82, 84, 119, 286n67; custody under, 261–62; desertion and child abuse, 61, 63–65, 282n103; nineteenth-century changes in, 29–33; responsibilities of fathers under, 258; working women under, 156, 157–58. *See also specific laws*
Leary, Lewis, 97, 291n46
Lee, John, 247
Leibowitz, Samuel, 210

Leisure time: children's time at home for, 26, 139–40, 141, 306n71; commute of fathers and, 139, 305n55; immigrant fathers and, 42, 73–74, 77–80; individual approach to, 138–39; new fatherhood and, 93, 98–99, 103–4, 292n56; 1950s fathers and, 204–5, 212, 327n80; quality time in, 202–3; rural life and, 26; urban life and, 26; working-class fathers and, 42–43, 278n28

Levine, James A., 224, 225

Levy, David, 173, 175

Lynch, Peter, 224

Lynd, Helen, 136, 197, 226

Lynd, Robert, 135, 136, 137, 197, 226

MacDonald, Martha Wilson, 96

Mace, David, 198, 202–3, 207

MacKenzie, Catherine, 174

McNarney, Joseph E., 168

Mangione, Jerre, 84–85

Manhood: baby-boom fatherhood responsibilities as hallmark of, 189; fatherhood equated with, 221, 247; out-of-wedlock births and, 240, 241; providing for family as definition of, 147, 308n24

Marriages: baby boom in 1950s and, 188–89; changing social views of, 116–17; consumption and success and, 198; feminist views of, 245–46; reorganization of men's lives and, 219–20, 228–29; slavery and, 20, 54; unemployment and, 151

Masculinity: identification with father and, 207, 208, 251–52; masculine and feminine traits and, 95–96, 110–11; "masculine domesticity" concept of, 89, 116–17, 286n2; men's movement redefinitions of, 265–67; new fatherhood redefinitions of, 88–89, 90, 115, 244, 247, 287n12

Massachusetts Society for the Prevention of Cruelty to Children, 61, 65

Maternal leave policies, 224–25, 246

Mather, William, 29

Mathews, William H., 153

Maxwell, William H., 82, 83

May, Elaine Tyler, 190, 191, 197

Medical professionals, 124–25, 131–32

Melzer, Milton, 80–81

Men's liberation movement, 247–48, 250, 261

Middle-class families: breadwinning and, 4; child abuse and, 61; child-rearing practices in, 211–12; consumption and, 89; ideal family model based on, 66; industri-alization and changes in, 13, 15, 16; leisure time activities in, 138–39; parent education for, 103–4

Middle-class fathers: alienation of, 141–42; breadwinning and, 4, 33; child study and expert advice followed by, 103, 108–9, 295n82; leisure time with children and, 42, 93; new fatherhood concepts and, 89–91, 102, 103, 253–54; Patri papers reflecting experiences of, 108–15; unemployment and, 309n33; wartime draft of, 170; work and children as preoccupations of, 3

Middletown study, 3, 136–37, 139, 140, 141, 226, 305n60, 306n71, 307n6

Migration: black fathers and supplemental wage work and, 52–54; of blacks to cities, 237–38, 338n75; from farms to cities, 27, 29

Miller, Arthur, 189, 199–200

Mobility: unemployment and, 45, 279n40; working-class fathers and, 40–41, 277n19

Moral development of children, 12–13, 139, 251, 252

Mother-child relationships: absent fathers during wartime and, 179–80, 181–82; child-support payments and, 221, 231–32, 332n6, 335n48; family life reformers and, 62–63; 1950s fathers and, 212; rural life and, 26, 29; scientific mothering concept in, 32–33; Southern white plantation economy and, 18; working-class families and, 43. *See also* Mother-daughter relationships; Mother-son relationships

Mother-daughter relationships: changes in work force and, 16–17; 1950s fathers and, 212

Mothers: black families and, 214; child abuse and, 254–55; child-rearing as work of, 3, 101, 130–32, 187, 226; children's preferences for, 132–34, 142, 303n33; consumption and success and, 198; continuity of traditional views of, 227–28, 334n33, 334n35; custody of children and, 233–34, 243; immigrant families and, 69, 282n3, 283n18; incest and, 255; leisure activities and, 79; new fatherhood concepts and, 6, 115–18; 1950s fathers on place of, 192; nineteenth-century status of, 12, 30; out-of-wedlock births and, 239–42; parent education emphasis on, 126–27, 128–29; postwar marriages and, 228–29; as role models, 94, 95, 289n29,

290*n*35; wartime and, 167. *See also*
Working mothers
Mother-son relationships: absent fathers
during wartime and, 180–81; fears of
overfeminization in, 94–95, 172–73, 181;
homosexuality in son and, 209–10; juve-
nile delinquency and, 210
Movies, 139–40, 253, 305*n*60
Mowrer, Ernest, 91
Moyers, Bill, 237, 266
Moynihan, Daniel P., 213–15, 216, 217
Moynihan Report, 213–15, 216, 217, 260,
331*n*123
Murray, Charles, 237

Naming practices, 4, 11, 20–21, 19, 273*n*25
National Congress of Mothers, 127
National Convention for Men, 243
National Organization for Women (NOW),
245, 246
National Recovery Administration, 154
Nazism, 208, 209, 212
New Deal, 148, 159
New fatherhood: class identity and, 89–90;
competing versions of, 6–7; criticism of,
244; cultural contradictions of, 119–42;
disciplining children and, 104, 296*n*87;
education and, 112–14, 298*n*106; emotional bonds in, 6, 88, 101–2, 105–6,
297*n*93; emphasis on personal life and,
91–92; expert advice and, 98–102, 103,
120–26, 295*n*82; feminists and, 90, 186,
217, 244–47, 287*n*12; future success of
children and, 111–12, 113; individualism
emphasized in, 100–2, 293*n*65, 293*n*67,
293*n*70; invention of, 6, 88–118; leisure
time and, 103–4; male feminists redefinitions of, 246–47; masculine domesticity
in, 89, 116–17, 286*n*2; middle-class reactions to, 89–91, 102; 1950s fatherhood
and, 186; parent education and, 126–32;
Patri papers reflecting attitudes in,
108–15, 119–20; personality development and, 104–5, 110, 296*n*90, 296*n*91;
psychological benefits of, 248–49; reality
of experience of, 103–8; second redefinition of, 245–47; sex-role identity and,
93–97, 110–11; sexual behavior of children and, 106–7, 109–10; women and
domestic sphere and, 6, 115–18; work
force changes and, 89, 90, 287*n*10
Newsweek (magazine), 230–31, 233, 263
New York City, 69, 72–74, 151, 153, 238
Nixon, Richard, 8, 197

Occupational mobility: children of immigrant fathers and, 41; unemployment
and, 45, 279*n*40; working-class fathers
and, 40–41, 277*n*19
O'Malley, Frank Ward, 131
Orsi, Robert, 69
Osherson, Samuel, 142
Out-of-wedlock births, 231; fathers' responsibilities and, 236–37; postwar changes in
rates of, 229, 230; teenage fathers and,
239–42
Oversey, Lionel, 190

Parental leave policies, 224–25, 246
Parent education: courses in, 248, 249, 250;
current redefinitions of fatherhood and,
248–49; emphasis on experts and,
120–26, 301*n*22; fathers' relative separation from, 129–30, 302*n*27; ironies in,
130–31, 132; motherhood emphasized in,
127, 128–29; new fatherhood and, 6,
103–4, 248, 295*n*82; organizations supporting, 127–28; therapeutic culture and,
126–27
Parents. *See* Fathers; Mothers; *and related
headings*
Parents' Magazine, 95, 97, 98, 144, 176
Parent-teacher associations (PTAs), 103,
127, 128, 129, 295*n*82, 302*n*24
Paternal leave policies, 224–25, 246, 250
Patri, Angelo, 108–15, 119–20, 122–23, 136,
139, 144
Patriarchy: fatherhood and defense of,
257–60; incest and, 255–57
Peer society: immigrant fathers and, 77–78,
79; unemployment of father and, 149
Personality development: absent fathers during wartime and, 175; divorce and, 234;
expert advice on, 122, 125–26; family
definition and, 93, 94, 99; interacting
personalities theory of, 93, 94, 99, 104;
masculine and feminine traits and,
95–96, 110–11; new fatherhood concepts
of, 104–5, 110, 296*n*90, 296*n*91; 1950s
fathers and, 8, 203, 205; parent preferences and, 134, 303*n*36; Patri papers and
expert advice on, 109–10; unemployment
and, 147–48, 309*n*29, 309*n*35
Planned Parenthood, 163
Plantation economy, 17–22, 52
Play, 42–43
Pleck, Joseph, 95
Pogrebin, Letty, 250
Polikoff, Nancy, 264–65

Power of father. *See* Authority of father

Pregnancy, 79, 167; new fatherhood and, 248; postwar changes in rates of, 229. *See also* Out-of-wedlock births

Progressive reform movement, 57, 60, 61, 63

Psychological factors: children's development and, 93, 122–23, 175, 177; new fatherhood and, 248–49

Psychologists, 124–25, 250–52

Public opinion: absent fathers during wartime viewed in, 174–75; fathers and child rearing viewed in, 224, 227; wartime draft of fathers and, 170–71; working women viewed in, 156–57, 158, 188, 311*n*71

Puner, Helen, 203

Quayle, Dan, 5, 231, 236

Racism, 53, 54, 213

Radin, Norma, 252

Radio shows, 103, 109, 129, 295*n*82, 302*n*24

Reading to children, 42, 103–4, 278*n*28

Reagan, Ronald, 237

Rebel without a Cause (movie), 185–86

Recreation activities. *See* Leisure time

Religious attitudes: children in nineteenth century and, 11–12; of immigrant Jewish families, 72–73; slavery and black families and, 21; Southern white plantation economy and, 19; wartime drafting of fathers and, 171

Republican mother, 12

Richman, Julia, 83

Riesman, David, 201

Robertson, Pat, 6, 269

Robinson, Bryan, 240–41

Robinson, John, 10

Rockwell, Norman, 164

Role models. *See* Sex-role models

Roosevelt, Franklin D., 7, 143, 146, 147, 148, 164

Rotundo, E. Anthony, 14

Rubin, Lillian, 2, 3

Rural life, 23–29; children's preferences for parent in, 133; children's views of, 29, 275*n*61, 275*n*63; intergenerational unity at heart of, 23–25; migration patterns and, 27, 29, 237–38, 338*n*75; personality adjustment and, 105; urban life compared with, 25–26

Russell, Diana, 256

Rustin, Bayard, 216

Ryan, Mary, 16

Salls, Richard, 224–25

Saturday Evening Post, 88, 164

Savage, E. P., 62–63

Schizophrenia, 209, 328*n*97, 328*n*100

Schlafly, Phyllis, 258–59

Schools. *See* Education

Schroeder, Patricia, 225

Schulberg, Budd, 75–76

Scientific mothering concept, 32–33

Scott, Michael J., 167

Sears, Robert, 191, 194

Self, emphasis on, 91–92

Self-respect: breadwinning central to, 2, 144, 159, 307*n*6; new fatherhood's emphasis on expert advice and, 125–26; unemployment and, 45–46, 155; wages earned by children and, 151; working-class fathers and, 66–67

Sex education, 106–7, 239

Sex-role models: absent fathers during wartime and, 168, 172, 174, 175, 315*n*30; current research on, 251–52; effects of divorce on, 234; fathers as, 96–97, 175, 243; masculine and feminine traits and, 95–96, 207–8; mothers as, 95, 290*n*35; new fatherhood and, 6, 93–97, 110–11, 251; 1950s fatherhood and, 186; overfeminization in, 94–95, 172–73, 181; social changes and, 95

Sexual behavior of children: absent fathers during wartime and, 167; children of immigrants and, 79–80; courtship and dating and, 140, 306*n*65; new fatherhood and, 106–7, 297*n*97; out-of-wedlock births and, 239–42; Patri papers on, 109–10; unemployment related to, 153–54

Simon, Robert, 55

Simpson, Margarete, 133

Slavery, 20–22, 54

Smart, Carol, 263

Smith, Daniel Blake, 18

Smith-Rosenberg, Carroll, 17

Social changes: absent fathers during wartime and, 168–69; courtship and dating and, 140, 306*n*65; emphasis on personal life and, 91; middle-class fatherhood and, 90, 92, 93, 115; reorganization of men's lives and, 230–31; sex-role model changes and, 94; unemployment and, 151–54, 157

Soldier-fathers, 172–76; advertisements portraying, 161, 164–65, 166; birth of first child during absence of, 177–78, 320n79; birth of second child after return of, 182; children's feelings about, 178–79, 320n82; closeness to children felt by, 180–82, 183, 321n97; draft and, 167–72; family instability and, 167, 168–69, 314n26; morale of, 169, 316n36; public opinion on, 170–71, 174–75; return of, 176–82

Sons: dating behavior and economic independence of, 140–41; fathers as role models for, 93–94; parent preferences of, 132–33; sports and leisure activities and, 73–74, 77–78, 79. *See also* Father-child relationships; Father-son relationships; Mother-son relationships

Sorokin, Pitirim, 23–26, 171–72

South: black migration from, 237–38, 338n75; slavery and black families in, 20–22, 54; white plantation economy in, 17–19

Spanking, and discipline, 104, 296n87

Sports, 73–74, 77–78

State government: desertion and child abuse and involvement of, 61–65; involvement in family life, 7, 92, 268; middle-class conceptions of family life and, 66; nineteenth-century authority of father and, 31–32; public schooling growth and, 31; working-class families and, 56–66; working mothers and, 65, 158

Steffens, Lincoln, 10, 72–73, 101, 117

Stern, Elisabeth, 70

Stimson, Henry, 168

Strecker, Edward, 173, 174

Support groups, 248, 249

Swartz, Arthur, 157

Tasch, Ruth, 191, 195, 196, 203, 205

Teachers, impact of, 83–84

Television: portrayals of fathers on, 191, 253; segmentation of family consumption by, 196

Therapeutic culture: changing concepts of fatherhood and, 6, 121–22, 126, 248, 250; juvenile court system and, 60; nineteenth-century changes in, 32–33; parent education and, 126–27, 129–30

Thoreau, Henry, 189

Thurow, Mildred B., 29

Ueda, Reed, 78

Uhlenberg, Peter, 221, 229–30

Unemployment: authority of father and, 50–51, 145–46, 279n63, 308n16; changes in fatherhood concepts and, 7; children's reactions to, 148–50; coping with, 44–45; dependence on children's wages in, 47–48; effects on men of, 309n33, 312n2; family relationships affected by, 48–50, 145, 307n9, 308n13, 308n17; geographical mobility due to, 45, 279n40; Great Depression and, 143–46; personality changes related to, 147–48, 309n29, 309n35; social order and, 151–54; working-class families and, 43–51, 67; work relief programs for, 154–56

Urban life: black families and, 22, 237–38, 338n75; children in central cities and, 238–39; migration from farms to, 27, 29; personality adjustment and, 105; rural life compared with, 25–26

Values: family as symbol of, 162–63; feminism and redefinitions of, 5–6; immigrant fathers and, 74, 76–77

Veiller, Lawrence, 74

Venereal diseases, 153, 154, 313n21

Veroff, Joseph, 229

Vidal, Gore, 199

Violence in families, 254–57

Voth, Harold, 257

Wages: children's independent control over, 55, 79, 315n29; family's dependence on children's earning, 36, 38–39, 47–48, 85–86, 150–51, 156, 277n13; increase in number of working women and trends in, 222–23, 325n53; working-class fathers and, 36

Waldman, John, 174

Wallace, Henry A., 27

Waller, Willard, 187

Wallerstein, Judith, 232, 234–36

War bond advertisements, 161, 313n15

Watson, John B., 301n22

Weber, Michael, 55

Weiss, Robert S., 2

Weitzman, Lenore, 232

Welfare agencies, 130, 152, 153, 157, 310n50

Westbrook, Robert, 164

Weyl, Walter, 87

Wheeler, Burton, 168, 169, 170, 171–72, 317n53

White House Conference on Families, 246

Whyte, William, 201, 202

Wilkie, Jane, 222–23

Williams, Aubrey, 156

Williams, James, 153–54

Wilson, William J., 237–38, 239

Women: families headed by, 21, 53–55, 217, 231, 280n77, 280n79; new fatherhood concept of roles, 6, 115–18. *See also* Mothers; Working mothers

Work: definition of manhood and, 147, 308n24; father-child relationships and impact of, 2–3: time spent with children and hours of, 224, 245

Work force: black fathers in, 23; black migration to cities and, 237–38; cultural meaning of fatherhood related to, 89; family leave policies in, 224–25, 246; Great Depression and, 143–44; immigrant fathers and children in, 74, 77, 78; industrialization and changes in,13–14; men's monopoly of most desirable jobs, 3–4; new fatherhood and, 89, 90, 287n10; 1950s fathers and success in, 201–2; occupational ties between fathers and sons, 14–15, 16, 21–22, 23, 37–38, 134–35, 276n7; postwar employment of women, 187–88, 321n3; rural migration to cities and, 27–28, 29. *See also* Working mothers

Working-class families: child-rearing practices in, 211–12; industrialization and changes in, 13–15

Working-class fathers, 34–67; authority of, 50–51, 65–66, 279n63; black families and, 52–56; child labor laws and, 57–59; children's earnings and, 36, 38–39, 47–48, 55, 277n13; desertion of family by, 61–65, 282n103; home ownership and, 40, 277n15; juvenile court system and, 59–61; legal enforcement of breadwinning obligations of, 62–63, 64–65; masculine identity among, 35–39; occupational mobility of, 40–41, 277n19; relationships between children and, 42–43, 48–50; schooling and, 55–56; self-respect and breadwinning by, 66–67; slavery and, 22–23; sons entering the work force and, 37–38, 276n7; state involvement in family life and, 56–66; supplemental wages earned by, 52–54; unemployment among, 43–51, 309n33; wages and strate-

gies for survival of, 36–37; working mothers and, 37, 47, 53, 65, 282n118

Working mothers: breadwinning role and, 4, 156–57, 222–23, 244; child care and, 3; division of labor and, 4, 163; family leave for, 225, 246; new fatherhood redefinitions and, 244, 245; pensions earned by, 65, 282n118; postwar employment of, 187–88, 321n3; public opinion on, 156–57, 158, 311n71; reasons for increased numbers of, 222, 325n53; reorganization of men's lives and, 219–20, 222–28; unemployment and need for wages of, 47–48, 156; working-class families with, 37, 47, 53, 65, 282n118; work relief programs for, 154–55, 311n57; World War II and, 4, 160, 163–64, 187

Work relief programs, 154–56, 311n57

Works Progress Administration (WPA), 154, 155, 156, 268

World War II: absent father during, 167, 168–69, 314n26; changes in breadwinning role during, 4, 8; draft and, 167–72; fatherhood redefinitions and, 8; images of fathers in, 164–65; instability of family during, 167, 313n21, 315n30; popular iconography during, 161, 164–67, 183, 313n15, 313n16; working women and, 4, 160, 163–64, 187. *See also* Soldiers

Worrell, Margaret, 159

Wyatt-Brown, Bertram, 19

Wylie, Philip, 172, 173, 265

Yates, Richard, 199, 200–201

Yezierska, Anzia, 70, 71, 74, 76, 80

Youth culture: authority of father and, 140; consumerism and, 137–38, 196–97; courtship and dating in, 140, 306n65; immigrant fathers and, 77–81; leisure and recreation activities in, 79–80; rural life and, 27–28, 274n52; sports and, 73–74, 77–78

Zachary, Caroline, 97

Zaretsky, Eli, 56

Zelizer, Viviana, 59

Zimmerman, Carle C., 23–26, 100

Zunz, Olivier, 40